THE RESTORATION
OF THE ROMAN FORUM
IN LATE ANTIQUITY

T0385444

ASHLEY AND PETER LARKIN SERIES
IN GREEK AND ROMAN CULTURE

THE RESTORATION
OF THE ROMAN FORUM
IN LATE ANTIQUITY

TRANSFORMING PUBLIC SPACE

GREGOR KALAS

University of Texas Press

AUSTIN

Copyright © 2015 by the University of Texas Press
All rights reserved

First edition, 2015

Requests for permission to reproduce material from this work
should be sent to:
    Permissions
    University of Texas Press
    P.O. Box 7819
    Austin, TX 78713-7819
    http://utpress.utexas.edu/index.php/rp-form

∞ The paper used in this book meets the minimum require-
ments of ANSI/NISO z39.48-1992 (R1997) (Permanence of
Paper).

LIBRARY OF CONGRESS CATALOGING-IN-PUBLICATION DATA

Kalas, Gregor, author.
    The restoration of the Roman Forum in late antiquity :
transforming public space / Gregor Kalas. — First edition.
        pages   cm — (Ashley and Peter Larkin series in Greek
and Roman culture)
    Includes bibliographical references and index.
    ISBN 978-0-292-76078-3 (cloth : alk. paper)
    1. Roman Forum (Rome, Italy). 2. Forums, Roman—
Conservation and restoration—Italy—Rome—History—
To 1500. 3. Rome—Politics and government—284–476.
4. Rome (Italy)—Antiquities, Roman—Conservation and
restoration. I. Title. II. Series: Ashley and Peter Larkin series
in Greek and Roman culture.
    dg66.5.k35 2015
    937'.63—dc23   2014031606
    ISBN 978-1-4773-0993-3 (pbk.)
    DOI:10.7560/760783

TO ANDREA, JUSTINE, AND RAYNA

CONTENTS

ILLUSTRATIONS

ACKNOWLEDGMENTS

ONE OF THE GREAT PLEASURES OF WORKING ON A PROJECT SUCH AS THIS IS TO REFLECT back upon the support of friends and colleagues. I received the most attentive and insightful scholarly direction I could have possibly imagined while writing a doctoral dissertation, with a very different focus from this book, under the direction of an exemplary intellectual model, Dale Kinney of Bryn Mawr College.

A proposal to produce a digital reconstruction of the late antique statues in the Roman Forum received the enthusiastic support of Diane Favro of UCLA and an award from the National Endowment for the Humanities in its Fellowships at Digital Humanities Centers program. The staff at the Experiential Technologies Center and other colleagues at UCLA provided wise input, including Zoe Borovsky, Chris Johanson, Yoh Kawano, Maya Maskarinec, Kathryn McDonnell, Kevin McMahon, Ece Okay, Todd Presner, Claudia Rapp, Mike Rocchio, Marie Saldaña, David Shepard, Lisa Snyder, Pelin Yoncaci, and Itay Zaharovits.

I have had the privilege of responses from colleagues who read the manuscript. Diane Favro and Brenda Longfellow, who read the book for University of Texas Press, made terrific, substantive recommendations for which I am truly grateful. Christine Shepardson, writing a book on late antique Antioch in the campus building next to mine, read the entire manuscript and provided truly smart and timely advice during critical phases, delivered with her wonderful energy that kept me motivated. Julian Hendrix, with whom I shared initial drafts of each chapter, gave me extremely productive feedback. Additional friends and colleagues shared useful assistance after reading sections of the manuscript, for which I thank Elisha Dumser, Kristine Iara, Joseph Jewell, Rayna Kalas, Ben Lee, Anthony Mora, Jim Rosenheim, and Alan Rutenberg. Maura Lafferty shared engaging conversations and generously provided help with Latin.

At the University of Tennessee, I have been fortunate to receive the warm support of friends and colleagues. The congeniality of Knoxville deserves mention. In particular, the Faculty Seminar in Late Antique Studies has provided a stimulating context for research. The group read chapters of the book in draft form, and a particularly resounding thanks goes to the members of this group, including Matthew Gillis, Thomas Heffernan, Michael Kulikowski, Maura Lafferty, Jacob Latham, and Christine Shepardson. Dorothy Metzger Habel is an extraordinary colleague whose deep knowledge about Rome has helped me in so many ways. Other colleagues have offered friendship and support, for which I thank Brian Ambroziak, Katherine Ambroziak, Tom Burman, Marleen Davis, T. K. Davis, Bob French, Florence Graves, Tim Hiles, Heather Hirschfeld, Laura Howes, John McRae, Amy Neff, Max Robinson, Avigail Sachs, Mark Schimmenti, Clerk Shaw, Ted Shelton, Tricia Stuth, Aleydis Van de Moortel, Scott Wall, and Suzanne Wright.

I have had the extraordinary privilege of working with an amazing group of students at the University of Tennessee and Texas A&M University. I am happy to recognize in particular the contributions of the talented Brian Doherty, who drew upon his skills as a writer and as a graphic designer while providing excellent illustrations and furnishing attentive editorial advice for the book. Andrew Ruff taught me to see Rome in new ways and ably assisted with ground plans. D. Tyler Thayer discussed Constantine with enthusiasm and diligently produced additional architectural drawings. Cameron Bolin prepared two drawings that display his impressive abilities. Discussions in seminars with David Berry, Tyrone Bunyon, Ashley Chadwick, Marianela D'Aprile, Cayce Davis, Justin Dothard, Chuck Draper, and Jacob Stanley sharpened my critical skills.

While conducting research, I benefited from advice, assistance, and productive conversations with colleagues and friends; for this, I extend my sincere appreciation to John Alexander, Tommaso Astarita, Niall Atkinson, Doug Boin, Jeremy Braddock, Jill Carrick, Arlene Chapman, David Defries, Danilo Di Mascio, Drew Dudak, Marcel Erminy, Jan Gadeyne, Karl Galinsky, Nerina Giuliani, Joe Hutchinson, E. J. Johnson, Shannon Kelley, John Kessler, Susan Lippold, Kathy Mountcastle, Ekaterina Nechaeva, Michael Neuman, Diana Ng, Kirstin Noreen, Amy Papalenxandrou, Vivian Paul, Patricia Pierce, Betsey Robinson, Cecile Ruhe, Philipp von Rummel, Despina Stratigakos, Pier Luigi Tucci, Ann van Dijk, and Nancy Vorsanger. Franz Alto Bauer talked through a number of important issues, sharing his amazing knowledge and sending me publications with exemplary generosity. Jim Burr has been an extremely helpful and congenial editor.

I received generous financial assistance from the National Endowment for the Humanities, the Office of Research at the University of Tennessee, the University of Tennessee's College of Architecture and Design, and Texas A&M's Melbern Glasscock Center for Humanities Research. A residency as the University of Tennessee Affiliated Fellow at the American Academy in Rome granted me access to an amazing facility, for which I am truly appreciative. The Humanities Center at the University of Tennessee generously aided in the costs of publishing illustrations.

I gratefully acknowledge the kind assistance I received while conducting research in Rome from Gianpaolo Battaglia, Alessandra Capodiferro, Lavinia Ciuffa, Irene Iacopi, Paolo Imperatori, Giuseppe Morganti, Pina Pasquantonio, and Maurizio Rulli.

My parents, Jim Kalas and Barbara Nelson, have been constant sources of good counsel, and I wish to express my profound appreciation for all that they have done. My treasured friend Paul Justin Johnson died from complications related to AIDS long before the book's completion; his encouragement of my scholarship truly motivated me. I also wish to acknowledge the inspiration I receive from my nieces and nephew—Astrid Kalas Braddock, Sylvie Kalas Braddock, Max Reeves, and Sophie Reeves—who make me so optimistic about their generation. Now more than ever, I appreciate the support I receive from three amazing sisters: Andrea Kalas, Justine Kalas Reeves, and Rayna Kalas. Their accomplishments, humor, and intelligence have inspired me; to them I dedicate this book.

ABBREVIATIONS

CIL   *Corpus Inscriptionum Latinarum*, ed. Theodor Mommsen et al. (Berlin, 1862–).

Cod. Theod.   *Theodosiani Libri XVI cum Constitutionibus Sirmondinis*, ed. Theodor Mommsen and Paul Krueger, 2 vols. (Hildesheim: Weidmann, 2000). First published in 1905. Translation by C. Pharr: *The Theodosian Code and Novels and the Sirmondian Constitutions* (Princeton, N.J.: Princeton University Press, 1952).

CSEL   *Corpus Scriptorum Ecclesiasticorum Latinorum.*

ILS   *Inscriptiones Latinae Selectae*, ed. Hermann Dessau, 5 vols. (Berlin: Weidmann, 1892–1916).

LP   *Liber Pontificalis*, ed. Louis Duchense, 2 vols. (Paris: Boccard, 1981). First published 1955.

LTUR   *Lexicon Topographicum Urbis Romae*, ed. Eva Margareta Steinby, 6 vols. (Rome: Edizioni Quasar, 1993–2000).

MGH   *Monumenta Germaniae Historica.*

MGH AA   *Monumenta Germaniae Historica, Auctores Antiquissimi.*

PLRE   *The Prosopography of the Later Roman Empire*, ed. A. H. M. Jones et al., 3 vols. (Cambridge: Cambridge University Press, 1971–1992).

RIC   *Roman Imperial Coinage*, ed. Harold Mattingly et al., 10 vols. (London: Spink, 1923–1994).

THE RESTORATION
OF THE ROMAN FORUM
IN LATE ANTIQUITY

THE LATE ANTIQUE
ROMAN FORUM
UNDER RESTORATION

GENEROUS BENEFACTORS OF LATE ANTIQUE ROME SPONSORED CIVIC MONUMENTS AND public structures to forge the semblance of a well-run state. Elite Romans of the late empire, seeking to appear to be guardians of Rome's past, reinstated historic ideals of munificence in the Roman Forum by rebuilding structures more often than they initiated new construction (fig. I.1). Thus, architectural conservation flourished in the late antique Forum, where civic-minded aristocrats experimented with architectural formats for sustaining historical memories and thereby worked to counteract time's passage. These late antique transformations raise important questions. How did these changes revise the significance of the Roman Forum as a civic space? What role did architectural restoration play in advancing the status of prominent individuals? This book explores the significance of the piecemeal interventions that influenced the memories of important Romans who renewed the buildings and monuments of the late antique Forum.

In the fourth century, most legitimate rulers resided outside of Rome in alternate capitals, leaving Romans to deal with the inaccessibility of their emperors. Particularly after Constantine took charge of Rome in 312, the absent emperors no longer effectively served as the city's preeminent patrons; yet local senators continued to maintain the built environment, the public buildings, and the state monuments in acts dedicated to the rulers. Late antique inscriptions preserved the memories of the local nobility, who demonstrated their support for the frequently distant rulers. Thus, the Forum's monuments and statues constructed an image of how elite Romans wished official politics to be remembered.

Of course, Rome never regained its position as the primary capital of the empire. Despite this, the buildings and monuments of the Roman Forum constructed an architectural language that honored the return of the past by commemorating those prominent individuals who were proud to revive the city's earlier traditions. Rome's nobles advanced historical claims by conserving architecture as a link to the past, and they revived the Forum as a center for officially sanctioned memories.

The expressive strategies of late antique restoration can be understood by looking at historical evidence that completes the picture of the Forum, a picture that is currently diminished due to the inevitable effects of time. Archeological rediscovery commenced with full force in the nineteenth century, with the initial goal of recovering nearly all phases of the Forum prior to the third century CE. The most vigorous phase of the Forum's excavations occurred before archeologists realized that a few Republican-era remains and the vast extent of the imperial buildings had been preserved and, subtly yet importantly, amended during late antiquity.

REDISCOVERY

The excavations that uncovered the pavement of the Roman Forum's main plaza began at the turn of the twentieth century with the objective of revealing Rome at its ancient peak. In 1906, the archeologist Giacomo Boni completed the excavations in the central area of the Forum. Much of the pavement for the Forum's central plaza and the adjacent sections of the Via Sacra that he unearthed had been hidden for centuries beneath the terrain once known as the Campo Vaccino, Rome's Renaissance cow pasture (fig. I.2). As director of the Forum excavations, Boni sought to reinstate the ancient past by peeling away successive layers in keeping with the most advanced scientific procedures.

In 1813, almost a century before Boni completed his archeological campaign, part of an important bronze inscription inserted into the pavement stones came to light. It included testimony to the square's benefactor from the late first century BCE.[1] During his excavation, Boni uncovered some of the remaining inscribed pavement slabs, with letters that indicated to the archeologist that Lucius Naevius Surdinus, a praetor appointed under Augustus around 7 BCE, had sponsored the pavement of the Forum's central plaza (fig. I.3).[2] Armed with this evidence, Boni claimed to have revealed the Forum of the Augustan age. The archeologist then hastily discarded much of the material resting upon the pavement that could have documented the late Roman and early

medieval phases at the site. The physical recuperation of the Forum during the early twentieth century thus exposed the pavement slabs of the central piazza and the cobblestones of the Via Sacra after Boni had eliminated much of the contextual evidence with which to understand the chronology of the paved surfaces.[3]

The late antique interventions disturbed by Boni must have presented testimony to both the preservation and the transformation of the Forum. In Boni's search for the Augustan layer, he failed to notice a series of major repairs of the pavement during the reign of Septimius Severus (193–211). This is significant, because Boni exposed the Forum in a way that reveals a great deal about restoration concepts. Much of the surface currently visible in the central area shows evidence that the zone had been refurbished with the insertion of many new pavement blocks in the early third century, so that the surface could be integrated into a comprehensively renewed precinct at that time. Indeed, Boni did not take note of the signs that the Surdinus inscription had been excised from its original blocks during the third century and inserted into newer ones (see fig. I.3).

In the 1980s, Cairoli Fulvio Giuliani and Patrizia Verduchi published their discovery that pavement slabs lying atop earlier layers can be dated through the chronology established by the Rostra at the western end of the Forum's central area. They documented the sequence of repairs to the plaza, since the different layers of pavement intersect at the Rostra with the lower level of weathered paving stones dating to the first century BCE.[4] Above these weathered stones, Giuliani and Verduchi identified the smoother surface currently visible near the inscription. The now-exposed pavement of the plaza belongs to the same phase as the Severan cobblestones of the Via Sacra. The clear reintegration of the old letters into the newer blocks of the smoother pavement indicates that the Surdinus inscription was reused by Severus, who revived the memory of the Augustan-era praetor.[5]

Severan-era repairs masked decay in the Forum pavement, returning it to its pristine state by restoring the appearance of the Augustan age. Filippo Coarelli, writing in a volume issued in 1985 and having consulted only a preliminary summary of the in-

Figure I.1. Roman Forum, General View. Photo courtesy of Fototeca Unione. © American Academy in Rome.

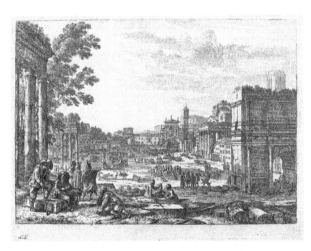

Figure I.2. Claude Lorrain, *The Roman Forum* (*Le Campo Vaccino*, 1638). The National Gallery of Art, Washington DC, Rosenwald Collection. (1968.8.460). © National Gallery of Art.

Figure I.3. Inscription of L. Naevius Surdinus in the Roman Forum. Photo courtesy of Fototeca Unione, Neg. 20548. © American Academy in Rome.

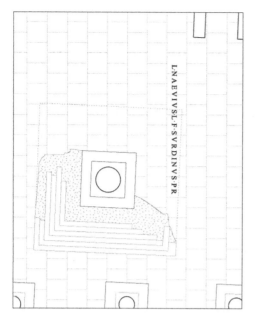

Figure I.4. Drawing of the L. Naevius Surdinus inscription in the pavement of the Roman Forum. Drawing by Brian Doherty.

vestigation by Giuliani and Verduchi that they issued prior to the release of their fully documented publication in 1987, disputed that an early third-century campaign would have reinstated the memory of a relatively unknown praetor; but he offers no archeological evidence to counter the Giuliani and Verduchi proposal.[6] Yet Coarelli concedes that "it remains probable that many of the blocks were reused in the course of the pavement's very long life."[7] Maintaining the inscription honoring Surdinus on the third-century pavement allowed the renewed surface to continually correlate with another monument in the Forum: the prominent and proximate inscription set into the parapet of the Lacus Curtius, which also displayed Surdinus' name.[8]

The Severan repairs of the Forum pavement both revived the Augustan plaza and transformed it conceptually, since the work led to cutting and pasting the bronze letters from the Surdinus inscription into a new physical context that established Severus'

Figure I.5. Arch of Septimius Severus in the Roman Forum. Photo by the author.

connection with a patron of the first century BCE (fig. I.4).[9] This process of recontextualization can be considered a type of revision, since the installation effaced the signs that the text was repurposed, much as textual revision typically masks the process of editing. In the third-century reuse of inscribed fragments, Severan builders memorialized the past in order to celebrate the civic munificence of a senator who had advanced the urban infrastructure at the outset of the principate. Clearly, the Severan conservation of the Surdinus text, integrating the old blocks seamlessly into the newly paved Forum square, implied a strategic link to the early empire.

Severan builders also transformed the Forum through major additions. The Surdinus inscription was physically overwhelmed by the scale of the nearby Arch of Septimius Severus (fig. I.5), a monument measuring nearly twenty-one meters in height and originally capped by a chariot drawn by six horses, flanked by statues of the emperor's sons. With the ambitious construction of the arch close to the spot where the Via Sacra reaches the far western point of the paved plaza, Severan builders formalized a spatial boundary for the Forum's central area.[10] The legitimacy of Severus and the acclaim he received for military victories, as presented in the sculptural reliefs and the large-scale inscriptions on the arch, associated imperial triumph with recovery from damage to the Forum caused by a fire that blazed around 191 CE, during the reign of Commodus.[11] As a result, the arch's inscription, with its dedication to Severus for the "restitution of the state and the amplification of the empire of the Roman people," alluded to the political context in which audiences were to consider the physical restoration of the Forum square.[12] During the third century, Severus' comprehensive project to restore the Forum plaza to its pristine state allowed the rebuilt urban environment to advance the emperor's ideals. Indeed, physical restoration in the Forum delivered authority to Severus and reinforced his legitimacy by means of the link to Augustus.

In the plaza, the installation of an equestrian portrait of Septimius Severus triggered associations with a legendary dream that made Severus' accession appear to be divinely sanctioned. In Herodian's account of Severus' dream, Pertinax, who had pre-

ceded Severus briefly as emperor in 193, was thrown from a horse and fell to the ground near the eventual location of the Severan arch. Severus then climbed onto the horse in the dream and rode toward the center of the Forum square.[13] The new equestrian monument of Severus was plausibly situated directly adjacent to a large indentation in the Forum square formerly identified as having held the equestrian monument of Domitian (fig. I.6). The pre-Augustan date of the indentation and evidence that the Severan repairs of the Forum plaza surface accommodated the new equestrian monument seem to indicate that the monument was installed on top of the early third-century pavement just north of the indentation (fig. I.7 [A]).[14] Together with the early third-century interventions in the paved central area, Severus' arch consolidated the Forum as a realm for imperial rituals and established it as a zone that retained the memory of Septimius Severus' triumph procession. Severus therefore solidified the ceremonial focus on imperial honors after rehabilitating the Forum.

As a result of their careful research, Giuliani and Verduchi revolutionized the study of the Forum's late phases. Significantly, the two archeologists attentively documented the different restoration projects that occurred after 211 CE, prompting a reconsideration of the Roman Forum that attends to revival efforts that took place long after the Severan reconstruction campaign. Unlike the Severan restoration, which returned to an Augustan target date, an important series of rebuilding efforts starting with the co-emperors Diocletian and Maximian (joint rule, 286–305) created a different and specifically late antique mode of recording the memories of imperial achievements in the Forum. These campaigns did so by particularly stressing the limited display of visible decay, asserting at once both perseverance and partial loss. Fourth-century interventions rebuilt the Senate House and instigated architectural restorations at the Basilica Julia, the Rostra, the temples of Concord, Saturn, Vesta, and Castor and Pollux, and the Porticus Deorum Consentium (fig. I.8). Subsequently, around the turn of the fifth century, one of the *tabernae* of the Forum of Caesar became the Secretarium Senatus, and the Basilica Aemilia received a repaired façade in the wake of fires that damaged the

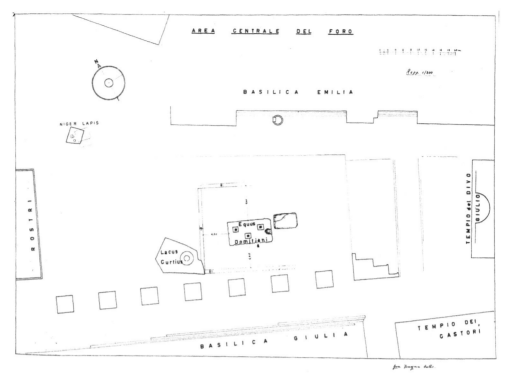

Figure I.6. Plan of the pavement in the central area of the Roman Forum showing the equestrian statue of Domitian ("Equus Domitiani") as identified by Giacomo Boni. Photo courtesy of Fototeca Unione, Neg. 5205. © American Academy in Rome.

Figure I.7. Aerial view of the pavement in the Roman Forum, with "A" indicating the location of the equestrian statue of Septimius Severus. Photo courtesy of Fototeca Unione. © American Academy in Rome.

structure in 410. Thus, the Roman Forum revealed by Giacomo Boni exhibited some of the most meaningful restoration initiatives in premodern Rome, the product of significant rebuilding campaigns postdating the third century.

The late antique restorations in the Forum beginning around the turn of the fourth century were distinguished by the appearance of a textured and fragmented past that was not entirely refurbished. It should be noted that the major interventions in the Forum considered here begin with the reforms of the emperor Diocletian after 284, when increasingly elaborate imperial rituals began to transform emperors into remote, autocratic overlords. The tumultuous empire of the third century had disrupted the already tenuous claims of legitimacy by emperors.[15] In the wake of a series of third-century crises, Diocletian proposed the Tetrarchic system of multiple emperors, all of whom were to follow career paths along highly orchestrated sequences so that the two junior rulers received joint promotions when the two senior colleagues retired in unison. The Tetrarchs promoted their quasi-divine status and expressed their exalted rank in court rituals, with emperors exhibiting such apparently minor yet highly significant prerogatives as the exclusive right to wear shoes of red- or purple-dyed silk bedecked with jewels.[16] The regalia offered lasting symbols of the co-ruling emperors' close identification with the gods. These symbols were to remain constant, even as the individual identities of specific emperors changed, setting up a concept of permanence.

An important shift in imperial authority occurred when Diocletian began to dismantle the tradition that an emperor would appear to be equivalent in status to Rome's aristocrats. Instead of ruling as a *princeps*, a leading figure among the senators of similar rank, and thus a ruler who received power granted by the elite, Diocletian began to appoint aristocrats to prestigious administrative posts. These posts offered status that was exalted yet lower than imperial rank, while Diocletian and his imperial colleagues claimed

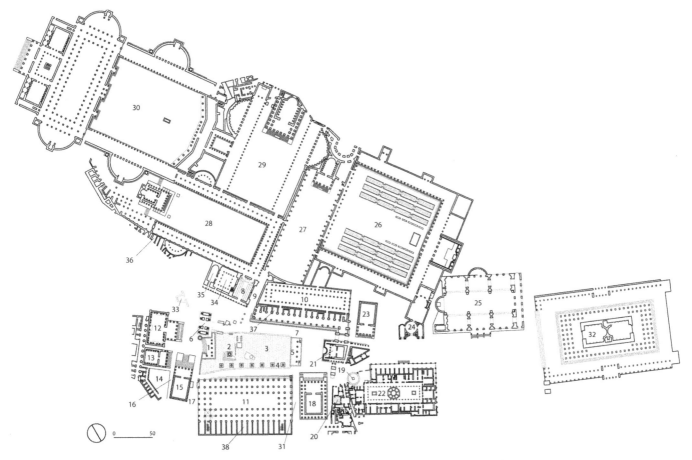

Figure I.8. Plan of the Roman Forum and the imperial fora in c. 400 CE: (1) western Rostra; (2) Column of Phocas; (3) plaza in the central area of the Roman Forum; (4) row of seven columns; (5) eastern Rostra; (6) Arch of Septimius Severus; (7) Via Sacra; (8) Senate House (Curia Senatus); (9) Argiletum; (10) Basilica Aemilia (nave); (11) Basilica Julia (nave); (12) Temple of Concord; (13) Temple of Vespasian; (14) Porticus Deorum Consentium; (15) Temple of Saturn; (16) Clivus Capitolinus; (17) Vicus Jugarius; (18) Temple of Castor and Pollux; (19) Temple of Vesta; (20) Lacus of Juturna (Lacus Iuturnae); (21) Temple of the Deified Julius Caesar; (22) Atrium of the Vestals; (23) Temple of Antoninus and Faustina; (24) Rotunda on the Via Sacra (the so-called Temple of Romulus); (25) Basilica of Constantine; (26) Temple of Peace; (27) Forum of Nerva (Forum Transitorium); (28) Forum of Caesar; (29) Forum of Augustus; (30) Forum of Trajan; (31) Vicus Tuscus; (32) Temple of Venus and Roma; (33) Mamertine Prison (Tullianum); (34) Atrium of Liberty (Atrium Libertatis); (35) Secretarium Senatus; (36) *tabernae* (shops) of the Forum of Caesar; (37) *tabernae* (shops) in the portico of the Basilica Aemilia; (38) *tabernae* (shops) in the portico of the Basilica Julia. Drawing by Brian Doherty.

supreme authority for themselves.[17] The Tetrarchs inserted images of rulers on top of free-standing columns so that they appeared to hover above all else in the Forum's paved plaza. Diocletian reportedly was angered by the "liberty" of the Romans when he visited the city in 303, probably alluding to prominent senators voicing bitter complaints,[18] but tension between rulers and Rome's nobility was not displayed in public monuments.

There is abundant evidence showing that Rome's aristocrats sponsored a wide array of restoration projects in the Roman Forum; yet they did so in honor of emperors. A senator required an imperial appointment to gain a prized office, and his aristocratic status thus hinged on his personal connection to the emperors. Apparent alliances between senators and emperors were on display in the Forum, even when this picture of harmony was far removed from reality. In addition, because they were unable to sponsor new civic buildings independent of the emperors, Rome's local elite turned increasingly toward architectural restoration projects. Thus, the astute archeological analysis of the Roman Forum by Giuliani and Verduchi invites a revised chronology in which to explore how and why individuals updated the built environment during late antiquity.

Yet Giuliani and Verduchi's precise investigations have been overshadowed by the search for Rome's origins. The visible testimony of restoration in the Forum's central area after the third century CE has not been fully integrated into scholarly discussions.[19] Instead, the bulk of recent archeological work in and near the Forum has focused on documenting the city's mythic emergence during the so-called Romulean age. After discovering part of a wall surrounding the Palatine Hill, Andrea Carandini interpreted its eighth-century BCE date as proof that Romulus actually inaugurated Rome's sacred boundaries, as recounted by Ovid and Tacitus.[20] While Carandini's archeology establishes a sound chronology for what his team unearthed, the claim that Romulus should be credited as the real founder of Rome is based on no evidence from inscriptions or other excavated material that positively attests to the legendary king as a historic individual.[21] Filippo Coarelli's important and comprehensive two-volume analysis of the

Roman Forum, meanwhile, focuses on the Republican and early imperial phases and does not extend into late antiquity.[22]

Even though legends of Rome's foundation remain a key point of interest to both archeologists and the wider public, these audiences must also confront the Roman Forum's existing ancient infrastructure, which features a wide array of late antique interventions. Major campaigns of restoration occurred during the fourth and early fifth centuries CE, when rebuilding shaped the precinct's appearance and ensured the survival of architecture into the present day.[23] Rome's historical memories underwent important transformations to become topographically rooted cultural markers protected by aristocrats, whose pride in the city's past offered a local addendum to the empire's "globalism" during late antiquity. This raises questions about how these late antique transformations came about and who sponsored these activities. As we shall see, during meaningful restoration campaigns, late antique aristocrats evaluated the extant features of the Forum to carefully excise certain memories while preserving other important features of the past.

THE SIGNIFICANCE OF RESTORATION IN THE LATE ANTIQUE ROMAN FORUM

The persistent vitality of the Roman Forum during the fourth and fifth centuries CE becomes clear from the physical testimony to the continued maintenance of Rome's public buildings and areas in which the community could assemble. Throughout this period, the judges held court in the civic basilicas of the Roman Forum, the populace gathered in the Forum's paved central area, and the senators assembled solemnly in the Senate House (Curia Senatus). In short, the Forum continued to embody Rome's state apparatus and received consistent upkeep until at least the breakdown of the western empire in 476.

Public statues, civic monuments, and their inscribed plinths provide a context for considering the architectural restoration that occurred in the late antique Roman Forum. Statue displays, for example, help to explain the Forum of this period because the publicly presented portraits were official monuments that advanced the impression that those who conserved buildings returned the state to tranquility. Late antique restoration featured the reuse of building materials and the recycling of statue bases for civic monuments, in part because the emperors and the aristocrats of Rome who sponsored the projects celebrated their respect for the past while projecting that they had mitigated the effects of decay. By the fourth century, the centuries-old Forum had already been updated many times; yet the critical role played by displaying old material in connection with recording individual memories distinguishes the late antique approach to restoration from its predecessors.

Public spaces of late antique cities featured monuments that presented the identities of those individuals who supported civic ideals through their patronage; statue displays in civic areas required consistent renewal and became reactivated by each successive installation that indicated the relevance of the past to the concerns of the present.[24] Documenting the accomplishments of prominent figures from various periods, the arrangement of imperial portrait statues reinforced the values passed down by previous generations. Visitors to late antique Rome came into contact with "the extensive population of statues and also the vast herds of equestrian monuments," according to Cassiodorus, a prominent member of Rome's sixth-century senatorial aristocracy.[25] The 101 inscriptions originating from statue monuments in the late antique Forum mostly accompanied imperial portraits as well as relatively few images of highly honored senators; artworks and masterpieces by famous artists were also on display. Most of these installations also recorded memories of the aristocratic benefactors in the affiliated inscriptions. Senators receiving imperial appointments to high-ranking positions, such as consul or urban prefect (*praefectus urbi*), typically honored the rulers by setting up statues in front of buildings in the Forum that rendered legitimacy to the emperors, who, during the fourth century, typically resided in other capitals.

It remains an open question whether emperors specifically generated buildings and honorific monuments, given the evidence that aristocrats took the initiative for the projects in Rome.[26] Prior to the third century CE, senatorial munificence had followed the model provided by the emperors, leading the aristocratic sponsors of statues to bask in the same glow as the rulers.[27] The later Roman empire ushered in an era of heightened hierarchical divisions between emperors and senators, with the aristocrats independently sponsoring monuments that honored emperors to demonstrate their agreement with the ruling authorities in exhibitions that essentially documented the administrative hierarchies of the state. This resulted in displays of imperial portraits in the Forum's central area and in the plaza in front of the Senate House. There is also evidence, nonetheless, that emperors and the local elite of Rome corresponded in letters and otherwise collaborated to create monuments in the late antique Forum.

Some statues were transported to the Forum by senators during late antiquity. The interest in these statues comes in part from inscription evidence that the works either were collected from elsewhere or were set up after having fallen down.[28] Those that can be considered artworks, some by famous Greek artists, stood apart from imperial portraits; they demarcated cultural zones where they were on display at the façades of the Basilica Aemilia and Basilica Julia flanking the Forum plaza (fig. I.8 [10] and [11]). The statues attributed to important artists functioned culturally as artworks in part because the surviving inscriptions, which lack the epigraphic characteristics of the honorific displays, suggest that the works belonged to a distinct category from the portraits. The senatorial initiatives to establish late antique exhibitions at the Basilica Aemilia and the Basilica Julia differed from the overtly political messages featured in the Forum square, since the works on view at the two basilicas sought to restore the cultural values associated with the earlier generations of aristocratic senators. Even though there was a topographical separation between artworks under senatorial sponsorship at the edges of the Forum and the imperial portraits that predominated in the central plaza, mutually beneficial alliances between aristocrats and emperors indicate that the installations in general refurbished both public space and the status of Rome's elite. Thus, Rome's senators must have pursued local projects that communicated ideas about the city's cultural renewal. The many connotations of restoration included references to the leadership of the empire, with statue installations representing important individuals as if they had reinstated the accomplishments of past rulers.

Civic architecture and public space in late antique cities have only recently benefited from new interpretive paradigms that attend to the meanings of reused sculptures and architectural fragments, called *spolia*.[29] Although structural repairs were consistently pursued throughout Roman antiquity, the legal status of individual marbles, columns, epistyles, and other publicly owned fragments as civic property caused them to be retained by the state during late antiquity. The valued pieces promoted new formats for creating pastiches out of the old architectural elements.[30] The cultural significance of restoration during the fourth and fifth centuries CE shaped the patchwork-like arrangements of old fragments; thus late antique reconstruction strategies differ radically from renewal as it is practiced today.[31]

The late antique restoration of both buildings and monuments in the Roman Forum brought concrete expression to the politicized restitution of the past. *Restitutio*, with connotations of reinstating, giving back, or restoring that which had been taken away, was the term used to describe many architectural or monumental restoration projects.[32] Innovation often had to be disguised as restitution in ancient Rome. Thus, it could be argued that the disdain for novelty was implicit in the verbs *resituere* and *reddere*—both of which connote either giving back or restoring— which, when applied to a building or a monument, suggested that the restored structure was repaired at its proper location or that a replacement structure stood in the same spot as that which it replaced.[33] Another term, *reparare*, designated the renewal of a still-intact building.[34] Restoration activities expressed reverence for the past, but the benefactors who supported the repairs in the pursuit of individual status hid the personal desire for social transformation under the cloak of restitution.

When applied to public buildings in Rome, the word *restitutio* indicated the obvious renewal of structures, together with the agenda of reinstating the sta-

tus of the elite benefactors who were financing the repairs. During the late Republic and the early imperial era, magistrates held the strategic responsibility of maintaining Rome's built infrastructure, so crucial to warding off decay and projecting the message that the city was culturally renewed. As seen at the Basilica Aemilia, which was ornamented in 78 BCE with ancestral portraits to record a patron's lineage, the Republican Forum had been built up as a result of families investing in the public sphere to mark status or pedigree.[35]

Restoration as a late antique architectural practice correlates with orations and literary products that communicated imperial prestige by promoting specific virtues. The texts of late Roman panegyrics lavished praise on emperors who were said to have reinstated history, subtly implying that the rulers renewed justice and protected the rights acquired by Romans over the centuries. Pacatus, writing in praise of the emperor Theodosius I in 389, celebrates the ruler for having vanquished his rival Maximus, emphasizing that no revenge was taken against the enemy's former supporters: "All were restored to their homes, all were restored to their wives and children, all finally—which is sweeter—were restored to innocence. See, Emperor, what this clemency has obtained for you."[36] The emperor's justice was deemed to restore proper privileges to those guilty of having previously collaborated with Theodosius' enemy. By implication, such praise advanced the sense that conserving old architecture actually reinstated the virtues of past benefactors. One can conclude that structural repairs in the Roman Forum made the rulers shown in public statues appear to stand in their proper places. This sense of propriety was strengthened by the revival of historical memories.

To be sure, there was no unanimity over the goal of preserving the Forum. Writing in the aftermath of the Visigothic sack of Rome in 410 CE, Orosius proposed jettisoning pagan antiquities in the Forum, since they potentially attracted divine retribution: "The Forum with its vain images, which by a wretched superstition gave God a human shape, was smitten by lightning bolts; all those abominations which the fire let loose by the enemy did not reach, heaven-sent fire destroyed."[37] Orosius argues vehemently against renewal, implying that the upkeep of pagan statues in the Forum impeded the goals of Christians. Orosius' rhetoric seems not to have worked, however, for evidence from the Forum suggests that benefactors invited the public to reconceive rather than to reject antiquities.

Orosius stands at the outset of the long tradition that sees ancient architecture as doomed to ruin after the fifth century. One group of modern historians has consequently turned to texts such as the one by Orosius to characterize fifth-century Rome as having suffered an irrecoverable loss.[38] Presenting an alternative view, Alan Cameron has offered a highly nuanced account of how late antique elites retained their Hellenistic cultural interests, even while Christianity emerged as normative.[39] Historic individuals with their names inscribed on monuments inserted their identities into the historical record, and their memories appeared in images on public display in many Mediterranean cities. Public enemies might also be forgotten when the regulations that led to obliterating the names of the condemned were enforced.[40] The potential for individual rehabilitation after such erasure from public monuments has been brilliantly explored in Charles W. Hedrick Jr.'s analysis of the official restitution of memories that undid the condemnation of Flavian the Elder (Nicomachus Flavianus, 334–394), a hero to Rome's traditionalists.[41] Civic architecture in late antique Rome emphasized the interplay between memory and public benefactions that launched a symbolic revival of the ancient capital; one recent study, for example, has demonstrated that the late antique walls resurrected Rome's status through imperial campaigns to remake the circuit not just as a rampart, but as an emblem of the city.[42]

Building upon careful attention to memory in the analysis of ancient Rome, I present the case that reinstating the past provided the key strategy through which benefactors negotiated Rome's cultural position during the later Roman empire. My investigation of the Roman Forum during the fourth and fifth centuries carefully entwines discussions of reconstructed architecture with considerations of artworks, epigraphy, literature, and public monuments, an approach that draws upon Paul Zanker's argument that civic projects advertised the new ideology

pioneered by Augustus at the outset of the empire.[43] Careful analysis of the Forum's inscriptions and their accompanying portrait statues bolsters the claim that senatorial installations recaptured traditional aristocratic virtues, ostensibly reinforcing each emperor's legitimacy while subtly reinvigorating the norm of consent among the rulers, the people, and the elite benefactors. The pages to follow underscore how different temporal concepts regulated the commemoration of memories in the Forum, where public fame proceeded from the appearance that each newly inserted portrait statue supplemented earlier installations, and that rebuilt structures likewise continually updated the past.

The book addresses a fundamental question about the preservation of the Roman Forum as a built environment: How did sponsors and imperial authorities revise urban experiences through the subtle changes—the restoration of buildings and the renewal of monumental installations—that reactivated important memories? The Forum was rebuilt over various campaigns in the wake of a devastating fire in 284, after which the refurbished structures featured decorations and inscriptions emphasizing the late antique preoccupation with reinstating lapsed time. I engage with current debates concerning the gravity of late antique urban catastrophes by documenting that the Forum's resilience occurred with the coinciding goals of displaying honorific statues and pursuing the structural restoration of significant buildings.

Recently, innovative considerations concerning the experiential dynamics of Rome's urban space have emphasized how the physical environment constantly changed, thereby calling attention to the diachronic evolution of the cityscape.[44] Considerations of Rome as a complex urban environment have led scholars to avoid isolating the discrete phases of structures, instead emphasizing that late antique continuities and early medieval transformations allowed memories to persist over time at significant sites in the city.[45] In sum, buildings were never conceived as fixed in time during late antiquity; a dynamic process of revising conceptions of the past resulted from the fragmentary reuse of ancient building materials and the integration of buildings with the prominent display of public statues.

USING DIGITAL ENVIRONMENTS

Capturing the spaces of ancient cities in digital formats facilitates research on statues and their accompanying inscriptions, indicating that the urban topography triggered recollections of significant events or the accomplishments of key individuals. Statues functioned as physical markers of memories, and the coordination of images with inscribed texts reveals how audiences experienced public space in late Roman cities. An exemplary digital project pursued by an Oxford team that presents both late antique statues and the associated inscriptions underlines the importance of considering them in unison.[46] A further concern is to connect ancient inscriptions with precise geographic locations, which has led scholars to map out public texts in their original urban contexts.[47] With regard to investigating the Roman Forum, researchers have introduced three-dimensional environments that facilitate research about urban space, and digital reconstruction has approximated the appearance of buildings and monuments.[48]

One important benefit of digital reconstruction is the ability to connect the layers of the past with the spatial implications of historic sites.[49] As the *Rome Reborn* project demonstrates, video formats have advanced considerations of movement through an ancient city, even though the animated films present urban reconstruction from a bird's-eye view rather than at ground level.[50] An alternative method of conducting research on historic cities exploits a Google Earth interface, featuring digital reconstructions that maintain both accurate geographic coordinates and precise dates while allowing one to browse the digital models as one chooses rather than having to follow preset itineraries.[51]

This book was developed in tandem with a digital research project I conducted together with Diane Favro and Christopher Johanson, *Visualizing Statues in the Late Antique Roman Forum*.[52] The digital project confronted a key issue: almost none of the statues originally situated in the Forum survive, even though numerous inscriptions remain to attest to the displays. Many sculptural monuments commemorated the emperors and members of the aristocracy. Yet important works attesting to the dynamic role of

memory within the Roman Forum have been separated from their original topographical contexts, opening up the potential for research that digitally rejoins the statues and monuments with their original display spots.

An initial step in producing the digital reconstruction of the late antique Forum entailed collecting archeological evidence of inscribed statue bases so as to identify their original display locations. These places for the original installations do not always match where modern archeologists rediscovered the plinths. To be sure, the find spots of the inscriptions offer important insights, but indentations in the pavement and other extant physical evidence offer additional clues as to where the statues were initially installed. After determining where many of the works were displayed, we used the names of known individuals from the inscriptions to establish the chronological sequence of the displays.[53] The scale of each statue was reconstructed on the basis of its surviving plinth.[54]

An important feature of the website is to provide a navigable simulation of the spatial experience of walking through the reconstructed Roman Forum.[55] Some of the illustrations in this book are captured from the digital environment of *Visualizing Statues*; these offer glimpses of how the website frames experiential and spatial considerations of the Forum. A database of all the late antique inscriptions, including geographic coordinates for the known or hypothesized display spots in the Roman Forum, are also featured on the website.[56] Thus, *Visualizing Statues* allows viewers to understand movement through the Forum in an environment featuring precisely localized data together with the exact dates associated with many of the reconstructed statues.[57]

The epigraphic record suggests that the publicly displayed portrait statues of the Forum conserved memories of individuals whose identities were presented in Rome's ceremonial space. *Visualizing Statues* captures how memories were localized at the specific locations where the statues were on view. The portrait statues clustered around the Rostra, the plaza in front of the Senate House, and at the edges of the Via Sacra. When individuals moved through the late antique Forum, they must have interpreted the significance of statue installations by noting the dialogue among adjacent works or those arranged along sight lines. This has elicited the observation that rituals such as open-air processions and civic assemblies provided a functional basis for understanding the statues and inscriptions of the Forum. One case study available on the website focuses on the statues visible during the procession conducted by the emperor Honorius at Rome to celebrate his consulship in 404 CE.[58] It is hoped that the ability to browse the architecture of the late antique Forum together with the statues and other monuments that were integral to the precinct will allow other scholars to conduct further research using *Visualizing Statues*. Since the digital environment can be considered as a context in which to pursue further investigations, it facilitates reflections about the space of the Roman Forum and generates questions about the exhibitions of statues, such as who determined the arrangements.

IMPERIAL AND SENATORIAL REPRESENTATION IN THE ROMAN FORUM

The statues displayed in the late antique Forum were assembled in exhibitions, and there is evidence that senators corresponded with emperors about the statues.[59] Even though it cannot be precisely defined who dictated the content of many statue exhibitions in the public areas of the Forum, the groupings presented political concepts, such as the concord among imperial authorities and aristocratic officeholders. Further, the alignment of older statues with newer ones hinted that the values of the past contributed to the cultural vitality of the present, signaling a peaceful, flourishing age. Perhaps because the fourth-century emperors were usually absent from Rome, their words in praise of the most esteemed senators, whether spoken or written, were presented in certain inscriptions as if in archival documents. Some imperial speeches appeared in inscriptions honoring Rome's aristocrats after some senators had taken the initiative to set up statues depicting emperors. To be sure, higher status was accorded to emperors than to senators in the monumental displays of the

late antique Roman Forum. Yet the senators who set up statues in the Forum served in such posts as consul, urban prefect, praetorian prefect, or governor. These posts required appointment by the emperors, so these aristocrats were fully integrated into the leadership of the state. In Rome and elsewhere in the empire, local elites demonstrated their appreciation of emperors in statue displays confirming that imperial governance was normative.[60] Emperors and senators thus shared the language of power, and both groups acknowledged the role of the past in establishing precedents for their purported harmony.

Tropes characterizing good government mentioned in the inscriptions capture images of peace and virtue. Traditionally, emperors received terms of praise in coins, inscriptions, and panegyrics. Key words linked wise rulership to individual virtues: *liberalitas* or "generosity" was a personal quality that led to actual distributions to the public; *providentia* or "having foresight" connoted the wisdom that allowed one to see the correct path.[61] Traditional expressions of praise also applied to the built environment, with terms mentioning such virtuous roles as *conditor* (founder), *conservator* (conserver), and *restitutor* (restorer).[62]

A major virtue on display was that of concord, demonstrating that senators worked together with emperors. In the Forum of Trajan, a number of statues depicted particularly distinguished senators. Several inscriptions accompanying the senators' portraits feature the texts of speeches delivered by emperors approving the honors. These orations, filled with praise and transcribed word for word on certain statue bases, offer testimony to what Robert Chenault aptly characterizes as the "rhetoric of consensus" among the rulers and the aristocracy.[63]

An important statue display that documented the public rhetoric practiced in either the Roman Forum or the Forum of Trajan survives only in the form of a damaged statue base that originally featured an inscribed quotation from a public speech.[64] In 379 CE, Avianus Symmachus, father of Quintus Aurelius Symmachus, emphasized his imperial connections and his skill at oratory in an inscription for his honorific portrait statue, plausibly installed near the Senate House; only the damaged plinth survives

Figure I.9. Inscribed statue base of Avianus Symmachus (*CIL* 6.1698). Vatican Museums. Photo by the author.

(fig. I.9). The inscription indicates that Avianus served as an ambassador who represented the senate to the former emperors,

and who, being usually the first to state his opinion in the senate, has given to this esteemed institution a great deal of authority, wisdom, and eloquence to match the dignity of his rank; our victorious rulers have ordered the [bronze] statue shining with gold, which the distinguished senate by numerous decrees obtained from our lords, the emperors, to be set up together with an affixed text of a speech, which contains a full list of his positions in proper order; and, to add to this great honor, their unerring judgment has also decreed that a second statue of equal magnificence should be set up also in Constantinople.[65]

Avianus Symmachus' statue was rare, in that it was a public statue from late antiquity that featured a portrait of a local aristocrat, for which the senate as well as the emperors granted the required permission. Further, the inscription celebrates the official services Avianus Symmachus provided to the current and previous rulers. In a fascinating display of historical documentation, the statue featured the inscribed speech on one side, indicating an archival impulse that preserved a record of Avianus' achievements for posterity. (This face of the marble block does not survive.) Implicitly, the "affixed text of a speech" (*adposita oratione*) maintained memories of the honors bestowed upon the senator that only augmented his erudition, virtue, eloquence, and civic contributions, for which Avianus sought to be remembered by subsequent generations. The techniques of scholarly authors—quoting from a letter or a speech as an archival activity—were applied in the inscription honoring Avianus Symmachus, burnishing his own reputation as an author of panegyrics. As this example demonstrates, senators adduced the memories of civic virtues while attesting to the bonds between aristocrats and emperors in the monuments of the late antique Roman Forum and the Forum of Trajan.

The main historical memories presented in the public texts of the late antique Roman Forum were those recording the specific identities of rulers and those senators who had received the most prestigious appointments, setting up the monumental honors to individuals in civic space as a visual analogue for laudatory orations.[66] Perhaps the decision of Diocletian in the 280s to set up two co-emperors of roughly equivalent power, neither of whom lived in Rome, started the process of documenting the emperor's power by means of letters rather than speeches delivered in person. Quoting excerpts of letters and other documents in Rome's open-air displays, then, acknowledged the changing circumstances—namely, the absence of emperors who had to send letters to Rome from afar—while attesting to the maintenance of social bonds that tied imperial authorities to the local aristocrats. The orations documented in some late antique inscriptions were significant in recording the speeches delivered at meetings of the Senate, which eventually occurred in both Rome and Constantinople. In fact, Avianus Symmachus installed statues in both cities.

The archival records of speeches presented in inscriptions and the statues preserving memories of specific individuals constitute a historical record of worthy deeds. That the activities recorded in the Forum's public space were individual appointments to distinguished offices, and to imperial positions in particular, leaves us with an impression that political commemoration dominated the Forum. Statues displayed in the Forum's public space and their accompanying inscriptions offer Carlos Machado evidence with which to argue that late antique sponsors revived cultural memories of the historical past in the Forum.[67] Yet there is ample evidence that, due to the preponderance of imperial portrait statues accompanied only occasionally by images of senators and generals, the late antique Roman Forum remained a zone that celebrated rulership overall; the documented memories of politics, therefore, overshadowed cultural memories in the civic center.[68] Studies of the epigraphic record have led John Weisweiler to emphasize that it was the highest-ranking senators who dedicated the portraits of the exalted emperors in the late antique Forum; the sponsoring aristocrats received a measure of status in return.[69] Self-pride, then, was the motivation for most of the installations recording the identities of the elite. The central zone of the Roman Forum began to shift away from the legends of the city's distant past after the Tetrarchic age in favor of recording the memories of individual late antique power brokers.

Detailed information concerning how imperial policies were communicated to aristocrats and high functionaries throughout the later Roman empire appears in the Theodosian Code (*Codex Theodosianus*). The Code is a compilation of legislation generally excerpted from the letters issued by emperors starting with the time of Constantine up to the year 438, when the emperor Theodosius II, who oversaw the project, collected and distributed the texts. The laws assembled by Theodosius II indicate each critical imperial legal decision in its final form. The compilers noted the precise year of each law and assembled the juristic statements chronologically so that the most

recent decisions had the greatest validity. Different legislation was often sent to the East than to the West, implying that laws were enforced differently in the two realms of the later Roman empire.[70]

The documentary inscriptions displaying the texts of imperial letters were therefore in many ways as binding as imperially disseminated correspondence. This suggests that public displays enforced official concepts. Yet not all of the inscriptions featured the precise terms that the emperors had sent out. Instead, the displays of statues provided subtle reminders of the eloquence of Rome's aristocrats, who invented clever terms of praise for emperors. These aristocratic orators gained lasting fame by inscribing catchy phrases in stone. Tiberius Claudius Severus, a senatorial aristocrat of the highest rank, set up two aligned works that honored Diocletian and Maximian in the 290s with the same dedicatory phrases, "To the strongest and most flourishing," an alliteration in Latin (*fortissimo ac florentissimo*).[71] Later, in 353, Neratius Cerealis, the senator holding the post of urban prefect—the leader of the senate with responsibility for overseeing the public buildings of Rome—set up an equestrian monument for the emperor Constantius II. Neratius Cerealis used the dedicatory phrase, "To the restorer of the city of Rome and the world," featuring an internal rhyme (*restitutori urbis Romae adque orb[is]*).[72] These elegant phrases attest to public rhetoric.

There was a further dimension to the aristocrats' concern for documentation: the revival of the past launched by senators remained explicitly political in maintaining testimony to the skills of delivering speeches in the Senate House and recording that Rome was a center of eloquence and power. Thus, a senator plausibly identified in a highly damaged inscription as Ceionius Rufius Albinus, an urban prefect, also applied a text to a plinth that quoted from a "decree of the most illustrious senate" that sanctioned his statue's display in the Forum, set up in 391 and approved by the emperor Valentinian II. This is a further example of an "archival" document affixed to the secondary side of an inscribed statue base.[73] Documents inscribed onto late antique statue bases advanced the Forum's role as a realm for official history by preserving the names of emperors accompanied by the identities of senators who, by association, upheld their own exalted prestige.

Fed by the hunger for status and power, senators such as Avianus Symmachus and Ceionius Rufius Albinus established in the Forum's monuments a chronology of most emperors from the last decade of the third century until the early fifth century. Prior to the fourth century, displays had associated emperors, gods, and high-ranking aristocrats.[74] After Constantine (r. 306–337) introduced legislation that curtailed certain forms of sacrifice, senatorial patrons returned to using in inscriptions the traditional term of "restorer" (restitutor), which had been used to praise emperors for centuries. Yet the term no longer connoted the renewal of earlier emperors' divine qualities or the return to a mythic Golden Age. In the fourth century, imperial inscriptions using terms for restoration took on new meaning: late antique rulers instead communicated that they had brought back the peaceful times of cultural vitality. In a statue base honoring Constantine, for example, the inscription, set up in the Roman Forum at some point during his reign, praised him as the "fortunate restorer, founder, and extender of peace and the promoter of tranquility."[75] The late antique preference for terminology designating an emperor as a restorer (restaurator in the Constantinian inscription and restitutor in others) linked the ruler's identity with the virtue of bringing back calm, which in turn legitimized the restoration of buildings by the ruler.

Late antique rebuilding has received additional documentation in the recent excavations attending to postclassical layers at the imperial fora that flank the modern Via dei Fori Imperiali, the street passing over parts of Rome's historic center.[76] New discoveries, together with the epigraphic testimony to the rhetorical claims that promoted the fame of restorers, suggest that concepts of time and the late antique sensitivity to the trajectory of history can shed light on the importance of architecture in the Roman Forum.

CONCEPTS OF TIME

The late antique Roman Forum featured carefully preserved civic structures surrounding the central plaza, where the open-air displays documented the vitality that restoration brought back to Rome. Surprisingly, some temples were rebuilt or received major repairs as cultural monuments during the fourth century CE, even as laws to prevent sacrifice drastically curtailed the use of pagan altars.[77] Major streets—the Via Sacra, the Argiletum, the Vicus Jugarius, and the Vicus Tuscus—all intersected at the low-lying terrain of the Forum bounded by the Capitoline and Palatine hills (see fig. I.8). In the Forum, political life competed with commercial activities: official speeches were delivered on top of the Rostra at either end of the paved central area, whereas the south-facing side of the Basilica Aemilia accommodated markets for goods and services. Rome's aristocrats of the late empire must have paraded about the Forum to maintain their visibility before the populace, much as Cicero in De oratore described Manius Manilius traversing the public square during the Republic, doling out advice to those he met.[78] In sum, the Roman Forum during late antiquity continued to function as a zone to seek out popular support and as a place where audiences appreciated the return of the favored eras of the past.

Imperial policies ensured that the aristocratic elite would connect their revival of history with the virtue of generously restoring civic structures. This prompted Rome's populace to see the physical recuperation of old buildings as a return to traditional euergetism.[79] One can assume, then, that the ubiquity of building renewal was not necessarily an indication of the breakdown of the architectural industry. Indeed, images of Rome's degradation had long fostered the reputation of the late antique city as diminished; yet the fall of Rome must not be anticipated too hastily. In addition, the familiar trope of cultural renewal due to imperial initiatives had traditionally situated the public buildings of Rome, and particularly the civic architecture of the Roman Forum, as emblems of virtuous governance. These considerations call attention to the vigor of late antique restoration and emphasize how senatorial and imperial sponsors sought to promote an ideological return to the past by triggering responses to repairs.

The preservation of civic life in the Roman Forum, together with the restoration of buildings and monuments, raises issues about concepts of time, namely, whether the past was divided up into periods, progressed through stages, reemerged in a cyclical fashion, was subject to renewal, or was transmitted into the present by means of updates. Vestiges from the past remained crucial to the late antique Roman Forum, which, by means of architectural reuse, indicated the importance of restitution. Yet the Forum's archaic traces memorializing the city's origins, including the commemoration of Rome's foundation at the Lapis Niger, which remained visible during the fourth and fifth centuries CE, were overshadowed by the late interventions.[80] Architectural strategies and monumental projects inserted into the Forum after 300 CE featured such approaches to renewing the past as *spolia* displays and repairs that recorded the process of conservation. In addition, late antique methods of historical documentation, such as the inscriptions with excerpts from archival sources, established that recording the past allowed memories to remain viable and meaningful for generations to come. In other words, the past could lay the groundwork for the anticipated future. According to Charles Hedrick Jr., the epigraphic preservation of names was of fundamental importance to establishing the historical record; by this means, the venerable activities of upstanding citizens remained on view for generations in public texts. Similarly, open-air exhibitions presented the affiliations among individuals living in different eras.[81] Concepts of the past were physically documented in the public areas of the Roman Forum so that powerful and prestigious elite benefactors could usher in periods of peaceful tranquility through their generosity.[82]

The major issues raised by the late antique Roman Forum concern how rebuilding reiterated the memories of those whose names were carved in stone and for whom the appeal of reinstated honors launched architectural revival efforts. In the fourth century, the virtues tied to munificence flourished; yet the commemoration of the past no longer instilled a desire for a return to the Golden Age. Bringing back this ideal era had been predicated upon restoring the rule of Saturn, with the comingling of humans and the gods.[83] For example, images of the deities displayed together with representations of mortals

communicated politicized cosmic symbolism at the early imperial Temple of Concord, which Tiberius orchestrated at the western edge of the Roman Forum.[84] After Constantine altered the religious centrality of the state-sanctioned gods, public monuments rarely anticipated a return to the mythic past or the Golden Age. Yet there was no physical marker in the Forum that explicitly expressed the Christian sympathies of most post-Constantinian emperors prior to the sixth century. Nonetheless, Christian apocalyptic predictions introduced a preoccupation with a temporal endpoint that contrasted with the ancient concern for an original age of mythic closeness among mortals and the deities.[85] It can be argued that the recapitulation of lapsed time evident in the architecture and monuments of the late antique Forum—in avoidance of the tainted concept of a Golden Age—resulted from the civic commitments of senators and the political interests of imperial authorities wishing to emphasize the civil restitution of the happy eras of the past. An aura of political stability resulted from architectural projects and monumental displays that demonstrated legitimacy through attentive restoration.

Collecting *spolia*, displaying inscriptions, assembling statues, and repairing buildings were cultural activities comparable to the editing of texts.[86] To characterize how the textual approach crossed over into architecture and urban space, I use the term "revision," which captures updates to the written record of the past. Revision further implies that a core text, after receiving emendations, remains fundamentally intact. Historical writing in late antiquity incorporated the preservation of letters, documents, petitions, responses, and legal rescripts. The letters of Quintus Aurelius Symmachus or the legal texts witnessed in the written responses to queries concerning policy as assembled in the Theodosian Code offer examples of texts transmitted to us by archivists.[87] The process of collecting, maintaining, and editing these letters in late antiquity was a historical impulse that also shaped the appearance of public inscriptions.

Not all of the documents and speeches that late antique senators collected were excerpted from old texts; late antique archivists preserved memories very publicly and at topographically meaningful spots through the display of statues in the Forum. Pierre Nora has identified fragmented memories as residing at sites of commemoration (*lieux de mémoire*); he says that significant locations become enveloped by the past to function as historical places that are meaningful for a society for whom shared experiences become cultural memories.[88] In his analysis of monuments attesting to memory practices in the late antique Roman Forum, Carlos Machado ponders whether non-elite communities retained cultural memories different from those of emperors and senators; he infers from the lack of evidence for popular responses that senators and emperors competed in different ways over a range of places where each high-status group took possession of memories.[89] Rather than examining these shared memories that provided the cultural capital of the late antique Roman Forum, I focus on the documented events and individual achievements that were attested in inscriptions and representations, which, I argue, made the public space of the Roman Forum into a "text" that was constantly under revision.

The Tetrarchic emperors Diocletian and Maximian were responsible both for undertaking major rebuilding campaigns in the Forum after 284 CE and for fundamentally altering the concepts of imperial rule, two phenomena that I propose were inextricably linked. Diocletian and Maximian used new representational strategies for emperors that caused audiences to remember specific pre-Tetrarchic emperors as having been updated by the new ideologies put in place around 300. The sites of the Forum became places for the specific emperors and senatorial officeholders to be memorialized during late antiquity. In other words, restored architecture provided a context for remembering individuals as opposed to recording cultural memories. The commemoration of individuals offers us a useful method for understanding how the past promoted lasting memories of personal accomplishments recorded in the inscriptions.[90]

The meanings associated with late antique architectural restoration in the Roman Forum emerge from a consideration of statue displays, imperial rituals, and epigraphic habits. The late antique dynasties, from Diocletian's Tetrarchy until the end of the rule by members of the Theodosian house, coordinated the restoration of buildings with the politicized attempt to resurrect civic virtues. On a practical level, the emperors appointed the urban prefects of Rome to year-long terms to oversee the senate and administer all civic architecture in the city, generating a chain of allegiances in which aristocrats honored emperors in inscriptions.[91] In 376, the legal restrictions preventing local senators, and urban prefects in particular, from instigating new civic buildings in Rome without imperial approval were solidified in a letter from the emperors Valentinian I, Valens, and Gratian that was read out in the senate. It asked for all urban prefects to abstain from pursuing "any new structure in the renowned city of Rome." The emperors articulated that the care of the city resulted from restoring and from avoiding new construction. They used highly specific terms and demanded that urban prefects "focus on improving the old buildings . . . without digging up the substructure undergirding noble buildings, without obtaining from the public recycled stones, and without despoiling buildings by stripping away pieces of marble."[92] This legislation clearly attests to the efforts by emperors to control the building activities pursued by local senators.

The character of late antique architectural restoration indicates imperial presumptions concerning time that were apparent in the ceremonial activities of emperors. By reinstating the past, imperial rituals from 284 until 312 emphasized the cyclical rather than the linear passage of time. With the vows (*vota*) traditionally taken by each new emperor upon accession, still celebrated during the Tetrarchy, imperial rituals anticipated five- and ten-year increments of rule that were renewed upon the fulfillment of each pledge.[93] It is usually suggested that Constantine's favorable attitude toward Christianity prompted a fundamental rupture in the ritual life of the empire, even though imperial rites, aside from sacrifices, remained consistent in most ways. Although Constantine himself shied away from the traditional rites associated with vows, the celebrations of jubilees at ten-year intervals continued.

In an important article, Adam Gutteridge examines the evidence that a series of Christian emperors rejected pagan rites associated with taking vows at regular intervals in favor of a late antique concept of "perpetual restoration."[94] The transition in temporal concepts from the fulfillment of the past to the late antique restoration that envisioned perpetuity implies for Gutteridge "a longing to strive towards (and even to catch up with) the future."[95] The fundamental importance of this insight pertains to identifying renewal as a key political concept. For example, Constantius II, whose equestrian statue base set up in the Forum in 353 presented him as the "restorer of the city of Rome and of the world," overstated the case so that the ruler would belong to a historically meaningful trajectory; in other words, furnishing the emperor with a past that he restored also established a path toward an anticipated future.[96] The remarkable historical consciousness appearing in the citations from letters and speeches on inscribed statue bases also preserved memories in a forward-looking way and advertised the virtue of reinstating the past. Further, the fourth-century shift toward documentation in the fragmented appropriation of architectural and sculptural elements or *spolia* recognized the present viability of the past; these fragments also anticipated the future. Yet implicit in the need for recuperation was the presence of decay, which taints the theme of perpetual renewal by pointing toward the inevitability of loss.

Methods of rebuilding that cast political ideas onto restoration projects during Constantine's reign placed the Roman Forum at the center of discourse concerning architectural recuperation. When the emperor Maxentius was deposed, Constantine had to address the architectural projects that his enemy had begun. In general, one can infer that merely preserving these architectural projects would have been insufficient. Instead, small-scale changes pursued during the restorations allowed Constantine to accrue fame as a restorer who transformed the explicitly despised memory of Maxentius, yet appropriated the rival's architecture.

The senators of Rome may have instigated some of the restorations in Rome's monumental center during Constantine's reign, thereby inviting the emperor to reconsider the city's legacy.[97] Despite Constantine's abandonment of Rome (with the exception of

brief visits for jubilees), the emperor's images took on urban prominence, as local senators reinvigorated the appeal of the past by situating Constantine's imagery in contexts indicating that he had revived the accomplishments of earlier rulers, particularly Trajan.[98] The aristocrats of Rome introduced a language of architectural restoration that maintained Rome's traditions in light of Constantine's ambivalence toward the old Roman state rites. With the premise that a legitimate emperor fulfilled the destiny established by earlier generations in assuming the role of *Augustus*, the imperial position remained embedded in the concept of reviving the past. Consequently, the senate designated Constantine as the legitimate emperor and restorer of the past, in contrast to Maxentius' role as a tyrant. The initiatives in Rome, probably undertaken by local authorities, allowed Constantinian honors in the Roman Forum to supersede the memories of Maxentius, gracefully sidestepping the painful truth that Constantine had triumphed in a civil war.[99] Thus, the Roman populace must have perceived the Constantinian "restorations" of Maxentius' buildings as appropriations that erased the memories of strife.

Even the members of the Valentinian dynasty who avoided Rome altogether ensured that the Roman populace received food distributions and ordered that the public buildings be restored.[100] Due to tense relations between the senators of Rome and the emperor Valentinian I (r. 364–375), imperial legislation offered strict guidelines that maintained the balance between senatorial pride and imperial authority, with urban upkeep as the civic benefit.[101] The tradition of maintaining Rome eventually fostered claims that the city reemerged stronger after misfortune. Rutilius Namatianus, an orator from Gaul who came to Rome and reached the esteemed position of urban prefect in 414, addressed the city directly when he wrote, in the wake of the sack of 410: "The time that remains is unlimited, just as the earth remains stable and the stars are fixed at the poles; you are renewed by that which upends other realms: to grow stronger out of misfortune is the principle of your rebirth."[102] In Rutilius' words, we witness the important concept that revival results from having displayed grit in the face of challenges. Thus, restoration flourished during the fourth and fifth centuries because it conveyed the strength of perseverance, which benefited both imperial authorities and the senatorial elite.

Even though some aristocrats identified with Christianity, others maintained the temples of the Forum in ways that established temporal continuities despite the religious transformation of the empire. For example, in 367, the praetorian prefect Vettius Agorius Praetextatus sponsored the securely documented restoration of the Porticus Deorum Consentium, which transformed the temple into a cultural artifact.[103] Efforts to preserve the monumental remains of the traditional cults clashed with the Christian perspectives of emperors and many members of the senatorial elite; the disputes particularly erupted during the 380s in the aftermath of the altar of Victory being removed from the Curia Senatus.[104] While there were no explicitly Christian buildings in the Forum prior to the sixth century, texts voice a Christian perspective about architecture. Hagiographic narratives, such as the apocryphal *Acts of Silvester*, narrate the activities of saints and papal authorities in the Forum. In the *Acts*, Pope Silvester I is said to have descended beneath the Temple of Vesta in the Forum to imprison a pestiferous dragon in a cave.[105] Even this act, which effectively deactivated the Vesta shrine, did not damage the structural integrity of the temple. Thus, Christians participated fully in maintaining the architectural integrity of the Forum during the fourth and fifth centuries.

TRANSFORMING PUBLIC SPACE

Open-air statues, preserved temples, imperial monuments, and civic structures all contribute to an understanding of architectural restoration that participated in reconfiguring the late antique Roman Forum. Building conservation, I contend, introduced the strategic coordination of architecture with both statues and the city's preexisting heritage to establish that public structures provided spaces where the virtues of the past could be maintained.

Chapter 1 here commences with a focus on the Tetrarchic installations in the Forum that advanced new temporal concepts in keeping with political changes.

At the outset of the fourth century, Diocletian and Maximian, as co-ruling senior emperors, celebrated a significant imperial anniversary in the Forum in order to cast their novel system of governance in traditional terms. The two speakers' platforms at either end of the Forum's central area supported facing rows of columns capped by statues depicting two co-reigning senior emperors flanked by their junior colleagues. The lasting installation of statues implied that collegial rule entailed fixed terms of office and projected an image of political stability. Specifically, inscriptions attest that the column monuments celebrated the twenty-year jubilees of the senior emperors in tandem with the ten-year jubilees of their two junior colleagues in a nod to the regular schedule defining that succession was to occur upon the retirement of the senior rulers. Diocletian, I argue, set the stage for the subsequent transformations of the Forum that reasserted the ideal of time's permanence amid the physical evidence of change.

Chapter 2 introduces how Constantine took possession of monuments in the Forum using a variety of approaches for delivering *restitutio*, the term for restoration that connotes returning something to its proper place. For instance, new inscriptions or architectural transformations marked that Constantine had taken over the Basilica Nova and the Rotunda on the Via Sacra, projects that Maxentius had constructed. With the politicized monuments now linking the victory over Maxentius with the restitution of Rome, Constantine at once appropriated and revised the claims that his rival was the *conservator* of his city.

The statues installed publicly in the Forum documented historic individuals in portraits that displayed their identities and emphasized their virtues. In Chapter 3, the emergence of constantly revised exhibition schemes indicates how the public space of the Forum received updates, often in ways that correlated with architectural repairs. The serial nature of the displays transmitted associations from the past that were altered by the installation of each new work. Most of the statues depicted emperors and were accompanied by inscriptions that specified their virtues as having accrued by association with earlier statues, since the cumulative nature of the displays resulted from implied cross-generational affiliations. Research on the original display spots attests that installations triggered memories along the major pathways as well as in the Forum square and the piazza facing the Senate House; portrait statues were thus able to personalize the ways in which the topography of the Forum transmitted the past to late antique viewers.

Chapter 4 confirms that senators moved artworks to the façades of the Basilica Aemilia and the Basilica Julia starting in the 370s. It can be argued, then, that the installations celebrated the virtues of Rome's aristocracy at the civic structures housing legal proceedings. Evidence connects the repairs at the two basilicas with the shifted statues that were not portraits; some of the statues were masterpieces by Greek sculptors. It is tempting to contemplate the implications of these works, whose subjects are not specifically identified in inscriptions. The statues moved to the basilicas' façades could broadly fit into the category of art, whether taken from private homes or from the interiors of temples. Thus, senators launched the reevaluation of art that was previously private, or perhaps pagan, at the sites of local authority in the Forum. This was significant in creating what might be considered an open-air museum along the façades of the two basilicas. There, cultural revival occurred almost as a sign of material abundance at these civic structures for a public who sought out sites for leisure activities with amenities such as artworks or civic ornament.

Chapter 5 explores the contested eternity of the Forum's temples. Reconstruction campaigns at the Temple of Saturn, sponsored by the senate, together with repairs at the Porticus Deorum Consentium by the senator Vettius Agorius Praetextatus, modified the temples through the evident reuse of older architectural elements in ways that at once advertised the restitution of the past and the acknowledgment of time's passage. The explicit display of *spolia* hinted to audiences that pagan buildings had been restored to match the altered circumstances of the fourth century. Even the podium of the Temple of the Dioscuri was restored during the fourth century. Legends of saints, written during the fourth and fifth centuries, demonstrate that Christian authors shared the value of preservation in the Forum. Pope Silvester, as re-

counted in hagiography, eliminated the threat of a dragon inhabiting the Temple of Vesta in the Forum by containing the beast behind a closed door, suggesting that the shrine remained undamaged. Implicitly, Pope Silvester purposefully curtailed the demon without harming pagan architecture.

In Chapter 6, I explain that the Senate House, rebuilt under Diocletian and Maximian at the turn of the fourth century, created a building signaling Rome's local control. The termination of imperial support for senators serving in pagan priesthoods coupled with the state appropriation of temple endowments effectively withdrew cult affiliations from the honorific positions senators occupied. The situation culminated in Christian senators orchestrating the official removal of the altar of Victory from the Senate House, an act that was contested in letters sent to the emperor Valentinian II in the 380s by the pagan senator Q. Aurelius Symmachus. St. Ambrose, bishop of Milan, also sent letters to Valentinian II demanding that the altar never be returned to the Senate House. The dispute over the removal of the altar sets forth evidence that pagans and Christians actually agreed to conserve the statue of Victory, which had never been removed. Senators also transformed a hall that originally belonged to the Forum of Caesar into the Secretarium Senatus, a space where aristocrats received exclusive and advantageous judicial hearings. Latin hagiographic texts about the life of St. Martina coupled with epigraphic testimony to the honor paid to a St. Epiphanius at the Secretarium Senatus attest to the ways Christians maintained yet transformed memories of an early fifth-century senator, also named Epiphanius, who had restored the building within the senatorial compound. Another hagiographic narrative recounting St. Peter's contest with Simon Magus on the Via Sacra suggests how hagiographic texts contested the monumentality of statues, since the saint was honored with either footprints or kneeprints that were legendarily etched in the street's pavement stones to mark humility rather than statuesque pride.

This book reflects on the Roman Forum as a ceremonial stage for emperors during late antiquity. An analysis of how ceremonies elicited responses from audiences that registered a need for renewed space demonstrates that rituals appropriated the past as a way of reinforcing the themes of imperial pride projected in both buildings and inscriptions. The book engages with current debates about whether vitality or decrepitude characterized late antique Rome; it documents that the Forum's resilience was poised at the confluence of both decorative and real restoration. The significance of this today lies in recounting that late antique conservation transmitted ancient architecture down to us. Indeed, I argue that *restitutio* as expressed in buildings and monuments remade the Forum to appear timeless. The different perceptions of the Forum originating from late antiquity not only reoriented the discourse on ancient architecture, but actually shaped the physical appearance of the buildings and monuments through which we now assess the Roman past.

COLLECTIVE IDENTITY AND RENEWED TIME IN THE TETRARCHIC ROMAN FORUM

THE TETRARCHS, RULING WITHIN A SYSTEM OF MULTIPLE EMPERORS WHO OPERATED IN unison, communicated concepts of recurring time in the Roman Forum to promote a highly ordered scheme for reviving governance. The Tetrarchs were supposed to adhere to temporal cycles in which imperial succession followed regular patterns; this regularity staved off the vulnerability of the emperors to haphazard events. In the 290s, the co-rulers Diocletian and Maximian established a supposedly eternal pattern of orderly transitions in rulership that—despite internal conflicts that doomed their original system—was mapped out in the Forum. Specifically, to support the Tetrarchic goal of setting up collegial emperors who gained office together, builders in Rome constructed column monuments presenting one group of rulers whose images paralleled companion statues of their intended replacements.

Practical concerns also prompted a comprehensive rebuilding of the Forum by the Tetrarchs. The fire of Carinus in 284 seriously damaged the buildings and monuments of the Roman Forum and altered the site where senators and imperial authorities had competed over the right to display portrait statues.[1] A fourth-century report concerning the fire indicates that "public structures of Rome burned, specifically the Senate House, the Forum of Caesar, the Basilica Julia, and the Graecostadium."[2] This list has prompted the observation that the fire proceeded along one trajectory leading from the Basilica Julia to the Graecostadium immediately to its south, as another branch raged from the Senate House toward the Forum of Caesar (fig. 1.1).[3] Emperors Diocletian and Maximian (joint rule, 286–305) instigated repairs of the Forum's buildings around the turn of the fourth century, as documented in historical accounts, at the Basilica Julia, the Senate House, and the Forum of Caesar.[4] This architectural transformation corresponded with new strategies for representing the emperors, particularly in the integration of reused materials into monuments honoring them.[5]

In the Forum plaza and in front of the Senate House, the Tetrarchs and their fourth-century successors received acclaim in displays of portrait statues—sometimes plated with silver or gold—presented at greater than life size.[6] Despite the prominent imperial representations

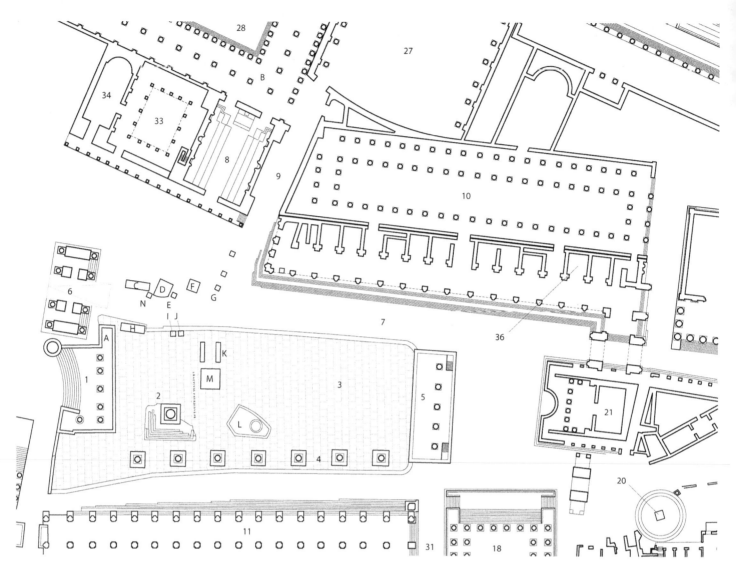

Figure 1.1. Plan of the Roman Forum in c. 400 CE: (1) western Rostra; (2) Column of Phocas; (3) plaza in the central area of the Roman Forum; (4) row of seven columns; (5) eastern Rostra; (6) Arch of Septimius Severus; (7) Via Sacra; (8) Senate House (Curia Senatus); (9) Argiletum; (10) Basilica Aemilia (nave); (11) Basilica Julia; (18) Temple of Castor and Pollux; (20) Temple of Vesta; (21) Temple of the Deified Julius Caesar; (27) Forum of Nerva (Forum Transitorium); (28) Forum of Caesar; (31) Vicus Tuscus; (33) Atrium of Liberty (Atrium Libertatis); (34) Secretarium Senatus; (36) *tabernae* (shops) in the portico of the Basilica Aemilia; (A) extension to the western Rostra; (B) Atrium of Minerva (portico of the Forum of Caesar); (C) equestrian statue of Constantius II; (D) Lapis Niger; (E) statue of Mars; (F) statue group of the Theodosian dynasty; (G) three statues in a row of Constantius II; (H) equestrian statue of Constantine; (I) statue of Stilicho; (J) statue of Honorius; (K) travertine supports for the "Arch" of Honorius; (L) Lacus Curtius; (M) display spot of the statue of Marsyas and the Ficus Ruminalis; (N) statue of Maxentius. Drawing by Brian Doherty.

Figure 1.2. Digital reconstruction of the western Rostra in the Roman Forum, c. 303 CE. Experiential Technologies Center, UCLA. © Regents, University of California.

Figure 1.3. Sculptural relief showing Constantine standing on the Rostra and the Hadrianic roundels from the Arch of Constantine. Photo by Mary Ann Sullivan.

dominating the fourth-century Forum, aristocrats continued to have their identities featured in public space. Suggesting that senators had forsaken virtuous activities in the pursuit of lasting fame, the late fourth-century historian Ammianus Marcellinus in his account of Rome poked fun at those senators who sought to set up excessively formal statues symbolizing the survival of their class above all else: "Some of these desire statues, out of the belief that they will be recommended to eternity, as if they will earn more rewards from bronze images, lacking feelings, than from the knowledge of honorable and just actions."[7] Senators were criticized for pursuing high rank over contributing to the public good when they desired statues presenting static time to preserve a frozen class system.

The Tetrarchs reworked the Forum's central area in anticipation of an important imperial jubilee in 303 that utilized the space they had physically transformed.[8] Their ritualized ideas about time appeared in methods of construction that furnished an appropriate context in which to celebrate revival.

An individual standing in the plaza of the Roman Forum during the fourth century and facing the western Rostra saw five columns rising above the speakers' platform. These columns were added just prior to 303 by Diocletian and Maximian (fig. 1.2). With these columns and other additions, the Tetrarchs had transformed the old Augustan Rostra. Statues installed above the columns on the speakers' platform advertised Tetrarchic ideas about rulership in a generic fashion, and, as I argue below, the images seem to have been intended as a lasting backdrop for emperors who would use the tribune during the upcoming generations. Fourth-century visitors facing the western Rostra gained a view that is also captured in a relief on the Arch of Constantine that documents the installation of now-lost statues on top of the columns (fig. 1.3).

THE TETRARCHIC SYSTEM

In the decade following the fire of 284, Diocletian and Maximian divided the empire in two under the joint rulership of two senior emperors, or *Augusti*, who implemented the Tetrarchy, a collegial system of governance. Diocletian named Maximian as his ally and co-emperor in 286; both eventually claimed divinely sanctioned positions. In the Forum, this Tetrarchic system was represented in the column monuments produced for Diocletian and Maximian, which featured statues on top that captured both their eternal concord and their politicized system of reviving the past. The column installations, which showed emperors in pairs, represented collegiality as generated by joint succession: each cohort of two *Augusti* anticipated the two who were to follow them. Inscriptions, rituals, restored buildings, and sculptural reliefs localized in the Roman Forum all worked together to make exemplary moments from the past appear to return under the Tetrarchs, as if their cyclical concept of time resounded throughout public space. The Tetrarchic monuments in the Roman Forum thus implemented a particular vision of temporal stability in which the imperial positions were believed to remain constant while the individual officeholders changed.

Though the restored buildings and newly installed column monuments in the Tetrarchic Forum lack clear indications of sponsorship, brief mentions in the *Chronograph of 354* lead us to presume that they were a result of imperial directives.[9] This apparent imperial acquisition of sponsorship privileges correlates with the growth in rulers' prerogatives under the Tetrarchs. Under the autocratic rulership that Diocletian introduced, imperial images began to appear more grandiose than images of other aristocrats; meanwhile, elite sponsors had to give up their traditional forms of self-representation to pursue projects that emphasized the exalted positions of the emperors.[10] Judging from inscribed statue bases, the Tetrarchic Forum was meant to sustain the supposedly eternal system of rulership that the emperors pioneered.

The concern for permanence also prompted the Tetrarchs to initiate other reforms. Diocletian and Maximian reorganized the empire's administration by dramatically expanding the number of prestigious posts available and opening up new opportunities for those with distinguished military careers. Many of the newly appointed officials came from outside the senatorial ranks, subjecting the aristocratic elite to heightened competition in their pursuit of esteemed positions. Ambitious military leaders were systematically encouraged to switch to civilian career paths and therefore provide a support network for legitimate emperors. In fact, to prevent usurpers from gaining the formidable support of numerous troops in the large provinces, the Tetrarchs revised the empire's territory by doubling the number of provinces, each under the new leadership of a civil vicar (*vicarius*). Designating civilians rather than military officers to collect taxes for distribution to soldiers, Diocletian effectively prevented the commanders from gaining the full loyalty of their troops by paying them.[11] This diminished the potential for military leaders to threaten the emperors.

An important political shift occurred in 293, when the senior emperors appointed their first two junior *Caesares*, Galerius and Constantius I, as the chosen successors to the *Augusti*. Mystery still surrounds how the *Caesares* were chosen: perhaps secrecy enhanced the religious aura of each emperor, pegged as an avatar of either Jupiter or Hercules.[12] Each *Caesar*, as *Augustus*-designate, acquired some authority by taking vows and performing rites at imperial jubilee ceremonies that, though rooted in imperial traditions, took on new meanings during the Tetrarchic age. In setting forth regular patterns of ritual renewal during imperial anniversaries, the Tetrarchs created the appearance of political stability, with highly orchestrated celebrations commemorating imperial succession.

Urban space and state monuments seem to have been of tremendous importance to the Tetrarchs. Rituals performed in public areas of the cities throughout the empire, after all, could allow many Romans to participate in the festivities commemorating the itinerant rulers. It is plausible that Diocletian and Maximian intended Rome to be the ritual center for jubilee celebrations that united all four emperors; but there is no evidence that all four Tetrarchs ever actually appeared there together.

The Tetrarchs maintained control over the vast Roman empire by traveling to meet military challenges at the various frontiers. Consequently, Rome was denied its customary position as the residential capital.[13] Despite this, the Roman Forum seems to have received commemorative monuments for all four Tetrarchs, who thereby designated the Roman plaza as a place to celebrate the rule of the four over the entire empire, fractured though it was. With none of the Tetrarchs living in Rome, no single emperor could gain preeminence in the traditional capital. The empire was definitively divided between east and west: Diocletian ruled in the east, together with the *Caesar* Galerius; Maximian served as *Augustus* in the west, with Constantius I as *Caesar*. After expanding the size of the imperial bureaucracy and increasing the number of provinces, the Tetrarchs instigated a growth in assemblies and rituals that highlighted the global dominion of emperors; but the most significant imperial anniversaries seem to have been localized at Rome and celebrated with events that culminated in the Forum.

Despite the split between east and west, the Tetrarchic emperors projected the message that the individual rulers operated as one, and they relinquished their individuality to advance the cause of concord. In keeping with the principle of collegiality, any single emperor who was victorious in battle would share the credit with all four.[14] The conceptual unity also required that each individual emperor issue laws in the name of all of the reigning Tetrarchs.[15] Alliances among the rulers were made by marriage, but an *Augustus* was prevented from appointing his son to the position of *Caesar*. Diocletian thus broke the chain of dynastic succession by denying the birthright of emperors' sons, and he named two new *Caesares* in 305 who were not related to the members of the imperial college.[16]

Despite the efforts at coordination, Tetrarchic emperors did not specify in imperial documents the precise lengths of their terms in office. What mattered most was the appearance that the emperors operated jointly; this togetherness was projected in coins, public inscriptions, and honorific monuments.[17] In Rome, installing images of the co-rulers in pairs particularly designated a sequence of succession that appeared well ordered and predictable. Thus, the original Tetrarchic system regulated time through orderly imperial appointments, earned through merit rather than by birth, to create the appearance that accessions adhered to a fixed schedule. But those who had dynastic hopes of joining the imperial college, particularly Constantius' son Constantine and Maximian's son Maxentius, eventually rebelled against their exclusion from power. By 306, the nonhereditary system had fallen apart.

The Tetrarchs developed the idea of temporal repetition in reaction to the third-century crisis of imperial legitimacy: short-lived reigns had disturbed the empire's patterns of rulership. As a result of numerous third-century setbacks, the Forum seems to be without a sequential array of monuments originating from the era immediately preceding the Tetrarchs. Civic sponsorship had decreased during the tumultuous third century; the benefactions that did emerge in the western empire were cobbled together from fragments of earlier installations.[18] The Tetrarchs did not reinstate the memories of esteemed historical aristocrats; instead, they turned to divine protectors as prototypes. Each emperor was identified by name with Jupiter or Hercules (with the rulers designated as either *Iovius* or *Herculius*). Roman concepts of historical time were reinforced by the sense of replicating divine traditions, since celebrating the well-chosen exemplars from the past also anticipated a bright future. Diocletian and Maximian thus celebrated their identities as reiterating an everlasting, immortal pair of gods, a rulership principle that successive generations of emperors were expected to replicate.[19]

At the turn of the fourth century, the Roman Forum became a site for ceremonies tied to the Tetrarchic cycles. Festivities celebrated in Rome in 303 honored Diocletian and Maximian on the twentieth anniversary of their rule; as was customary, the anniversary was celebrated a year in advance. Formal addresses by emperors had traditionally been delivered from the Rostra in the Forum, causing audiences to think of the speakers' platform as a site for imperial oratory. Yet by the fourth century, given the abandonment of Rome by emperors, the occasions for speeches by rulers were rare. Nonetheless, the

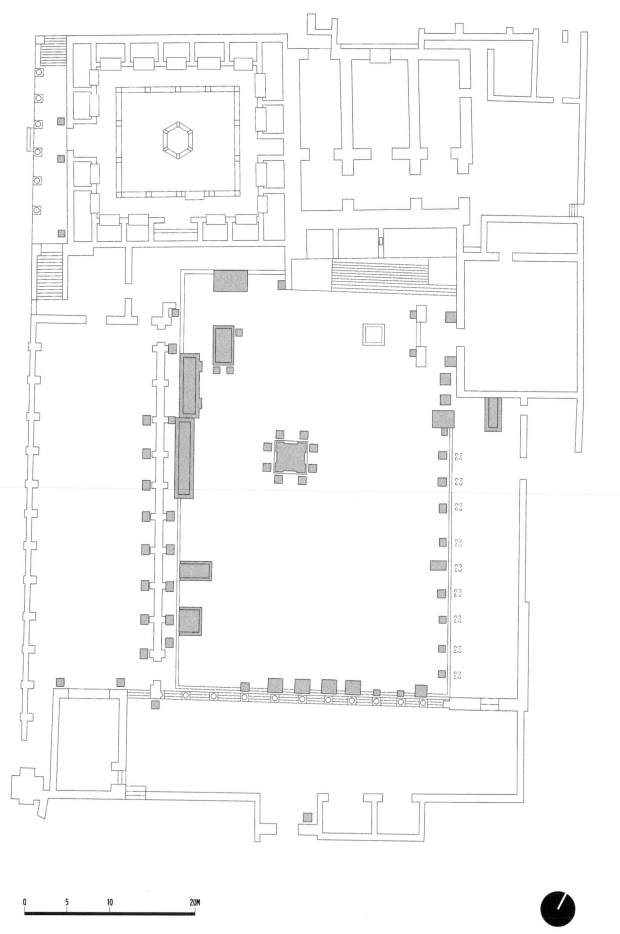

0 5 10 20M

Figure 1.4. Plan of the old Forum in Cuicul (Djemila, Algeria), after Gerhard Zimmer. Drawing by Cameron Bolin.

Forum's paved plaza acquired particular significance, since the statues contributed to the imperial purpose of the civic center. Statues lined each edge of the central Forum plaza, but only a few installations were aligned with the northern edge of the precinct along the Via Sacra; together, the statues marked off the plaza as a unified space (see fig. 1.1). Such an arrangement of statues surrounding the spots for the populace to gather can be deduced by comparison to other examples, particularly the forum of Cuicul, now the Algerian city of Djemila (fig. 1.4).[20]

IMPERIAL PANEGYRICS AND THE RENEWAL OF TIME

In 303, when the Roman Forum was activated by Tetrarchic ceremonies, the permanent installations commemorating Diocletian and Maximian resounded with the words spoken from the Rostra. Unfortunately, these speeches are not recorded. In a series of orations delivered in cities other than Rome, the well-ordered Tetrarchic state received praise for replicating the rhythms of nature. Ideas of cyclical patterns in the surviving texts of speeches provide a context for considering the Tetrarchic decorations of the Forum. Since Diocletian and Maximian received explicit praise for their concept of reconstituted time in panegyrics, their commitment to political stability and its clear benefits influenced generations of rulers who succeeded them.

The corpus of panegyrics praising Roman emperors includes four orations read before the members of Diocletian's first college of four emperors. The concept of temporal renewal particularly permeates the encomium honoring Constantius I, the western *Caesar*, delivered at Trier in 297. The panegyrist, whose name is not recorded, associated the rule by four collegial emperors with the orderly succession of the four seasons in an annual cycle. Proposing that the two *Caesares*, Constantius and Galerius, had reinstated the past, the panegyric stressed that the traditional 1 March start of the new year coincided with the rulers' shared moment of imperial accession (*dies imperii*) in 293. According to the text, as a result, political events occurred in tandem with the seasonal

cycles, commencing with the 1 March springtime renewal. Addressing Constantius and Galerius together, the orator stated:

O time at which our beliefs establish that everything was born, since we now see that all is confirmed by this season [spring]. O kalends of March, just as you were the beginning of the revolving years, so now you mark the beginning of the eternal emperors. How many ages, most unconquered emperors, do you generate for yourselves and for the state by sharing your amplification of the world?[21]

Even though the Julian calendar, used in 297, commenced each year on 1 January, celebrations known as the Natalis Martis continued during late antiquity on 1 March, and the traditional rites of renewal acquired political resonance because the Tetrarchic emperors appointed *Caesares* on the March date.[22] Beginning the cycles in the spring set in motion the theme of regeneration for the emperors. Identifying joint accession dates further made the co-ruling emperors appear to operate in complete concord during the Tetrarchic age, even when backdating was required to make the anniversaries coincide. All of the emperors theoretically operated in unison and aimed to celebrate their anniversaries of rulership together.[23] In fact, the imperial bond was reactivated on anniversaries, such as when Constantius and Galerius marked their five-year jubilee (*quinquennalia*) in 297.

The four collegial emperors mapped their notion of time onto a single empire that was divided physically but unified conceptually. The panegyrist who delivered the speech in 297 praised all four emperors together, because the four sectors of the world mirrored both the four seasons and the four essential elements. Addressing Constantius directly, the orator stated:

Indeed all the most important essences depend upon and rejoice in the number contained in your divine being: there are four elements and just as many seasons in a year. The world is divided into four by a double ocean. The cycle of years starts over again after four revolutions of the sky, the sun's chariot is drawn by four horses, and the sky features two lights, Vesper and Lucifer.[24]

The last phrase alludes to the harbingers of daytime and nighttime respectively: the morning star, Lucifer, and the evening star, Vesper. Accompanying the solar deity Sol as he was pulled across the sky by a chariot, the two stars in the panegyric represent the two *Caesares*, Constantius and Galerius, who benefited from the same daily renewal as the rising sun. Nature further justifies that the four Tetrarchs instigate renewal after "four revolutions of the sky," because they also derive their number from the four elements of air, earth, fire, and water, as well as the four land masses.[25] The references to nature augment the aura of divinity surrounding each emperor; the oration casts each ruler as maintaining the natural order willed by the gods.[26]

Panegyrics refer to Diocletian and Maximian adopting the pseudonyms of Jupiter and Hercules, respectively, to indicate that the divine identities would remain permanently intact, particularly when the individual officeholders confronted challenges. In Tetrarchic rhetoric, the emperors were presented as mortals who reflected the eternal identities of the immortals. The coordination between rulers and divinities appears in an oration read before Maximian in 289 in which the author turns imperial triumph into a reiteration of Hercules' labors. With reference to Maximian's victory over the Bagaudae, the orator addressed the *Augustus*, stating:

You [Maximian] came to the help of the Roman name, as it faltered, at the ruler's side, with the same urgency as your Hercules once provided to your Jupiter, when he was plagued by difficulties while battling the Sons of the Earth [giants]. Hercules then earned most of the victory, and established that he had not so much acquired heaven from the gods as restored it to them.[27]

In the panegyric, Maximian's victory primarily brought back honor to the Roman name. But Maximian's triumph also renewed the power of Diocletian and ultimately restored the proper respect for Jupiter and Hercules.

Since the Tetrarchic military successes were celebrated mostly during imperial anniversaries, the cycle of jubilees gained in importance by providing a regular calendar for ritual expressions of joint victory. The anniversaries, celebrated at decade-long intervals, generated new types of honorific installations for the Tetrarchic Roman Forum.

THE TETRARCHIC TRANSFORMATION OF THE ROMAN FORUM

The fire of 284 created an urgent need to refurbish the Roman Forum during the first years of the Tetrarchy. After the devastation, the ability to govern was compromised: senators could no longer gather in the ruined Curia Julia, and judges were unable to preside over courts of law in the damaged Basilica Julia. Thus, in the last decade of the third century, Diocletian and Maximian instigated a project to reverse the Forum's disrepair, rebuilding the Augustan Rostra, the Senate House (Curia Senatus), the Basilica Julia, and the structure aligned with its southern flank, the Graecostadium (see fig. I.8).[28] Recent excavations provide evidence that the ambitious Tetrarchic project at the Curia expanded the senatorial complex by linking it to a refounded *Atrium Libertatis* in the portico adjacent to the senatorial assembly hall and adding to the compound to the west of the Senate House with insertions into the narrow halls (*tabernae*) of the Forum of Caesar (see fig. I.8).[29] As a counterpoint to the enlarged senatorial compound, Diocletian and Maximian turned the Forum's central area into a site for imperial messages and revised the old Augustan Rostra at the plaza's western end (fig. 1.1 [1]). They also inserted the second Rostra at the eastern end of the square (fig. 1.1 [5]).

This architectural restoration had ritual implications. An analysis of the two Tetrarchic Rostra with lofty columns supporting statues suggests that the installations symbolized the cyclical patterns of the gods that were particularly relevant during the occasional imperial rituals practiced in the Forum. The most important Tetrarchic ceremony practiced at Rome commemorated the twentieth jubilee of the *Augusti* in November 303. That occasion also turned into an anniversary celebration for the *Caesares* Constantius and Galerius, who had postponed by a year the date of their ten-year anniversary. The Rostra installations celebrated Diocletian and Maximian—

only these two appear to have actually arrived in Rome—as the instigators of a newly conceived empire, a message that was amplified by the renewal of the Forum's buildings.[30]

Diocletian and Maximian exploited the restoration projects to suggest that they had vanquished the decay inherent in the passage of time. In recognition of this, high-ranking senators honored Maximian as the emperor of the west with statues set up publicly in the Forum calling him "unconquered" (*invictus*).[31] Since the fire of Carinus probably destroyed many of the statues and public inscriptions that had ornamented the Forum prior to 284, the honorific monuments set up thereafter for rulers featured epigraphic texts announcing the reversal of fortune. Throughout the fourth century, inscriptions in the Forum attest that senatorial patrons set up imperial statues that used such terms as *reddere* ("restore," "give back") and *restituere* ("restore," "replace," "put in its former place"), implying that military victories also helped bring the empire back to its former glory.[32]

REARRANGING THE FORUM'S CENTRAL AREA

The architectural campaign undertaken during the reign of Diocletian and Maximian dramatically renewed the Roman Forum by redefining the Forum's central area as an imperial zone in which elevated images about rulership towered over the space. This paved area was physically separated from the plaza in front of the Senate House. Archeologists Cairoli Fulvio Giuliani and Patrizia Verduchi argue that streets effectively separated off the Forum's central area; the separation was increased when the Tetrarchs framed the paved plaza with Rostra monuments (see fig. 1.1).[33] The Tetrarchs shortened the Forum plaza by installing at the eastern end of the square a platform that supported five monumental columns (see fig. 1.1 [5]).[34] This eastern Rostra clearly consolidated the paved plaza of the Forum, since the new Rostra contracted the space that had previously extended to an older tribune integrated into the Temple of the Deified Julius Caesar (see fig. 1.1 [21]).[35] At the western end of the Forum square, the preexisting western Rostra received an extension that matched

approximately the width of the newly installed tribune. The two speakers' platforms faced each other directly (see fig. 1.1 [A]).[36]

Named for prows taken from ships conquered in naval battles, the Rostra at the Forum's western end, originally completed under Augustus, began as a monument crediting emperors with Roman military victories (fig. 1.5). It was expanded under the Tetrarchs with an addition that extended the tribune to the north. With a patchwork of reused materials giving it a textured appearance, this addition produced a dialogue between loss and recuperation (fig. 1.6). Masonry blocks, haphazardly gathered to compose the extension, express temporal concepts by visually exposing a process of assembly, creating the appearance of a restoration project. Modern historians have tended to apply pejorative terms to this honest assembly of reused material. Yet the vocabulary of fitting old material into a new context at the Augustan Rostra matched fragmentation with restitution. In other words, it should not be presumed that the rough-hewn recomposition of reused stones was a sign of decrepitude; instead, the Rostra proudly attests to its repaired status. The Tetrarchic campaign at the Augustan Rostra manifestly celebrated restoration to emphasize the attempt of the jointly ruling emperors to bring back the past. As a result, the Tetrarchic concept of restoration ushered in strategies of composition using textured and fragmented but recuperated pieces.

It is clear that the tribune's extension was constructed prior to the year 334, during Constantine's reign, because a Constantinian equestrian statue base overlaps on top of the base for the tribune (fig. 1.7).[37] This evidence, together with the formation of the five-column monument, indicates that the Tetrarchs were responsible for widening the Rostra. There had been some question about this. Archeologists discovered four fragmentary inscribed blocks that were likely arranged as a frieze on the Rostra with an inscription that was determined to commemorate a victory over Vandals during the reign of the emperors Marcian and Avitus (joint rule, 455–456). This prompted Christian Hülsen to designate the extension as the "Rostra Vandalica."[38] The only name surviving in the fragmentary inscription,

Figure 1.5. View of the western Rostra in the Roman Forum. Photo courtesy of Fototeca Unione. © American Academy in Rome.

Figure 1.6. The Tetrarchic extension to the western Rostra in the Roman Forum (the so-called Rostra Vandalica). Photo by the author.

Figure 1.7. Marble foundations that supported the plinth of the equestrian statue of Constantine overlapping the base of the western Rostra. Photo by the author.

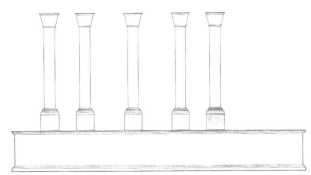

Figure 1.8. Elevation showing a reconstruction of the Tetrarchic five-column monument at the western Rostra. Drawing by D. Tyler Thayer.

however, is that of Iunius Valentinus, who served as an urban prefect at an uncertain date, but probably after 456.[39] The inscription, which does not actually mention a triumph over Vandals, was obviously produced long after the campaign to widen the tribune. In addition, the total dimensions of the inscribed blocks—the extant portions of which measure almost ten meters across—would span approximately the entire Rostra's width; they were not restricted exclusively to the northern addition.[40] The text on the frieze, therefore, must be dissociated from the earlier widening of the tribune. The misconception that a campaign to extend the Rostra occurred in the fifth century must be replaced by the correct chronology, that a Tetrarchic addition dating to c. 300 was supplemented by an inscription incised into the preexisting frieze in honor of Marcian and Avitus after 456.

Diocletian and Maximian further transformed the western Rostra so that it could support five columns capped by statues of the *Augusti* and the *Caesares* together with a divine namesake (fig. 1.8).[41] The proposal that an image of Jupiter stood on top of the central column at the western Rostra with a directional link to the Temple of Jupiter on the Capitoline Hill, situated to the southwest of the column monument, is appealing.[42] Viewers facing in the opposite direction, looking at the eastern Rostra, could see the Temple of the Deified Julius Caesar only by looking through the columns on top of the podium.

A likely assumption is that the organization of the two Rostra showcased both the harmony among emperors and their organized plan to synchronize collegial rulership.[43] There is little doubt that the display asserted key points of Tetrarchic ideology. Indeed, surviving epigraphic evidence suggests that the two Rostra were tied to jubilees, during which the schedules of imperial anniversaries for Tetrarchic rulers were aligned so as to lay the groundwork for the succession to new *Augusti*.

Earlier in the empire, the Rostra had linked imperial traditions with cross-generational affiliations among the elite of Rome.[44] Augustus exploited historical topography to commemorate subtly his own ancestry by completing Julius Caesar's project, which shifted the Rostra from the Comitium to the western end of the Forum square (see fig. 1.1 [1]). To finalize the project, Augustus added another speakers' platform projecting from the front of the Temple of the Deified Julius Caesar. The central area of the Forum, then bounded by the Augustan Rostra at the western end and the Rostra in front of the temple honoring Caesar to the east, created a rhetorical space marking Augustus' allegiance to Caesar, his uncle and adoptive father. Finally, with the shift of the Rostra away from its original position near the Senate House at the Comitium, the site of participatory consensus by the populace, Augustus moved the center of government away from the precinct associated with the Republic.[45] Although Diocletian and Maximian updated the Forum, their pairing of the renovated western tribune with the new eastern Rostra referred back to Augustus' inheritance from Julius Caesar. By adding to Augustus' Rostra, the Tetrarchs implied that they had refounded the principate under new imperial guidelines.

TETRARCHIC COLUMN MONUMENTS IN THE ROMAN FORUM

The Tetrarchic column monuments installed on the Forum's two speakers' platforms framed the precinct with a concise visual presentation of the system Diocletian had introduced (see fig. 1.2). Specifically, two five-column monuments on either side of the Forum set up a context for displaying facing images of four rulers—each foursome presumably shown with a divine counterpart—illustrating the Tetrarchy's principles. The absence of individual names on any of the recorded inscriptions likely indicates that each imperial statue elevated on top of a column represented the generic aspect of the divinity (*genius*) inherent in each emperor rather than his actual likeness.[46] From this, it can further be inferred that the five columns were not intended to support honorific statues dedicated to specific emperors, but rather provided a context in which to advertise collective rule.[47] Physical evidence suggests that the installation of the five-column monument was integral to the restoration of the western Rostra; thus, column monuments were components of the vast restoration program of Diocletian and Maximian.[48] That the five-column monuments lack any epigraphic evidence of senatorial sponsorship accords with the evidence that the Tetrarchs recast the Forum's central area in anticipation of celebrating the twentieth anniversary of imperial rule there in 303.

An understanding of the eastern and western Rostra in the Tetrarchic Roman Forum relies upon archeological evidence together with inscriptions and pictorial testimony from the fourth-century relief on the Arch of Constantine (fig. 1.9).[49] This Constantinian sculpture shows the five columns in the background and furnishes visual testimony to the placement of statues on top of the free-standing columns. Judging from the relief, H. P. L'Orange has interpreted the visual distinctions between the central statue and the four flanking representations as indicating that Jupiter's image stood on the central column.[50] Archeological investigations have revealed that masonry blocks reinforced the interior of the western Rostra, helping to support the five columns.[51] Investigations by Patrizia Verduchi into the late antique modifications to the Augustan Rostra prove that the Tetrarchic columns stood directly on top of rather than behind the platform, as had previously been hypothesized.[52] One can also extrapolate the approximate height of the columns from the size of the one extant plinth; the tops of the columns would have towered nearly thirteen meters above the Rostra floor, including the capitals and plinths, without factoring in the height of the statues.[53] Recovered material might indicate that pink granite monoliths held porphyry statues on the Rostra, but these discoveries cannot be definitively linked to a Tetrarchic five-column monument.[54] The dimensions of the columns at the eastern Rostra are impossible to reconstruct with precision, but the Forum's two tribunes must have been comparable in scale.

The Tetrarchs installed the two five-column monuments as backdrops for those delivering public addresses in the Forum, since the columns were recessed to provide space for speakers. The late antique regionary catalogues speak of three Rostra (*rostra tria*). The first was the western Rostra. The second was probably the platform extending in front of the Temple of the Deified Julius Caesar.[55] The third speakers' platform was the one at the eastern end of the Forum square (see fig. 1.1 [5]). Much of what had survived from the eastern Rostra was jettisoned by Pietro Rosa, director of the Forum's excavations, in 1872–1874.[56] Some of the brick construction from this structure remains at the southeast corner of the paved plaza (fig. 1.10) and shows evidence of once having been fitted with ships' prows. An analysis of the remains from the eastern Rostra and the discovery of a brick stamp plausibly dated to Diocletian's reign led Giuliani and Verduchi to assert that the original construction campaign occurred in the Tetrarchic period.[57]

A single column base survives from the western Rostra in the Forum. Its inscription indicates that it

Figure 1.9. Sculptural relief showing Constantine addressing the populace from the Rostra in the Roman Forum, detail from the Arch of Constantine. Photo by the author.

Figure 1.10. Brick construction surviving from the Tetrarchic eastern Rostra in the Roman Forum. Photo by the author.

was set up for the joint celebration of an imperial anniversary. On one side, scattered pieces of armor shown in the background accompany depictions of crouching figures conquered in battle, with a vague reference to military success (fig. 1.11). In addition, two personifications of Victory with wings are represented holding an oval shield inscribed with testimony to a festivity for the *Caesares*: "To the *Caesares*, good fortune on the ten-year jubilee" ("*CAESARUM DECENNALIA FELICITER*").[58] The statue base must originally have been produced to mark the ten-year anniversary of the *Caesares* Constantius and Galerius. Yet the lack of particular identification for either junior emperor is noteworthy, given the honorific function of most other comparable inscriptions. In celebrating unspecified *Caesares*, the epigraphic text hints that the five-column monument was intended for any individual who legitimately served as junior emperor for ten years. Consequently, the five-column monument anticipated the continuity of joint rulership beyond the first Tetrarchy. Now-lost inscriptions from additional plinths supporting columns on the Rostra were rediscovered during the Renaissance. One commemorates a twenty-year anniversary and states, "To the *Augusti*, good fortune on the twentieth jubilee"; the other is inscribed, "To the emperors on the twentieth jubilee."[59] Since the recorded inscriptions commemorate both the tenth jubilee of the *Caesares* and the twentieth jubilee of the *Augusti* in a single monument, the installation coordinated jointly celebrated rituals for all four members of the imperial college.

An image of traditional rites from the surviving Decennalia base shows one of the Tetrarchic emperors sacrificing together with senators and emphasizes the traditional practices that solidified coalitions among aristocrats and rulers (fig. 1.12). This side of the plinth depicts an imperial figure, presumably one of the *Caesares*, ritually sacrificing at an altar. The personification of Victory is shown crowning the *Caesar*, who faces Mars wearing a helmet; two youths, one holding a box and the other playing pipes, serve as acolytes at the altar. To the far right is a seated figure of Roma under the bust of the solar deity Sol, a conventional grouping that signifies eternal Rome.[60] Two senators wearing togas accompany the group at

the sacrifice. The image of lustration with the emperor making an offering at the altar before the figures of Mars, Victory, Sol, and Roma links Tetrarchic success with Rome's eternity. Another side of the statue base depicting a pig, a sheep, and a bull—accompanied by a priest and those about to perform the sacrifice—illustrates preparations for an offering during the rite called the *suovetaurilia* (fig. 1.13). The animal sacrifice must have further sanctioned the fulfillment of vows by *Caesares* and *Augusti* to reign for ten additional years.[61] The fourth side of the column base features a sculptural relief that depicts a procession of military officials, four of whom carry banners decorated with insignia (probably of the empire), hinting that the parade honored all four rulers (fig. 1.14).

Emanuel Mayer has noted that the procession of sacrificial animals on the one side of the base progresses as if toward the scene of the sacrifice; similarly, the soldiers carrying banners march in the direction of the sacrificial scene.[62] The sequential movement implied by the three sides of the base suggests that the scenes capture ritual events that moved through the city. The reliefs on the single surviving plinth and the recorded inscriptions on the other bases connect ritual triumphs with the well-coordinated jubilee celebrations of Tetrarchic rulers by mentioning their synchronized anniversaries. Inscriptions use the plural form of dedication "to the senior emperors" ("*AUGUSTORUM*") on one base and the honors paid "to the *Caesares*" ("*CAESARUM*") on the other. The reliefs reinforce the collegiality of rule by indicating the different religious duties involved in taking the vows in anticipation of ten more years of rule.

Taken together, the epigraphic testimony and the sculptural reliefs of the Decennalia base indicate that the five-column monument was initially used for the known anniversary observed by Diocletian and Maximian in Rome on 20 November 303. Schedules were in fact rearranged to synchronize the anniversaries of all four emperors for this event. Though Constantius and Galerius did not physically arrive in Rome for the occasion, as military duties kept them close to the empire's frontiers, the ten-year anniversary for the two junior emperors may have been planned for their participation in the western capi-

Figure 1.11. Inscribed face of the Tetrarchic Decennalia base. Photo by the author.

Figure 1.12. Imperial sacrificial scene on the Tetrarchic Decennalia base. Photo by the author.

Figure 1.13. *Suovetaurilia* scene on the Tetrarchic Decennalia base. Photo by the author.

Figure 1.14. Imperial procession on the Tetrarchic Decennalia base. Photo by the author.

tal. Yet the jubilee of Constantius and Galerius, by tradition scheduled for the conclusion of the ninth year, namely 302, was actually celebrated in 303.[63] The manipulation of dates implies that, just as each individual Tetrarchic victory was shared by all four emperors, the entire college benefitted from the commemoration of a jubilee earned by one or more of the group. In fact, Diocletian began his imperial reign in 284, appointed Maximian in 285, elevated Maximian to an *Augustus* in 286, and welcomed the *Caesares* into the college in 293. Yet the five-column

monument illustrates that a revised chronology allowed Maximian effectively to backdate his accession to 284 and the *Caesares* to adjust their anniversaries by a year in order for all four to celebrate at once on the same schedule.

The grouping of five columns installed upon the western Rostra presented the coalescence of Tetrarchic *Augusti* and *Caesares*, which perhaps indicated the fulfillment of vows taken to rule continually as inscribed on the now-lost plinth, "VICENNALIA IMPERATORUM."[64] Martina Jordan-Ruwe argues that

Figure 1.15. Porphyry statue group of four Tetrarchic rulers, Venice, S. Marco. Photo by Nino Barbieri.

the four emperors were arranged symmetrically on the columns with the statues representing the *Augusti* exhibited on the inner flanks and images of the *Caesares* on the outer two columns, perhaps with each senior emperor introducing a junior successor.[65] The five-column monument thus focused on the peaceful succession of *Caesares*, who were slated to be promoted to *Augusti* after fulfilling their initial vows. The five-column monument negated the imperial cult of personality, favoring the new identities of the Tetrarchs under a divinized bond with either Jupiter or Hercules.

Considered together, the two five-column monuments anticipated future jubilee rituals. The Roman pair of tribunes is distinct from the independent four-column monument that the Tetrarchs set up to commemorate the specific members of the first Tetrarchy in Alexandria; a similar arrangement of just four columns was displayed in the Egyptian city of Antinoopolis.[66] The two Rostra in Rome implied the hope for an everlasting series of joint promotions by configuring two sets of four imperial images, as if each Tetrarchic group anticipated another. The near-divination of each emperor charted a path to imperial office through links to the gods; religious rituals confirmed this au-

thority while solidifying the vows. Senators of Rome were shut out of the process of affirming imperial appointments, since Diocletian, in violation of precedent, never asked the aristocrats to ratify his own nomination as emperor. Imperial succession for Diocletian was derived exclusively from the gods, and the five-column monuments raised the Tetrarchic *Augusti* and *Caesares* closer to the heavenly realm to celebrate this theoretically permanent system.

It is possible that each of the statues situated on top of the columns at the Rostra presented images of an emperor's *genius*, or quasi-divinized spirit.[67] Even if the individual portraits stood on top of the columns, the statues were to be seen from far below, where the individual traits of physiognomy could not be easily distinguished. As mentioned above, the surviving relief from the Decennalia base shows that the *genius* of the Roman people accompanied the *Caesar*, who lacks the identifying attributes of portraiture (see fig. 1.12). There was, in fact, a golden statue of the *genius populi Romani*, the divinized spirit of Roman people, situated on the western Rostra; it had originally been placed there by the emperor Aurelian (r. 270–275).[68] This gilded image seems to have received a new base during the reign of Diocletian and Maximian.[69] The Tetrarchs, then, seem to have restored Aurelian's *genius* as the eternal, quasi-deified protector of Rome's populace. The placement of the renewed statue symbolizing the people indicated the role of the Rostra as the place from which to address audiences; the people were closely associated with the ground level. Consequently, the images supported by the columns presented an elevated cohort of rulers juxtaposed to the *genius populi Romani* below.

Individual likenesses are not a feature of the imagery presenting the Tetrarchs as a college of four. In the Venetian porphyry group of Tetrarchs originally from Constantinople, each senior *Augustus* looks like an elder version of the junior *Caesar* (fig. 1.15). In addition, two porphyry columns that originate from Rome and are now on view in the Vatican Library feature images of all four Tetrarchs shown in very high relief. These Vatican columns do not clearly distinguish between elder and younger members of the imperial college; this is a distinct difference from the Constantinopolitan group.[70] Both sets of stubby, nonparticularized images of the Tetrarchs visualized the authority shared by the rulers, suggesting representations of a permanent system that erased individual identity, and thereby proposed ritualized roles linked to either Hercules or Jupiter.

Roman senators did not respond with favor to the first Tetrarchy. Senatorial aristocrats expressed their disdain to Diocletian and Maximian in 303, according to Lactantius, even though the emperors restored numerous buildings in Rome.[71] The *Augusti*'s 303 visit was a disaster: 13,000 spectators reportedly perished in a stampede at the Circus Maximus.[72] Aristocratic Romans apparently muttered complaints during Diocletian's visit, indicating that the newly supreme rulership of the Tetrarchs made the elite feel that they were not welcome to participate fully in the operations of the state. Though none of these senatorial grumblings is specifically documented, one has to imagine that the occurrence of imperial appointments without even the nominal participation of Roman senators provoked further objections. The quasi-divinized Tetrarchic emperors eliminated the senatorial system of checks and balances, which had the potential to counteract the dictatorial impulses of rulers.[73] Some senators must have additionally objected to the ceremonials that treated the living emperors as nearly divine without the Senate having granted the rulers this status.

JUBILEE RITUAL IN ROME

When Diocletian and Maximian appeared in the Forum in 303 to commemorate their twentieth jubilee beneath the towering images on top of the two Rostra, the emperors themselves were inaccessible and surrounded by advisors.[74] The populace, as a result, could not easily see the emperors up close; the two rulers appeared all the more unapproachable due to their newly magisterial trappings of office. Fourth-century sources credit Diocletian with developing the formality of royal clothing, which featured purple-dyed silks, elaborate jewels, and the insignia of office. Eutropius explains Diocletian's ceremonial dress as the regalia of someone obsessed with his divine status, stating that the ruler "commanded that he be worshipped, where

all previous emperors had been greeted. . . . He ornamented his shoes and robes with precious jewels."[75] Diocletian and Maximian during their jubilee celebrations, then, presented themselves in royal finery that clashed with the tradition that emperors appear on par with senators.

Diocletian and Maximian arrived in person for the jubilee, purposefully renewing the past by means of rituals that emperors had practiced for centuries. Each new emperor traditionally took a public vow (*vota*) at the outset of the reign and petitioned for another decade of successful rule, known as the *susceptum*. A moment called the *solutum* marked the fulfillment of the vow, as if a reinstatement of the past. Since the brief reigns of most third-century emperors had left the vows unfulfilled, the anniversary of 303 was a noteworthy twenty-year completion of the vows or *vota soluta*.[76] The religious rites sanctioning renewal at the conclusion of ten years, a prerequisite for divine approval of Tetrarchic rule, allowed the *Augusti* and the *Caesares* to consecrate the pact for all four emperors at once. Since all of the imperial colleagues operated under the same vow, Diocletian and Maximian could nearly guarantee the fulfillment of their own oaths together with those of the *Caesares*. Thus, collegial rule offered the potential of longevity in that the death of a single ruler would not preclude the surviving co-rulers from fulfilling the *solutum* vows.

In Rome, Diocletian and Maximian must have processed along the conventional triumphal route that progressed southward along the Via Lata, the modern Via del Corso, following a pathway that accorded them the status of victors in the context of jubilee festivities (fig. 1.16). The route must have passed through the Arcus Novus, a now-lost triumphal arch constructed in 293 for Diocletian and Maximian, mentioned in the regionary catalogue.[77] One surviving fragment from the arch depicts two female personifications, probably representing the empire's eastern and western halves, supporting a shield upon which a third figure writes the text, "VOTIS X ET XX."[78] This inscription identifies the religious oaths taken for the completion of the tenth year, for which the emperors did not arrive personally in Rome, and resembles in format the text in-

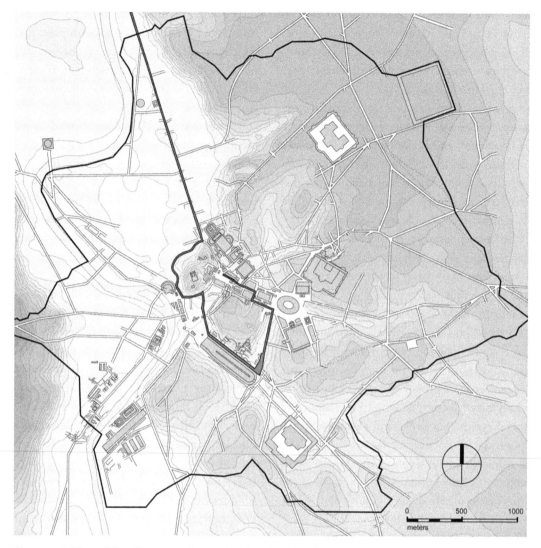

Figure 1.16. Map of fourth-century Rome showing the imperial processional route. Map by Marie Saldaña.

scribed within the shield on the Decennalia base. It is assumed that another now-lost inscription on the arch mentioned the slightly distinct wording "VOTA X ET XX," which would be appropriate to the *suscepta* vows taken in anticipation of a twentieth anniversary (looking forward to a second successful decade of rule).[79] Given that anniversaries were celebrated on the ninth year, the Arcus Novus was set up in 293 for a celebration of Maximian, who could synchronize his rule with Diocletian (not in attendance) and backdate the accession to 284.[80] The inscriptions on the Arcus Novus emphasize that the Tetrarchic rites of renewal both synchronized and conflated the vows taken by jointly ruling emperors.

The visit to Rome in 303 by Diocletian and Maximian provided the sole opportunity for the two to address the populace of Rome from the newly reconstructed tribunes. The jubilee ritual was the particular focus of the Tetrarchs' five-column monuments; but other rites practiced in other places, such as the *adventus*, or arrival in a city, also gained in importance during the first Tetrarchy. The increase in the number of provinces together with the expanded ranks of emperors led to many more orations produced for presentation at a greater number of *adventus* celebrations.[81] Panegyrics prepared for these Tetrarchic events in various cities praised emperors for the restitution of the empire, arguing for a Tetrarchic refoundation of Rome. Such rhetoric can be witnessed in a panegyric for Maximian presented in 291 in Trier on 21 April, the birthday of Rome:

In truth you celebrate the foundation of the city as if you achieved immortal piety as its founder. One might justifiably call you in particular and your brother the founders of the Roman empire, for you are, which is comparable, its restorers (restitutores) and although on this day, the city's birthday, which goes back to the origins of the Roman people, it is the first days of your rule which mark the beginning of its salvation.[82]

Even though Maximian's 291 oration was read in Trier, it anticipates the manner in which the two *Augusti* addressed Rome's populace in 303, as rulers who restored the city's foundation by Romulus and Remus.

Other aspects of the procession of 303 indicated that the *Augusti* celebrated their achievements in anticipation of their joint retirement, which Eutropius tells us occurred "after a magisterial triumph over many nations."[83] Even though Constantius and Galerius appear not to have arrived in Rome, the *Caesares* received commemoration in absentia, as the *Augusti* performed the *solutum* vows for the entire imperial college and commemorated Galerius' victory over the Persians in 298, among other triumphs.[84] Evidence from earlier panegyrics implies that emperors postponed victory celebrations after battle to consolidate triumphs for commemorations during the regularly scheduled anniversaries.[85] In the procession of 303, a diverse group of conquered peoples was paraded through the streets, as if to perform their subjugation to the triumphant emperors. Presumably, the participation of the vanquished prisoners communicated that the two Tetrarchs, marching through Rome, had the right to stage a triumph. A fourth-century description of the conquered Persians dragged along in the procession mentions that they were accompanied by an international group of war prisoners subjected to humiliation. The same source accounts for largesse in silver and gold distributed to the public, together with the emperors bringing into the city "thirteen elephants, six drivers, and 250 horsemen."[86] The exotic animals figured into the same theme of globalization as the interna-

tional assembly of prisoners, referring to numerous successful wars at the empire's borders. The characterization of the Tetrarchs as global rulers emerged in imperial propaganda as early as 291, when a panegyric for Maximian pondered the issue of globalism with a pointed reference to Romulus and Remus, asking: "Which twins or close brothers share an undivided inheritance with as much equivalence as you share the Roman world?"[87] The ritual event of 303 in Rome illustrated that together, the Tetrarchs were ever-victorious over the whole world.

The ritual practices of Diocletian and Maximian emphasized that their togetherness extended into synchronizing their activities. Eutropius mentions that the captured children, wives, and sisters of the defeated Persian general Narses proceeded in front of the imperial chariot. The author also implies that the two emperors rode in a single vehicle, and that the rulers planned their joint abdication on that very day.[88] The procession, after passing through the Forum, ascended the Capitoline Hill for the culminating rites at the Temple of Jupiter Optimus Maximus, where the two Tetrarchs may have discussed retirement. A panegyric praising Constantine recalls that Maximian looked back with regret at having joined Diocletian's plan to retire, since the Tetrarchic emperor of the west "lamented having taken an oath to him in the Temple of Jupiter on the Capitoline."[89] To be sure, the oath could have simply renewed the vows of the two emperors to be closely identified with Jupiter. But this was the only event at which the two senior emperors could have met in person to confirm their joint plan to step down. Reports imply that Diocletian, facing health concerns that caused him to see his days as numbered, came to Rome after planning to leave office. Although the stated reason for the trip was the jubilee, Lactantius asserts that, "when good fortune had deserted him, Diocletian proceeded at once to Rome in order to celebrate there his *vicennalia*."[90] A series of jubilee rituals, then, synchronized Tetrarchic rule and culminated in an unprecedented jointly scheduled retirement.

The two Rostra that were prepared for the joint anniversary of Diocletian and Maximian in 303 were intended as permanent installations. Initially, they united the celebrations of the first Tetrarchs during the

Figure 1.17. Digital reconstruction of the central area of the Roman Forum in c. 303 CE, showing the two Tetrarchic five-column monuments. Experiential Technologies Center, UCLA. © Regents, University of California.

same event; they also anticipated that additional jubilees would regularize the cycles of the rulers' successors. The two groupings of five figures elevated upon columns from the two facing Rostra at either end of the Forum depicted the alternation from one Tetrarchic college to another; presumably the rulers were accompanied by Jupiter on the western Rostra and Hercules to the east. The emphasis on framing the Forum plaza as an assembly site by pairing two speakers' platforms supporting colonnades can be illustrated with a digital reconstruction of the area in 303 (fig. 1.17). Of course, the rituals were rarely practiced in Rome. Thus, column monuments and statues offered a permanent representational scheme that mapped the transition from one co-ruling college of four emperors to the successive quartet.

THE REVISION OF THE TETRARCHIC ROMAN FORUM

The strict coordination between the columnar displays at the eastern and western Rostra framing the Roman Forum's central area presented regulated cycles that sustained the Tetrarchy of Diocletian and Maximian. Lining the south edge of the Forum were seven additional free-standing columns that defined the edge of the paved central area and demarcated an imperial zone (see fig. 1.1 [4]). While it is possible to imagine that Diocletian and Maximian ordered the seven free-standing columns to complement the two Rostra with their own colonnades, adding an odd number of column monuments to the Forum seems illogical, given the Tetrarchs' preoccupation with pairs of emperors. There is every reason to believe that portrait statues surmounted each of the seven towering columns, which stood directly on the Forum pavement, even if there are no surviving inscriptions and no specific physical evidence to indicate whom the monuments honored. However, there is little reason to consider the seven columns as belonging to a cohesive project that originated with the two facing Tetrarchic Rostra. With the two paired sets of four imperial statues on the tribunes, linked most probably with either Hercules to the east or Jupiter to the west, the central area of the Forum clearly demonstrated Tetrarchic imperial succession. By contrast, seven columns disturbed the clear coordination between the two Rostra, since seven emperors do not fit within the logic of Tetrarchic succession. Even more problematic would be to conceive of the Column of Phocas as a Tetrarchic installation, since the free-standing column disrupted a view toward the western Rostra and supported a single image of an emperor (see fig. 1.1 [2]). This solitary column also cannot be easily contextualized in the Tetrarchic ideology of collegial rule. Analysis of the Column of Phocas, discussed in Chapter 3, sees the monument as plausibly dating to the reign of either Constantine or Constantius II and as marking the sight line for visitors entering the Forum from the Argiletum, which led to the densely inhabited neighborhood to the north, the Suburra.

During the nineteenth-century excavations of the Forum, the remains of the seven gigantic column bases were discovered in front of the Basilica Julia.[91] These seven honorific columns (see fig. 1.1 [4]) consolidated the central plaza into a unified space bounded on three sides by tribunes or columns.[92] Today, one can still see the brick construction of their massive plinths, measuring about four meters in height. Two felled columns, one of pavonazzetto and another of gray granite, were re-erected in 1899 after their rediscovery near these monumental bases (fig. 1.18); the other columns did not survive in situ.[93] In late antiquity, the plinths were sheathed with marble slabs, as indicated by dowel holes. Three different brick stamps from these plinths appear comparable to those used during the reign of Constantine, indicating that their installation could have

occurred decades after Diocletian and Maximian retired in 305.[94] Franz Alto Bauer has entertained the possibility that the brick stamps dating plausibly after 312 and found in the seven columns could be explained if Constantine had reworked a preexisting set of honorific columns.[95] It is also important to recall that column monuments capped by statues appear to have been a domain for imperial imagery and ideology; the evolving conceptions of imperial rulership can be charted through the shift from the glorification of a sole emperor at Trajan's column, for example, to the commemoration of collegiality in the five-column monuments sponsored by the Tetrarchs.[96] Martina Jordan-Ruwe proposes that the seven columns in the Forum suggested an imperial concept distinct from that connoted by the five-column monuments.[97] The initial framing of the Forum by the Rostra surmounted by column monuments advertised imperial succession at regular intervals, whereas the seven columns

Figure 1.18. Column monuments from the southern side of the Roman Forum. Photo by the author.

distorted the regular patterns of alternation among four rulers that Diocletian envisioned. Indeed, seven emperors could not be paired up or assembled into groups of four for an imperial college such as that of the highly regulated first Tetrarchy without an awkwardly extraneous statue. The seven columns, then, are best contextualized in the political events that occurred after 305.

Visually, the late antique column monuments framed urban space much as the triumphal arches punctuated the major thoroughfares and marked ritual entrances at the edges of the Forum. Today, the Forum's only surviving arch is that of Septimius Severus, dedicated in 203 CE (see fig. I.5).[98] In late antiquity, the Arch of Tiberius and the Parthian Arch of Augustus remained standing, as did the Arch of Gaius and Lucius.[99] The Arch of Tiberius is represented to the left of the western Rostra in the fourth-century relief on the Arch of Constantine showing the emperor's triumphal address to the citizenry (see fig. 1.9). On account of this relief, as well as written sources and archeological finds, it is clear that the Arch of Tiberius was aligned with the Rostra on the western end of the Forum square.

The Rostra and the arches formed meaningful juxtapositions in the Forum. At the western end of the square, the Arch of Septimius Severus presented a striking visual pairing with the adjacent western Rostra, fitted with its Tetrarchic columns. The Constantinian relief illustrates that the columns atop this Rostra continued the line of the engaged columns on the Severan arch (see fig. 1.9). During late antiquity, the western Rostra emphasized the ritual significance of imperial jubilees, whereas the Arch of Septimius Severus featured reliefs depicting battles. As Jordan-Ruwe points out, the triumphal arches asserted victory ideology associated with individual emperors, whereas the Rostra's columns connoted group celebrations in jubilee rituals as developed by the Tetrarchs.[100] In the Constantinian period, however, the individual form of rulership was restored after 325 and celebrated in the Forum.

The coordination between a column-bearing platform and the engaged columns on the triumphal arches further illustrates how late antique additions transformed the Forum. After its installa-

tion, the Tetrarchic five-column monument at the western Rostra altered perceptions of the Arch of Septimius Severus by suggesting that the continuity of rulership could be illustrated through visual linkages among the different imperial constructions; it thereby legitimized the imperial lineage. This was achieved not by suppressing older monuments, but by adding new elements to the Forum that converted the previous structures. By juxtaposing the preexisting structures with the more recent installations, a new mode of imperial commemoration was created.

The space between the eastern and western Rostra was marked off as a political zone. At the western end of the Forum square, the installation of the five Tetrarchic columns upon the Augustan Rostra introduced a clear-cut visual terminus for the plaza (see fig. 1.1 [1]). Augustus used the speakers' tribunes to commemorate his family history in the Roman Forum, establishing a precedent for the subsequent use of the platforms.[101] Diocletian and Maximian criticized the formerly hereditary path to imperial authority as they transformed the Forum; this created a ritual space emphasizing cycles of time to sanction the rescheduled jubilees of the multiple rulers appointed because of merit rather than by birth. The eastern Rostra identified by Giuliani and Verduchi also presented a screen of columns that sectioned off the opposite end of the Forum. Thus, the five-column installations redefined the central area of the Forum and emphasized the distinctly Tetrarchic concepts of collegial rule in this square. Within decades of the joint abdication of Diocletian and Maximian, the breakdown of the first Tetrarchy prompted a revision of their approach to imperial collegiality in the Forum. After 305, when Diocletian and Maximian retired in unison, it is plausible that the row of seven columns was installed in front of the Basilica Julia, diminishing the focus on the two sets of Tetrarchic groupings in the Forum.

THE TETRARCHIC LEGACY

After the retirement of Diocletian and Maximian, the succeeding Tetrarchs struggled to uphold the precepts of joint rule. By 306, the scheme of orderly succession had disintegrated, as Maxentius, Maximian's son, took over as a usurper. Diocletian's failure to ensure the continuity of a nondynastic college of emperors after 306 does not diminish the extraordinary influence of his reforms, particularly in orchestrating administrative changes and dividing the empire into east and west. In Rome, Diocletian and Maximian introduced temporal renewal as the theoretical basis for restoring public buildings and updating urban space, a theme that persisted long after the first Tetrarchy. To advertise the temporal cycles, Diocletian and Maximian used the Tetrarchic monuments on top of the Rostra at either end of the Forum's central area as new interventions juxtaposed to preexisting features, transforming the plaza into a precinct that supported the cyclical renewal of the past. The images on top of the columns in the Forum allowed Diocletian and Maximian to make amends for the absence of emperors from Rome by creating a permanent representation of their ideology. The Rostra monuments also suggested the importance of all four Tetrarchs celebrating jubilees together. The Tetrarchic reconfiguration of the old Augustan Rostra provides a clear instance in which repairs shaped political experiences. The Tetrarchic transformations in the Forum originated with the synchronization of jubilee celebrations to renew continually the collegial bonds among the emperors.

The ideology of Diocletian and Maximian became palpable with the exhibitions of statues situated close to restored buildings. Reusing Rome's historical monuments by turning them into advertisements for joint rulership, the first Tetrarchs instigated a novel approach to the Forum that made their collegial rule appear as if it were inherited from their illustrious predecessors. Specifically, Diocletian and Maximian transformed the tradition of the solitary column monument into a communal display under four Tetrarchs that located emperors under the stewardship of Jupiter and Hercules. Tetrarchic rituals and orations also celebrated cyclical renewal; for Diocletian and Maximian, restoration fostered political stability.

In analyzing the Forum of this period, it must be considered that Diocletian had prevented Maximian from appointing his son Maxentius as emperor, which fueled the son's antipathy to the system outlined for the first Tetrarchy. Indeed, Maxentius, specifically excluded from the legitimate college of four, received no acclaim whatsoever within the Tetrarchic five-column monuments. Did Maxentius respond to this exclusion by constructing the seven-column installation in the Forum during his rule? The extant physical evidence does not allow us to reach a conclusion on this issue. Yet it must be remembered that Maxentius, who ruled a diminished western empire centered on Rome until 312, pursued new construction as an independent ruler who challenged the traditions of the first Tetrarchy. After 305, it must have appeared slightly ironic that Diocletian and Maximian had used the Forum's Rostra to set up a permanent system of collegial rule by four that had already become outdated.

In the end, the original Tetrarchic system could not fully coordinate succession within a nonhereditary scheme, causing the imperial college to fall apart. Despite their failed ambitions, the Tetrarchs did produce urban-planning successes that promoted the late antique ideology of collegial rule. The Tetrarchic emphasis on imperial ideology was unsuccessful in its specifics, but it introduced restored time as a key imperial message of the Forum's central area.

CHAPTER 2

CONSTANTINE
THE RESTORER

THROUGHOUT CONSTANTINE'S RELATIVELY LONG AND INFLUENTIAL REIGN, LASTING from 306 until 337 CE, changes in the empire had profound consequences for Rome. Constantine set in motion a policy shift favorable to Christianity, instigating dramatic cultural transformations; but the shift in religion did not immediately alter the fourth-century buildings and monuments of Rome's civic center. Nonetheless, Roman elites credited the significant repairs of specific buildings to Constantine and thereby forged his reputation as a restorer. In this manner, Constantine acquired the built heritage constructed initially for his rival and predecessor Maxentius (r. 306–312)—a usurper whose Rome-based reign, though illegitimate, offered an architectural legacy that Constantine inherited. It seems odd that senators, who sponsored most of the buildings, established Constantine's fame by conserving structures once linked to the illegitimate Maxentius. Yet the restoration of the usurper's preexisting buildings signaled Constantine's liberation of Rome, as he carefully regulated the memories of Maxentius and returned imperial governance to its proper form. This chapter frames Maxentius' projects through a Constantinian lens, underlining the reuse of Maxentius' buildings that shaped Constantine's identity and, more importantly, exploring the ways these restoration projects delivered messages that destabilized the Tetrarchic concept of stasis achieved through repetition.

Constantine gained the support of Rome's powerful aristocrats in 312, when he triumphed over the usurper Maxentius, whose name was subsequently erased from the public monuments of Rome in official acts of condemnation. Even as defeat relegated Maxentius' identity to oblivion, the victorious Constantine drew upon his rival's Rome-centered projects in a comprehensive campaign to acquire a favorable reputation in the Roman Forum. Inscriptions placed on statues praising Constantine as the "restorer," either of civic governance or of peace, signaled a return to a positive relationship between an able emperor and Rome's aristocrats.[1]

Conserved buildings appeared to be a by-product of the attention paid to running the empire properly. By adopting the Maxentian buildings, Constantine addressed the city under a vast program that redefined the public realm as a place of tolerance and good governance. Constantine further returned to a rhythm of life that encouraged senators to join administrative positions and invited the people to participate in civic rituals. Projects featuring the reuse of architecture together with adaptations to civic space recalled the unified rule of the principate and eventually charted the path toward the leadership of a single *Augustus*.

Patronage during the reign of Constantine set forth the temporal idea that the present had emerged as an addendum to the past, a concept that displaced the repetitive patterns of the Tetrarchs. Even though Constantine dimmed Maxentius' reputation, the reported hostility between the two has been reconsidered in light of clear evidence that together they had objected to their initial joint exclusion from Diocletian's Tetrarchy.[2] As sons of Tetrarchic emperors, both Constantine and Maxentius had been overlooked when new *Caesares* were appointed in 305. After the initial rejection, the two launched an additional critique against the correlative damage caused by Tetrarchs who, assuming god-like identities, imposed sacrificial rites as obligations for all those who operated in civic space. The Tetrarchic promotion of Jupiter and Hercules had been associated by some with the persecutions of religious minorities, particularly Christians.[3] As the usurper governing Italy and North Africa, Maxentius agreed to ratify the appointment of one new bishop of Rome while restoring ecclesiastical properties that had been alienated during the Tetrarchic persecutions of Christians; his approach to religious policy, then, could be characterized as renouncing the close identification of an emperor with Jupiter or Hercules.[4]

Constantine's strong affiliation with the Christian community instigated an approach to urban public life that was distinct from that of Maxentius; indeed, after 312, Constantine worked to redefine civic space as a truly common ground. Constantine promoted a partnership with Rome's senators, an engagement with the aristocratic elite that also echoed Maxentius' policies. Constantine inherited many of the buildings that his former rival had constructed, even as he advanced policies that, by no longer alienating the Christian populace, helped to make the Ro-

man Forum truly public. Thus Constantine's identity as one who both restored and transformed came to be displayed in the architectural projects of the Roman Forum and the Via Sacra district to the east.

Maxentius' coinage featured his portrait on the obverse, as well as an image of a temple occupied by a statue of Rome, with the she-wolf who had nurtured the city's founder decorating the pediment and presenting the phrase, "the conserver of his city" ("CONSERVATOR URBIS SUAE").[5] In a significant shift, coins named Constantine as the "restorer of liberty" ("RESTITUTORI LIBERTATIS"), a numismatic phrase referring to the emperor and accompanied by an image of the personified Roma.[6] Other coins issued under Constantine presented an even closer parallel to those of Maxentius, whose identity was subtly altered with the phrase identifying Constantine as "liberator of his city" ("LIBERATOR URBIS SUAE").[7] With this claim to have been a liberator, Constantine publicly decried the period of Maxentius' usurpation. Despite applying censure to his vanquished predecessor, however, Constantine upheld his long-standing history of cooperating with Maxentius. His careful attention to Rome has led Elizabeth Marlowe to observe that Constantine condemned Maxentius in the aftermath of a civil war; yet policies after the victory of 312 maintained the architectural monuments in the Roman Forum of the defeated rival.[8]

Policies instituted by the Tetrarchs, including new taxes on Romans and the threat of dismantling Rome's praetorian guard, had led to Maxentius receiving the backing of aristocrats and soldiers when he proclaimed himself emperor in 306. But Maxentius never received official recognition by the legitimate rulers belonging to the second generation of Tetrarchs. In establishing his role as an imperial patron, Maxentius may have aimed to amend the Tetrarchic imagery that pervaded the Forum plaza, since the messages of the five-column monuments were so unfavorable to him. Although Maxentius had the legacy of his father, Maximian, available to him, this memory was complicated by Maximian's rejection of his son as a dynastic heir. As discussed above (see Chapter 1), Maxentius (or members of the Constantinian dynasty) probably installed the

Figure 2.1. Digital reconstruction of the central area of the Roman Forum in c. 320 CE, showing the column monuments on three sides of the central plaza. Experiential Technologies Center, UCLA. © Regents, University of California.

seven columns flanking the Forum's south side (fig. 2.1). The seven columns, supporting an odd number of imperial portraits, gestured toward a system that differed from the Tetrarchy, which always showed the collegial system advancing co-rulers in pairs (or foursomes). With the seven columns cordoning off the Forum, the predominant parallels between the two sets of four rulers with their divine avatars in the column monuments at the two Rostra were folded into a new, less Tetrarchic scheme. Indeed, brick analysis of the plinths supporting the seven columns on the south side of the Forum opens up the strong likelihood that the row of self-standing columns was built after Diocletian and Maximian retired in 305.[9] Though it cannot be proven, it is compelling to think

that Maxentius added the seven columns to the Forum as an anti-Tetrarchic installation.

Maxentius also had an important impact on the area to the east of the Roman Forum, along the Via Sacra. Though formally outside of the Forum's precinct, the eastern Via Sacra featured buildings at the Velia Hill sponsored by Maxentius that fundamentally framed the route along which many visitors approached the Forum's central area. It also provided the pathway for the last phases of the triumph processions. At the high point of the Velia, Maxentius restored the Temple of Venus and Roma. He also constructed the Basilica Nova and a Rotunda immediately to its west, with entrances addressing the Via Sacra (see fig. I.8).

The architectural practices that emerged in Rome around the turn of the fourth century displayed fragmented architectural *spolia* in buildings, a practice that explicitly entailed the proper and legal transmission of pieces from Rome's built heritage placed into newer contexts that honorably respected the past.[10] Recent approaches to investigating Rome have attentively considered the transformations of ancient buildings after their initial construction phases. Reused buildings that feature individual fragments or that had been reworked through restoration are now recognized as having memorialized Rome's history in keeping with the discourse on *spolia*.[11] Constantinian buildings—many of which were sponsored by senators—exhibited old architectural fragments that documented the reappropriation of favorable eras in the past, signaling abstractly the return to proper governance. Statues set up publicly during the reign of Constantine in the same space as the repurposed buildings of the Forum clearly prompted viewers to react critically to the Tetrarchic installations. The addition of Constantine's images regulated the memories of collegial rule by shaping viewers' responses to Tetrarchic projects, providing a guide for considering architectural reuse. One example of this—the large, equestrian statue of Constantine that extended forward into the Forum plaza from the north end of the western Rostra—will be considered in detail below.

During his reign, Constantine reformed Rome's administration, clarified the aristocratic rankings of the senators, and reestablished justice by granting liberty and restoring properties to Christians and other religious minorities.[12] These actions underscored the message that Constantine had liberated and restored the empire. To deliver this message, Constantine, together with the senators of Rome, working often with different agendas, reactivated the pre-Tetrarchic past and created both architectural and monumental installations in which old and new building materials were purposefully interrelated. Even though Constantine did not choose Rome for his residence, the emperor's reputation was promoted by senatorial sponsors along the Via Sacra and in the Roman Forum in ways that returned to the past and introduced the important concept of regulating memories by preserving them.

Thus, the projects of Diocletian, Maximian, and Maxentius were by and large left standing. This established a relational identity for Constantine that was forged by juxtapositions and new additions rather than by destruction.

CONSTANTINE AND THE MONUMENTAL CENTER OF ROME

Even though Constantine changed Rome with his pioneering sponsorship of a grand Christian basilica near Rome's outskirts at the Lateran, begun as early as 313, the Constantinian projects in the Roman Forum and along the Via Sacra demonstrate that the emperor sought to establish continuity with his predecessors by providing traditional civic benefits.[13] How, then, can we reconcile Constantine's prominence as someone who brought back the past with the dramatic changes he introduced?

Constantine's projects in the Roman Forum suggest that the reuse of architectural elements and the transformation of entire preexisting buildings coopted the achievements of the Tetrarchs and Maxentius; yet, by exhibiting earlier *spolia*, the evident signs of ruination also suggest the partial fragmentation of that past.[14] Concurrent with these new projects, the senatorial aristocracy erased the memory of Maxentius by physically effacing inscriptions; Aurelius Victor, in an account of Constantine's achievements, recounts that "all the monuments constructed magnificently by [Maxentius], the city's temple and basilica, the senate had dedicated to Flavius [Constantine] because of his worthy service."[15] The senate thereby provided Constantine with the vanquished predecessor's architectural legacy. The statement by Aurelius Victor also indicates how Constantine and the senatorial elite of Rome pursued architectural restoration projects that regulated memories in the recently rebuilt Basilica of Constantine and the Temple of Venus and Roma; Victor does not mention the nearby Rotunda on the Via Sacra, which will also be considered here.

Constantine's Christian foundation at the peripheral Lateran has generated the hypothesis that no

Constantinian churches appeared in the Forum because pagan aristocrats maintained their stronghold there, a view Richard Krautheimer advanced in light of the power of senatorial traditionalists.[16] Judging from the inscriptions in the Forum, however, early fourth-century senatorial sponsors actually pursued civic euergetism along traditional lines, with clear announcements celebrating aristocratic connections to Constantine.[17] Thus, surviving epigraphic testimony from the political commemorations on inner-city civic monuments gives the impression that local aristocrats were sidestepping religious controversies during the age of Constantine, rather than aggravating the polemics over urban space.

Though he claimed membership in the imperial college founded by Diocletian, Constantine only gained acceptance as an *Augustus* in the Tetrarchy after a number of military victories. Senators in Rome must have shared Constantine's distaste for the memory of the first Tetrarchy, recalling the disasters such as the stampede in the Circus Maximus during the twenty-year jubilee for Diocletian and Maximian in 303 (see Chapter 1). Further, Constantine practiced imperial rituals in a manner that set him apart from the Tetrarchs. Marching through the city as if on a triumph procession the day after the victory at the Milvian Bridge, Constantine may have declined to sacrifice at the Temple of Jupiter Optimus Maximus on the Capitoline Hill at the procession's end, if the report of the sixth-century author Zosimus is credible.[18] Whether or not Constantine cancelled the sacrifices to Jupiter in state rites, he did launch an affront on the Tetrarchic ritual veneration of both Hercules and Jupiter. Though the dearth of fourth-century evidence precludes stating that Constantine definitively avoided the Capitol in 312, subsequent emperors processing through Rome—Constantius II, Theodosius I, and Honorius—clearly terminated their rituals at the Forum's central area and avoided sacrificial rites.

In the triumphal topography of Rome, a now-lost colossal statue of Sol, originally set up during Nero's reign, dominated the space to the north of the Arch of Constantine. The Neronian associations with Sol had long disappeared from the colossus; a fourth-century transformation and an inscription added by Maxentius were eventually dismantled by the senate in conjunction with setting up the Arch of Constantine.[19] The colossus of Sol during most of the Constantinian era stood at a position where it could be seen through the Arch of Constantine along a sight line marked by the imperial processional path progressing from the south. Looking above and through the central passageway of the arch, a viewer understood that Constantine's identity was to be experienced as literally leading toward that of Sol.[20] In its urban context, the long-standing colossus of Sol appears to have been an element of the old topography that acquired new meaning once the Arch of Constantine framed views of the giant statue. Although Constantine benefited from his support for Christianity, the configuration of the Arch of Constantine and the colossus of Sol affirmed the ritual route along which the emperor processed and led toward the Temple of Venus and Roma, the Basilica Nova, and the Rotunda on the Via Sacra, emphasizing imperial urban ceremonies while essentially displacing the Tetrarchic veneration of Jupiter and Hercules.[21]

During the reign of Constantine, the Forum's paved plaza, which Diocletian and Maximian had transformed, received installations that addressed the populace at the ground level, unlike the Tetrarchic installations, which had elevated the emperors to the realm of the gods. An important sculptural relief from the Arch of Constantine produced around 315 illustrates Constantine distributing coins to the people in the Forum as a formal act of generosity (fig. 2.2). Another sculptural relief on the arch depicts Constantine's official address in the Forum before the populace, showing the emperor on the Rostra between enthroned portraits of Hadrian and Marcus Aurelius and in front of the Tetrarchic five-column monument (see fig. 1.9). As mentioned earlier (see Chapter 1), the relief records the statues installed on top of the Tetrarchic columns. This representation is also important for illustrating that Constantine appeared without co-emperors in the arch's relief. Thus, the Arch of Constantine prepared by the senate and completed in 315 implicitly denied that Constantine shared his position with Tetrarchic co-emperors at the time.

Figure 2.2. Sculptural relief showing Constantine distributing coins to the populace in the Roman Forum, Arch of Constantine. Photo by the author.

Figure 2.3. Arch of Constantine, north face. Photo by the author.

The relief from the Arch of Constantine also contextualizes the representation of Constantine's activities within the sculptural program of the arch as a whole (fig. 2.3). An assembly of sculptural reliefs reused from other monuments produced during the reigns of Trajan, Hadrian, and Marcus Aurelius appear as *spolia* in the Arch of Constantine so that the fourth-century ruler assumed qualities of the illus-trious emperors of earlier generations.[22] The senatorial sponsors of the arch assembled a sculptural program of *spolia* that invoked the honored reigns of these earlier emperors, much as Constantine appeared when he was shown standing on the Rostra together with images of Hadrian and Marcus Aurelius (see fig. 1.9). The term *spolia*, which in antiquity indicated plundered objects, has acquired modern connotations that, with respect to scholarly discussions of fourth-century reuse, imply the transmission of old fragments into newer contexts filled with richly textured meanings.[23] Senators created a close identification between Trajan and Constantine by recarving what was originally a Trajanic portrait into one resembling Constantine in one relief from the arch.[24] Rome's aristocratic sponsors produced the arch using *spolia* from honored rulers to palpably affirm that Constantine inherited an exemplary past. Senators who reused sculptural fragments suggested that the disjunctures of these broken pieces were restored under Constantine; *spolia* reveal both the decomposition of the past and its recomposition.

The open-air installations of Constantine's statues in the Roman Forum affirmed his close alliances with senators and celebrated his forgiveness for those aristocrats who had received lofty positions during the period of usurpation. Three senators who had already served under Maxentius were appointed by Constantine to new terms in the urban prefecture.[25] Aurelius Victor alludes to the clemency of Constantine in the aftermath of Maxentius' so-called tyranny, presumably referring to the same forgiveness offered to Maxentius' former associates: "Since it is true that nothing is welcomed more than eliminating tyrants, one's popularity only increases once one has offered proof of restraint."[26] Constantine's respect for senators earned him both status and legitimacy. In 313, the senate granted Constantine the title of senior *Augustus*, a position that Maximinus Daia had formerly held.[27]

Senators seeking to display their status by publicly installing statues or other monuments recognized Constantine for his attention to elite participation in the administration. Constantine reinvigorated the senatorial aristocracy of Rome, which entitled members of the elite to receive appointments to high-ranking offices that let them play significant roles in the imperial administration. The aristocrats who received prestige from being appointed to the esteemed posts were often those who inscribed their identities onto statue bases dedicated to the emperor in the Forum, restoring the sense that the civic center upheld imperial imagery with the explicit consensus of the senate. In an important set of administrative decisions, Constantine dramatically expanded the ranks of those who could receive these high-ranking offices as a practical benefit of "liberation." Constantine allowed someone of equestrian rank, who was previously excluded from the highest class dominated by the old senatorial families, to receive a nomination or appointment to high office, which came with the title *vir clarissimus* (literally, "a most famous man"). A status-seeker could thereby access a path to ascend the senate's hierarchy.[28] As a result, the senate increased its membership more than threefold over the course of the fourth century. Though the competition and the dilution of status must have been bothersome to some, those serving in key posts acquired new opportunities to achieve high rank in the imperial administration that effectively renewed the senatorial body by welcoming new talent. Thus, religious changes and aristocratic reforms instituted by Constantine did not dissuade Rome's senators from making close affiliations with the ruler. Indeed, Constantine claimed that he had reestablished justice, and his legitimacy was furthered by the senate's commitment to restoring the past and reusing Rome's sculptural and built legacy.[29]

Public monuments praising Constantine in the Forum contained hints that their senatorial sponsors were aware of changing religious policies, but avoided potentially offensive references to traditional cults. By praising the emperor for restoring Rome under the aegis of a single, traditional deity, senators anticipated his reactions in a manner that displayed their slight confusion. The senate as a whole dedicated the arch adjacent to the Colosseum to Constantine at the "instigation of divinity and the greatness of his mind," as Noel Lenski translates one phrase of the inscription. While invoking Rome's tutelary deity, Lenski claims, the senators implied that Constantine took proper and traditional ritual precautions before crossing the *pomerium* to free the city from Maxentius' usurpation.[30] Recognizing Constantine for putatively respecting Rome's protective deity, senators in Rome presented honors to the emperor that linked him to an unspecified god. This lack of specificity extended into the Forum precinct. The avoidance of religious contention helped to make all welcome in the public arena.

The common ground that senators carved out in

the Forum created a space for communicating their close ties to the emperor. An anonymous orator praised Constantine after 312 by mentioning that "the senate has recently dedicated to you [Constantine] a statue of a god."[31] In the same oration, Constantine's clemency toward senators appears to have already gained traction as a benefit of ending Maxentius' usurpation. Addressing Constantine, the orator asked:

Now why should I mention your decisions and acts in the Curia, by which you restored to the senate its former authority, refrained from boasting of the salvation which they had received through you, and promised that its memory would rest eternally in your breast?[32]

For the restitution of the senate to its proper position, Constantine received praise from the orator: "You restored to the senate its former authority" (senatui auctoritatem pristinam reddidisti).[33] It is ironic to reflect upon Constantine's creation by the year 330 of a separate senate in Constantinople, but the institution in the East did not replace Rome's senate.[34] Thus, the religious policies of Constantine did not disturb the types of benefactions local senators in Rome pursued; rather, civic space was defined as an area where neither Christians nor those who followed the traditional cults would encounter affronts to their religious sensibilities.

Constantine's reforms also had consequences for the public display of statues in the Roman Forum. In 331, Constantine eliminated the position of curator aedium sacrarum, curator of the temples, with some of the responsibilities shifted to the newly formed position of curator of statues (curator statuarum). The holder of this new post cared for old public monuments and installed new portraits in the fora and other open areas. The curator of statues also kept an inventory of the works in the temples.[35] The urban prefect, with oversight of the curator of statues, received the right to inscribe lasting epigraphic testimony to his affiliation with the emperor on statue bases.[36] Plausibly, the curator of statues took stock of the city's statues: one source from the first half of the fourth century recorded twenty-two equestrian stat-

ues together with eighty gilded statues of gods and seventy-four ivory cult statues in Rome.[37] In return for the services provided to the state, a curator of statues could also set up works in public. One benefit of the position was the exalted honor of being able to identify oneself in inscriptions as one who cared for statues (curavit), a highly coveted privilege that seems to have been desirable for consuls once their year-long position had concluded. The artworks that the curator of statues exhibited in public space during the reign of Constantine included at least one from the Roman Forum: a statue base that identifies Maecilius Hilarianus, who probably organized the installation just after 333, when he served in Rome's curator post.[38] The expansion of senatorial ranks at Constantine's instigation, together with the restored aristocratic control over Rome's public exhibitions, bureaucratized in the office that cared for statues, brought about a renewal of open-air displays preserving the city's heritage in public areas of the city.[39]

CONSTANTINE AND THE RITUAL USE OF THE ROMAN FORUM

Constantine marched without the company of co-emperors when he paraded through a Roman Forum that was dominated by Tetrarchic symbolism in 312. The two sets of five-column monuments in the central area had carved out a zone in which to commemorate an orderly imperial transition between co-reigning pairs of collegial rulers. In the Tetrarchs' jubilee ritual of 303, all four members of the imperial college had received commemoration, with four insignia paraded through the city. Each standard designated one of the rulers (see fig. 1.14). In 2006, Clementina Panella discovered on the slope of the Palatine Hill three lance tips from ceremonial standards and three scepters, two holding a single sphere and one presenting two spheres. These had been made for Maxentius and had perhaps been tucked away at his conquest, prior to which this emperor had continued Diocletian's tradition of emphasizing the insignia of office.[40] Like Maxentius' trappings of office, monumental symbols of Tetrarchic authority incorporated into the five-column monuments recorded aloof, imperial power. The Tetrarchic images in the central area of the Forum did not depict the personal bonds between elite senators and emperors, since the column monuments produced for Diocletian and Maximian denied individuality for the sake of emphasizing the concord and similitude among members of the college.[41]

Constantine approached public space in a slightly less remote manner. Constantinian patrons introduced an equestrian statue and completed the work of installing non-Tetrarchic ideas by finalizing construction of the seven column monuments, which plausibly supplemented the preexisting memories recorded in the Forum.[42] The exchange of favors among the senators of Rome and Constantine illustrated dialogue and the participation of the elite in imperial power arrangements.

Despite Constantine's all-too-brief stay in Rome and his refusal to establish himself permanently in the Italian capital, the emperor celebrated three significant ceremonies there. The first occurred the day after the victory at the Milvian Bridge, in 312. The second commemorated his ten-year jubilee in 315.[43] The last visit occurred in 326, when Constantine belatedly celebrated his twentieth year of rule (*vicennalia*); he did not come to Rome for his thirtieth jubilee in 335.[44] Panegyrists had long articulated the desire of the city's residents to welcome the emperor in person. On the several occasions when emperors did visit, the residents of Rome rushed to greet the rulers in gestures of affection that matched the campaigns to set up public statues in honor of imperial authorities.

All of the imperial processions in Rome as practiced during the Constantinian dynasty drew upon themes of the triumph ritual.[45] Thus, imperial visits to Rome marked the "everlasting victory" (*victoria aeterna*) for a ruler, and festivities repeatedly commemorated the act of conquering.[46] The day after Constantine defeated Maxentius, Constantine was greeted by senators and the populace outside the city limits.[47] Senators played a prominent role in the procession, and this positioned Rome's aristocrats as colleagues of Constantine.

Constantine seems to have established the itinerary for fourth-century emperors through Rome: commencing at the Milvian Bridge, the procession progressed into the Campus Martius and along the Via Lata, passing along the Circus Maximus to the south of the Palatine, and turning toward the Colosseum in order finally to follow the Via Sacra westward and into the Roman Forum (see fig. 1.16).[48] The initial Constantinian procession in Rome resembled a triumph in the display of the dismembered body of Maxentius and, more importantly, in the use of the pathway that called attention to the triumphal route along the Via Sacra, using an ideologically important sequence that passed through the Forum.[49] One could speculate that Constantine terminated the processions in the Forum because he was omitting culminating sacrifices at the Temple of Jupiter Optimus Maximus. In all likelihood, then, the ritual path proceeded along the Via Sacra and through the Arch of Septimius Severus, turning immediately to the east so that the emperor could easily climb up the steps onto the Rostra without continuing any further along the Clivus Capitolinus, which earlier emperors had followed to ascend the Capitol. Constantine's ritual path in 312 probably culminated in the emperor distributing coins to the populace and making a formal address from the western Rostra in the Roman Forum, since these scenes were depicted on the Arch of Constantine. The implied viewership of Constantine by the populace in the sculptural relief from the arch and the evidence of senatorial participation in the 312 ritual indicate the importance of the Forum to performances of allegiance between the emperor and the people, and between the emperor and the aristocrats.

The triumphal themes of the Constantinian procession in 312 were reiterated in the annual commemorations of the tyrant's defeat (*evictio tyranni*) on 28 October.[50] Other public feasts that used public space into the middle of the fourth century—including the *Vestalia* and other celebrations for Vesta at the Forum's Temple of Vesta held 7–15 June—established that civic rites of all types continued to bring the populace into the Forum.[51] Other late antique public ceremonies employed the area of the Temple of Venus and Roma in a manner that avoided offending nonpagans in the fourth century and indicated that outdoor festivals continued to be celebrated near important monuments and temples. Specifically, senatorial aristocrats demonstrated their affiliations with emperors by conducting the civic rites of Roma, Roma Aeterna, and Natalis Urbis, the last commemorated on 21 April.[52]

Monuments with inscriptions clustered around the ritual space of the fourth-century Forum. Indeed, some statues were intended to remind viewers of past urban celebrations or to reiterate the political messages expressed during imperial processions. Fourth-century rituals symbolizing the coalitions linking emperors to senators were concentrated in the Forum, where civic architecture and public monuments maintained memories of these alliances. Writing decades after Constantine's reign in a letter to the emperors Theodosius I and Arcadius, the urban prefect of 384, Q. Aurelius Symmachus, implied that statues offered permanent traces of the bonds between senators and emperors that matched the ritual activities.

This noble order of senators has discovered a pleasant way of making a return to prove its gratitude [to the emperors]. It has solemnly honored with equestrian statues, and has thus enrolled among ancient names, the author of your family and line who was formerly general in Africa and in Britain. . . . This is the honor given to men whose children by their birth benefit the state. Indeed, the people, sated with the benefactions given by imperial generosity, with a swift tilt of the balance have swung strongly in your favor. When it learnt from my preliminary announcement that the good things sent by the parents of the state would soon arrive, it broke from every gate and poured out for quite long distances, thinking that luck was with the man who was the first to see these good things. So, whereas these imperial benefactions are usually waited for, now they have arrived at call. I say nothing about the day when a procession led royal elephants through packed lines of magnificent horses.[53]

From Symmachus' perspective, writing in the 380s, the orderly arrangement of imperial statues had been sanctioned by the aristocrats of Rome to demonstrate their affiliations with the rulers. Some of the monuments seem to have been prepared locally in anticipation of an emperor arriving in person. After the Tetrarchic emperors had created installations indifferent to Rome's elite in which the imperial likenesses dominated city space from positions on top of columns, Constantine reestablished links with the aristocracy.

Anicius Paulinus Iunior, an aristocrat of lofty status, participated in a community of honors when he transformed the space in front of the western Rostra in the Forum by installing the equestrian statue of Constantine there. At this busy site in the city, reciprocal honors between Constantine and Anicius Paulinus Iunior revised the significance of the Forum's installations. The equestrian portrait, which was specifically situated next to the five-column monument so as to thwart Tetrarchic collegial ideology without causing any harm to the Rostra installations, also proclaimed that Constantine hoped for a return to solitary rule.

Senatorial initiatives in the Roman Forum during Constantine's reign can be witnessed in inscriptions mentioning senatorial benefactions that celebrated the emperor's authority while elevating the status of elites.[54] Under Constantine, imperial appointments to exalted offices established positions in the city's administration with nuanced ranking in ascending degrees of honor.[55] In recognition of Constantine's interest in establishing his own status as the most exalted of all, another double-sized portrait of the emperor was dedicated to "Constantine Augustus" by the senate for display on a statue base rediscovered in the Basilica Aemilia.[56] The large-scale images of Constantine allowed local senators to participate in the emperor's expanded authority, which Constantine achieved by giving many positions to the elites, who had felt excluded from Diocletian's court.[57]

One inscription recovered from the Forum seems to indicate that a local aristocrat had restored a statue, since the inscription states that a bronze work (*ex aerario*)—possibly a togate figure—had been repaired as a gesture honoring Constantine. The indications of reuse hint that the return to an earlier senatorial order provided an administrative benefit to the city.[58] Constantine received credit for handing back authority to senators by appointing an increased number of aristocrats to important posts.[59] Accordingly, it is striking that another statue of Constantine displayed in the Forum recorded a dedication by the entire senate. The senatorial inscription praises Constantine, along with an unspecified co-ruler, for "invincible strength and divine power; [this statue was dedicated] by the senate and people of Rome, to the liberators from offensive tyrants and restorers of the state, to our Lord Constantine the Great."[60]

Epigraphic statements generated good publicity for Constantine by using such phrases as "generator, founder, and restorer of peace," as was written on another statue base in the Forum.[61] Newly added displays in the central area of the Forum introduced points of dialogue with the older monuments, at times demonstrating how Rome's senators both transformed and respected the past. Portrait statues depicting Constantine at an overblown scale in the Forum's central area established that his dynastic power enabled him to expand imperial authority, which also lifted up the status of senators serving in his administration.[62] The epigraphic terms and exhibition practices used for these statues asserted that social hierarchies brought benefits to Rome's elite.

A CONSTANTINIAN INTERVENTION IN FRONT OF THE LACUS OF JUTURNA

The arrangement of displays, together with the inscriptions belonging to Constantinian statues from the Forum, called attention to the civic responsibilities of aristocrats at significant locations. An example of the provocative installation of a statue inscribed with an individual's civic position occurred next to the aquatic shrine, the Lacus of Juturna, a pool fed by a spring that was dedicated to the goddess of fountains (see fig. I.8 [20]). The front side of a base found close to Juturna's spring indicates that a statue depicting Constantine was set up there by the curator of aqueducts (*curator aquarum et Miniciae*), Flavius Maesius Egnatius Lollianus.[63] On one of the sides, the statue base indicates that Lollianus dedicated both Constantine's portrait

and the administrative office (*dedicata cum statione*) on 1 March 328; the inauguration of waterworks (*statio aquarum*) occurred on the archaic start of the new year.[64] Lollianus displayed the statue of Constantine outdoors in order to create a visual juxtaposition with the aquatic shrine; in fact, the portrait of the emperor at the waterworks stood right in front of the old shrine. Some have speculated that the administration of the aqueducts moved close to the Lacus of Juturna in the Forum during late antiquity, but it appears that inaugurating the work of administrating the waterworks is distinct from setting up an office complex.[65] Thus, under Constantine, the pool at the Lacus of Juturna remained intact and was implicitly rendered civic when Lollianus' inauguration as supervisor of the waterworks was staged there. A different inscription found near the Lacus of Juturna from the same period or slightly later actually mentions an ornamental restoration.[66] The decorative addition of each statue, then, updated the significance of the installation spot.

Lollianus provided a statue of Constantine to celebrate the emperor through the use of a provocatively sited installation. Specifically, Lollianus opened up his year-long term of office supervising the aqueducts with a statue hinting that the Lacus of Juturna had been made more amenable to civic life. One consequence of the installation was that the preexisting features of the Forum were preserved; yet the installation of the new statue revised the meanings of the older monuments standing nearby, and essentially restored public space under the auspices of Constantine's administrative vision.

CONSTANTINIAN DISPLAYS IN THE PLAZAS OF THE ROMAN FORUM AND IN FRONT OF THE CURIA

With the emperor's probable elimination of sacrifices to Jupiter during state ceremonies, Constantinian rituals that utilized the Roman Forum were more political than religious, as his processions brought new emphasis to civic areas. As argued in the preceding chapter, the Tetrarchic festivities, with the rites that accorded divine and permanent authority to emperors, had limited the opportunities for the aristocrats of Rome to appear ritually prominent. In addition, the Tetrarchic imperial system had given powerful positions to individuals of relatively modest social status and thereby deprived the upper aristocracy of exclusive opportunities to earn the highest ranks.[67] Distinct from Diocletian's Tetrarchy, Constantine's displays in the central area of the Roman Forum and the plaza in front of the Senate House coalesced with the restoration of ritual gestures by which senators demonstrated their participation in the administration and their consent to the emperor.

The ritual space of the Forum featured a prominent Constantinian portrait statue on horseback, the Equus Constantini, that can be interpreted as intruding upon the spectator's view of the northern section of the Tetrarchic Rostra. Specifically, the equestrian statue of Constantine was aligned with the Via Sacra (fig. 2.4).[68] The equestrian monument honoring Constantine was said to be near the Rostra, since a fourth-century source, the *Notitia urbis Romae*, implies that it was close to the Rostra and mentions it on the same line as the statue of the *genius populi Romani*, which was exhibited directly on the tribune; the source records the horseback statue prior to mentioning the Senate House (see fig. 1.1 [H]).[69] The report of an equestrian monument of Constantine had also been written down in the eighth century by an anonymous visitor to Rome known as the Einsiedeln pilgrim.[70] Since the early medieval text specified that the equestrian statue was situated close

Figure 2.4. Digital reconstruction of the equestrian monument of Constantine in the Roman Forum. Experiential Technologies Center, UCLA. © Regents, University of California.

to the Arch of Septimius Severus, the monument apparently occupied a spot within the Forum's central area.[71]

Large concrete foundations lined with blocks of marble at the southwestern corner of the Forum's central area have the dimensions of an equestrian statue base. On the basis of textual evidence, as well as stratigraphic data, Giuliani and Verduchi assert that this plinth, now supporting the Decennalia base, once held Constantine's equestrian monument (fig. 2.5).[72] The final piece of evidence that links Constantine's equestrian statue with a display location near the western Rostra is the discovery on the northern edge of the Via Sacra near the Senate House of an equestrian base for Constantius II, Constantine's son, who clearly created a dynastic link with his father (see fig. 1.1 [C]).[73] In 334, after Constantine had celebrated two imperial jubilees in Rome, the consul Anicius Paulinus Iunior set up Constantine's equestrian statue. Almost touching the northern extension of the western Rostra, Constantine's equestrian statue was positioned so that viewers would contemplate the ruler on horseback as superseding the collegial rulership presented in the five-column monument next to it. The extant foundations for the equestrian statue reveal that this was a colossus, double life-size if not larger.[74] The now-lost statue inscription articulates the honors for the emperor that were earned as a result of consolidating the entire empire under his solitary leadership:

To our lord Constantine the Great, pious and ever-triumphant emperor, [who] gladly earns divine blessings for enlarging the state to encompass the whole world by his plans and actions for the senate and people of Rome, dedicated by Anicius Paulinus Iunior, of the highest aristocratic rank, consul (*consul ordinarius*) [and] urban prefect.[75]

In contrast to the Tetrarchic installation on top of the Rostra, Constantine's image projected a message of triumph by a solitary emperor who received proper recognition from the highest-ranking senator in his role as urban prefect and consul; the entire senate must have sanctioned this installation as well. Further, Anicius Paulinus Iunior was showered with

Figure 2.5. Foundations for the plinth supporting the equestrian monument of Constantine in the Roman Forum. Photo by the author.

prestige by Constantine, since he received the highest possible honor, a consulship.⁷⁶ As a work juxtaposed to the western Rostra, Constantine's equestrian portrait documented how Anicius Paulinus' own exalted status had been elevated by association with the emperor.

Constantine's equestrian statue was situated at a high-traffic spot, where all those walking along the Via Sacra would note that this emperor had vanquished the Tetrarchic system. Constantine's inscription must have faced the Via Sacra, since a subsequent statue of Honorius, which remains to this day at its display spot, also addresses the street (fig. 1.1 [J]). The emperor on horseback was oriented to face the

direction in which the inscription was read, which is the same direction in which the emperor progressed during processions. The link between the equestrian representation of Constantine and the ritual path, therefore, became a declaration of the emperor's significant visits to the city.

A viewer standing near Constantine's equestrian statue on the Via Sacra could turn to the north and view the plaza in front of the Senate House, which featured statues that associated the accomplishments of Rome's elite with Constantine's administration. One act that benefited Rome was Constantine's reform of the tax and fiscal administration. A statue base rediscovered just in front of the Senate

Figure 2.6. Plaza in front of the Senate House.
Photo by the author.

House—its original display spot remains ambiguous—presented a dedication to Constantine by the chief fiscal administrator (*rationalis summae privatae*), named Appius Primianus. The inscribed text alludes with vague terms to Constantine's economic measures, such as introducing the gold *solidus* as a standard denomination and requiring that tax payments be made in coin rather than in kind, both of which bettered the lot of Rome's aristocratic landholders.[77] Appius Primianus alerted viewers to the kind of praise that might be proclaimed publicly in front of the Senate House, such as identifying Constantine as "loyal, luckily unconquered, and most fortunate." As a patron, Appius Primianus wished also to identify Constantine as belonging to a dynasty, with the mention of the emperor's father by name. The sides of the statue base feature erased words documenting its previous life, underlining the material presentation of reuse. The inscription reads: "To our Lord Constantine, perpetual Augustus, loyal, luckily unconquered, and most fortunate, (and) the son of the divine, loyal Constantius I; (set up by) Appius Primianus, of senatorial rank, the chief fiscal administrator; in devotion to his divine nature and majesty."[78] The installation thus signaled that an administrative appointment for Appius Primianus had made him proud.

The idea of practical services provided for citizens coalesced with preservation efforts that guaranteed the maintenance of the city—linking administrative

acts to the plaza in front of the Curia—where sponsors regulated the past through the public displays. In order to shape memories in public space, patrons either preserved preexisting materials or strategically removed evidence of perfidy. During the reign of Constantine, senatorial sponsors reconsidered the plaza in front of the Senate House, which Diocletian and Maximian had repaved when they rebuilt the Curia.[79] The project of appropriately honoring Constantine at the senatorial plaza (fig. 2.6) updated a significant memorial to Rome's foundation at the Lapis Niger, a monument with black paving stones surrounded by a parapet at the legendary location of Romulus' burial (figs. 2.7 and 1.1 [D]).[80] There, Romulus had been commemorated by Maxentius, who was distinct among the later Roman emperors in his great admiration for the founder of Rome. Romulus justified Maxentius' Rome-centered rule, as was witnessed in the installation of two statues in front of the Senate House at the Lapis Niger. Mars, perhaps accompanied by the she-wolf, was displayed prominently in the installation, which reactivated the narrative and ritual memories connected to the foundation of Rome (fig. 2.8).

Senatorial sponsors working after 312 advanced imperial policies regulating the critical reception of Maxentius by erasing his name from the statue base displayed at Romulus' memorial (fig. 2.9). With the selective excision of Maxentius' identity, the statue and the monument installed next to the Lapis Niger preserved most of the text and the statue, but not the role of the condemned usurper.[81] The inscription initially recorded the dedication, "To unconquered Mars and father of his eternal city and to its founders; [set up by] our lord Maxentius, unconquered *Augustus*." Maxentius' name is now effaced.[82] On the right side of the Mars monument, an older inscription lists members of the carpenter's guild (*collegium fabrum tignuariorum*) from the reign of Antoninus Pius in 154 CE, indicating that the base had had a purpose prior to holding the statue of Mars.[83] The financing for the Mars statue had been provided by Furius Octavianus, who sponsored the installation during Maxentius' reign and inscribed his own name on the same side as the text mentioning the

Figure 2.7. View of the Roman Forum from the plaza in front of the Senate House showing the Lapis Niger (in the foreground). Photo by the author.

Figure 2.8. Digital reconstruction of the statue of Mars and the portrait of Maxentius displayed near the Lapis Niger. Experiential Technologies Center, UCLA. © Regents, University of California.

Figure 2.9. Inscribed base for the statue of Mars displayed adjacent to the Lapis Niger with the name of Maxentius erased (*CIL* 6.33856). Photo by the author.

Figure 2.10. Rotunda on the Via Sacra (the so-called Temple of Romulus). Photo by the author.

collegium.[84] Preserving the memory of the carpenters linked the respect for Rome's foundation with the important organization of builders and their contributions to the built environment. Ceremonies also must have accompanied the dedication of the Mars statue, recorded on the statue base as occurring on 21 April, the birthday of Rome, which marked the annual celebration of the *Parilia* ritual. During the reign of Constantine, the recollections of the usurper's earlier dedication had been diminished, yet the installation to Mars and honoring the foundation of Rome remained intact. Constantine, then, affirmed memories of Rome's foundation, yet decisively obliterated Maxentius' role in consolidating that tradition.

A second statue depicting Maxentius appeared in conjunction with the Lapis Niger, as inscription evidence attests (fig. 1.1 [N]). The surviving text records the dedication, "To our Lord Maxentius with the ancient qualities necessary in a censor and with an outstanding sense of piety."[85] The Maxentius statue also stood on top of an Antonine statue base.[86]

Maxentius' name was not thoroughly excised from this inscription during the Constantinian era, but then, the sanctions applied to those whose names were erased from the public record occurred haphazardly. Constantine probably removed the statue representing the vanquished emperor from the Lapis Niger display, however, since the surviving base for the portrait was recovered from the Basilica Julia.

Constantine regulated Maxentius' memory through erasure, but also preserved the Lapis Niger monument as well as the memory of guilds. In the end, the partially destructive measure actually contributed to a larger project of conservation.

THE ROTUNDA ON THE VIA SACRA

During the Constantinian era, it became important for the emperor to acquire links to imperial predecessors after regulating these memories. As a result, architectural restoration became particularly promi-

Figure 2.11. Portal of the Rotunda on the Via Sacra. Photo by the author.

nent. Constantinian transformations revised historical concepts by adapting buildings using some of the same procedures through which public statues were updated. Constantine, for example, received glory as the chief patron in Rome with specific connections to the most accomplished imperial builders when the senate rededicated the Rotunda on the Via Sacra (often mislabeled as the "Temple of Romulus") to him after the structure was built initially for Maxentius (fig. 2.10).[87] Constantine revised the Rotunda, a circular structure that led toward a vast apsidal hall and from there provided access to the Temple of Peace (fig. I.8 [24] and [26]). Indeed, the Rotunda served as a vestibule to a precinct rather than as an independent structure; it therefore opened up access to an important urban district. The Rotunda had neither functioned as a temple nor commemorated Romulus, whether the name designated the founder of Rome or Maxentius' son of that name.[88] The Rotunda's true purpose was to connect visitors with the Temple of Peace beyond it, thus providing a façade

on the Via Sacra that welcomed audiences to a most awe-inspiring assembly of statues and marvels, assembled for public enjoyment.

When acquired by the senate in honor of Constantine, the Rotunda's façade featured a portal, produced during the initial construction of the Rotunda under Maxentius, that displayed recomposed architectural fragments (fig. 2.11). Maxentius assembled architectural *spolia* for the doorway by carefully reconstructing a seemingly incongruous assortment of elements, such as Severan jambs, a reused bronze door, and lavish porphyry columns. Originally, the metaphor of reassembly applied to the complex as a whole, with the Rotunda configured as an addition to the Temple of Peace. Entering the Rotunda from its main portal, a visitor encountered a domed interior capped by an oculus with two side doorways, each leading to a narrow, apsidal hall. These two lateral halls flanking the Rotunda had their own façades facing the Via Sacra, with two monolithic columns of green marble elevated upon massive bases framing each of the two subsidiary entrances. The two apsed interiors to either side of the domed space may have featured sculptures, but there are no physical remains from the displays. During the third century, Septimius Severus had extended a preexisting space at the southwest corner of the Vespasianic Temple of Peace, creating a hall with an apse projecting to the west (fig. 2.12). When the Rotunda was inserted, around 310, the third-century apse had been removed from the western wall of the Severan *aula*, and a new apse was constructed on the opposite side of the structure, projecting to the east (fig. 2.13).[89] This reorientation allowed the Rotunda to offer the main entrance to the apsidal hall and thereby fundamentally transformed the complex.

Constantine's identity was soon linked with the Via Sacra Rotunda. The rededication to Constantine, featured in a now-lost inscription, was added after the evident signs of Maxentius' patronage had been removed.[90] Two sixteenth-century antiquarians separately described an epistyle on the façade featuring the Constantinian inscription. Onofrio Panvinio transcribed the text as, "To Constantine the Great" ("CONSTANTIN[o] . . . MAXIM[O]").[91] The second transcription appears in a drawing by

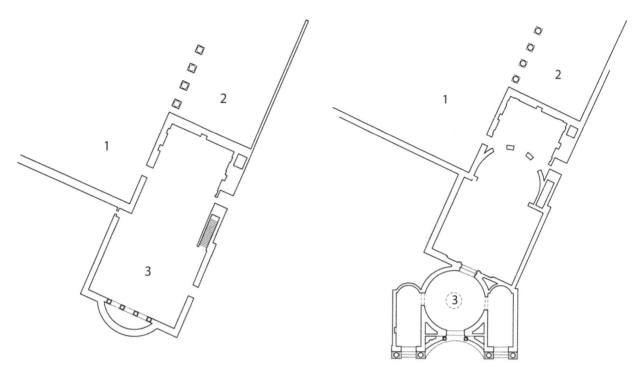

Figure 2.12. Plan of the complex at the southeastern corner of the Temple of Peace in the Severan age: (1) Temple of Peace courtyard; (2) hall exhibiting the marble plan of Rome (*Forma Urbis Romae*); (3) apsidal hall. Drawing by Brian Doherty.

Figure 2.13. Plan of the complex at the southeastern corner of the Temple of Peace courtyard in c. 310 CE: (1) Temple of Peace courtyards; (2) the hall exhibiting the marble plan of Rome (*Forma Urbis Romae*); (3) the Via Sacra Rotunda. Drawing by Brian Doherty.

Pirro Ligorio, who is often thought to be much less credible than Panvinio. Ligorio apparently filled in some missing letters to furnish an extended version of the text that Panvinio had also seen: "IMP CAES CONSTANTIN[o] . . . MAXIM TRIUMPH."[92] Unfortunately, the subsequent loss of the inscription and the conjecture caused by the variations in the two sixteenth-century transcriptions only allow for Constantine's name to be securely associated with the building, with no clarity as to where or how the inscription was displayed upon the façade.[93]

Aligned with the adjacent entrance to the Basilica Nova, just to the east along the Via Sacra, the Rotunda from its inception was designed to provide a monumental portal facing the street leading toward the Forum (see fig. I.8). At the entrance, a marble paving block below the bronze doors is framed by fourth-century brick construction.[94] Analysis of the foundations beneath the paving block and of the extant brickwork has determined that originally, the

central façade for the Rotunda featured a flat wall.[95] Constantinian architects designed a new, curvilinear façade featuring niches for the Rotunda that replaced the original, flat façade. The additions reached out toward the Via Sacra (fig. 2.14).[96] Analysis of the brickwork from the second phase added to reframe the portal confirms that the curved wall was introduced during the Constantinian period.[97] The transition from a flat façade to a curvilinear one completely transformed the Rotunda's main entrance, with the rededication inscription crediting the project to Constantine in the end.[98] Moreover, the epigraphic evidence appears to echo the report by Aurelius Victor that the senate rededicated all of Maxentius' structures so that they honored Constantine.[99]

Fundamentally, Constantine constructed a historical argument for inheriting the past by effacing the memory of the condemned Maxentius and rehabilitating the Temple of Peace, which was associated with Vespasian, its founder, and Septimius

Severus, its restorer.[100] By adding the inscription and new façade to the Rotunda, Constantine appropriated a complex of buildings adjoined to the circular structure (see fig. 2.13). The spatial progression led toward the Temple of Peace, where a particular highlight was the marble plan of Rome (*Forma Urbis Romae*), symbolizing the whole city, which Septimius Severus had replaced after the Vespasianic original had been destroyed (fig. 2.15). The Rotunda encouraged visitors to progress toward a grand assembly hall, which terminated with an apse; yet this hall was skewed in orientation with respect to the Via Sacra and required a substantial shift in orientation to the west.[101] Thus, the Rotunda functioned as an elegant pivot among linked spaces. The core of the fourth-century apsidal hall still survives, though it now belongs to the church of SS. Cosma e Damiano.[102] A small doorway in the apse of the fourth-century *aula*, located to the northwest of the two larger openings, led to the portico belonging to the Temple of Peace; from there, one could gain access to the marble plan of Rome (see fig. 2.13).[103] Thus, the domed structure on the Via Sacra functioned as a vestibule through which one could reach a secular basilica, and from there, the Temple of Peace, with a display of numerous treasures that seemed to turn this precinct into a museum, the most prominent treasure being Rome's marble map. But the Temple of Peace also featured a remarkably luxurious pleasure zone, with rose beds and water courses along which were displayed many masterpieces and statuary including those that Nero had once collected for his private enjoyment and that Vespasian had rendered public thereafter.[104] Constantine acquired the identity of an emperor who refurbished these extraordinary urban ornaments and reasserted their public availability when his name was installed on the Rotunda.

It is important to keep in mind, as John Osborne has pointed out, that the Rotunda on the Via Sacra and its adjoined basilica together furnished access to additional features of the Temple of Peace, including the candelabrum, the silver tables, and other treasures taken from the temple in Jerusalem.[105] Many of these were exhibited in the Temple of Peace precinct. One masterpiece, the calf sculpted by Myron, elicited numerous responses to its verisimilitude over the centuries, including an account from the sixth century by Procopius:

During the time when Athalaric the grandson of Theoderic ruled Italy, a herd of cattle came into Rome in the late evening from the country through the Forum which the Romans call the Forum of Peace; for in that place has been situated from ancient times the temple of Peace which was struck by lightning. And there is a certain ancient fountain before this Forum, and a bronze bull stands by it, the work, I think, of Pheidias the Athenian or of Lysippus. For there are many statues in this quarter which are the works of these two men. Here, for example, is another statue which is certainly the work of Pheidias; for the inscription on the statue says this. There too is the calf of Myron. For the ancient Romans took great pains to make all the finest things of Greece adornments of Rome. And he said that one of the

Figure 2.14. Pirro Ligorio, drawing of the façade and plan of the Rotunda on the Via Sacra in 1550, from Biblioteca Apostolica Vaticana, Vat. Lat. 3439, fol. 13. © Biblioteca Apostolica Vaticana.

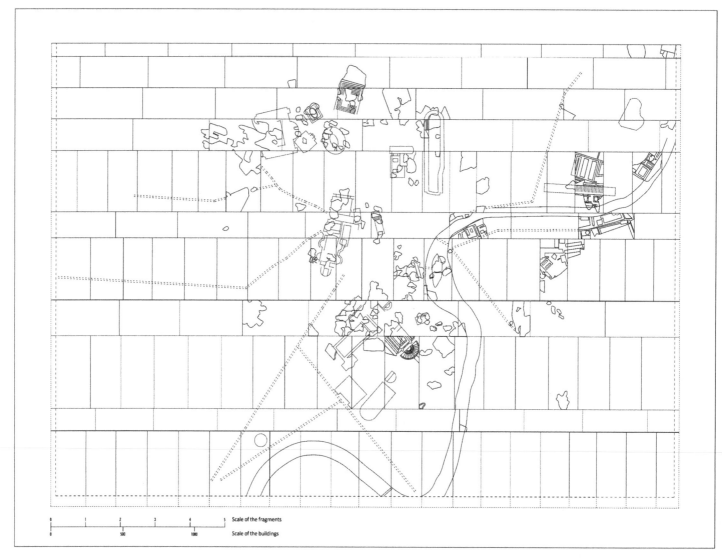

Scale of the fragments

Scale of the buildings

Figure 2.15. Drawing of the marble plan of Rome (*Forma Urbis Romae*), after Emilio Rodríguez Almeida. Drawing by Cameron Bolin.

cattle then passing by—a steer—left the herd and mounting this fountain stood over the brazen bull.[106]

Procopius documented the continued display of masterpieces in the Temple of Peace. Ever since Vespasian had exhibited these Greek works for public enjoyment, the display had retained its function as a benefit given by the emperor to the people, ornamenting the porticoes, the walkways between fountains, and the beds of roses. One statue base identifying a sculpture by Polykleitos of the athlete Pythokles was rediscovered decades ago; it probably was one of the Neronian works that Vespasian turned

over to the people.[107] Recently discovered fragments of statue bases have established that famous works by Parthenokles and Praxiteles, as well as another still-unattributed work, were all on view in the Temple of Peace.[108] Constantine connected these works to the portal he reclaimed facing the Via Sacra.

The significance of the marble plan of Rome lies in its capturing the city through graphic means, which perhaps offered a conceptual alternative to the experience of negotiating urban space to reach the Temple of Peace. Incised marble panels were fastened to the rear wall of the apsidal hall by bronze clamps. The map resulted from remarkably precise measurements produced during a comprehensive urban survey, depicting the city accurately at a scale of 1/240.[109] The precision used to produce the marble plan secured its graphic verisimilitude, one of the criteria that Procopius uses to praise Myron's bronze calf that allegedly attracted the interest of a steer. Impressive in its scale, the marble plan loomed over its spectators and offered a permanent testimony to the early third-century city; it filled an area of about 13 by 18 meters on the rear exterior wall of the basilica (see fig. 2.15). The plan existed as a spectacular visual showpiece of accurate mapping permanently etched in marble. It was not produced as an urban prefect's practical tool for keeping cadastral records or for organizing the maintenance of public buildings; therefore, it does not substantiate claims that the office of the urban prefecture used the apsidal hall. In fact, changes in property ownership could not be registered on the showpiece.[110] The Severan marble plan illustrated precisely all of Rome's roads, fora, public buildings, and private houses, replacing and updating the earlier Vespasianic plan damaged in the fire of 192 CE.[111] As a result, the Severan plan continued to deliver Vespasian's message that the emperor provided urban accoutrements for the public.

Vespasian's marble plan, situated among the sculptural masterpieces, invited a consideration of civic ornament as integral to Rome's infrastructure, as if representing the vast landscape of Rome on a map contextualized public marvels in the dynamics of an evolving city overseen by the emperor.[112] Septimius Severus' updated version of Vespasian's marble plan, with an insistence on revised accuracy by the third-century emperor, renewed the treasures of the Temple of Peace in the context of a prominent symbol of Rome.

The Via Sacra Rotunda invited movement through the city by welcoming visitors to a sequence of spaces linking the eastern sector of the Roman Forum with the Temple of Peace. The joined spaces were experienced after passing through the Rotunda, leading visitors to encounter marvels, masterpieces, a public garden, and the colossal map. The path leading from the Rotunda to the apsidal hall and from there to the Temple of Peace suggested that negotiating a complex of public structures matched the variety of the spaces with the diverse artworks and marvels on

view. Further, the configuration of showpieces in the Temple of Peace called forth significant memories of Nero's private collection being turned over to the public realm. In sum, the use of interventions to reaffirm a connection to the marble plan and the Vespasianic Temple of Peace by means of the renovated Rotunda allowed Constantine to acquire the lasting memory of the city's publicly displayed artworks and the variety of interlinked spaces.

The installation of the Rotunda's curvilinear façade and inscription, both of which framed a portal composed of *spolia* (see fig. 2.11), led to Constantine being celebrated as the guardian of the memories recorded in the Via Sacra complex. The Rotunda's bronze doors had been produced originally for another building during the Severan period, as were the marble jambs that precisely frame this door.[113] The cornice directly above the marble door frame was arranged during the Maxentius phase and is composed of four parts, the central two of which are reused pieces originating from the first or second century CE, flanked by two pieces produced in the fourth century.[114] The white marble bases for the porphyry columns rest upon lower foundations than do the door jambs and therefore must have been part of Maxentius' initial portal design.[115] It is important to emphasize that medieval and modern transformations have updated the portal's original composition: the architrave supported by the porphyry columns, for instance, has been altered over the centuries. In fact, with the rising medieval terrain, the doorway had been elevated, and then was repositioned in 1880, after excavations had lowered the ground level once again.[116] And although the Severan door with its jambs had been framed by the porphyry columns in the fourth century, the architrave resting upon the porphyry columns was probably added after the sixth-century transformation of the complex into the church of SS. Cosma e Damiano.

During the Constantinian era, the Rotunda communicated many ways of inheriting fragments of the past. Evident references to the architectural and ornamental heritage of Rome were linked sequentially at the Via Sacra complex as one proceeded toward the marble plan. The domed vestibule capped by an oculus provided a miniature version of the Pantheon

THE RESTORATION OF THE ROMAN FORUM IN LATE ANTIQUITY

without replicating the original and was attached discordantly to the apsidal hall and the Temple of Peace. The reused pieces arranged in the portal gestured toward the historicity of various architectural elements, recognizing that the complex was arranged like a text, with citations to earlier works. The Via Sacra complex, therefore, operated as a microcosm of the city, and it featured fragmented elements or *spolia* joined with references to architectural masterpieces to celebrate renewal under Constantine. The idea of updating the past was central to the Constantinian project at the Rotunda, as if revising and supplementing the complex transmitted Vespasian's Temple of Peace into a context relevant to the fourth century.

The Via Sacra complex regulated memories, much as inscriptions for monuments in the Forum indicate how the Constantinian additions transformed the past. The Constantinian Forum was governed by the juxtaposition of new interventions with preexisting monuments, such as the equestrian bronze that interrupted the view of the western Rostra. The Rotunda's façade provided access to an entire complex that encouraged visitors to enjoy Rome's cultural heritage. In a panegyric delivered at Rome, probably not in the presence of the emperor, Nazarius characterized the benefits of civic structures in allowing people to enjoy urban amenities:

There is leisure for more relaxed spirits to employ the amusements of peace. All the most celebrated things in the city gleam with new work, and not only are those which have been worn out through age distinguished with renewed splendor, but the very ones which were formerly considered the most magnificent betray the unseemly parsimony of the ancients now that they shine with golden light.[117]

Nazarius' statement indicates that spaces for public enjoyment also were provided with new functions, hinting that Constantine tried to shift attention away from the "unseemly ancients" (*indecoram maiorum*). Nazarius seemed to notice the type of intervention that subjected old marvels to new interpretations, underlining their status as amusements for the people. The senatorial sponsors who transformed the Via Sacra Rotunda in honor of Constantine suggest-

ed that the emperor cared for the whole city, which was achieved by altering the entrance leading toward the marble plan of Rome. Was the emphasis on the curved façade of the Rotunda a way to redouble the emphasis on the trajectory from the Via Sacra to the Temple of Peace along a bent axis, one that necessarily deemphasized the shrine at the center of Vespasian's Forum? It is hard to discern a religious agenda in the Constantinian Forum, yet the restorations certainly emphasized the cultural pleasures derived from rendering to the public that which was once "unseemly."

CONSTANTINE'S BASILICA

Immediately adjacent to the Rotunda, the Basilica Nova was rededicated to Constantine after its construction for Maxentius (fig. 2.16). The senate took over the ambitiously vaulted interior in Constantine's name after 312. The mammoth structure, resembling the vast interior spaces of late imperial baths, functioned at important moments for legal proceedings (fig. 2.17). As a supplement to the visual experience of the Rotunda next door, where one encountered the cultural benefits of Constantine's program, the repurposed Basilica Nova indicated that justice was bestowed by the emperor within a law court. Transformed into the Basilica of Constantine, the building featured on the interior a colossal portrait of Constantine, the fragments of which survive in the Capitoline Museums. This statue was displayed in the Basilica's western apse (fig. 2.18). The colossus presented what can be considered a local aristocratic perspective on Constantine's identity, since the building was rededicated in honor of the emperor at the behest of the senate, according to Aurelius Victor.[118] It is clear that the colossus, recarved from an earlier imperial portrait, was transported from elsewhere in the city for display in the basilica. Since the colossal portrait of Constantine was probably recarved from Hadrian's image and not Maxentius', there is little reason to think that the original basilica had contained a mammoth portrait. The new insertion of the emperor's likeness at a colossal scale within the basilica's western apse gave

Figure 2.16. Basilica of Constantine. Photo by author.

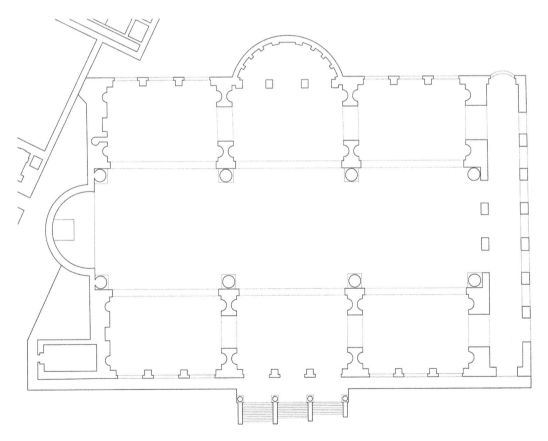

Figure 2.17. Plan of the Basilica of Constantine. Drawing by Brian Doherty.

a sense of a major transformation during the age of Constantine.[119]

It appears that the Constantinian architectural interventions to rededicate the mammoth structure were restricted to the northern apse. It used to be widely believed that the southern portal with a grand staircase providing direct access from the Via Sacra and featuring four porphyry columns was an afterthought, produced for Constantine (fig. 2.19).[120] An investigation by Susanna Buranelli Le Pera and Luca D'Elia uncovered a visible projection of the foundations for the entire basilica underneath the south-facing staircase, clearly defining the entrance as integral to the building's original plan.[121] The Constantinian interventions thus did not include the entrance from the Via Sacra, nor did the apse projecting to the north correlate with this portal as

Figure 2.18. Colossal portrait of Constantine, Capitoline Museums, Rome. Photo by the author.

an interrelated construction phase. Nonetheless, the clear indications in the exterior brickwork of the curved sections supplementing the flat wall surface show that the northern apse was indeed added after the initial building campaign, though not in conjunction with the Via Sacra façade (fig. 2.20). As a result, Constantinian transformations had the benefit of the practical addition of the northern apse, which was exploited for a juxtaposition on the interior with the colossal portrait displayed to the west.

Structural analysis indicates that inserting the northern apse was one of a series of additions that bolstered the entire structure, which had become unstable after the foundations had settled.[122] Though it did not belong to the original campaign, the northern apse furnished a practical rather than conceptual transformation.[123] Extending to the north beyond a coffered, barrel-vaulted section of the aisle, the apse was separated from the aisle bay by an architrave supported by columns. Once completed, the apse accommodated judges or perhaps magistrates.[124] As a result, the transformation that bolstered the stability of the northern wall by adding an apse provided an opportunity to particularly frame the judicial activities in the apse.

A significant approach to conservation emerged when Constantine reused Maxentius' basilica. Constantine's transformed original requires a consideration of the interior. After the work that reinforced the structure was completed, Constantine's colossal portrait was installed in the western apse to provide a looming reminder of the imperial presence. Inserting the second large apse at the center of the northern wall during the reign of Constantine provided a juxtaposition between the two apses. There is circumstantial evidence that law courts associated with the appellate judges appointed by the emperor met within the basilica. The emperors had administered law courts publicly in the Roman Forum until the second century CE, when, after the reign of Hadrian, there are no sources specifying that the imperial judicial practices continued to occur there.[125] As a law court, the Basilica of Constantine, and its northern apse in particular, probably functioned for the judges. Constantine innovated a system in which judges supervising the appellate courts operated in

Figure 2.19. Remains of the porphyry columns from the southern portal of the Basilica of Constantine. Photo by the author.

the place of the emperor.[126] After the reforms of Diocletian, letters and legal rescripts from the emperor were received by the urban prefect as part of the judicial responsibilities of that office. In 331, Constantine organized the legal system so that those who heard appeals on behalf of the emperor (*vice sacra iudicans*) were the urban prefects of Rome.[127] This new legal system seems to have been accommodated within the Basilica of Constantine, where the colossal portrait of the emperor would have been a dominating presence for the judges.

The drama and the scale of the interior, with its cross-vaults towering thirty-five meters above ground, placed dual emphasis on the two apses, the northern one for the judges and the western one with Constantine's portrait depicted at a scale appropriate to the vast interior.[128] Colossal portraits populated Rome during Constantine's reign; the impressively large fragments of another portrait in

bronze still survive.[129] The reports about the mammoth portraits in historical texts present challenges of interpretation, since the sources do not always match up precisely with the surviving fragments. Senatorial patrons may have inserted a symbol onto the colossus shown inside the basilica with a purposefully vague reference to the sign Constantine claimed to have seen prior to the triumph over Maxentius. The ambiguity rested in a conventional victory symbol acquiring equivocal Christian resonance.

Eusebius wrote that, immediately following the victory over Maxentius, Constantine ordered a portrait statue in the most frequented part of Rome with the emperor's hand holding "a trophy of the savior's passion."[130] The mammoth right hand associated with the colossus and originally exhibited in the basilica has a closed fist with a hole on the top into which a staff or spear probably had been inserted.[131] A presumably earlier version of the right hand,

71

Figure 2.20. Overlap of the eastern apse where it was added to the preexisting wall of the Basilica of Constantine. Photo by the author.

discovered on the Capitoline Hill in the eighteenth century, probably belonged to the original portrait; it seems to confirm that the colossus had been transformed to accommodate the likeness of Constantine and his trophy.[132] This suggests that the "trophy" was a feature of the colossus exhibited in the basilica. An inscription presented the claim that Constantine had restored Rome under the aegis of a banner or a sign, yet the epigraphic text has only been recorded by late antique historians, and the original does not survive. Eusebius wrote that the inscription accompanied the portrait of Constantine, directing the viewer's attention to the symbolism of a "sign": "By this salutary sign, the true proof of bravery, I saved and delivered your city from the yoke of a tyrant; and moreover I freed and restored to their ancient fame and splendor both the senate and the people of Rome."[133]

If the statue carried a conventional Roman military banner or standard, then its format was that of a spear with an intersecting crossbar.[134] In this case, an alternate transcription of the text provided by Rufinus might be more accurate: "Under this unique banner (*singulari signo*), which is the distinguishing mark of true virtue, I restored the city of Rome, the Senate and the Roman people, seized by the yoke of tyrannical power, to the earlier conditions of liberty and nobility."[135] The lack of clarity in the presentation of the "banner" seems to have resulted from senators remaining confused about the implications of Constantine's ties to Christianity. If the statue held a spear with a crossbar in its right hand, the standard retained a traditional military format as well as a resemblance to a Christian cross. That senators embraced dual readings of the symbol appears to accord with the vague language of praise used in most late antique inscriptions. Given the repeated epigraphic testimony to Constantine's administrative reforms elsewhere in the Forum, the installation at the Basilica Nova presented renewal symbolism to indicate that judicial practices within the space advanced liberty under the aegis of the emperor. Restoration offered the perfect metaphor in that returning to the earlier splendor downplayed Constantine's victory in a civil war and the uncomfortable novelty of his religious policies. The erasure of Maxentius from the Basilica Nova allowed the building to be reborn as a site that indicated that Constantine had not only conserved Rome, but also restored the city as a reconceived version of the past in which justice was strengthened.

Given the degree of documented architectural transformations for the Basilica Nova, together with the appropriation of an earlier imperial colossal portrait, it is clear that Constantine consciously maintained the preexisting urban infrastructure to honor Rome's history. Conserving buildings became particularly meaningful; under Constantine, the use of newly installed imagery maintained the past while prompting revised perceptions. Converting the preexisting colossus to commemorate Constantine's imperial identity within the basilica established the conceptual similarity between physical repairs and the restoration of the ruler's individual status. In other words, the importance of the recarved colossal portrait was embedded in matching the emperor's identity with the Basilica of Constantine. The return to a system of justice favorable to the aristocrats instigated by a sole emperor, with senators receiving appointments as appellate judges who ruled favorably on behalf of the other members of the elite, was implicit in the basilica once the Constantinian portrait was installed.[136] Constantine's imperial identity in Rome emerged from his administrative and judicial reforms, his early attempts that proclaimed tolerance of religious diversity, and his victory over Maxentius, all of which were expressed at the basilica. Once transformed, the Basilica of Constantine presented the judges as participants in the city's restoration to its proper place within the larger empire.

CONSTANTINIAN REVISION

Constantinian activities in the Roman Forum were pursued by the city's aristocratic patrons and maintained the architectural and monumental infrastructure, but designating these initiatives as conservation must come with an understanding of restoration as a culturally vital activity. Given the importance of epigraphic testimony in late antique urban space, revision, as an important process of transforming texts, must be considered in any analysis of Constantinian architecture.[137] The erasure of Maxentius' name, as from the statue of Mars, offered a model of transformation in which most of the preexisting monument remained intact; only the name of the condemned individual was removed. Likewise, rewriting urban space occurred with physical juxtapositions in which an inscription or an inscribed statue compelled viewers to revise their perceptions of what had been there previously. Constantinian architects added the emperor's name to the exterior of the Via Sacra Rotunda and his identity to the interior of the Basilica of Constantine; the latter was transformed through the practical insertion of the northern apse and the recarved colossus. The editorial process also was applied to the city with the creation of a system of fragmentation and citation. At the Via Sacra complex with the Rotunda adjoined to the marble plan of Rome,

the references to the Pantheon and Greek statues had also belonged to Maxentius' scheme. But Constantine rewrote and reclaimed this complex when his name was inserted onto the Rotunda façade. Thus, unlike the Tetrarchs, for whom restoration offered a way to permanently install their authority, Constantine proposed that restoration updated Rome's built heritage as a process that combined conservation with transformation and anticipated subsequent changes. Constantinian transformations were subtle additions, slight editorial corrections that maintained the meaning of the core text by leaving the urban fabric intact.

It is also important to consider the status of Christianity. Constantine's policies required audiences to see the temples in a new light. The entire peak of the Velia Hill to the east of the Forum's central area, for example, was taken up by the double temple dedicated to two goddesses, Venus and Roma (fig. I.8 [32]). Aurelius Victor specifically identified the "temple of the city" (*urbis fanum*) as one of the structures that the senate rededicated to Constantine after his triumph.[138] The *Chronograph of 354* specifies that the building had burned during the reign of Maxentius and that it had been repaired shortly thereafter.[139] Even though transformations during the Constantinian era remain difficult to trace in the available archeological evidence, it is clear that some of the repairs undertaken by Maxentius remained for his successor to appropriate. Investigations of the building are hindered by the extensive reconstructions undertaken during the Fascist era, which led to a partial reconstruction rather than careful archeological study. In addition, some of the ancient building remains inaccessible beneath the cloister and church of S. Francesca Romana. Despite the challenges, it has been determined that the two interior cellae, rebuilt in all likelihood by Maxentius after a fire that was concentrated at the structure's core, had received additions during the Constantinian period that filled in the square niches flanking the apses and provided a giant architrave in the western cella.[140]

The late antique accounts of the Temple of Venus and Roma celebrate it as a spot for commemorating the heritage of Rome. Cassiodorus, writing in the sixth century, mentions that long after "the temple of

Venus and Roma had been built, it is now called the temple of the city."[141] The change in name suggests that the building had become less a functional shrine than a monument to the past; yet this shift might not have occurred until after the Theodosian legislation of the 390s.[142] Reports about the temple indicate that the vast podium held up more than 100 free-standing columns facing north and south. The temple was accessed from the Via Sacra by proceeding up eleven white marble steps, eventually leading to a podium without columns at the western end of the precinct. The entrance to the Temple of Venus and Roma from the Via Sacra provided urban ornament at the location where imperial processions continued to be practiced during late antiquity.

An early fifth-century account by Prudentius set forth anti-pagan complaints about statues displayed at the temple. In *Contra Symmachum*, Prudentius described viewing the scene from the Via Sacra: "the lofty Capitoline Hill, the priest wearing a laurel wreath standing at the temples of their gods along the Via Sacra, and the valley resounding with the cattle lowing on their way to the temple of Roma." Prudentius then expressed particular concern about the statues seen from the Via Sacra, imagining that they would make a strong impact on an impressionable boy viewing them: "He would think that what is done by the senate's authority must be genuine, and so he gave his faith to the images and believed that the figures standing in a row, which he shuddered to look at, were the lords of the heavens."[143] The images were identified as the statues of many gods: Hercules (Alcides) and Castor and Pollux (sons of Leda), among others.[144] What is notable is the objection to statues that could be seen outside, as if the cult images had

been moved to a spot on the western podium of the temple so that they could be viewed from the Via Sacra. They faced the processional route of the Via Sacra and therefore reinforced the path along which imperial processions progressed. Even though this evident transference of statues to the exterior of the temple might not have occurred under Constantine, it is striking that the works were both recontextualized and preserved.

Considered together, the Constantinian transformation of the Roman Forum particularly featured monuments that lined the Via Sacra. From the top of the Velia Hill, where Constantine "restored" the Temple of Venus and Roma by perhaps shifting smaller statues outdoors to the locations facing the processional route, the last phase of an imperial ritual commenced at the eastern end of the Via Sacra before proceeding into the Roman Forum. Heading westward along the Via Sacra, the processions passed by the Basilica of Constantine and the Rotunda, both of which had been restored under Constantine. Even the equestrian statue of Constantine faced the Via Sacra, where the procession reached its culmination, if indeed emperors had ceased to ascend the Capitol due to objections to sacrificing at the Temple of Jupiter Optimus Maximus. Repairing the buildings and monuments along the Via Sacra emphasized the imperial rituals. For Constantine, this urban reconfiguration provided space in which he brought back just governance and reasserted that civic administration as well as urban rituals were the joint endeavors of the emperor and the senators. The connected ideas of restoring and reforming were communicated by Constantine's projects in the Forum, which revised attitudes toward the past while maintaining the city's heritage.

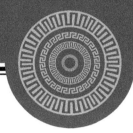

CHAPTER 3

STATUES IN THE LATE ANTIQUE ROMAN FORUM

THE LATE ANTIQUE ROMAN FORUM FEATURED MANY STATUES, THANKS TO ACTS OF SENA-torial munificence that encouraged viewers to see the topography as consistently updated. These public statues also recommended to viewers that they consider the civic center as if under restoration, since the individual portraits implied that each new installation revised what had stood there before. Many late imperial statues exhibited outdoors featured reused plinths, and many new works were juxtaposed to older statues, inviting comparisons among the various esteemed figures represented in the portraits. Appropriating older monumental fragments by inscribing newer texts onto preexisting plinths hinted that physical strategies of rehabilitation gestured toward the wider rejuvenation of urban life. The metaphors of maintaining the state and guarding the civic realm suggested that disparate groups—from the populace at large to local aristocratic officials to the rulers who appointed them—achieved consensus over time as they created monuments in the Roman Forum. Once the individual works were fit into groupings, the many portrait statues in the Forum exploited the ad-ditive process through which they were assembled to indicate a sequential lineage among individuals.

Most of the late antique statues installed in the Forum represented those who had led the state. Details about both these leaders and Rome's aristocrats emerge in the texts inscribed on the plinths, indicating that the displays upheld (or occasionally excised) the memories of both local sponsors and the emperors honored by the installations. The find spots of the statue bases, along with indentations on the pavement from a few of the original display loca-tions, aid in reconstructing some of the displays. When the original sites of the installations are known, one can analyze sight lines and the alignment of significant portraits. From these observations, it is possible to see that each generation of rulers established links with other statues within a given viewshed, so that the portraits exhibited cross-generational affiliations.

There have been 101 inscriptions recovered from the Forum that belong to late antique statues from the period spanning 284–526 CE, but none of the associated portraits or art-

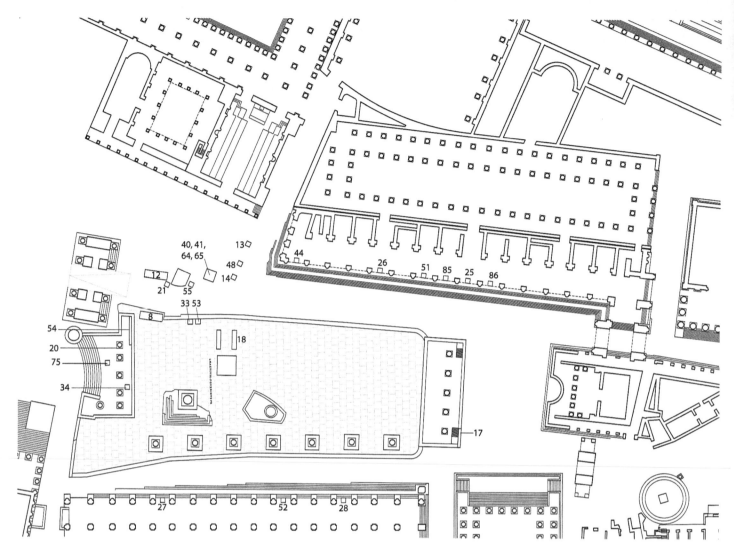

Figure 3.1. Plan of the central area of the Roman Forum showing the display locations of late antique statues, c. 476 CE. The numbers correspond to the catalogue available in Visualizing Statues in the Late Antique Roman Forum, http://inscriptions.etc.ucla.edu/index.php /mapping-statues. Drawing by Brian Doherty.

works survives.[1] The previous chapter addressed statues that Constantine used to regulate memories; this chapter looks at the Forum's statues installed from the reign of Constantius II (337–361) until the breakdown of the Western empire in 476. A representation of the statues in the Roman Forum featuring their geographic coordinates and a catalogue of the inscriptions is available online; these set forth both epigraphic evidence and display characteristics that explain how public inscriptions operated in the urban context.[2] Those late antique statues for which original display spots can be defined by archeologi-

cal or epigraphic testimony are represented in a plan labeled with the numbers from the online catalogue (fig. 3.1).[3] This chapter presents the case that local Roman senators struggled to elevate their own positions by exploiting the numerous connotations of restitution in Rome, typically memorializing the social connections among aristocrats and emperors that brought back the ideals of the heroic past. In fact, many of the Forum's late antique inscriptions reflect or anticipate highly orchestrated dialogue, whether in the exchange of letters or in real social interactions among emperors and members of the elite.[4] Processions and other imperial rituals staged in the Forum offered rare opportunities for physical encounters. As representations, the Forum's statues captured the ideals of harmony between Romans and the often distant emperors.

Each individual statue installed in the Roman Forum offered a piecemeal supplement to earlier installations, changing the previous iteration. A senator making a one-time installation responded to earlier works and helped to build up the exhibition through a process of accrual. The column monuments instigated this series of reactions. Diocletian and Maximian had rebuilt the Rostra and added the five-column monuments framing two ends of the Forum's paved central area to link architectural rebuilding with the imperial system they had pioneered. A critical reaction to the Tetrarchic Forum was elicited when the seven columns on the Forum's southern flank presented an alternative (see fig. 2.1).[5] The Tetrarchic nonhereditary system of Diocletian and Maximian met with resistance from Constantine and his son, Constantius II, whose family dynasty was featured prominently in the statues of the Forum. Even though Constantine reaffirmed dynastic succession after the Tetrarchs had suspended hereditary rulership, the Forum remained a nearly exclusive realm for imperial ideology, a mode of honoring emperors in public space that Diocletian had initiated. By the end of the fourth century, the paved sectors of the Forum and the plaza before the Senate House were dominated by images of emperors interspersed with a few portraits of very powerful senators. Alternate strategies were applied to the public façades of basilicas and the areas occupied by temples.[6] This dichotomy was by no means strict. Nonetheless, after Constantine, new additions of imperial monuments refined the political concepts that Diocletian had introduced to the Forum, so that the displays communicated to the populace that the Senate and its membership had returned to their proper roles in a state in which the ultimate authority rested in legitimate emperors.

A series of displays set up in honor of the emperor Honorius (r. 395–423) and apparently exhibited in anticipation of consular celebrations for the emperor in 404 presented a remarkable departure from the traditions of the Forum.[7] The correlation between Honorius' statues and a panegyric by Claudian, a poet working for the imperial court, indicates that the emperor and his closest advisors had requested certain installations in Rome. Thus, in the fifth century, there was a rupture in the tradition of senators anticipating the types of monuments that would appropriately honor the emperors. The statues installed for Honorius indicate that the emperor's advisors had negotiated the types of statues that were to be displayed in the Forum; yet local senators still took on the role of sponsoring these installations.

Because the sponsoring senators recorded their names in inscriptions that still survive, exhibitions maintaining and representing the social order of powerful emperors and their closely affiliated aristocratic officials can be documented in late antique Rome.[8] The waxing and waning fortunes of powerful individuals inserted distinguished people into a well-regulated historical record. Harriet Flower and Charles Hedrick Jr. have demonstrated that statues and their inscriptions placed individual identities in urban public space to preserve the memories of those who had withstood the test of time or to erase the names of those who had suffered disgrace, building up a picture of history that could be seen and experienced.[9] In the inscriptions, the superlative terms that local high-ranking senators used to praise the emperors, such as "most fortunate" or "most generous," hinted that the aristocratic virtues also came to the fore.[10] Because the Roman Forum, as a high-traffic area, was the site for presenting official messages to the public, the statues communicated that times of hardship had been superseded by wise governance, and that consensus had emerged among rulers and local elites.[11] Emperors, who are shown as overseeing this realm, predominated in the zone: as Franz Alto Bauer has demonstrated, each ruler from Diocletian until the end of the Theodosian dynasty except for Jovian was honored with a statue in the Roman Forum.[12]

To suggest that the provocative interplay among works in the Roman Forum was constructed through a series of one-time interventions begs the question of how any coherence could have been achieved. Indeed, it would be impossible to claim that any mastermind or set of guidelines set forth procedures that structured the late antique exhibitions. Rather, a picture emerged from a selective number of benefactors striving to establish links with earlier displays. Chronological changes in the late antique statue displays have prompted Carlos Machado to conclude that the gradual disintegration of imperial power in the West, commencing with the turn of the fifth century in his account, offered the urban prefects of Rome opportunities to gain local status through works that asserted aristocratic identity in Forum installations that did not feature imperial portraits.[13] Further insights can be gained by comparing the Roman Forum with other public display spots in Rome. For example, Robert Chenault has defined the late antique Forum of Trajan as a zone for aristocratic group definition, since the inscriptions record that portraits of highly esteemed senators by far outnumbered the images of emperors there.[14]

Analyzing the public exhibitions that ornamented late antique districts in Rome apart from the Roman Forum underlines the specificity of each urban context. A brief survey of the Forum of Trajan and the Temple of Peace sheds light on the distinct features of the Roman Forum. For instance, recent archeological research has determined that the impressive equestrian statue of Trajan in the Forum of Trajan was aligned against the southernmost end of the plaza on the central axis, providing a direct axial connection to the imperial statue on top of the Column of Trajan; this caused subsequent emperors to avoid installations at spots where they might appear diminished by comparison to Trajan.[15] One could argue based on the senatorial portraits that Rome's elite pursued new strategies for displays in Rome after the Tetrarchy, since a late antique power imbalance caused imperial authority to replace the more level playing field that had existed in the earlier principate. John Weisweiler has argued that late antique senators tried to exhibit their rapport with the overwhelmingly powerful rulers at the site where Trajan's images dominated over everything, but their status had been relatively diminished with the growth of imperial power.[16] The majority of the late antique displays in the imperial fora and the Roman Forum were initiatives undertaken by senators, however, and it seems unlikely

that the aristocratic patrons would have pursued works only to attest to their loss of status. Indeed, Chenault observes an alternate scenario, noting that the late antique senatorial installations in the Forum of Trajan commenced with the reign of Constantine and accordingly reflected the need to establish collective norms in the wake of Constantine's expansion of the senatorial aristocracy. Chenault identifies themes that include the emphatic prevalence of honors credited to late antique senators in the Forum of Trajan; status was earned there by displays attesting not necessarily to birth, but to holding high office or otherwise attaining elevated civic status. Rhetorical abilities and literary accomplishments particularly found expression in the Forum of Trajan, plausibly with displays concentrated near the precinct's two libraries, which featured statues of Claudian, Merobaudes, Aurelius Victor, Sidonius Apollinaris, and the philosopher Marius Victorinus; their achievements as authors rather than as holders of high office in the administration earned them the images.[17] Portraits of the authors of panegyrics joined with images of the most powerful aristocrats in the Forum of Trajan to establish that this display showed portraits of Rome's local elites—in contrast to the imperial images that predominated in the Roman Forum.[18]

Much of the impressive collection that had been assembled during the reign of Vespasian in the Temple of Peace, a forum often designated as a temple precinct, survived into late antiquity and marked the cultural benefits that accrued to Rome at the conclusion of the Jewish War in 70 CE. In light of recent discoveries, it can be determined that the open-air courtyard featured a series of six symmetrically arranged water courses that defined the space as a pleasure garden (see fig. I.8 [26]).[19] From Jerusalem came artworks and spoils of war, and from Nero's house came an extensive number of masterpieces by renowned Greek artists, together with the famous *Dying Gaul* and *Gaul Committing Suicide with His Wife* from Pergamon. The Pergamene works flanked the axial central walkway outdoors.[20] Much of the vast collection remained on view for public enjoyment into the sixth century: Procopius specified that the calf sculpted by Myron and the bronze bull attributed to Pheidias or Lysippus numbered among the works by illustrious Greek artists in the Temple of Peace, as discussed in Chapter 2 above.[21] Presenting impressive masterpieces from across the known world in a context of erudition and urban ornamentation, the exhibition assembled by Vespasian that survived into the sixth century communicated that the vast empire brought peaceful leisure to Romans, who understood that their happiness was increased by the cultural center featuring the world's most significant artworks.[22]

The inscriptions from the late antique Roman Forum feature mainly imperial dedications, but, as Franz Alto Bauer notes, this did not preclude others from having their statues shown there.[23] There are documented cases of officially sanctioned representations in the Forum that displayed images of local senators or other members of the elite. The gilded bronze statue of Avianus Symmachus discussed above (see the Introduction), although it possibly was displayed in the Forum of Trajan, originally included a now-lost citation from the letter that granted dispensation for the prominent senator to have a public statue. After the senate voted to honor the aristocrat Vettius Agorius Praetextatus with a statue in the Forum, Q. Aurelius Symmachus, the son of Avianus Symmachus, sent an official letter to the emperor asking for ratification.[24] A corresponding inscribed statue base has been discovered in the Roman Forum immediately adjacent to the Column of Phocas. Its text honors Praetextatus and records that, with senatorial approval and imperial confirmation, images of local aristocrats could appear within the paved central area.[25] Praetextatus, who was held in high regard for his service to the state, played a very public role as a proponent of the traditional cults; yet none of his pagan priesthoods are mentioned in the Forum inscription.[26] Thus, official permission was a prerequisite for any nonimperial portrait to be displayed in the Roman Forum and the accompanying inscriptions avoided references to controversial issues such as holding prominent priesthoods of the traditional deities.[27] The local elite, with their own funds and possibly the city's revenues, paid for the works exhibited in the Roman Forum prior to the middle of the fifth century, when the administrative concerns in Rome underwent drastic transformations.[28]

RESTORATION BETWEEN THEORY AND PRACTICE

Reinstating the civic values of Rome's aristocrats was a theoretical interest that informed the practical concerns of setting up statues. Inscriptions used traditional terminology, since the names entered the historical record when etched in stone. The sponsor's name was given in the nominative case in Latin, typically with the patron offering a dedication to the emperor(s); the name of each ruler appeared in the dative case.[29] Senatorial decree was needed to grant the emperor a portrait statue in the Forum; an emperor might earn this honor by receiving a prestigious appointment, such as the consulate, or by gaining victory in a military conquest, or by having ruled over a lengthy period of time. In turn, the emperors typically had to approve portraits depicting people of nonimperial status who were to be represented in the Forum's central area or within the plaza in front of the Senate House.[30]

The commemorative landscapes of late antique cities relied on the preservation of memories, which both sustained the achievements of earlier generations and projected them into the future. The formation of historical memories through monuments functioned particularly well when the honored individual had acquired a link to earlier generations, as Charles Hedrick Jr. has argued.[31] Each imperial dynasty also transformed perceptions of the past through the preservation and adaptation of Rome's built fabric. Those depicted in the statues were often the ones for whom urban ceremonies were conducted. Tradition designated civic areas for celebrations of the most important state events, such as imperial processions. Even a local Roman receiving an appointment as consul would march with assembled aristocrats from his home to the Forum.[32]

Because of the centrality of maintaining memories in the commemorative landscape of the Roman Forum, preserving Rome's built heritage emerged as a cultural value. Of course, the restoration of the past proceeded amid the struggle to confront formidable challenges: accidental destruction, acts of condemnation, or outright neglect. Given the importance of maintaining the historical record, with the names written in inscriptions together with the identities of architectural sponsors, it was considered better to conserve than to establish new buildings.

Aristocrats in Rome valued restoration for practical reasons, but the display of individual identities in portrait statues also suggests deeper meanings. Ideas about perseverance were applied equally to the sponsors of monuments and to the physically restored structures. The most elevated praise of individuals was accorded to those withstanding the test of time, either by overcoming adversity or by enduring despite a potential lapse into oblivion. The supplement to the Theodosian Code produced for the emperor Majorian (r. 457–461) condemned patrons who sought architectural fragments, but in so doing caused the destruction of old structures: "Under the pretence of modifying materials for public buildings, the esteemed buildings of the ancients are disintegrating, and great monuments are taken apart so that something small may be repaired."[33] Majorian reiterated in his policy of 458 the earlier legislation that preserved public amenities, including statues and architectural fragments. Later, in the early sixth century, the Roman senator Cassiodorus wrote a letter on behalf of King Theoderic drawing upon this tradition to praise restoration over new construction:

It is not worthwhile to initiate solid buildings if lawlessness will destroy the construction. For the things that wisdom has begun and care has maintained are sturdier. And therefore caution should be used in preserving rather than planning anew, since the plan at the beginning deserves praise, but from preservation we receive accolades for completion.[34]

The comparison between an individual's status and a civic monument, both of which could be reinstated, also appears implicitly in the argument advanced in 399 by Q. Aurelius Symmachus, speaking in support of restoring full status to Flavian the Elder: "It is better to restore honor than to give it."[35] Restoration allowed a sponsor to supplement the past, adding to the precedents in a manner that formed a historical argument or fleshed out individual status with respect to previous generations.

The late antique statues of the Roman Forum resulted from civic and senatorial benefactions in transactions resembling gifts.[36] Donors of elite senatorial standing furnished both the statues and the funds for buildings and monuments in exchange for exalted status, hoping to inscribe their identities into the city's landscape forever. A gift given appropriately came with the fiction that the benefactor's virtues, rather than his wealth, advanced the city's upkeep. An exception appears in a description by the historian Ammianus Marcellinus that indicates the abuse of donations in support of restoration. The urban prefect Caeionius Rufius Volusianus signo Lampadius used inscriptions installed upon buildings he had restored to inappropriately position himself "not as the renewer, but as the founder," according to Ammianus.[37] Lampadius, as depicted in Ammianus' account, did not fully grasp how appropriate restoration earned one fame only after one proceeded in a virtuous manner. Ammianus thus hinted that Lampadius had not grasped the fact that times had changed: in contrast to earlier times, when founding structures offered the highest esteem, during late antiquity conservation offered the most prestige, by clearly establishing that the restorer upheld civic values.

In Ammianus' narrative, Lampadius appears to have also misunderstood how to offer proper benefactions to the public. One misguided strategy he used was to distribute gifts indiscriminately by paying extravagantly for games and by distributing coins to the disenfranchised. Lampadius did not provide handouts to the people at large, however; rather, "he summoned some beggars from the Vatican and presented them with valuable gifts."[38] In addition, Lampadius wished to earn credit as the benefactor for repairing buildings, but he did so by stealing construction materials rather than by using civic funds. Ammianus describes Lampadius' illicit acquisitions: "He did not order the cost to be defrayed from the usual taxes, but if there was need of iron, lead, bronze, or anything of the kind, attendants were set on, in order that they might, under pretence of buying the various articles, seize them without paying anything."[39] The thefts and the offense to the poor particularly violated the norm of gifts proceeding from virtuous generosity. Lampadius ended up exiled and deprived of the fame he had sought on account of his corrupt actions. The Lampadius episode confirms that restoration was valued when the sponsor returned building materials to their proper and useful function in the civic realm as a sign of respect for the past.

CONSTANTIUS II AND IMPERIAL AUTHORITY

Though the fourth-century emperors after Constantine visited Rome only occasionally, they expressed a ceremonial revival of the capital when they did. Although they were rare, the public assemblies before rulers in the Forum's central assembly spot and the area facing the Curia were documented as the highlights of processions that emperors celebrated at Rome during the fourth century. In describing the ceremony of Constantius II at Rome in 357 commemorating his victory over Magnentius, Ammianus Marcellinus identified two separate formal meetings: "He addressed the nobles in the Senate House and the populace from the tribunal."[40] The typical late antique protocol required emperors visiting Rome to encounter the populace at the Rostra and meet with the senators in the Curia. Processions in Rome honoring Theodosius I in 389 and Honorius in 404 also featured these two separate meetings.[41] The importance of the Forum's central area and the plaza in front of the Curia for these imperial ceremonies explains the high number of imperial statues in these zones; in part, the installations preserved memories of the in-person encounters. The theme of restoration presented in some statues of the Forum also communicated that the physical presence of the emperor put the empire back into its proper place. Yet the theme of restoration granted Constantius II a particularly aggrandized appearance, as one who had exceeded the norms of the past.

The anticipation of an emperor's visit motivated aristocratic patrons to initiate the construction of publicly displayed statues. Local figures could be honored in other parts of the city, such as at the homes of senators.[42] It seems logical to assume that aristocrats pursuing honorific displays that commemorated emperors typically operated independ-

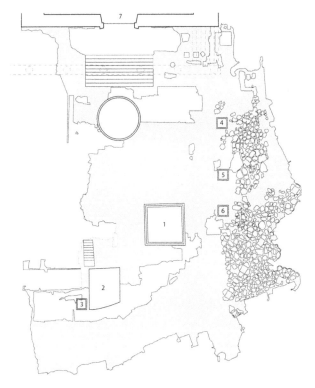

Figure 3.2. Plan of the plaza in front of the Senate House indicating the display locations of late antique statues and monuments. (1) Theodosian dynastic monument; (2) Lapis Niger; (3) portrait statue of Maxentius; (4), (5), and (6) three portrait statues of Constantius II; (7) entrance to the Senate House. Drawing by Andrew Ruff.

dent of the imperial bureaucracy.[43] Yet there were times when directives from the imperial court instructed Romans how to commemorate the rulers.

The public display of portraits received particular emphasis during the reign of Constantius II, who grappled with trying to appear statue-like when he undertook a ritual procession during his visit to the city. His task was to leave a lasting memory that captured the imperial persona of Constantine's son. The installation of three portraits of Constantius II at the plaza in front of the Senate House turned to redundancy in order to guarantee that Constantius was remembered (fig. 3.2).

The many statues of Constantius II in front of the Curia also asserted emphatically that the emperor's authority was ubiquitous, expansive, and ever-present. One of the statue bases still remains at its original display spot (fig. 3.3). Cavities at the

Figure 3.3. Statue base of Constantius II belonging to a row of three portraits from the plaza in front of the Senate House (*CIL* 6.31395). Photo by the author.

Figure 3.4. Surviving statue base flanked by the marble remains from two additional statue bases for an installation of three portraits of Constantius II at the plaza in front of the Senate House (*CIL* 6.1161, 1162, 31395). Photo by the author.

top of the remaining statue base held the feet of the bronze portrait. Judging from these indentations as well as the measurements of the plinth, Brigitte Ruck has calculated that this portrait, like the other two identical bronze portraits accompanying it, was 2.7 meters tall.[44] Given that the inscribed part of the one block that remains at its original location faces toward the plaza, it should be assumed that all three portraits were oriented in the same direction. Further, marble fragments in the pavement are traces of the additional two inscribed statue bases (fig. 3.4).[45] Thus, it appears that the three identical bronze installations depicting Constantius II stood in a row at a larger-than-life scale (see fig. 3.2). Each of the three plinths accompanied a statue of Constantius, and all replicated the same text, noting sponsorship by the urban prefect Memmius Vitrasius Orfitus: "To the one who expanded the empire, our lord, the great Constantius II [Flavius Iulius Constantius], victor over the entire world and ever-triumphant Augustus, [set up by] Memmius Vitrasius Orfitus, of the highest senatorial rank [and] imperial judge hearing tertiary appeals, in devotion to his divine nature and majesty."[46] Orfitus revealed his own hunger for power by sponsoring this set of three identical statues to aggrandize Constantius II. Through their expansive scale and the blatant repetition of the bombastic inscriptions, the monuments presented Constantius II such that the multiple likenesses pervaded the space in front of the Senate House, much as his triumph extended to "the entire world."

Framing the plaza in front of the Senate House with the three statues of Constantius II points toward the dominant role of imperial imagery in public space. The overly emphatic insistence on the authority of Constantius II seems to have struck Romans as indecorous. Orfitus as the sponsor was himself accused of arrogance by Ammianus, who records that his failure to solve a wine shortage caused riots protesting his policies.[47] Since Ammianus was writing more than thirty years after Orfitus provoked outrage and civil unrest, it is plausible that memories of the urban prefect's insensitivity had survived.

The physical presence of Constantius II at Rome

in 357, marking his victory over Magnentius, plausibly elicited a negative response on account of his insensitivity to the public and his remote appearance, according to Ammianus. Yet Ammianus asserted that the emperor was overwhelmed by Rome's impressive sights: "And when he came to the Rostra, he looked out with amazement at the concentration of marvels on every side of the Forum."[48] Ammianus, writing in the 380s, thus indicated that Constantius II was struck by the impressive installations, which presented an imposing past that humbled the emperor. In describing the procession of Constantius II, Ammianus highlighted the emperor's wish to imitate the monuments he saw, which led the living emperor to behave as a statue. Ammianus reported that

being saluted as Augustus with favoring shouts, while hills and shores thundered out the roar, he [the emperor] never stirred, but showed himself as calm and imperturbable as he was commonly seen in his provinces. For he stooped when passing through lofty arches (although he was very short), and as if his neck were held in place, he kept his eyes facing straight ahead, turning his face neither to the left nor to the right like a human statue, neither did he nod when the wheel jolted nor was he ever seen to spit . . . or move his hands about.[49]

The oddity of an emperor who could not live up to the expectations created by his representations suggests that the dialogue between rituals and statues was critical to creating meaningful displays. Ammianus humorously reduced the emperor on procession to an inert representation devoid of life and displaying none of the spitting or head gestures that would make him human. Thus the statues of Constantius II can be considered as going too far in competing with earlier imagery. Ammianus implied that the emperor was overly concerned with his reputation, as his statues surpassed the preexisting displays with the augmented scale that made his appearance overbearing. Ammianus also suggested an irony that Constantius II, although described as short, fooled himself into thinking that he was as tall as his colossal portraits, as if imperial authority had substituted the statue-like public persona for the actual individual. But Ammia-

nus acerbically hinted that Constantius II was satisfied by his remote demeanor.

The legacy of Constantius II resulted from his oversized statues presenting ideas of restoration. Epigraphic testimony on an equestrian statue of Constantius II advanced the emperor's claim to have restored Rome (fig. 3.5). The urban prefect Neratius Cerealis sponsored this statue, which matched in position and format the statue of Constantine on the opposite side of the Via Sacra (fig. 3.1 [8] and [12]). The inscription speaks to the eloquence of the conceit, since the son was paired with the father in a manner that established Constantius II as a replication of Constantine:

To the restorer of the city of Rome and of the world, and the eliminator of poisonous tyranny, our lord [Constantius II] Flavius Iulius Constantius, victor and always triumphant *Augustus*; [set up by] Neratius Cerealis, of the highest senatorial rank, urban prefect (of Rome) and judge hearing imperial appeals, in devotion to his divine nature and majesty.[50]

The sponsor further compared Constantius II to his father by suggesting that the victory over the tyrant Magnentius paralleled that of Constantine over Maxentius. The benefaction was credited to Neratius Cerealis, who had convinced the senate to condemn Magnentius' usurpation and thereby helped to restore the legitimacy of Constantius II in the West.[51] Cerealis is a definitive example of a senatorial sponsor who wished to advertise his agreement with the emperor. Restoration (*restitutio*) in its several meanings gained political connotations when the term was applied to Constantius II as if he had reinstated the wise governance of Constantine, a message that resulted from the close visual links between statues of the two emperors.

The political displays in the Roman Forum and the inscriptions that accompanied the monuments formalized the arrangement by which both conceptual and physical restoration allowed emperors to appear to be the culmination of those who had ruled before. Constantius II's images may have overextended the grandeur of imperial authority, but through scale

Figure 3.5. Base for the equestrian statue of Constantius II (*CIL* 6.1158). Photo by the author.

and repetition his statues created a dialogue among the monuments in public space. Thus, the concept of restoration for the Constantinian dynasty crossed over from a political ideal to a material expression. In the end, the restoration of the monuments of the past was interrelated with the establishment of displays that featured updates and new additions inserted over time. Physical additions such as the installations of Constantius II allowed the emperor to appear to be improving upon the legacy of the past.

THE PROBLEMATIC LEGACY OF THE VALENTINIAN DYNASTY

Installations in the Forum during the Valentinian dynasty hint at the problems of an emperor gaining a reputation as a restorer of Rome without the proper involvement of the city's senators. It is striking that the first generation of the Valentinian dynasty, specifically the emperors Valentinian I and Valens (joint rule, 364–375), avoided visits to Rome and

received the honor of relatively few statues in the Roman Forum. During the joint reign of those two emperors, the strained relations between rulers and the aristocrats of Rome led to formulaic installations in downtown Rome without the attentive involvement of the imperial court.[52] Religious disputes were one cause of this strain, but they should not be presumed to be the only one; Valentinian I did confirm the appointment of a prominent pagan, Vettius Agorius Praetextatus, as proconsul of Achaia in 364, and granted his request to allow night sacrifices for the Eleusinian mysteries in Greece.[53] But accusations of aristocrats practicing the occult led Valentinian I to bring Rome's senators to trial, and the resulting tensions might have caused the city's aristocrats to provide less-than-prominent monuments in honor of the Valentinians.[54] During the Valentinian dynasty, then, Romans generally would not have viewed advertising connections to the imperial court as the way to achieve lasting fame.

Perfunctory senatorial loyalty to the emperors did continue during the Valentinian dynasty, however. A statue base from a monument honoring Valens was found in front of the Senate House.[55] At the same plaza in front of the Senate House, presumably, was displayed a statue of Valentinian I.[56] The sponsor of both works was the urban prefect of 365–366, C. Caeionius Rufius Volusianus (usually known simply as Lampadius), mentioned above as the one who had flagrantly violated the norms of civic benefactions in Rome.[57] According to Ammianus, as noted earlier, Lampadius completely disregarded the code of conduct defining a benefactor's role as one who upheld virtue.[58] The two documented monuments that Lampadius sponsored to honor Valentinian I and Valens in the Forum attempted to give credit to the urban prefect, who earned a reputation for being both corrupt and excessively power hungry. Lampadius was renowned for not understanding that proper connections to emperors and the correct pursuit of virtue played significant roles in preserving an individual's memory. Lampadius as described by Ammianus was a thief who restored buildings in an illegal fashion; thus his sponsorship was likely an attempt—probably unsuccessful—to curry favor with Valentinian I and Valens by asserting that they could envision gaining local support due to the urban prefect's support.

Outside of the Forum, senators paid strategic attention to the city's built infrastructure by constructing or repairing bridges over the Tiber, with proper credit given to the Valentinian emperors. One, the Pons Aurelius, was repaired by Avianus Symmachus (father of Q. Aurelius Symmachus) in the late 360s; by 370, the senate had dedicated a new bridge to all the members of the Valentinian dynasty, including Gratian, the newly appointed *Augustus* and young son of Valentinian I.[59] Produced in anticipation of an imperial arrival into Rome, the bridges were made to encourage an official visit by Valentinian I that never occurred. Nonetheless, a mission to Trier seeking to formalize the ties between the senate and the court of Valentinian I particularly benefited the emissary sent from Rome, Q. Aurelius Symmachus.[60] Members of the Symmachi family seem to have organized the practical upkeep of Rome without devising a grand exhibition to celebrate the Valentinians in the Forum. Yet the repairs of monuments such as the

bridges particularly highlighted that the Symmachi exploited maintenance to display their attempts to influence the imperial court for the benefit of Rome. By contrast, the statues of the Valentinians in the Forum exhibited improperly constituted links with the shady senator Lampadius, since the corrupt urban prefect sought personal fame illegitimately from a putative connection to the emperors. Lampadius' reputation as a thieving restorer and as a violator of senatorial customs demonstrates that honor did not accrue from illicit deeds.

THE RETURN TO COLLEGIAL RULE UNDER THEODOSIUS I

A period of instability in the West during the usurpation of Magnus Maximus, who had evicted the emperor Valentinian II from Italy, was reversed after Theodosius I (r. 379–392) insisted on both family lineage and joint rulership by related emperors as the path to imperial legitimacy. Some senators, including Q. Aurelius Symmachus, initially sought an alliance with the illegitimate Maximus. Yet after the defeat of Maximus in 388, senators established monuments in the Roman Forum that celebrated Theodosius' victory. His family lineage, military successes, and orthodox Christianity enabled Theodosius I to craft a new imperial identity during a procession he conducted at Rome in 389, at which point the emperor demonstrably respected aristocratic traditions and virtues. Both the ritual commemoration in a procession and the monuments displayed in the Forum honoring Theodosius indicated the return to collegial rule, yet now under the leadership of a family dynasty. The Theodosian dynasty, as a result, was commemorated by displays in the Forum that created visual juxtapositions to the Tetrarchic monuments as they established precedents for collegiality.

Early in the reign of Theodosius I, prior to the usurpation of Maximus, an urban prefect of Rome named Lucius Valerius Septimus Bassus set up a monument honoring three co-ruling emperors. It was located at the back of the eastern Rostra (fig. 3.6). The statues of the three emperors were displayed prominently, but the works did not directly

Figure 3.6. Digital reconstruction of the eastern Rostra in the Roman Forum with the statue monument of Gratian, Valentinian II, and Theodosius I (*CIL* 6.1184a). Experiential Technologies Center, UCLA. © Regents, University of California.

face viewers standing in the Forum's central area. An investigation by Franz Alto Bauer has determined that an inscribed epistyle from this display featuring the names of Gratian, Valentinian II, and Theodosius I was originally situated above the Rostra's doorway, through which one reached an interior staircase (fig. 3.7).[61] Placed above the door frame, the marble epistyle block has surviving indentations for inserting the feet of the bronze statues, indicating that all three upright figures were shown as if standing on the Rostra. The three emperors' statues, which faced away from the Forum, were positioned to be viewed by those ascending the platform. Further, the three statues appeared far less remote than the four Tetrarchs commemorated on top of the columns. By

Figure 3.7. Inscribed architrave from the statue monument of Gratian, Valentinian II, and Theodosius I (*CIL* 6.1184a), originally installed at the eastern Rostra. Photo by the author.

placing the three statues so that the emperors' backs were turned to the Tetrarchic emperors elevated on top of the columns far above the Rostra, Bassus distinguished Theodosian governance from that of Diocletian.

The epistyle block was an old architectural fragment that Bassus had elevated on top of columns as the upper frame of the doorway, an act of spoliation asserting that the urban prefect sponsored a rigorously critical appropriation of the past. Once installed in the Rostra, the old epistyle also created an evident adaptation of the preexisting speaker's platform. Clearly, turning their backs on the Tetrarchs allowed the Theodosians to be honored for negating the aloof positions of colleagues of Diocletian. The architectural language employing *spolia* allowed Bassus to advance the built environment of the Forum through his well-informed knowledge that refining the past appropriately honored Gratian, Valentinian II, and Theodosius I.[62]

Some of the senators in Rome had supported Theodosius' foes. Q. Aurelius Symmachus allied himself with the illegitimate Maximus, as mentioned earlier, and Nicomachus Flavianus the Elder a few years later formed an even more dangerous tie with the usurper Eugenius. Theodosius penalized Flavianus with a memory censure that was eventually reversed, but Symmachus and the son of Flavian received clemency.[63]

Perhaps in preparation for an imperial visit after Theodosius I eliminated the threat of Maximus, Ceionius Rufius Albinus as the urban prefect set up around 389 a monument facing the Curia's façade dedicated to Thermantia, the Theodosian dynasty's matriarch, together with all three rulers—Valentinian II, Theodosius I, and Arcadius. In so doing, he used identical terms to honor each of the three emperors. The representation of Thermantia is noteworthy as a portrait of a woman; it asserts both the significance of lineage in the Theodosian dynasty and the importance of aristocratic women in late fourth-century Rome. A series of repetitive inscriptions, meanwhile, designated each of the three rulers as an "extinguisher of tyranny and founder of public security," as indicated on the inscribed panel dedicated to Theodosius I (fig. 3.8). The phrase "extinguisher of

tyranny" drew a comparison with the nearby equestrian statue of Constantius II, there identified as the "eliminator of poisonous tyranny."[64] The conceptual link with Constantius II drew upon the memory of a Constantinian family dynasty, since Theodosius had eliminated the threat of usurpation by establishing a new dynasty on the model of Constantine.

Dynastic messages can particularly be identified on a separate inscribed marble slab accompanying the statue representing Thermantia, mother of Theodosius I (fig. 3.9).[65] This was the only late antique portrait of a woman displayed in the open space of the Forum, and it celebrated her in the inscription as "a woman of the holiest and most noble memory, wife of the revered Theodosius the Elder, man of illustrious rank and count leading both branches of the military [infantry and cavalry], mother of our lord Theodosius [I], emperor forever, [and] grandmother of our lords Arcadius, the strongest ruler, and Honorius, the most pious youth."[66] Her late husband and the father of the dynasty, Theodosius the Elder, received some manner of rehabilitation in the inscription after his highly secretive execution. In his place, Thermantia became the family leader. Theodosius I and his son, Arcadius, featured prominently in the Thermantia inscription. Even though he was mentioned in the inscription, Honorius, the other son of Theodosius I, was too young to receive his own portrait in 389; yet a statue of Valentinian II was included due to his marriage ties with the family.

The three imperial inscriptions that Ceionius Rufius Albinus sponsored are identical in format: these inscribed slabs match the height of the marble bearing the inscription honoring Thermantia. These are not bases, but rather marble panels that lined the outer face of a larger monument. Rubble together with grooved marble blocks surviving in the pavement of the plaza in front of the Curia (fig. 3.10) indicate that the Theodosian family group had been installed close to the Via Sacra, slightly to the east of the Lapis Niger (see fig. 3.2).[67] A plausible reconstruction would suggest that the three emperors had been aligned in a row on one side, with their mother shown separately (fig. 3.11). If this was the case, Theodosius I and his co-rulers invited a contrast to the three identical portraits of Constantius II

Figure 3.8. Statue base for Theodosius I (*CIL* 6.36959), originally installed in the Theodosian dynastic monument in front of the Senate House. Photo by the author.

Figure 3.9. Statue base for Thermantia, mother of Theodosius I (*CIL* 6.36960), installed in the Theodosian dynastic monument. Photo by the author.

Figure 3.10. Marble supports and rubble surviving from the Theodosian dynastic monument in front of the Senate House as they appeared in 2007. Photo by the author.

Figure 3.11. Digital reconstruction of the Theodosian dynastic monument in front of the Senate House. Experiential Technologies Center, UCLA. © Regents, University of California.

shown at a slightly colossal scale and arranged on the east end of the Curia plaza with identical inscriptions. The repetitive inscriptions in each installation and the arrangements in rows of three suggest that the two statue groups were comparable. Viewers were invited to appreciate the Theodosians as closer to the people, less self-aggrandizing, and more attentive to their matriarch than was Constantius II, whose overly imperious representations in triplicate and at a scale larger than life made him appear too remote in retrospect. Nonetheless, Ceionius Rufius Albinus identified the Constantinian family as a precedent for the Theodosian dynasty. The Theodosian family group operated both by acquiring legitimacy from the past and by prompting critical views of the earlier emperors represented in nearby monuments.

The Theodosian monument was set up adjacent to the statue depicting Mars probably shown with the she-wolf, which had linked Maxentius to memories of Rome's foundation at the Lapis Niger, the legendary site of Romulus' burial (see fig. 3.2).[68] The elevated platform supporting statues of the rulers of the Theodosian dynasty shown adjacent to the Lapis Niger suggests that the Theodosians wished to be viewed as new founders who displaced Mars and Romulus. In a panegyric praising Theodosius that was delivered during the emperor's ritual celebration at Rome in 389, the author Pacatus fashioned a literary conceit that embraced sculptural decoration as pre-

senting history rather than myth. In words envisioning Theodosius' portrait statues, Pacatus directly addressed Rome's sculptors: "You artists, scorn those hackneyed themes of ancient fables. Turn your skillful hands to these historic exploits. . . . With these let the forums be decorated."[69] While receiving a high degree of honor, Theodosius avoided seeming overbearing in the statue group by sharing the honorific stage with his co-ruler Valentinian II and his son Arcadius. The relative modesty of the statue of Theodosius I contests the legends and fables that had once prevailed in front of the Curia.

The clear function of the Roman Forum as a ritual space to advance the emperor's wise adherence to tradition also receives mention in Pacatus' panegyric. Theodosius' arrival in Rome in 389 earned the following terms of praise, addressed directly to the ruler:

What took place in Rome; the impression you made on the day you first entered the city; how you behaved in the Senate House and on the Rostra; now in a chariot, now on foot, distinguished in either mode of progress, triumphant now in war, now over pride; how you showed yourself to all as a ruler, to individuals as a senator; how in your frequent and unpretentious public appearances you not only visited public buildings, but hallowed with your divine footsteps private dwellings as well.[70]

Pacatus allowed Theodosius to have it both ways: he appeared at once as a lofty, victorious emperor, and as a humanized ruler who shared the same status as the nobility of Rome.

Theodosius came to Rome in 389 to receive ritual honors for his triumph over Magnus Maximus and the emperor processed through the city in a manner that demonstrated his willingness to appear as a regular citizen and as the founder of a dynasty.[71] Marching through Rome, Theodosius carried his five-year-old son Honorius through the streets to introduce to Romans an important member of the dynasty.[72] Coordination between Theodosius' imperial procession and the installation in front of the Senate House suggests that the imperial ritual continued to shape perceptions long after the emperor's departure. In the panegyric that commemorated Theodosius, Pacatus identified the emperor as conducting the customary speeches for the populace from the Rostra and afterward addressing senators in the Curia. In recognition of the high status of senators, Theodosius stepped out of the processional chariot to walk with the rest of the cortege. Theodosius' ritual behavior demonstrated that he may have ruled the empire, but in Rome he was a citizen.

THE LAST TRIUMPHAL PROCESSION IN ROME

One emperor in the Theodosian dynasty, Honorius, received commemorations with references to restoration that made the ruler appear to have inherited the past in Rome. Honorius began his rule as a child; even as a teenager, he operated in a constricting alliance with the military general Stilicho.[73] The most extensive array of statues displayed in the Roman Forum since the Tetrarchic age set the stage for the triumphal procession celebrating Honorius' consulship. Making a grand ritual entrance on 1 January 404, Honorius proceeded along the triumphal path that culminated in the Forum for the last imperial ritual of this type celebrated at Rome. He marched through the streets to claim honors for two victories: an effective defeat of Gildo, an African nobleman who had threatened the grain supply and who had been eliminated through negotiations rather than battles; and a stand-off with Alaric, who was blocked from entering Italy without actually being defeated. Both achievements were credited to the topmost general (*magister utriusque militiae*) of the West, Stilicho, a half-Vandal and husband of Theodosius' niece, Serena. There was a unique display of statues depicting Honorius with Stilicho that used display contexts in the Forum to make the two appear to be co-rulers. Given that the Forum's installations honoring Constantius II and Theodosius I had insisted on family lineage, dynasty had become an important theme for statues by the late fourth century. Though related only by marriage alliances, Honorius and Stilicho were shown in two statue pairs that constructed their positions as if both were members of the ruling family.

Unprecedented status was offered to Stilicho in

the Roman Forum, where the preparations for inserting statues of the half-Vandal general in the central area required both senatorial and imperial consent. There is no surviving record of who requested the permission for Stilicho's statues, one of which was silver-plated and therefore invited comparison with images of emperors.[74] In fact, the silver portrait of Stilicho appeared on the Rostra together with a statue of Honorius sponsored by the urban prefect Flavius Pisidius Romulus. Evidence that Honorius also received a silver-plated statue comes from a fragmented inscription text specifying its display spot at the Rostra.[75] Presumably, given that it is unlikely that a senator would honor a general at this location on his own initiative, Pisidius Romulus received pressure from the imperial court to set up the Stilicho statue in addition to the statue of the emperor.[76] Stilicho claimed that he had been appointed as regent to Honorius directly by Theodosius I, which effectively restricted the young emperor's own power.[77] Still, in 404 Stilicho was clearly favored. More importantly, the paired statues of Honorius and Stilicho on the Rostra connected the theme of collegial rulership with an imperial jubilee, since the young emperor celebrated ten years of successful rule after the fact by partly crediting Stilicho for the accomplishment.[78] In 408, however, Stilicho stepped over the line, either by seeking to appoint his son Eucharius as emperor or by attempting himself to become the emperor of the East after the death of Honorius' brother, Arcadius.[79] Honorius responded as if Stilicho were a threat and executed him. After his death, Stilicho's name was erased from the inscribed plinth on the Rostra, but the text preserves the title designating the military commander (*magister utriusque militiae*) as an evident indication of Stilicho.[80] The survival of his title in the inscription likely reminded viewers of Stilicho's memory censure, casting his participation in the Theodosian dynasty as discredited treachery after 408.

The installation of the pair of statues depicting Honorius and Stilicho on the Rostra suggests that the two portraits either accompanied or maintained a memory of the emperor's ritual visit to Rome in 404, when the ruler ascended the platform in the Forum to address the assembled populace. Details of

Honorius' procession appear in an articulate verse panegyric that had been read aloud by its author, Claudian. Using a poetic style peppered with excerpts and historical references to the past that create a literary bricolage, Claudian indicated how the present reactivated memories from the past.[81] Describing Honorius at the Rostra, Claudian invoked the memory of the emperor's official visit as a boy with his father, Theodosius I. "This is the very boy, he who now summons the Romans of Rome to the Rostra and seated on his sire's throne of ivory reports in due order to the conscript fathers the causes and the outcomes of his deeds."[82] While celebrating Honorius in the panegyric delivered as part of the festivities in 404, Claudian effectively instructed the emperor on the significance of processional protocol.

With his sophisticated literary allusions, Claudian subtly appropriated the voices of Rome's literary traditions while signaling his awareness of Rome's built heritage. Claudian suggested that the towering statues held aloft by the freestanding columns in the Forum elevated the portraits at the height of the temples and too high above the human race, since from the Palatine one could observe "the statues soaring through the midst of the clouds."[83] With this image, Claudian shared with Honorius a process of responding to the city that matched literary terms with the experience of urban space.

Claudian's speech, written in advance of Honorius' procession through Rome, oddly offered the emperor a retrospective account of the event. Describing Honorius' speech from the Rostra, Claudian praised the lack of artificiality and accordingly shed a positive light on the emperor's apparently inelegant rhetoric.[84] Elsewhere, Claudian described the purpose of the procession, asserting that entering the Curia reinforced Honorius' bond with senators.[85] Further, Claudian informed the emperor that in the Curia was a statue depicting "Victory herself with its wings."[86] Claudian thus recorded that the statue of Victory remained in the Curia long after the associated altar had been removed in response to objections from Christian senators, and he indicated the viability of the statue once it was displayed apart from the associated cult implements. In fact, Claudian credited the statue itself for guarding Rome.[87]

Elsewhere, Claudian indicated that the doors of the Temple of Janus were closed. Presumably, the doors of this diminutive shrine, likely situated where the Argiletum intersects with the Via Sacra, were shut as the traditional response to the end of hostilities.[88] The antiquities of Rome functioned viably in Claudian's poem once disconnected from offensive cult practices and after the tainted altar was removed from a spot adjacent to the Victory statue.

The descriptive and didactic messages of Claudian's panegyric seemed to persuade Honorius that he belonged in Rome. Winding through the city's streets was a homecoming for the emperor, according to Claudian. Noting that Honorius proceeded from the Roman Forum to the palace on the Palatine Hill, Claudian stated directly to the emperor, "From here the Via Sacra, now truly named, brings you back to your ancestral home."[89] With reference to an earlier part of the imperial progression through Rome, Claudian reflected on Honorius' behavior that conveyed to the public that this ruler behaved as a citizen. Claudian stated that the emperor "prevented the senators of Rome from marching in front of his chariot. . . . [Honorius] has come as a citizen, his predecessors as lords."[90] Viewers focused their attention on the imperial chariot as it moved from the city's northern edge along the Via Lata, then headed southward around the Palatine Hill, and finally traveled westward along the Via Sacra for the procession's ritual climax in the Roman Forum (see fig. 1.16).[91] The ritual terminated among the numerous representations of emperors on view in the Forum.

The procession of 404 as recounted in Claudian's panegyric indicated that Stilicho appropriated historical precedents to justify the general's prominence in Rome. Stilicho accompanied Honorius in the chariot, earning the acclaim in the ritual triumph that usually only the emperor received during the late empire.[92] Historical sources record a fiction that Theodosius I privately requested that Stilicho serve as the guardian of his sons, Honorius and Arcadius, at a point when the latter did not require a regent. Stilicho's own marriage to Serena, niece of Theodosius, created a family alliance that was strengthened when their daughter, Maria, was wed to Honorius.[93] Stilicho even named his daughter Thermantia, after

Figure 3.12. Base for the statue of Honorius in the Roman Forum, with the name of Stilicho erased (*CIL* 6.31987). Photo by the author.

Figure 3.13. View of one side of the base for the statue of Honorius (*CIL* 6.31987), indicating the reuse of an equestrian statue plinth. Photo by the author.

the matriarch of the Theodosian dynasty; she became Honorius' second wife. When Claudian addressed Honorius directly and informed him that accompanying his father in 389 at the age of five anticipated the visit in 404 with his father-in-law Stilicho, the poet's goal was to aggrandize the role of the military general. To establish the parallel between Theodosius I and Stilicho, Claudian said to Honorius:

Citizen as you are, deign to enter this company and let us see once more the face we saw so long ago, so that recalling in his mind that earlier triumph, Tiber, who had welcomed you as your father's companion in the tender years of childhood, may now worship you as a young man under the guidance of your father-in-law.[94]

Claudian constructed highly literate justifications for Stilicho's full-fledged membership in the imperial family.

When Honorius and Stilicho paraded through

Rome together, they could not have failed to notice that a second pairing of their statues faced the Via Sacra close to the Curia's façade. The base for the statue of Honorius still remains at its original display spot, and the installation explicitly exposes the reuse of older monuments (figs. 3.12 and 3.1 [53]). An upturned equestrian statue base exposed the dowel holes on one side into which the horse's hooves originally had been inserted (fig. 3.13). The reused, upturned statue base communicated that the past was recomposed to justify the present, and Honorius and Stilicho were both implicitly legitimized by the general's portrait standing adjacent to that of the young emperor (see fig. 3.1 [33] and [53]). The two works directly addressed the Theodosian family monument, which dominated the plaza in front of the Senate House; together, they formed a sort of dynastic axis (see fig. 3.1 [33, 40, 41, 53, 64, and 65]). It is unclear whether Stilicho's statue stood on a reused plinth, since the inscription, which is now inserted into a wall and covered by glass at the Palazzo Capranica della Valle in Rome, is currently difficult to inspect. Stilicho's base was rediscovered close to the Arch of Septimius Severus. Presumably, Stilicho's statue was installed with senatorial consent just prior to the procession of 404, since the inscription mentions the victory in Africa that was celebrated on that date in Rome. It is likely that the statue was ordered by Honorius at the urging of Stilicho and ultimately confirmed by the senate, since the inscription advertised the latter's ties to the imperial family. With terms of praise, the text identifies Stilicho as

the exalted husband of the granddaughter of the lord, count Theodosius [father of Theodosius I], and chosen colleague of the lord Theodosius Augustus, victorious in all wars and defender of the same emperor, and similarly father-in-law of our lord Honorius Augustus, having liberated Africa and made provisions for its council, by decree of the Senate.[95]

The list of Stilicho's ties to the imperial family legitimized him as having both imperial power and dynastic authority.

The upturned plinth from an old equestrian monument helped to form Honorius' lasting legacy (see fig. 3.12). Interestingly, the inscription identifies the deceased Theodosius I as the founder of the dynasty and, with the official dedication by the urban prefect Pisidius Romulus, specifies both of the emperor's sons, Arcadius and Honorius, as the legitimate rulers. The text mentions a battle against the Goths, probably the one at Pollentia in 402, in which Stilicho prevented Alaric from entering Italy without a definitive defeat. The text, featuring an erasure, reads,

To the honor and virtue of the most loyal soldiers, our lords Arcadius, Honorius, and Theodosius, perpetual *Augusti*, at the end of the battle against the Goths through the good luck of the everlasting ruler, our lord Honorius, [and] the strength and advice of the distinguished count and [the erased section must have named Stilicho]; orchestrated on behalf of the senate and people of Rome by Pisidus Romulus, of the highest senatorial rank, [and] urban prefect. . . .[96]

Given that originally the inscription commemorating Honorius featured the names of both his family members and Stilicho, the installation also established a meaningful juxtaposition with the Theodosian dynastic monument that it faced. Regulating memories was a major component of the public display, since Stilicho's name, as originally inscribed on the base, had been erased by 408. Reusing the equestrian base provided Honorius with some fame as a restorer; but Stilicho, who had attempted to acquire a similar reputation by recycling a preexisting statue base, was clearly designated after 408 as an improper and therefore censured intruder into the commemorative space of emperors.

Gazing at the pair of statues depicting Honorius and Stilicho from a vantage point on the Via Sacra in 404, one would have seen them as shorter, but nonetheless elevated depictions that contrasted with the loftier statues atop columns that lined the south side of the Forum square (fig. 3.14).[97] The two statues of Honorius and Stilicho intimated that they were co-rulers at the time, presented on upturned plinths as if on top of columns. Given their display context in the Forum, the two statues depicting Honorius and Stilicho exploited the sight lines that configured them in the same space as earlier imperial imagery.

There is inconclusive evidence hinting that an equestrian monument for Stilicho may have been installed in the Roman Forum. A highly unusual inscription discovered close to the Basilica Julia indicates that the one depicted upon the statue base was an "advisor" to nobles and plausibly a general, using titles that seem to fit with Stilicho. It is a damaged and fragmented text that can be reconstructed as bearing a dedication, "to our most foresightful general [and] the most victorious of our lords and also the advisor to patrons of noble rank and in the name of Rome, [missing text reconstructed hypothetically as 'Flavius Stilicho of the highest senatorial rank']."[98] Heike Niquet concluded from the dimensions of the extant portion of the base that this was wide enough to support an equestrian portrait, which would have been a remarkable anomaly as a commemoration of a military general in the Roman Forum.[99] Stilicho clearly was using his marriage alliances and military position to acquire the honors traditionally bestowed

Figure 3.14. Digital reconstruction of the paired statues of Honorius and Stilicho facing the Via Sacra (*CIL* 6.1730, 31987). Experiential Technologies Center, UCLA. © Regents, University of California.

Figure 3.15. Two travertine slabs installed in the pavement of the Roman Forum to support the "Arch" of Honorius. Photo by the author.

Figure 3.16. View of the Roman Forum, c. 1900, showing the late antique installation of the Anaglypha Traiani placed on top of the travertine slabs. Photo courtesy of Fototeca Unione (neg. Gatteschi 95). © American Academy in Rome.

upon an emperor. If the surviving, fragmented inscription indeed originated from an equestrian statue of Stilicho, then his improper acquisition of status in the Forum was too bold and was ultimately condemned through erasure.[100]

The most impressive Honorius monument was installed on two surviving travertine supports in the Forum pavement upon which two sculptural reliefs made for Trajan, the Anaglypha Traiani, had once been arranged (fig. 3.15). When the Forum pavement was unearthed at the turn of the twentieth century, the reliefs remained on top of the two foundations (fig. 3.16).[101] The two travertine foundations established a passageway aligned with the trajectory of the Argiletum (see fig. 3.1 [18]). The Trajanic sculptural reliefs, reused for an installation on top of the travertine supports along this passageway, belonged to a monument that can be plausibly reconstructed as a highly idiosyncratic "arch" that commemorated Honorius.[102]

One indication that the Trajanic sculptures were used for Honorius' arch is a large-scale inscription whose text was copied during the sixteenth century; only fragments survive today (fig. 3.17). According to the text, the monument was set up by the senate to commemorate the elimination of Gildo, for which Honorius received credit: "To the unconquered and most fortunate emperors, our Lords, the brothers Arcadius and Honorius, protecting the senate and people of Rome from the rebellion and gladly rein-

stating Africa; mighty Honorius defended Libya."[103] It is striking that Stilicho's name does not appear in the inscription. Correlations between terms from the inscription and Claudian's panegyric provide the basis for concluding that this was an arch. On a small architrave that probably spanned the "arch," the text expresses that "mighty Honorius defended Libya," "(a)RMIPOTENS LIBY[c]UM DEFENDIT HONORIU(s)." In fact, strikingly similar terms in Claudian's text, with the personified Roma speaking to the emperor directly, state that the city's residents had "built an arch that featured your name through which you, in your radiant toga, might walk, and [Rome] was busy consecrating monuments to your battles with inscriptions honoring Libya's defense" (pugnae monumenta dicabam / defensam titulo Libyam testata perenni).[104] Claudian attests that Honorius marched through an arch to mark the triumph over Gildo, a Libyan. A digital reconstruction configures the arch so that it could have supported a quadriga, although freestanding imperial portraits might have been supported on top (fig. 3.18). Thus, the arch exclusively aggrandized only the legitimate emperors, Honorius and Arcadius, and subtly left out Stilicho.

The arch's reuse of the Trajanic sculptural reliefs connected Honorius with an earlier emperor. The reliefs represent Trajan in the Forum offering clemency by depicting tax records destroyed in a bonfire on the side that faced eastward (fig. 3.19). As installed on the late antique arch, both of the two

Figure 3.17. Inscription dedicated to Arcadius and Honorius (CIL 6.1187), originally integrated into the "Arch" of Honorius in the Roman Forum. Photo by the author.

Figure 3.18. Digital reconstruction of the "Arch" of Honorius in the Roman Forum. Experiential Technologies Center, UCLA. © Regents, University of California.

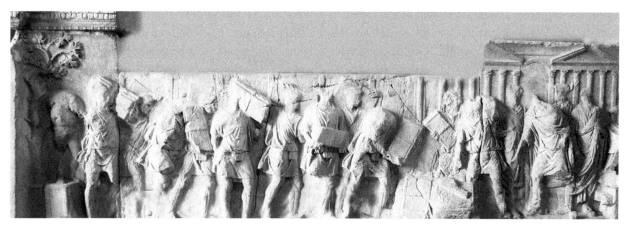

Figure 3.19. Trajanic sculptural relief (one of the Anaglypha Traiani) from the Roman Forum illustrating the burning of tax registers. Photo by the author.

reliefs depict statues of Marsyas and a fig tree (*ficus Ruminalis*)—the latter emerges from a statue base in the Trajanic sculpture—at positions adjacent to the actual works depicting Marsyas and the tree as configured in the paved central area in late antiquity (see fig. 3.18).[105] The site specificity provided a historical background for Honorius by rooting the young emperor in Rome as a fulfillment of Trajan's legacy. The Theodosian family to which Honorius belonged had originated in Spain, where, according to fictional accounts, the family descended from Trajan. In Claudian's panegyric celebrating Honorius' fourth consulship, the poet describes the emperor as a descendant of Trajan: "Not unworthy of reverence nor but newly acquainted with war is the Ulpian family [that of Trajan] and that Spanish house. . . . Hence came [Count] Theodosius, grandfather of Honorius."[106] The reuse of Trajan's sculptural reliefs hinted that an ancestral lineage was celebrated at Honorius' arch, even if the family history it presented was fictional.

The installations in the Forum allowed the youthful Honorius to inherit an imperial past. In the poem that Claudian presented to Honorius in 404, the Roman Forum served as the spot into which the emperor inserted his identity so that he could be compared to previous emperors. Claudian recalled Honorius' childhood visit to Rome, in which his father, Theodosius I, behaved as if he were a resident of the city: "With you at his side, when adding his name to the roll-call of the nobler princes, he [Theodosius I] played the part of citizen."[107] The public statues with

inscriptions thus appear together as if they are a roster of rulers.

The process of reading urban space by looking at reused fragments such as the repurposed equestrian base for the Honorius statue or the Trajanic sculptural reliefs for the "Arch" of Honorius can be understood through Claudian. The poet recomposed historical fragments and allowed the excerpts to be reinvigorated so that Honorius and Stilicho could inherit the literary traditions of the Roman empire that Ovid and Virgil had established. In this, Claudian drew from a literary procedure: excerpting lines from earlier sources and recomposing citations from other poems created a patchwork in the poetic form known as the *cento*. The *cento* was a creative activity of Claudian's literary circle, often featuring extensive quotations from Virgil.[108] Thus, the assembly of fragments offered late fourth-century individuals the opportunity to honor material pieces appropriated from the venerable past in a way that paralleled the citation of literary exemplars.

THE COLUMN OF PHOCAS

The additive process of constructing new monuments from preexisting pieces allowed the late antique Roman Forum to be continually updated into the seventh century CE. But whereas spoliation was used to connect the legacy of earlier emperors with the Theodosian dynasty, there seems to have been a different goal for the presentation of a solitary ruler in an isolated column monument, now known as the Column of Phocas, situated within the central area of the Forum. Phocas was a Byzantine ruler who was honored by an act of rededication in the early seventh century. In 608 CE, Smaragdus, the exarch of Italy, placed a gilded statue of the emperor (r. 602–610) on top of a preexisting column. Because of the benefits Phocas had offered Rome, the emperor received a statue installed at a highly prestigious position in the Forum—centrally located and elevated above all others. But the column had been constructed long before Phocas' reign: in 608, Smaragdus superimposed a new inscription onto a preexisting plinth, which had probably been produced originally in the fourth century. Phocas' memory was intended to be preserved much as the reappropriated column was restored.

The placement of the column is significant, since it marks the visual end point of the Argiletum as it proceeds into the Roman Forum (see fig. I.8 [2] and [9]).[109] This path was heavily used by the populace during late antiquity; it accommodated the traffic originating in the crowded neighborhood of the Suburra. The column—the only freestanding column from late antiquity to remain intact in the Forum into the modern era—drew those progressing along the Argiletum into the Forum's central area by providing a vertical signpost (fig. 3.20). It is important to consider the Column of Phocas in Rome as utilizing design ideas originating in Constantinople. In 328, the main artery of the eastern capital on the Bosporus, the Mese, was interrupted by the circular Forum of Constantine, the centerpiece of which was an honorific porphyry column capped by the emperor's bronze colossal portrait (fig. 3.21).[110] Placing an imperial column monument at the center of an important plaza in Rome applied urban-planning concepts developed for Constantine's Forum with its central monument marking the trajectory of the Constantinopolitan Mese. The placement was at odds with the earlier approach to imperial monuments in Rome, whereby Trajan and Antoninus Pius had asserted the emperor's role as the preeminent patron through portrait statues placed on top of monumental columns cut off from city streets. By inserting a column

in the middle of his circular forum in the eastern capital, Constantine pioneered a spatial condition for urban plazas in which major streets converged at a column to mark a visibly prominent destination.

The Column of Phocas provided Rome with a column monument as a linchpin between two significant urban spaces. Accordingly, it would be logical to assume that, in its original form, the Column of Phocas dominated the urban landscape as if the city were under the rule of a single emperor, an effect that Constantine had wished to achieve in Constantinople. Indeed, the independent column in the Roman Forum, with its wide, pyramidal base, effectively reconfigured the space where the public had earlier assembled to see those on top of the Rostra. Due in part to the reliance on a Constantinopolitan precedent, then, it can be theorized that the column was originally produced for either Constantine or his son, Constantius II. Unfortunately, no physical evidence confirms this supposition. Yet one can affirm

Figure 3.20. Column of Phocas in the Roman Forum. Photo by the author.

that the Column of Phocas marked the final addition to the series of column monuments and was installed after the demise of Diocletian's Tetrarchy, the period when collegial rule had been commemorated by the linked pairs of imperial column monuments.

The extant inscription records the honorific purpose of Phocas' statue. In a departure from fourth-century inscriptions, this text indicates that Phocas received his crown from God; in its clear Christian reference, this contrasts with the exclusively administrative content of the older imperial inscriptions. The text also emphasizes that only the statue was added by the exarch Smaragdus and specifies that the most elevated portrait in the Forum preserved Phocas' fame.

To the greatest, gentlest, and most pious of princes, our lord Phocas, an emperor eternally crowned by God, the triumphant and eternal *Augustus*. Smaragdus, former commander (*praepositus*) of the imperial palace, patrician, and exarch of Italy, devoted to his clemency, in thanks for the numerous benefits of his piety and for the peace obtained for Italy and for the preservation of liberty, dedicated this statue to his majesty, shining in splendid gold atop the highest column, placed there for his lasting glory on the first day of August in the eleventh indiction, in the fifth year after the consulate of his piety.[111]

Physical evidence does not provide adequate data with which to precisely identify the moment when the Column of Phocas was originally installed, as mentioned earlier. The column has a fluted white marble shaft surmounted by a Corinthian capital, both of which were reused materials originating in the second or third century CE.[112] An assembly of multiple bases, including a lower pedestal base made of marble blocks, was arranged as a stepped pyramid surmounted by a sub-plinth, which was composed of concrete faced with bricks and which supports the inscribed marble plinth (see fig. 3.20). Brickwork surrounding the concrete core lies directly on top of the Forum pavement and thus must postdate the Severan period.

There was an inscription for the original monument, the illegible traces of which can be observed today; it was erased so that Smaragdus could superimpose the dedication to Phocas. F. M. Nichols was the first to conclude from this evidence that the column had been constructed prior to Phocas' rule.[113] During the excavations at the turn of the twentieth

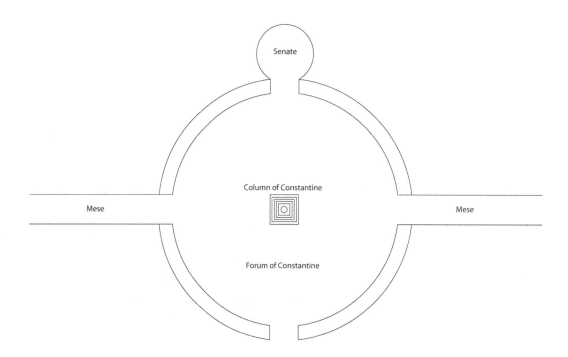

Figure 3.21. Plan of the Forum of Constantine in Constantinople. Drawing by Brian Doherty.

century, Giacomo Boni proposed that the steps were also added long after the construction of the original inner core.[114] Boni concluded that the column was first erected on top of the concrete base during the time of Diocletian, with the steps added at least two centuries later.[115]

In 1987, Giuliani and Verduchi published their observations on the physical evidence of the monument. Noting that the brick-faced concrete core rests directly on the third-century level of the Forum pavement, Giuliani and Verduchi asserted that the column was constructed during the reign of Diocletian in conjunction with the other column monuments in the Forum.[116] The soundings they conducted as part of an archeological investigation of the material composition for the base and the sub-plinth, however, reveal that the Column of Phocas was constructed using a different technique than was used for the seven columns on the south side of the Forum square. Those seven columns were all supported by solid bases of brick, whereas the singular, larger column rests upon a base of concrete faced with bricks, surrounded by steps. Giuliani and Verduchi base their argument that the Phocas monument originated during the Tetrarchy on their conception of a unified scheme among the Forum's column monuments.[117] Diocletian's Forum as envisioned by Giuliani and Verduchi may not be as coherent as they assert, however; for example, the Column of Phocas blocks the view of the western Rostra. A crucial issue is that the seven columns date to after the retirement of Diocletian, since Steinby's analysis of the brick stamps suggests a date during the reign of either Maxentius or Constantine.[118] Franz Alto Bauer analyzed the integration of the Column of Phocas with other monuments in the Forum, observing that the singular, tall column nearly intrudes upon the Surdinus inscription.[119] Bauer also noted that the brick section of the sub-plinth remained exposed without a marble facing, and there is no evidence of dowel holes to indicate that it was ever sheathed in marble.[120] Arguing that the brickwork of the sub-plinth was always visible, Bauer believes that this points toward a post-Tetrarchic date for the column.[121] Patrizia Verduchi subsequently came to the conclusion that the steps were added at the time of Smaragdus.[122]

The Column of Phocas co-opted and transformed the paved central area as if to suggest that the original honoree had acquired a history and superseded the traditions of previous emperors. The Forum then sanctioned the original emperor—still unidentified—who took possession of the civic space in which the portraits of earlier rulers were on view. All of the physical evidence for a post-Tetrarchic date corresponds with the ideological content of a solitary column that advanced a single ruler; whether this was Constantine or one of his successors remains an open question. By preserving the original column monument, Smaragdus linked the last imperial statue of the Forum to Phocas' refurbished identity. This was the ultimate act of inheriting memories in the Forum in the late antique manner. Remarkably, Smaragdus understood in the seventh century how transforming the solitary column monument could hint that Phocas had restored what the fourth-century emperors had advertised in the Roman Forum.

THE FIFTH CENTURY

The viability of the Roman Forum as the preeminent space for imperial commemoration in Rome indicates the continuity of civic and administrative activities in the precinct; yet a series of attacks and the political turmoil of the fifth century diminished the zone. Alaric's assault on Rome in 410 caused physical damage, including fires that ravaged the Basilica Aemilia and harmed the Curia Senatus. The epigraphic record indicates that these setbacks correlated with fewer monuments being set up in honor of emperors. In addition, fifth-century portraits of senators and military commanders were installed in the Roman Forum without testimony to imperial confirmation of the privilege. At least according to the surviving inscriptions, following the sack of Rome, the Forum reverted to its role as the site for presenting senatorial prestige, and the fifth-century emperors may have received a relatively small number of commemorations in the Forum's public areas. On the one hand, senators turned to written laws and Rome's ancestral traditions to sanction aristocratic prestige; on the other hand, emperors forged coalitions with senators and military commanders that are recorded in both monuments and textual sources from the fifth century.

The increase in portraits honoring senators and other non-imperial officials in the Forum is at odds with evidence that Rome returned to functioning as a residential capital for emperors in the fifth century. This included extended visits by Honorius and Valentinian III (423–455); the latter shifted the imperial court back to the old capital in 450. From 450 until 476, when Romulus Augustulus was deposed from his position as the last emperor of the West, the Western imperial court usually resided at Rome.[123]

Statues either sponsored by or dedicated to senators after 410 expressed how the senate as an institution revived its own traditions. It seems odd that the concept of consensus between emperors and senators had been more strongly expressed in fourth-century inscriptions, when emperors typically were not in Rome; yet the rulers' return to the capital in the fifth century corresponded with an apparent decrease in the statues at the Forum. Perhaps it was easier for senatorial sponsors to create an image of concord between the aristocracy and the emperors when the populace could not observe the reality. Fifth-century senators, meanwhile, confronted serious challenges, including episodes of usurpation, infighting among military commanders, and theological disputes that prompted the local aristocracy to increasingly emphasize their status in the city.

Against this messy political backdrop, the legal situation in the empire improved dramatically with the publication in 438 of the Theodosian Code, with which the emperor Theodosius II was able to eliminate conflicting laws applied differently in the East and the West. The real importance of the Theodosian Code in Rome pertained to the protections it offered senators. Epigraphic texts suggest that legal uniformity sanctioned those members of the local elite who upheld the law. In addition, the complex at the Senate House was significantly augmented as the location where aristocrats proclaimed their revived positions by installing statues, which often alluded to the legal protections for aristocratic interests. Inscriptions linked to the Curia and its adjacent structures subtly advanced how aristocrats enforced the rule of law as a senatorial concern.

There is evidence that the fifth-century aristocratic tradition was particularly celebrated in the public space around the Senate House. For example, in 438, Anicius Acilius Glabrio Faustus installed a statue honoring his father-in-law, Tarrutenius Maximilianus, either at the Forum's central area or close to the Senate House. Faustus, who delivered the Theodosian Code to the senate during his consulship in 438, reused a statue base and maintained its original inscription specifying a dedication to a deity, while adding the new inscription on the opposite face. Thus, a base originally intended for a cult image was transformed into a work that honored an aristocratic lineage, with the surprising maintenance of part of the original inscription asking the reader to "cherish the one who acts with the gods."[124] Though the name of the deity to whom the monument had been dedicated was erased and the side featuring a reference to the gods was flipped to become the reverse, Faustus also inscribed his own name and his highest office, consul, on the back of the statue base.[125] This type of reuse hints at an appreciation of learning and literary erudition, since the retained "citation" from the original dedication of an artwork deployed the concepts of memory that Claudian had crafted in his poetry, as mentioned above. The tradition of sustaining memories of ancestral religious practices would not be lost on viewers attentive to the signs of how aristocratic displays in Rome functioned. Faustus proclaimed that his father-in-law's eloquence earned him the togate statue. The text newly inscribed in 438 reads:

[Statue of] Tarrutenius. To Tarrutenius Maximilianus, of the highest senatorial rank and having served as the most eloquent consul of Picenum on the year when he turned nineteen, vicar of the city of Rome, and twice most distinguished legate for the Senate; Anicius Acilius Glabrio Faustus, of the highest senatorial rank, cheerfully offered the statue of his cherished father-in-law wearing a toga at this location.[126]

Our only indication about the original display location is the find spot where Lorenzo Pignoria rediscovered the statue base at the turn of the seventeenth century, which he recorded as being in the "Campo

Vaccino."[127] It is likely that the original installation was closely associated with the Curia, because the work so emphatically advances the importance of aristocratic traditions. Indeed, the inscription makes reference to the eloquence of Tarrutenius earning him the honor of a statue.

Also in the vicinity of the Senate House was the Atrium Minervae, which housed a statue of Minerva that needed repairs in the fifth century. The rear of the Curia communicated with a large portico belonging to the Forum of Caesar, which had been developed during the extensive repairs of Diocletian and Maximian (see fig. 1.1 [B]).[128] This portico had been divided into two sections by a central colonnade and communicated directly with the Argiletum. Here, during Diocletian's extensive building campaign, the Curia was fully integrated into the Forum of Caesar.[129] Subsequent restorations during the reign of Maxentius might have installed additional statues within the portico; at least one base originally honoring Maxentius shows evidence of secondary use during the fourth or fifth century.[130] Further documentation reveals that, during the late fourth or early fifth century, elaborately colored marbles provided a new pavement for the portico.[131] With the area behind the Curia redefined by a newly added second colonnade, a richly decorative marble pavement, and additional attention to the entranceway onto the Argiletum, the late antique efforts augmented the magnificence of the high-traffic zone connecting the southeast portion of the Forum of Caesar with the Argiletum.[132] In this area, the installations provided amenities and civic decor that supported public life.

One such monument was a statue of Minerva, restored in 472. Its inscription reads: "The statue of Minerva, broken by a falling roof destroyed by fire during an urban conflict, was restored by Anicius Acilius Aginantius Faustus, of senatorial status [and] aristocrat of the highest rank (inlustris), judge hearing imperial appeals, providing improvements and completing the work for the happiness of our times."[133] Setting up the image (simulacrum) of the goddess Minerva allowed the statue to reconnect with memories thanks to the fifth-century sponsor, implying that bringing back civic values occurred in conjunction with the repairs.[134] In fact, by reviving the artwork, Anicius Acilius Agi-

nantius Faustus brought back what he called the "happiness of our times."

Several topographers have speculated that the Atrium Minervae was connected with the Senate House, noting that the portico in the Forum of Caesar attached to the rear of the Curia created a space for the statue to be displayed. Other locations in the vicinity of the Curia are also candidates.[135] But the aristocratic patrons of late antique Rome were attentive to distinguishing the locations for displaying artworks from the places for political displays, as demonstrated by the paved central area of the Forum, the plaza in front of the Curia, and the areas flanking the Via Sacra, all of which were lined with imperial portraits. These paved open spaces were politicized and different from the locations for the display of art, including the Atrium Minervae and the Atrium Libertatis, which will be discussed in Chapter 6. The portico where Minerva's image was installed would therefore have featured the work of art within a lavishly ornamented covered walkway. Damage caused by the civil disturbances of Ricimer's assault on Rome in 472 provided the impetus for repairs, since the inscription indicates that Anicius Acilius Aginantius Faustus "restored" (restituit) the work.

Interestingly, the inscription accompanying the statue of Minerva calls the figure a simulacrum. This term, used in the Theodosian Code with reference to the exhibition of artworks in public spaces, hinted at the provisions made for the enjoyment of works of art based on concepts of quality or the craftsmanship. The pertinent law advocated public displays in places "where statues (simulacra) could be appreciated for their craft/artistic value rather than for their divinity."[136] After its restoration in conjunction with the portico's repaired roof, the cult image of Minerva provided a public space which was enhanced by the pleasure derived from viewing a work of art. It is important to underline that reversing structural damage provided a context that was appropriate for the display of a formerly cultic artwork. In other words, Anicius Acilius Aginantius Faustus, a Christian sponsor, had to somehow signify that he had altered the place for displaying Minerva's statue, and he accomplished this by restoring the atrium. Indeed, the repairs indicated the transmission of the past into the present under altered circumstances. Audiences constructed meaning by linking the physical restoration with the more conceptual "happiness of our times" (*beatitudine temporum restituit*). Implicitly, the statue of Minerva restored status to the cultural heritage of Rome rather than to an individual.

Prior to this restoration project, the emperors had guaranteed opportunities for public enjoyments and leisure activities in the fora and civic structures of Rome.[137] Providing places for learning or leisure for the populace was seen as a senatorial responsibility during the last quarter of the fifth century, after Rome had ceased definitely to be an imperial capital. Yet supporting a relaxed encounter with artworks in urban public space had a strong tradition in the late antique fora of Rome. There is clear evidence that senators used their sponsorship of monuments to seem to promote learning and constructive leisurely pursuits, including enjoying works of art. The senators, in the end, exploited connections with imperial bureaucrats and military leaders to ensure that the upper class could maintain property holdings, minimize tax burdens, and pass down senatorial status to their children; these issues were subsumed by the civic norms of maintaining honor and virtue while providing artworks that offered culture and beneficial leisure activities for the people.

STATUES AND BUILDINGS

An important premise of architectural restoration during late antiquity was that building repairs could honor the sponsors whose identities were preserved in inscriptions that accompanied statues. In Rome, maintaining memories through statues with their accompanying texts justified the production of inscriptions that maintained public records of civic activities such as building campaigns, urban rituals, military successes, and the appointments of individuals to prestigious offices.[138] Honorific statues, in celebrating the architectural munificence of aristocrats and emperors, traditionally had advertised that the city was built up by generations of virtuous individuals. Late antique policies further sanctioned restoration more

frequently than new construction due to the need to maintain the built infrastructure while preserving valuable building materials. As a result, building anew did not consistently carry the prestige that restoration did during the fourth and fifth centuries.

The Tetrarchic emperors Diocletian and Maximian from 283 until 306 CE formalized the ideological link between statues signaling political renewal and the restoration of civic structures. In his panegyric setting forth the reasons for restoring academic structures in Autun in 299, Eumenius addressed the Tetrarchic emperors: "Who could doubt, then, that the divine mind of Caesar, which chose a director with so much care for this gathering of youth, also wants the place devoted to its training to be restored and decorated?"[139] The intelligence of the sponsor and the expression of careful attention extended from the benefactor to the restored building.

Judging from inscriptions, with their limited yet crucial perspective on the significance of statue displays, the imperial portraits of the Forum expressed highly abstract values. Admittedly, that ambiguity has increased over the years, as the modern assessment of the statues in the late antique Roman Forum relies mostly on fragmented evidence. To compound matters, the statues themselves are largely lost. Yet even in antiquity, the epigraphic formulas turned to vague, general terms that glossed over the complexity of honorific displays. In one example, due to the survival of just a fragment from the original, we can only read the vague terms of praise without any knowledge of who received the acclaim: "To the preserver of the Roman Name; to the one who enlarged his world; to the destroyer of the tyrannical faction; to the conqueror over barbarian people; [this statue] of the blessed emperor. . . ."[140] Through the use of such topoi as "the preserver of the Roman Name" (*conservatori Romani nominis*) or "the one who enlarged his world" (*propagatori orbis sui*), inscriptions identified how a well-orchestrated exhibition of statue bases established links among those whose portraits appeared in public space. Finally, late antique epigraphic texts used the collective voice to articulate the shared ideals of civic authorities. Because of the attention to preserving both architecture and statues, monuments were able to express the unity among aristocrats and emperors across both time and urban space.

There were clear-cut divisions in the Forum as a space for the installation of public ornaments. Areas such as the paved central area of the Forum and the plaza in front of the Senate House were used for assemblies and featured monuments that charted the particularities of imperial ideology. The processional path of the Via Sacra likewise featured imperial portraits, especially configured along the north edge of the Forum square. The peripheral zones, such as the Atrium Minervae, were for educational pursuits and leisure as cultural activities. It is significant that the re-erected statue of Minerva in the atrium marked a different character for that space than was found in the zones for imperial imagery, since the transformed cult statue encouraged viewers to enjoy the artwork as a pleasurable activity, distinct from the admiration of social hierarchies perceived in the portraits on view in the Forum's politicized areas.

CHAPTER 4

RESTORED BASILICAS AND STATUES ON THE MOVE

DURING LATE ANTIQUITY, TWO BASILICAS WITH PORTICOES FACING THE ROMAN FORUM accommodated decorative statues that documented the civic benefits provided by senators for the populace. The aristocrats thereby offered a stark alternative to the imperial messages that dominated the paved central area and the senatorial plaza. The late antique reconstructions of both the Basilica Aemilia and the Basilica Julia, which lined the Roman Forum's north and south sides respectively, indicate that the revival of public architecture in Rome provided cultural amenities, which senators subtly claimed (see fig. 1.1 [10] and [11]).

The basilicas in the Forum remained spaces for the administration of justice throughout late antiquity, but as public buildings they also accommodated a wide range of activities. Both buildings featured stalls (*tabernae*) for commercial purposes. In addition, the façades of both basilicas addressed the busy central area of the Forum, with porticoes that protected people from the elements; these areas provided venues for public leisure.[1] Statues sponsored by senators were moved from other locations in the city to the porticoes of the basilicas during late antiquity, providing two displays along the façades. In both contexts, local aristocrats relocated the works to target wide audiences. The exact subjects portrayed in these statues are not specified in the inscriptions; yet epigraphic testimony to assembling and moving statues together with the inscriptions identifying famous Greek sculptors advance the claim that these façades presented viewers with works of art for enjoyment. The porticoes of the Basilica Julia and Basilica Aemilia, then, seem comparable to the Temple of Peace, where Rome's entire populace had access to the impressive collection of masterpieces by important Greek sculptors, featuring some initially assembled by Nero for his private house.

During the fourth and fifth centuries, senators were unable to determine the types of images presented in the central area of the Forum, where imperial portraits were emphasized. The senatorial aristocrats focused attention instead on providing civic benefits to the populace at the two basilicas, which featured material indications that the historic structures

105

had undergone adaptations. At the Basilica Aemilia in particular, the redecorated façade masked a compromised structure after a fire damaged the main hall. Senators sponsoring these cultural displays articulated that they provided spaces for Rome's populace to enjoy artworks, and the local aristocrats thereby made amends for the late antique emperors' failure to do so.

One important premise of this study is that statues accompanied by inscriptions offer significant testimony to the spatial context for identity, intonating in the exhibitions next to conserved structures that the reconstructed buildings survived the test of time much as worthy individuals persevered. Tracing inscribed statue bases to their late antique display locations, often by identifying the find spots, substantiates claims that aristocrats used the statues displayed in the porticoes of the two basilicas to claim that they—as opposed to the aloof emperors—countered impending ruin at the places where people enjoyed leisure. Admittedly, much of the actual reconstruction of the two basilicas had been undertaken by the Tetrarchs; yet after the reign of Constantine, the porticoes facing the Forum began to display artworks with inscribed bases in which senators claimed roles as cultural benefactors. Relocating statues was a widespread practice, particularly when considered as a parallel to the fragmentary reuse of old monuments, such as the secondary installation of the Anaglypha Traiani in the "Arch" of Honorius or the equestrian plinth upturned to become the vertical support for Honorius' statue (discussed in Chapter 3). On the basis of inscription evidence, the cultural displays in the Basilica Aemilia and the Basilica Julia indicate that local aristocrats continually encouraged the joys of civilized urban life that occurred in public space.[2]

Gabinius Vettius Probianus was the most frequently identified among senators who transferred statues to the Forum. This name appears twice in the historical record, first in 377 and then in 416.[3] The individual identified in the fifth-century documents has been dissociated from Gabinius Vettius Probianus. Given that it was unlikely for someone to work up the career ladder to achieve the exalted rank of urban prefect at a very young age and that the one who held this post in 416 had a similar but different name, the documentation likely refers to two separate individuals. One of the two individuals named Probianus moved the statues. Before considering which of the two sponsored the projects, however, it is necessary to outline the conceptual problems raised by shifting statues, since Probianus was not alone in adding ornaments to both basilicas in the Forum while claiming to have restored the buildings.

One of the reused statue bases illustrates Probianus' relocation strategy. A statue base states that Probianus repaired the Basilica Julia, a curious claim given that the assertion corresponds with no physical evidence and is not attested in other sources. The inscribed base, now unfortunately lost, was positioned at the façade of the Basilica Julia, where it called attention to an urban prefect fulfilling his designated duty of caring for civic architecture: "Gabinius Vettius Probianus, of the highest senatorial rank and prefect of the city [of Rome], added this statue to be an ornament for the Basilica Julia, restored anew by him."[4] The Probianus inscription affirms that sculptural ornament advanced highly potent symbols connected with concepts of restoration. Unfortunately, there is no specific indication as to what the statue depicted. Yet Probianus placed his inscription on a reused marble base whose alternate side recorded that Flavius Ursacius, a senator of impressive rank (and manager at the market for pigs), had written an honorific dedication to Constantine:

[This statue] of our lord Constantine, the strongest and most blessed Caesar, [was set up by] Flavius Ursacius, a high-ranking senator [who qualified for appointment as a prefect], tribune of the tenth, eleventh, and twelfth urban cohorts [a term that designates the chief of police], administrator of the pig market (forum suarium).[5]

The statue had originally been set up by Ursacius at some point between 306 and 312, when Constantine was a Caesar.[6] It is safe to assume that Probianus wished to recall Ursacius and the earlier oversight of the urban cohorts as a precedent for his later work maintaining the city. The older inscription also features the indication that Ursacius originally set up the statue of Constantine at the pig market (forum *suarium*) in the Campus Martius, where the senator was the administrator.[7] It is clear that Probianus moved the base, if not the statue as well.

Moving the statue base from the pig market provided meaningful ornament for the Basilica Julia, allowing Probianus to assert that he had contributed to the structure's restoration. It is worthwhile to ponder how the ornament created the semblance of repairs. Of course, the statue itself deserves consideration. Probianus might have reinstalled the portrait of Constantine, but the patron does not offer a second dedication to the emperor, and the reused base of Ursacius could have accommodated a different statue once relocated. When the base arrived at the Basilica Julia, the subject seems to have been of less importance than the change in context. Given the link between moving a statue and rehabilitating a public building, reinstating lapsed time allowed Probianus to acquire status from bringing back an earlier commemoration.

Further important issues are raised by the Probianus statue. The first concerns how Probianus and the statue can be linked to the evidence of repairs for the Basilica Julia, documented in the *Chronograph of 354* as occurring at the turn of the fourth century.[8] Since Probianus installed the statue as early as 377, at least 72 years after Diocletian and Maximian retired, why did he claim to sponsor its restoration? Did the transference of a statue provide an amenity that revived the Basilica Julia? What does it mean to consolidate civic ornaments such as statues at a public building in the Forum?

There was no legal impediment to hauling either a statue or an architectural fragment from one spot to another, provided both that it was properly acquired and that it remained within the public sphere and in its native city as a benefit for all. A legal pronouncement from the Theodosian Code issued in 357 forbade taking civic ornaments and public statues away from one city to benefit another.[9] Provisions in the legal code issued at a later date forbade in no uncertain terms harming extant structures in order to remove ornaments. A law issued in 398 implied that properly obtained works also had to remain in the public sphere and could be removed from the original location only if the structure had already decayed.[10] Consequently, the protocols legitimizing transference prevented buildings from crumbling further while implicitly admitting that each city had diminished civic structures. Moving statues within a city, then, was allowed when the built fabric was protected and when the relocated work continued to function as a public accoutrement of its city. Throughout the later Roman empire, elite patrons moved statues of the esteemed rulers of the past;[11] thus, the moved statues appeared localized as emblems of civic pride.

A further topic raised by the Probianus inscription concerns the nature of the senator's role as a sponsor, since he transferred at least six statues in addition to the one mentioned above that was destined for the Forum. Benefactions such as arranging public statues or repairing civic buildings augmented a patron's status; yet the gifts did not anticipate specific reciprocal gestures in ancient times. In the Roman empire prior to the third century, each exemplary ruler provided benefactions that in turn inspired local, senatorial ones. In the cities of the high empire, public displays of statues that joined rulers' portraits with those of senators illustrated that local aristocrats participated in a social order under the leadership of the emperor; the emperor's benefactions earned him the most prestige, with those of the senators following.[12] Paul Veyne has explored how popularity, social standing, and public favor accrued to patrons who donated generously to the city, whether their benefactions consisted of buildings, monuments, or public entertainment.[13] As a result, commemorative landscapes offered credit to the highest-ranking individuals by marking family lineages and specifying esteemed forerunners in the arrangements of portraits in open areas.[14] That Probianus and others who moved statues to the basilicas of the late antique Forum did not identify the subjects of these portraits is significant: these displays were distinct from those constructed to honor the emperor. Indeed, the relocated statues indicate that senators, who certainly measured their status with respect to that of emperors, pursued additional benefactions that did not contribute to imperial prestige. Probianus' gifts, finally, presented generalized ideals and broad concepts such as restoring urban ornament and providing benefits to the populace at busy locations that targeted wide audiences, not just the elite.

The augmented authority of late antique emperors, who had asserted their power by allowing only a select few portraits of senators in the Forum's central area, seems to have inspired local aristocrats to identify themselves as restorers. The porticoes of the Basilica Aemilia and Basilica Julia as well as the Forum of Trajan provided independent spaces in which Rome's senatorial elite could represent their achievements and virtues. The generic value of "restorer" (*restitutor*) had earlier been claimed by emperors; yet ongoing repairs to the structures, which provided visible and daily benefits to the populace of Rome, were the responsibilities of late antique senators.[15] Plausibly, the subtext for documenting fourth-century restoration by senators was that there had been a breakdown in the economics that had favored all civic benefactions during the third century, and that this corresponded chronologically with the rise of distant emperors who possessed overbearing power.[16] The fourth-century revival of benefactions by senators required a strategy for local leaders to characterize their values in the Roman Forum. In addition to reviving the civic displays that had focused on imperial imagery, Rome's senators provided benefits to the populace independently and presented local connotations for the title of restorer in the peripheral zones of the late antique Forum.

Restoring the decoration of the Forum allowed ornaments to display physically the eloquence of aristocrats. One such phrase that captured an emotional response to recovery after ruination was inscribed in 472 upon the reinstated statue of Minerva mentioned in Chapter 3. This statue, it was stated, was "restored for the happiness of our times" (*beatitudine temporum restituit*).[17] The phrase registers the degree to which "our times" hid destruction under the "happiness" of rehabilitation, placing a high value on renewal while imbuing recovery with the veiled and mournful emotions associated with time's passage. Moving statues created a material expression of the rhetoric that saw dilapidation over the ages as a basis for joyful reaction to rehabilitation, suggesting that relocation to a new context prompted complex riffs on the mixed pleasures of partly tarnished

beauty.[18] The statues such as those moved by Probianus further provided wide audiences with access to educated culture and fine art, which was attractive to both illiterate and literate audiences—with the former receiving verbal accounts of the contents of the inscriptions—so that both groups clamored for antiquarian displays.

It has traditionally been adduced from other inscriptions of Probianus that Romans moved cult statues away from temples to the public areas of the Roman Forum after ancestral rites had been legally curtailed.[19] Yet the interconnected activities of moving and restoring have no specific references to cult statues. One late antique statue originally displayed in the Forum, of unknown date and uncertain attribution (and without any explicit link to Probianus), hints on its inscribed base that the image had been moved from a ruined, squalid context to a new place.[20] Reuse was a valuable way for a sponsor to reclaim a threatened statue, no matter what it represented; the epigraphic record does not permit the conclusion that there was a widespread effort to create installations of secularized cult images.[21] Christian antipathy to cult images in temples did not necessarily cause statues to be moved—at least, none of the inscriptions from the Forum state outright that statues were moved from shrines to the Forum for purposeful deconsecration.[22] To be sure, cult statues may have been removed and reused, but it would be difficult to claim that the Forum was an unequivocally secular space in late antiquity.[23] Statues on the move deserve to be considered in light of the activities that restored monuments or promoted the reuse of older decorative materials—including redeployed architectural fragments—all of which focused efforts on consolidating the shifted statues at the highly frequented spaces within or near public buildings during late antiquity.

Inscriptions mentioning the movement of statues featured terms of praise that were also appropriate for celebrating cultural revival. If restoration was considered a more favorable activity than making anew, then recontextualizing statues increased the beauty of the works. The act of rehabilitating the once-censured Nicomachus Flavianus the Elder by restoring his statue in the Forum of Trajan was accomplished when the son, with imperial permission, claimed that the learned virtues of the father sanctioned the restoration of his memory.[24] The Forum of Trajan, with its exedrae for scholarly instruction and its Greek and Latin libraries, was a particularly favorable zone for celebrating literary erudition. The sophisticated spaces of the late antique city fostered the antiquarian fascination with the past and inspired highly trained orators.

The protected porticoes of the Roman Forum continued to provide an important context for citified activities. The porticoes of the Basilica Aemilia and the Basilica Julia provided commercial areas, but probably were less clearly for intellectual activities than was the Forum of Trajan, with its libraries and booksellers targeting ambitious students. The basilicas of the Roman Forum addressed a wide public having diverse interests; their audience was encouraged to look at impressive artworks as markers of high culture. Some of the works there on display were political portraits, taken from other parts of the city, that reinforced the public's participation in feelings of urban pride. Other works relocated to public venues, including masterpieces by famous artists, allowed the populace to enjoy works admired for their antiquarian details and for their connections to classical learning. Under the covered walkways of the Roman Forum, aristocrats made provisions for displays as public entertainment. Installations there targeted the masses, who viewed antiquities as the local emblems of earlier eras of cultural vitality. When statues were transferred to the porticoes of the Forum, crowds of varied classes were able to participate in learned culture symbolized in the relocated works that conferred splendor on the most frequented spaces of the city.[25]

THE BASILICA JULIA IN LATE ANTIQUITY

The original Basilica Julia was built during the middle of the first century BCE. The fire of 284 severely damaged the building; as it persevered, however, the structure became an emblem of architectural longevity.[26] This long-standing structure thus manifestly

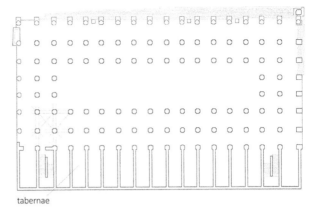

tabernae

Figure 4.1. Plan of the Basilica Julia. Drawing by Brian Doherty.

expressed that its various reiterations were intrinsic to its cultural position within the Forum.

The central, double-height nave of the Basilica Julia was surrounded by aisles on all four sides supporting second-floor galleries, and the north façade, at slightly more than 100 meters in width, spanned nearly the entire length of the Forum's central area (fig. 4.1). Along the north façade, a vaulted aisle provided a continuous passageway and furnished views of the Forum's paved plaza; the portico was somewhat wider and at a slight elevation with respect to the other aisles. Galleries surrounding the central nave at the upper level overlooked the Forum on the north side. The arcaded passageways featured a series of arched openings at the ground level that communicated directly with the Forum's public space. Along the steps facing the Forum, protruding from the basilica's north façade, were projecting platforms, some of which survive today and could have supported the statues transferred during late antiquity. The building was open on the north, east, and west sides at the ground level to provide ease of access into this highly public space where people walked as they approached the Forum's central area.

The Basilica Julia, already restored during the years 9–12 CE after a fire in the Augustan era, was consumed in the flames of 284, as mentioned above. After the restoration around the turn of the fourth century under Diocletian and Maximian as documented in the *Chronograph of 354*, the building maintained its previous footprint, with commercial facilities newly inserted along the south wall. The fire of

Figure 4.2. Remains of the Tetrarchic brick construction in the Basilica Julia. Photo by the author.

Carinus had spread immediately to the area south of the Basilica Julia and decimated the structure called the Graecostadium, which extended into the Velabrum and was replaced by a much smaller structure during the Tetrarchy.[27] The southern edge of the rebuilt Basilica Julia featured two staircases situated within two of the seventeen narrow halls aligned in a row for shops (*tabernae*) (see fig. 4.1). Judging from the fragmentary remains of the marble plan of Rome (*Forma Urbis Romae*), Franz Alto Bauer has determined that during the imperial period, the Basilica Julia had not been equipped with the *tabernae*.[28] When the Tetrarchic campaign reconstructed the Graecostadium at a diminished scale, some of its former commercial activities were shifted to the Basilica Julia, and specifically to the *tabernae*. Remains of brick arches at the southwest corner of the structure furnish lasting testimony to the basilica as rebuilt by Diocletian; the arches probably once continued further to the east, separating the *tabernae* from the rest of the structure (fig. 4.2).[29] The stalls for commercial uses clearly represented a change from the Basilica Julia prior to

its restoration. In all probability, the commercial *tabernae* were set back from the streets to maintain the old appearance of the basilica's façades. The change was fairly minimal; civil courts continued to meet throughout the fourth century, as commerce and legal proceedings coexisted in the same structure.

The central nave of the Basilica Julia, presumably lit by clerestory windows, held the civil proceedings of the centumviral court (a civil court consisting of 100 or more judges), which could have also spilled over into the two lateral aisles. Evidence for the staircases, located close to the southwestern and southeastern corners, suggests that visitors also used to ascend to the elevated galleries above the ground-floor aisles to obtain views toward the Forum on the north side as well as toward the interior nave, with the latter accommodating some of the spectators observing the courts (see fig. 4.1).[30] Legal proceedings argued before the *centumviri*, or judges for this court, occupied the basilica's tall nave with up to four concurrent sessions of forty-five judges or a single assembly of 180 judges, all inhabiting the tall nave of the basilica.[31] The prevailing concern was for making sessions open to the public; there were no architectural provisions made for audiences to be shielded from either the arguments of an adjoining session or ambient noise while listening to the proceedings.[32]

The Basilica Julia was easily entered from the Forum's central area, so its porticoes provided an attractive and shaded gathering place. The building's façade communicated directly with the Forum to welcome visitors, while full access was provided both to the civil courts and to the *tabernae*, tucked away along the south flank. On the interior, the Tetrarchic brick construction, parts of which still stand today, was the major feature that marked the transformation after the reconstruction that was initiated around 300 CE (see fig. 4.2).[33] At the edges of the structure, as recorded in inscriptions, one could have encountered money-changers.[34]

The most important evidence of crowded gatherings comes from the game boards that are inscribed all over the pavement of the Basilica Julia, with a particular concentration at the façade facing the Forum's central area. Boards for games of skill rather than for games of chance etched into the steps there plausibly indicate activities that were allowed in the public sphere, since gambling seems to have been frowned upon and was probably restricted to houses and taverns.[35] At the Basilica Julia, circular game boards documented at the steps facing the Forum's central area seem to have been intended for a game resembling the modern Merels that was not a game

of chance (fig. 4.3). Also, the arrangement of holes in the field of a game board at the Basilica Julia was intended for cups holding tokens of some sort that one would move so as to acquire a token in an opponent's cup, comparable to the modern game called Mancala (fig. 4.4).[36] Francesco Trifilò, who has analyzed the evidence of gaming boards inscribed onto the pavements in various fora, determined that games of skill were actually encouraged by civic authorities, who sponsored such public activities in acts of civic generosity that provided opportunities for leisure. The best evidence for the local benefactors sponsoring public boards for games of skill, while preventing games of chance and gambling, comes from Aphrodisias, where local aristocrats sponsored gaming surfaces at the Hadrianic baths with public inscriptions.[37] The Basilica Julia thus was a bustling structure that accommodated a varied public, which sought to participate in or observe games, shopping, and civil court cases.

THE BASILICA AEMILIA

Diocletian and Maximian also repaired parts of the Basilica Aemilia in the wake of the fire damage of 284, maintaining judicial spaces and ensuring through late antique restorations that civic life remained centered in the Roman Forum.[38] The Basilica Aemilia featured a clear distinction between its interior nave and its series of *tabernae*, protected by a deep portico that

Figure 4.3. Circular game board inscribed in the pavement of the Basilica Julia. Photo by the author.

Figure 4.4. Indentations from a game board inscribed in the pavement of the Basilica Julia. Photo by the author.

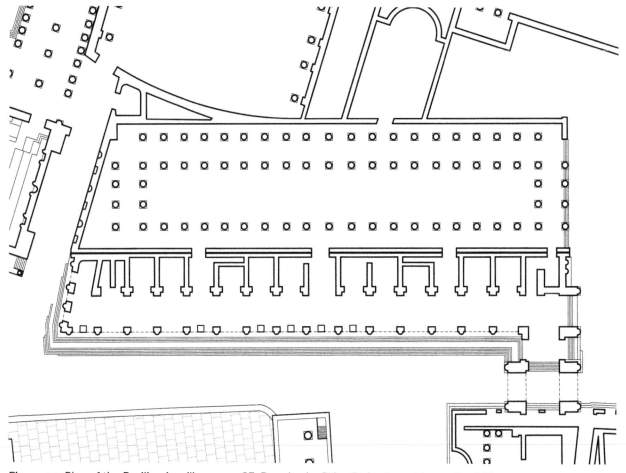

Figure 4.5. Plan of the Basilica Aemilia, c. 420 CE. Drawing by Brian Doherty and Jacqueline Miles.

faced the Via Sacra (fig. 4.5). The late antique restoration of the basilica framing the north side of the Forum retained many of the features that had been rebuilt after a fire in 14 BCE.[39] Throughout the fourth century, the nave was a double-height space surrounded by a single aisle, with an extra aisle added to the north. The colonnades separating the nave from the aisles and dividing in two the double aisle to the north were composed of high-quality purple- and white-speckled marble columns. Fragments of these columns still remain at the site. To separate the lavish nave from the portico, a massive brick wall was inserted with grand, arched openings (fig. 4.6). In a manner similar to the basilica across the Forum plaza, the late antique Basilica Aemilia featured massive brick construction on the interior. The wall features brick stamps bearing marks that are characteristic of the joint rule of Diocletian and Maximian, and other stamps dating into the Con

stantinian dynasty.[40] The early fourth-century brick wall with arched openings correlates with some of the remains of a new, late antique feature of the portico: a row of monolithic granite columns.[41] Two of the granite columns survive to their full height and have been reerected on their original bases, framing the entrance for one of the arched openings in the brick wall (fig. 4.7). The late antique portico of the Basilica Aemilia, therefore, was fully integrated into the design of the interior brick wall begun during the Tetrarchy. The portico and the brick wall were conceptually coherent, even if the late antique construction phases extended well into the fifth century.

The worst damage to the Basilica Aemilia occurring after the Tetrarchic period resulted from the sack of Rome in 410. Coins discovered during the excavations of the Basilica Aemilia included some that were fused to the pavement and others that had merely been jettisoned; most of the coins can be

Figure 4.6. Remains of the Tetrarchic wall at the Basilica Aemilia. Photo by the author.

Figure 4.7. Columns from the late antique portico at the Basilica Aemilia. Photo by the author.

dated to 350 at the earliest and 409 at the latest.[42] A layer of ash in the nave was documented during the excavations of the Basilica Aemilia; the correlation between the layer with the burnt remains and the layer with the coins indicates that physical damage occurred during 410.[43] Very few of the architectural remains were discovered touching the ash layer, leading to the supposition that the interior nave was abandoned after 410.[44] The portico, however, was revived and restored. Thus, as Franz Alto Bauer has determined, the evidence that the nave had been filled with rubble rather than undergoing repairs after 410, together with new additions to the portico, indicate that the portico was essentially a sham façade for the damaged basilica in the fifth century.[45]

Using the fixed-up exterior portico to mask the abandoned nave of the Basilica Aemilia disturbs the picture of urban vitality that late antique restorations sought to paint. It must be stressed that the rubble-filled interior was hidden, and that the portico had already been cut off dramatically from the nave by the Tetrarchic brick wall. To further conceal the damage from those walking along the Argiletum, a brick wall on the west façade was added in the fifth century, with niches that originally contained statues (fig. 4.8).[46] The new western wall and the reconstructed portico reveal an emphasis on activating the streets of the Argiletum and the Via Sacra by framing the damaged interior with well-maintained façades. A picture emerges of highly practical decisions that underscored the need to rebuild the commercial stalls in the portico of the Basilica Aemilia after 410; at the same time, the law courts that had once met in the basilica's nave could have moved to the facilities in the Forum of Augustus or elsewhere. Despite the expedient decision to abandon the Basilica Aemilia's damaged nave, the building was adapted to create the image of dilapidation having been repaired. At the fifth-century Basilica Aemilia, the ideal of reviving the past remained alive, if only by providing an illusion of architectural consolidation rather than the real thing.

Repairs to the damaged late antique façade of the Basilica Aemilia must have repeated the Tetrarchic design. In other words, the portico restored in the fifth century, fronted by monolithic granite columns,

makes sense only if it provided access to a functioning space. After 410, repairs addressed some of the damage but did not dramatically alter the early fourth-century portico.

The fifth-century restoration is documented in an inscribed architrave placed on the portico, presumably facing the Via Sacra (fig. 4.9). Dedicated by the urban prefect of 418–420, Aurelius Anicius Symmachus, the inscription honors Honorius and Theodosius II for the rebuilding undertaken by the high-ranking senator in their names.[47] The inscription might not have altered the overall senatorial connotations of the basilica, since it had originally been constructed by M. Aemilius Lepidus in the second century BCE and was rebuilt thereafter by a descendant of the same name, famously recording the history of this senatorial family in images placed on the façade.[48] The construction around 300 of the brick wall that divided the Basilica Aemilia's nave from its portico necessitated a major reworking of the tabernae and the colonnade facing the Via Sacra. This might have been only partly completed by the time of Alaric's attack, necessitating that Aurelius Anicius Symmachus finish the portico envisioned a century earlier. It is possible that the fifth-century portico provided access not to the nave, but to the tabernae and the covered walkway running parallel to the Via Sacra, which was a welcoming, protected area.

The granite columns arranged along the Basilica Aemilia's portico facing the Via Sacra were spoliated materials added onto the historic structure with material references to rehabilitation.[49] But the concept of amalgamation had been experienced at the Basilica Aemilia prior to 410, when one entered through the large arch of the Tetrarchic brick wall and into the nave with its radically different materials. In part, the disjunction between interior and exterior, also experienced at the Basilica Julia, articulated that the Basilica Aemilia had been reconstituted. The fifth-century structure provided a façade for show, yet it also held a covered portico that could be used. Thus, the spoliated granite columns assembled on the portico and facing the Via Sacra provided an appropriate context for the transference of statues from other parts of the city. The inscribed bases of the statues moved there added further nuance to the popular

Figure 4.8. Early fifth-century wall showing niches for statues at the western end of the Basilica Aemilia. Photo by the author.

Figure 4.9. Inscribed architrave dedicated to Honorius and Theodosius II (*CIL* 6.36962) at the Basilica Aemilia. Photo by the author.

appeal of reused materials and the splendor of the revived façade at the late antique Basilica Aemilia.

The Basilica Aemilia's portico exhibited late antique images with inscriptions stating that they had been relocated there, implying a change in significance. This engagement with recontextualized meanings at the Forum's basilicas gestured toward reviving the ideals of the past, but the display of statues at the façades of these two buildings also created a spatial contrast to the central Forum's imperial purpose. During the reign of Constantius II (337–361), one urban prefect of Rome, Fabius Titianus, set up seven bases in the Forum, mostly at the façade of the Basilica Aemilia, that do not seem to have featured portrait statues (fig. 4.10). In fact, the formula repeated on all of the inscriptions suggests that Titianus "curated" or rearranged statues, stating: "Fabius Titianus of the highest

Figure 4.10. Base for a statue sponsored by Fabius Titianus (*CIL* 6.1653a) at the Basilica Aemilia. Photo by the author.

senatorial rank, consul [and] urban prefect, curated the work."[50] All of these inscriptions designate reused statues, and all were installed during his first urban prefecture, from 339 to 341.[51] Not once does Titianus indicate the subject of the works displayed at the Basilica Aemilia, but he consistently claims a role as the curator. These works were not dedicated to Constantius II, even though it was a convention for senatorial benefactions to name the reigning emperor as the recipient of honors in the Forum.

Titianus was a controversial figure who wavered in his loyalties. He had supported an illegitimate emperor, the usurper Magnentius, after 350. This caused Constantius II to seek retribution. Indeed, after Constantius II halted the usurpation of Magnentius, Titianus himself suffered condemnation by erasure from the inscriptions at the baths of Titus that had honored the tyrant. Oddly, Fabius Titianus' name was not removed from the installations in the Forum that listed only the senator's name.[52] Even though Constantine had created the post of curator of statues, Titianus seems to have objected to the neglect of Rome's antiquities by that emperor's sons, Constans and Constantius II. Certainly, Titianus' disdain for Constantius II fosters a suspicion that he transferred important works of art rather than portraits of the emperor into the Forum. Together, these seven statues on the move reconceptualized the façade of the Basilica Aemilia that faced the Via Sacra, transforming it into a site for the display of significant statues. This provides strong evidence that the late antique portico with its granite columns had already been mostly set up by 339.

Constantine developed the role of the curator of statues for the oversight of artworks exhibited in Rome's public space, and it seems to have been a highly coveted position. It is not clear whether the curator of statues possessed the authority to set up statues independent of the obligation to honor the emperors in Rome's public space. Nonetheless, in Titianus' defiant position toward Constantius II and his allegiance with Magnentius, we see him challenging the official imperial court. We also see that Titianus sponsored statues with inscriptions lacking explicit imperial dedications, instead hinting that he placed these works at the Basilica Aemilia to make this a zone of public enjoyment under senatorial sponsorship, in contrast to the installations honoring emperors elsewhere in the Forum. Titianus' display presented an aristocratic perspective on the city in a manner that drew upon the Tetrarchic infrastructure while it presented images to revise the infrastructure's significance.

THE LASTING LEGACY OF TETRARCHIC REPAIRS

The large-scale rebuilding of the Roman Forum under Diocletian and Maximian provides a context in which to understand the transference of statues to the basilicas. During the Tetrarchic period, the Basilica Julia and the Basilica Aemilia both received substantive transformations that created a disjuncture between the façades and the interiors. To be sure, the ambitious construction projects at both buildings that were completed by 303 were financed by and credited to the emperors. The peripheral locations of the two basilicas, however, rendered them less central to imperial propaganda; further, the Tetrarchs may have initiated, but did not necessarily complete, the repairs at one or both of the basilicas, leaving senatorial sponsors to finish the projects. In any case, the long porticoes provided ample space for displays such as the seven statues set up by Fabius Titianus at or near the Basilica Aemilia. The cumulative effect of the installations was to present official adornments that reflected how Rome's local aristocrats furnished signposts of elite learning that the senators shared with the populace. In the second century, the jurist Paulus indicated that it would "usually be allowed for images and statues to be set up in public as ornaments to the state."[53] Civic buildings conveyed their manifold purposes through moved statues: public structures offered urban decor, and public access to the pleasures of contemplating literary ideas presented in artworks hinted that civic magistrates shared with the public their advanced learning and refined taste.[54]

There is no doubt that the dramatic rebuilding campaigns of Diocletian and Maximian had a lasting impact on the Forum: their campaigns extended to most of the precinct's significant buildings in a manner that displaced local senators from their roles as civic benefactors. Even though the Basilica Julia received major Tetrarchic restorations, two inscribed statue bases found within the basilica that set up dedications to Maximian as the Western emperor did not explicitly credit him for architectural conservation, despite the honors he received in the display of portraiture.[55] A different type of epigraphic testimony appears on a statue base for the deity Vortumnus, discovered along the Vicus Tuscus at the southeast corner of the Basilica Julia. The text seems to indicate the revival of one of the city's oldest cults during the Tetrarchy. Since the inscription identifies "Vortumnus during the time of Diocletian and Maximian" ("*Vortumnus temporibus Diocletiani et Maximiani*"), the statue of an Etruscan god with restoration credited to the Tetrarchs also renewed archaic religious traditions.[56] The Vortumnus statue hints at the connections to historic cult practices during the Tetrarchy, and thus prior to the time when artworks were displayed at the Basilica Julia. Nonetheless, the Vortumnus statue—displayed near and not precisely on the eastern façade of the Basilica Julia—added meaning to the Tetrarchic repairs as supporting the explicit revival of archaic practices during the first decade of the fourth century and emphasized how changed circumstances updated one of the Forum's treasured antiquities.

The reuse of an archaic statue and the repair of a building in Rome were neither unexpected nor a purely local phenomenon. Statue bases were reused throughout the later Roman empire.[57] In the early empire, removing the architectural fragments belonging to civic structures for transference to a distant town or taking publicly displayed statues from the original location to another city violated the spirit of community pride.[58] Late antique senatorial sponsors who moved artworks or architectural ornaments within a given city technically did not violate this traditional ethos. The subsequent imperial policies dating to the middle of the fourth century confronted dilapidation by specifying that "ornaments" (*ornamenta*) could be reused when the civic structures, including temples, were maintained. Based on a study of the legislation in the Theodosian Code,

Joseph Alchermes has made the important claim that the residents of each city had a right to enjoy public monuments as features that contributed greatly to the lasting honor of the locality. Implicitly, the imperial policies connected sculptural and architectural *spolia* with the civic structures where they were to be displayed.[59]

Late antique senators had to develop strategies other than dedicating statues to emperors to celebrate aristocratic civic munifence in Rome; yet they also had to retain the refined discourse of honorific inscriptions. Laws that prevented aristocratic inscriptions from claiming credit for benefactions curtailed senatorial initiatives to gain the highest possible honors. Still, there was a benefit from transferred materials, which has been noted by Hugo Brandenburg, who sees the shifted ornaments (*ornamenta*) as a category of objects that acquired aesthetic value on account of recontextualization.[60] One law sent to Mamertinus as the praetorian prefect of Italy in 365 by the emperors Valentinian I and Valens fostered efforts "to restore to their former appearance and to their suitable and useful service the ornaments of the cities (*ornamenta urbium*) and their marble embellishments (*decora marmorum*), if they are suffering the ravages of time."[61] This legislation clearly refers to architectural ornaments. In 376, Valentinian II and Valens wrote to the senate, ordering that "no one of the prefects of the city or other judges whom power has placed in a high position shall undertake any new structure in the renowned city of Rome, but he shall direct his attention to improving the old."[62] This restriction on opportunities for benefactions by local senators promoted the restoration of civic structures such as basilicas. The discourse on the city appearing in the Theodosian Code provides insights into the terms of praise that added beauty to public areas of a city: the ornaments of the cities elicited praise for urban space.

REDECORATION AS RESTORATION

The concepts of relocation and restoration coalesced with the exhibition of statues at the basilicas' porticoes, where civic concerns came to the fore. Urban public space still accommodated displays of the portraits depicting the highest-ranking state officials, as had occurred throughout the empire.[63] The ceremonial regions in the Roman Forum's central area and the plaza in front of the Curia were hierarchically the most important spots and were mostly reserved for images of emperors, whereas the porticoes of the basilicas featured artworks and ornamental statues. Dedications to emperors by Rome's aristocrats designated the space of the Forum as a realm of official imperial policies. Yet, unlike the residents of other cities, Roman locals continually pursued patronage of artworks independent of imperial dedications, particularly at the Basilica Aemilia and the Basilica Julia.[64]

Inscriptions in the Roman Forum calling attention to senatorial decorations, and specifically those not dedicated to emperors, facilitated cultural life under local patronage. Upon completion of a new public structure, a building inscription crediting the emperors was required, as recorded in a law from the Theodosian Code. Published in 394 (but reissuing an earlier proclamation), the law ordered that "if any of the judges should inscribe their names rather than the name of Our Eternity on any completed work, they shall be held guilty of high treason."[65] An implied benefit of architectural restoration undertaken without imperial funds was being able to avoid inscribing a dedication to the emperor. Restoration thus took on a particular connotation when applied to a statue moved by a senator: it documented that local benefactions advanced the public sphere for Romans. Additionally, the restoration undertaken by senators at the Basilica Aemilia and the Basilica Julia conveyed a vastly different agenda than the political *restitutio* that redounded to emperors.

Neither senatorial sponsor, Fabius Titianus or Probianus, seems to be a likely candidate for having completed extensive repairs at either the Basilica Aemilia or the Basilica Julia. Despite this, Probianus claimed to be a restorer. Epigraphic texts overstate but refrain from outright dissimulation in the words chosen to celebrate a benefactor.[66] It is plausible, then, that both Titianus and Probianus used their terms holding high offices to shift statues for the purpose of setting up cultural displays that created museological space, exploiting the architectural backdrop of basilicas.

Probianus set up his statues in either 377 or 416 at both the Basilica Aemilia and the Basilica Julia. Probianus' inscriptions in the Forum specify that he repaired buildings and set up damaged statues that had been toppled, which seems to accord with the devastation caused during the sack of Rome in 410.[67] Yet it appears that the individual holding the urban prefecture in 416 was named Rufius Probianus.[68] The sponsor of the statues, Gabinius Vettius Probianus, therefore, likely undertook the repairs in 377.[69] The earlier date for Probianus' urban prefecture makes particular sense if moving statues was an important pursuit that could be partly dissociated from repairing the physically devastated city. In other words, Rome's need for repairs had been a recurring issue throughout antiquity, and fourth-century senators who moved statues, including both Titianus and Probianus, did so for the betterment of urban public space as much as to remove works from their squalid settings.

Nine separate extant statue bases record that Probianus moved statues to a basilica, sometimes specified by name.[70] In all of his inscriptions, Probianus implies that he had saved the day, as if he had efficiently reversed the lack of decorations at the basilicas. He only specifies the Basilica Julia. The unidentified basilica, which he designates as distinguished (*inlustris*), must have been the Basilica Aemilia, given the find spots of the statue bases from there. There are slight variations in the wording of the inscriptions; one formula appearing twice does not identify the basilica by name: "Gabinius Vettius Probianus, of the highest senatorial rank and urban prefect, ordered [this] statue to be set in place so that it could ornament this distinguished basilica."[71] Probianus thus moved at least two statues to the Basilica Aemilia by alluding to the legally sanctioned process of furnishing ornaments for the citizens. Moving statues, then, resembled shifting around the *spolia* of precious building materials in that both, as ornaments of the cities (*ornamenta urbium*), were supposed to be enjoyed by the people as cultural property. By specifying the context in a basilica, Probianus definitively asserted that the reinstalled work entered a civic framework to be viewed by a wide public.

Recontextualizing a statue in one of the two basilicas changed the meaning of the work, which allowed Probianus to take control of the statue to advance his claim to be the virtuous repairer who helped his city and pleased the public. For this reason, the statue's subject is not mentioned, and Probianus' name is in the nominative case, since he claims to be the "restorer," not the recipient of a dedication by someone else. Another epigraphic text used twice by Probianus notes the busy foot traffic at the site of the installation (figs. 4.11 and 4.12): "Gabinius Vettius Probianus, of the highest senatorial rank and prefect of the city [of Rome], diligently repaired this statue that had fallen on account of fatal necessity in the busiest part of the city."[72] The new meaning of the work was that it had become civic ornament.

A larger issue is raised by the indications that Probianus saved the work from impending destruction. Stating that the statue had fallen on account of fatal necessity (*fatali necessitate*) has prompted efforts to pinpoint the event that toppled the monument. Even though the phrase invites curiosity about what tragedy occurred, it has to be admitted that Probianus used purposefully vague terms. In his various inscribed monuments, Probianus retains an unwavering commitment to restoration. Given the find spots for two of Probianus' bases at points close to the Senate House on the north side of the Roman Forum, these statues could have ornamented the Basilica Aemilia.[73] Others stood in front of the Basilica Julia.[74] The "necessity" to which Probianus refers might be the restricted imperial funds available for maintaining the city, a situation that was only aggravated by the shift in imperial residences away from Rome during the fourth century. Probianus and other senatorial benefactors would have wished to sustain Rome's infrastructure in response to imperial directives that ordered the maintenance of old buildings rather than the building of new ones. Further, moving statues seems to have allowed senatorial officials to work as collectors who installed works for the public good. Public buildings downtown received continual upkeep that was distinct from what occurred in other areas of the city; moving a statue to a basilica indicated that the Forum was well maintained.

Figure 4.11. Base for a statue set up by Gabinius Vettius Probianus (*CIL* 6.3864a). Photo by the author.

Figure 4.12. Base for a statue set up by Gabinius Vettius Probianus (*CIL* 6.3864b). Photo by the author.

Conserving architecture also allowed Probianus to achieve his primary goal: he was committed to displaying and preserving the honor that he and his predecessors had acquired over the ages by sponsoring monuments or public buildings. Yet, as Probianus contemplated the restoration of the Basilica Julia, he found himself constrained by finances. In the 360s, the coffers of the Roman empire no longer consistently supported buildings, causing the provincial governors and prefects of various cities to economize and avoid new construction projects; at the same time, architectural restoration was encouraged, as mentioned above.[75] Plausibly, legislation during the late fourth century began to encourage senators to put their names on the buildings they restored to encourage regional patrons to support architectural restoration. Senators started to opt for restoration, since only emperors could be named in inscriptions on newly constructed public buildings in the late fourth century. Despite this, the tradition of claim-

ing the role of restorer was an undefined and contentious issue in late antiquity, since there were imperial precedents for asserting in inscriptions that a building had been restored even though it had sustained only minimal interventions.[76] Thus, a presumed incentive for moving statues during late antiquity was that the emperor's name need not be attached, particularly if shifting the works of art required no funds to be allocated by the imperial court. Moving the statue to a civic location, further, could substantiate the vague claim that the building had been restored. Senators had greater freedom when acting as restorers rather than as builders, even if fourth-century aristocrats in the Western empire could not make the claim to be founders, either through the construction of new public buildings or through conservation efforts.[77]

Probianus continued a trend that Fabius Titianus had started. Both revised the Roman Forum by providing an alternative to the official and ceremonial realms framed by the two Rostra in the central area and the plaza near the Senate House. Probianus' claim to have restored the Basilica Julia would be surprising, unless it is understood that his interest was in revising the natures of both this basilica and the Basilica Aemilia. With promenades, shopping stalls, and shaded porticoes, the two basilicas of the Forum were for the populace of Rome and thus stood as prominent civic spaces. The shifted statues provided cultural benefits as markers that the senatorial aristocracy cared for the city and its citizenry, a role formerly provided by emperors.

CULTURAL DISPLAYS

One convention for exhibiting statues was to display the virtues of individuals. These qualities typically alerted the citizens of aristocratic traditions, which remained the subtext of those monuments whose origins were traced to generous benefactions. Artworks in the Temple of Peace or the Baths of Caracalla had long been enjoyed by the populace. Given that Probianus and Titianus were transferring works to the Basilica Julia and the Basilica Aemilia from mostly unspecified spots, it is also significant that three bases have been recovered identifying works by famous artists. The discovered labels indicate Greek statues by Polyclitus, Praxiteles, and Timarchus.[78] Today, two of the labels for the works by famous Greek artists are placed above the Probianus bases (see figs. 4.11 and 4.12). The bases were separated and identified as distinct works in late antiquity, however.

Ruling out Probianus as the clear-cut sponsor of the works by celebrated Greek artists still allows for the possibility of coordination among the unidentified works and the masterpieces of Greek sculpture on display at the Basilica Julia. The purpose of the exhibition resided in eliciting responses to the literary themes presented in a textured juxtaposition of works belonging to different genres and originating from different eras. The three masterpieces formed a coherent triad with attributions to famous Greek sculptors, but they were set amid a heterogeneous array of works, some of which were identified as relocated on the bases. Probianus and Titianus therefore moved statues to the basilicas to make provisions

for the populace to enjoy the sophisticated ideas of recuperation in well-appointed, civilized zones.

In the fifth century, moving statues continued to assert the positive consequences of consolidating partly tarnished works at the Forum's basilicas. There is no particular evidence to suggest that the sack of Rome created the exclusive conditions for moving statues, although it could have been a contributing factor. The son of Macrobius, the author of the *Saturnalia*, installed a work in the Forum as late as 472 that had been moved, not necessarily to keep it from harm, but in order to sustain the cultural health of the civic zones downtown. The inscription indicates that the work originated "from a remote location" (*ex abstrusis locis*).[79] The emphasis on the spot from which the statue was taken elicited appreciation for new meanings, indicating that viewers gained access to the poetics of recuperation while gazing at the recontextualized statue.

The cultural nature of the displays at the Forum's basilicas tacitly but pointedly supplemented the imperial control over the open areas of the Roman Forum. Texts honoring emperors for reversing urban decay are slightly distinct from the inscriptions celebrating the shifting of statues to the Forum basilicas: the moved statues describe the transference of power and articulate that cultural property was consolidated under civic authorities, specifically under the senate in the case of Rome.[80] There is a distinction between the aristocrats, who repaired specific monuments such as statues, and the emperors, who received full credit as patrons of rebuilt structures. Further, Rome presents an urban context distinct from that of Constantinople, to which Constantine had shifted the masterpieces of sculpture from other cities in the empire.[81] Notwithstanding the issues raised when he deprived cities of their own statues, Constantine as a collector advanced his authority by providing public ornaments, such as statues, for Constantinople. By contrast, the aristocratic sponsorship of public art in Rome appears to have reiterated in serial displays that the Forum's basilicas were senatorial venues.

Perhaps the most striking example of a senator moving statues to co-opt imperial space was undertaken by the most power-hungry urban prefect of

Figure 4.13. Base for statue originally inscribed in honor of Valens and later reused by Petronius Maximus (*CIL* 6.36956). Photo by the author.

the fifth century, Petronius Maximus. The competition to acquire power took a particularly dangerous turn with Petronius Maximus, since he orchestrated the murder of Aëtius in 454, putting the blame on the emperor Valentinian III. He also apparently hired assassins to kill Valentinian III in 455. Petronius Maximus ruled as emperor for 77 days in 455, indicating conniving and violent strategies pursued by a senator with ambitions to become the emperor but without family ties to the imperial house. Prior to his short-lived imperial rule and during his second urban prefecture, dated to either 421 or 439, Maximus transferred a statue (or reused the base) originally dedicated in 365 to the emperor Valens for an installation at the Basilica Aemilia (fig. 4.13).[82] On an alternate side of the base dedicated to Valens, Maximus claimed that he had "curated" (*curavit*) the statue

and used the same verb as is found on the fourth-century installations of Fabius Titianus.[83] Another statue base originally set up in 242 for the emperor Gordian III was also reused by Petronius Maximus; it was arranged at the façade of the Basilica Aemilia.[84] A third installation at the Basilica Aemilia sponsored by Maximus shows signs of having been erased, since the short-term emperor was condemned after 455 and killed by a crowd as he attempted to flee the city.[85] The repairs that advanced civic pride and the "curated" installations that expressed noble care for the city seem hardly applicable to Petronius Maximus. Despite his disregard for the traditions of propriety associated with moving statues, Maximus during his urban prefectures confirmed that the act of transference asserted senatorial control over the Forum's basilicas.

STATUES AND THE CONSOLIDATION OF CIVIC SPACE

When Probianus served his year-long term as urban prefect, which indications suggest was in 377 CE, Roman aristocrats were reacting to the restrictions upon senatorial munificence in the civic center. Senators remained eager not to give up the "epigraphic habit" in fourth-century Rome, since a series of public squares near aristocratic houses emerged as sites for senatorial portraits.[86] Senators typically did not air their grievances at their near exclusion from having their portraits displayed in the Forum, and they downplayed their disputes with the nonresident emperors.[87] As a result, Rome's local elite seemed to approve of the Forum's use mostly for statues of emperors in the open spaces; indeed, the names of senators continuously appeared in epigraphic texts as the local benefactors. It was an affront to the aristocrats that the emperors did not physically reside in Rome; but an even greater slight was the dislocation of most local senatorial representations from the Forum's central area, given the prominence of nobles in civic life.

One fascinating aspect of the topographical conditions for patronage in the late antique Roman Forum concerns the status and authority maintained by senators. Traditionally, the identity of each city was closely linked to the virtues of elite patrons whose status had been reinstated over time.[88] Drawing upon the imperial encouragement of restoration, and implicit support for moving statues away from degraded parts of the city as documented in the Theodosian Code, senators of Rome were able to designate two of the basilicas in the Forum as civic spaces for aristocratic displays. This was distinct from other cities in the empire, where the fora accommodated civic activities in which only emperors gained credit for patronage and public honors.[89] Moving statues to the Forum's basilicas in a manner that exhibited how senators advanced civic life was thus unique to the aristocrats of Rome. Elsewhere in the empire, emperors received honors for shifting statues to busy locations, as was the case of a monument displayed in Verona. The Veronese statue base states, "With praise for the happiness of the times [and in dedication to] our Lords Gratian, Valentinian II, and Theodosius I, the senior emperors, the governor [of Verona and the region] ordered that a statue that lay for a long time on the Capitolium be placed in the busiest spot in the Forum."[90] In Rome, senators held a unique role as those who increased the happiness of the public by re-erecting toppled statues without crediting the emperors.

Creating a cultural realm in the basilicas of the Forum allowed aristocrats to emphasize the virtues of learned culture and an appreciation for art, which they shared with the masses. The display of artworks at the porticoes invited the public to enjoy sophisticated masterpieces and other treasures at the locations where they shopped and gathered. In Rome, a unique set of conditions encouraged senators to exploit the permission they had received to be restorers who transferred statues and carved out civic realms at the basilicas. Instigated initially with the legislation issued in the 360s requiring that imperial funds be dedicated only to restoration and not to new construction in Rome, this valorization of repaired infrastructure took on the meaning of aristocratic concern for the city. In public buildings, the reuse of old architectural fragments, today known as *spolia*, conveyed nuanced meanings, among which the ideals of restoring past vitality figured prominently.[91]

Late antique restoration pertained to the renewal of civic pride that public citizens enjoyed at specific locations. There is no evidence that the sack of Rome in 410 caused the widespread need to re-erect statues. The shifted statues must be dissociated from artworks that had been toppled as a result of urban tumult. Raids caused damage, and degradation harmed statues, to be sure; but moving statues was part of a vast project of recontextualization. In fact, the most effective statues and the most expressive inscriptions indicated that transference of public art resulted from the civic generosity of prominent aristocrats at the busiest spots in the city. A statue on the move brought redoubled honor to the one who transferred it to a beautiful, crowded space such as the Forum. The movement of artworks also indicated that aristocratic concerns for lineage and tradition were to be read as beneficial to the populace, since the shifted statues projected aristocratic concerns at the populated areas.

The Forum was not the only part of Rome that benefited from linking architectural repairs with decorative concerns. Cassiodorus, a Roman senator working as the spokesperson of Theoderic, the Ostrogothic king of Italy, wrote around 510 CE to a member of Rome's illustrious Symmachi family, praising his restoration of private villas and the Theater of Pompey downtown: "And therefore I have decided that the fabric of the Theater [of Pompey], buckling under its great weight, should be reinforced by your counsel. This will make [the theater], which—as everyone knows—your ancestors donated to the country as ornament (*ornatus*), not appear to have diminished under their more noble descendants."[92] The ornamental additions allowed late antique senators to reclaim their roles as cultural benefactors whose old families kept the city vital.

Probianus' reuse of statue bases and his restoration of the Basilica Julia integrated his commitment to restituting the partly lapsed honors of the aristocracy with his commitment to enhancing architecture through the placement of statues. Probianus and numerous others carefully preserved the old inscriptions, rotating the reused plinths so that old benefactions remained continually visible, though clearly less prominent than before. Patterns of reuse in the statue bases exhibited in civic areas such as the basilicas of the Roman Forum signaled that memories of long-standing aristocratic traditions, including the pleasure of viewing a work of art, returned when a moved statue appeared on a preexisting plinth. Restoration captured the texture and even maintained some of the diminished appearance caused by the passage of time, honestly expressed in the gestures of reappropriation. Senators moved statues to the façades of the Basilica Aemilia and the Basilica Julia to launch an implied critique of the imperial displays elsewhere in the Forum. Reviving artistic displays enabled aristocrats to claim an alternative: to have delivered a restoration of culture.

THE CONTESTED ETERNITY
OF TEMPLES

A BYZANTINE SOURCE FROM THE SIXTH CENTURY RECOUNTS CONSTANTINE'S RELOCA-
tion of the Palladium, a powerful talisman that had once safeguarded Rome and that was supposedly hauled away from the Temple of Vesta in the Roman Forum and given a new home in
Constantinople. John Malalas reports in his *Chronicle* that the Palladium, the statue of Athena
that had purportedly been carried to Italy from Troy by Aeneas, was inserted beneath the
porphyry column in the eastern capital's Forum of Constantine.[1] In Constantinople, the Palladium provided a foundation story of a legacy transferred from Rome.[2]

The talisman's mythic removal from Rome is remarkably informative about architectural
preservation in late antiquity, raising key points of interest concerning historic shrines such
as the Temple of Vesta. Specifically, cult implements (and temples) remained intact even after ancestral rites had been curtailed, and shrines reemerged, playing public roles if signs of
transformation were displayed. Temples provided emblems of eternity in the sense that commending Rome's ancestral legacy to lasting memory required a certain amount of forgetting:
selective change ensured that only the treasured past was embodied in shrines.[3]

Malalas implies that a secret talisman hidden in a cavity underneath the Temple of Vesta
brought danger to the empire; yet the Palladium became considerably less dangerous once it
was shifted to a civic context beneath a column monument. Additional threats emerged: according to the tale in the *Actus Silvestri*, a legendary dragon inhabiting the cavity beneath the
Temple of Vesta prompted Constantine to ask Pope Silvester to contain the beast. But after
blood sacrifice was outlawed, officials sustained temples as public buildings functioning viably
in late antique Rome as backdrops for outdoor processions. Since the Temple of Vesta itself
survived, its potential for preserving only the favored memories of civic festivities and suppressing the disdained memories of secretive cult activities indicates how and why temples
were actually conserved in the fourth century.

The fourth-century renovations of temples in the Roman Forum offered subtle but meaningful alterations that maintained the eternal status of some, but certainly not all, ancestral
traditions, with the proviso that these memories did not instigate improper practices. Major

fourth-century renovations of traditional shrines in the Roman Forum overhauled the Temple of Saturn and the Temple of Castor and Pollux, as well as the Porticus Deorum Consentium; all were revered as part of Rome's cultural patrimony. Other temples were preserved, including the temples of Concord, Vesta, and Vespasian. The consolidation and restoration of temples demand explanation, because performing sacrifices and entering these buildings was increasingly problematic during the fourth century. The edicts outlawing sacrifice and forbidding people from using the interiors of temples were definitively codified in 391, but these prohibitions were anticipated as early as 356.[4] Yet public and outdoor celebrations that continued into the fifth century required an architectural context provided by temples. Open-air festivals devoid of sacrifices were important to the ritual life of fourth-century Rome, and the Forum's temples took on a new value as backdrops to these civic celebrations.

Laws prohibited sacrifice, and beliefs were contested as well. Those favoring ancestral practices commemorated Rome's persistence at the shrines located at critical spots in the city. Christian imperial authorities who outlawed sacrifice, however, took over the endowments and properties that supported cult activities during the fifth century, causing a rupture in the protection that the gods had once offered.[5] In the fourth century, temples had been physically reconstituted using evident signs of restoration: they exhibited *spolia* recuperated from ruin to sanction a concept of eternity in which selective loss was favored for contributing to the overall persistence of memories. Roman traditionalists at first embraced this approach, preserving the physical remains of temples for the long haul by retaining fragments of the past that had been visibly recuperated but definitively historicized; but Christian legends also suggested to viewers that they look critically upon shrines that had been decisively altered but clearly preserved.

PUBLIC RITUALS

In late antiquity, retaining temples was defensible because they supported civic life, including proces-

sions. Some Roman residents who had never converted to Christianity sought to retain the civic role of legally sanctioned and publicly celebrated ancestral traditions. Christian authorities, by contrast, objected vocally to sacrifice but were unable to erase other civic celebrations.

In the late fifth century, there may have been little opportunity for Pope Gelasius I (492–496) to prevent the Lupercalia—a wild rite that featured nude men running around the Palatine Hill and the Forum, striking elite women. Gelasius' only option seems to have been to excommunicate an elite sponsor of the celebration, as asserted in a letter the pope sent to the offending senator, Andromachus.[6] Indeed, Gelasius' attack on patrons supporting the Lupercalia suggests that public festivities were elite benefactions that effectively competed with the patronage of rites by the pope, since the laity gained social standing and public support from providing traditional civic celebrations.[7] The fifth-century pope contested the Lupercalia's purported ritual goal to purify the city. But Gelasius himself stood on shaky moral grounds; he admitted in his letter that he was responding to accusations that he had been lax in failing to punish a priest who had committed adultery.[8] Moreover, as a bishop, Gelasius had no civic authority at the time to end the Lupercalia, a rite that probably continued despite his objections.[9]

The laws written by Christian emperors provided the legal basis for civic festivals that utilized temples. In 399, the emperors Arcadius and Honorius jointly issued a decree that ensured the distinction between profane rites and the approved "festal assemblies of citizens," since, as it stated, "according to ancient custom, amusements shall be furnished to the people, but without any sacrifice or any accursed superstition."[10] Late antique struggles over pagan topography exposed the fissures in religious epistemology; yet pagans and many Christians agreed upon the upkeep of the city's public festivals and the built heritage of Rome, which included temples.

The rites deemed vital to late antique Rome were those practiced outdoors for the benefit of the public. As popular practices, their true value for both participants and spectators went beyond providing entertainment: ancestral rituals had been passed down to protect crops, to ensure fertility, to guarantee health, and, most important, to commemorate nobles who supported such festivities as public games or the inaugural rites of the consulship.

The benefits of purification were ascribed to the Lupercalia, celebrated annually on February 15. In this rite, young aristocratic men wearing only the pelts of goats on their heads circumnavigated the Forum and the Palatine and traveled down the Via Sacra into the Forum.[11] In a gesture thought to ensure women's fertility, the nearly naked Lupercals running along the Via Sacra slapped aristocratic women using pieces of goatskin.[12] This practice supposedly purified the city and offered fecundity to its citizens. The rite was seriously contested only at the late date of 494 by Gelasius. In the pope's all-out attack upon the Lupercalia, as articulated in the letter to the senator Andromachus, Gelasius refuted beneficial claims advanced by the rite's sponsors: "Is it to chase away the plague? . . . Even before my reign . . . a terrible plague struck down men and flocks, both in the city and in the countryside."[13] Gelasius also rejected an assumption that the Lupercalia was able to protect the city from attack: "Were there not still the Lupercals when Alaric sacked the city? . . . Why did they not serve any good under these circumstances?"[14] But the real force of the pope's attack was focused on the traditional ritual spaces in the monumental center of the city where the lay members of Rome's nobility received public acclaim for providing pre-Christian ceremonies, since, in recognition of sponsoring the Lupercalia, Andromachus might have appeared enthroned on the Rostra in the Forum where his predecessors had once held commanding views.[15] In the late fifth century, the pope attempted to influence the city after the political breakdown of the Western empire left Rome's bishop with a greater standing in the civic sphere. In the end, however, the issue of who controlled the Roman Forum and its temples was left unsolved; it was plain to all that the temple buildings themselves deserved no harm.

Clearly, Gelasius was well informed about the purposes of the traditional Lupercalia ceremony. Earlier, the rites of the Dioscuri had focused attention on the Temple of Castor and Pollux.[16] The continuation of traditional outdoor rites into the fifth century pre-

supposes that the sacrificial components had already been removed. Attractive features of traditional civic celebrations, such as feasting, seem to have sparked popular participation. In Antioch, Libanius' *Orations* record an interesting speech from the 380s in which he argued that traditional festivities featuring convivial banquets with a slaughtered animal were to be enjoyed legally and really did no harm whatsoever, since no bull was sacrificed. He claimed that the butchered beef could be the centerpiece of a lawful and fun gathering of people "for a banquet, and a meal, and a feast." Libanius asserted that "no altar received the blood, no part was burned, no offering of meal preceded, nor libations followed."[17] Libanius' comments give the impression that in Antioch, altering traditional rites was a significant development, but one that hoped to guarantee the continuity of ancestral practices with only the slightest nod to avoiding sacrifice. In Rome, the popular appeal of the old civic festivals, which probably differed from those in Antioch, guaranteed their survival. Finally, prior to Gelasius' papacy, bishops had little power to curtail traditional celebrations in the open-air precincts of Rome that persistently protected fertility, health, and the food supply.

THE LEGAL STATUS OF PAGANISM

After Constantine severed the bond between the state and its official cults that for centuries had flourished at the temples in the Roman Forum, Rome physically "moved away from its home base," as Jerome, writing in Jerusalem around 403, commented about the lapse in attention paid to the Capitoline Hill.[18] Constantine set the stage for late antique laws by forming a distinction between hidden acts, which he disavowed, and public celebrations, which appeared less tainted. The Theodosian Code indicates wavering imperial positions on juristic matters concerning traditional cults. Weak enforcement resulted from the inherent contradictions among the policies.[19] Making accommodations in 319 for citizens who wished to uphold the rites of their ancestors, Constantine issued a legal provision directing people to "go to the public altars and shrines and celebrate the rites of your custom; for we do not prohibit the ceremonies of a bygone perversion to be conducted openly."[20] Later, Constantine's sons, Constantius II (337–361) and Constans (337–350), issued legislation that curtailed pagan sacrifice. For example, one legal restriction imposed in 341 ordered that the "madness of sacrifice will be abolished."[21] A year later, a legal code sanctioned outdoor rituals to reverse the neglect of traditional shrines. The law, issued by Constantius II in 342 CE and sent to a praetorian prefect of the West, safeguarded extramural temples, which were deemed to be integral to maintaining ancient public spectacles:

Although all forms of superstition must be completely eradicated, nevertheless it is our will that the temples situated outside the walls shall remain untouched. For since certain plays or spectacles of the circus or contests derive their origin from some of these temples, such structures shall not be torn down, since from them is provided the regular performance of long-established amusements for the Roman people.[22]

Given the official caveat articulated by the emperor granting tolerance of some shrines in the West, it is little wonder that the attempts to ban pagan sacrifice issued in 341 by Constans, the brother of Constantius II, went mostly unheeded.[23] Further attempts by Constantius II to abolish sacrifice were also ineffective in the West, perhaps because he continued the ancestral tradition of being Rome's chief priest (*pontifex maximus*).

Fourth-century pagans sought to retain publicly celebrated civic rites. Privately conducted or illicit sacrifices, by contrast, received particular condemnation during the reign of Constantine. Nocturnal and secretive sacrifices were abhorrent because they were tainted with superstition. Restrictions on entering temples—which did not preclude outdoor festivities—were rigorously pursued in the Western empire starting in the second half of the fourth century. For example, Constantius II sent a legal decree to the West around 355 stating, "It is our pleasure that the temples shall be immediately closed in all places and in all cities, and access to them forbidden."[24] This decree contradicted other legislation securing the preservation of temples, however, leading to speculation that Con-

stantius II had not actually formed a coherent policy on the cultic shrines.[25] Meanwhile, there were prestigious Roman aristocrats who wished to retain some of the traditional rites. As a result, preventing entry into the buildings and curtailing the veneration of cult statues did not restrict the nonsacrificial events, such as feasting, that occurred outdoors.

The reign of Valentinian I (364–375) marked a period that recognized the authority of the past. During this time, officials legislated the preservation of unused public buildings so that imperial bureaucrats could accrue the political benefits. In 364, Valentinian I, together with his co-ruler and brother Valens, made the imperial position clear to the urban prefect of Rome: "Public officials shall not construct any new buildings in the eternal city of Rome. . . . However, we grant permission to all to restore the buildings that are said to have fallen into unsightly ruins."[26] Implicitly, the status of temples as public buildings guaranteed their survival.

Despite protective legislation in the Theodosian Code for all public structures, the financing and endowments of temples were threatened during the second half of the fourth century.[27] State subsidies for temples were first diminished under Constantius II; despite being temporarily reinstated by Julian prior to 363, they were further curtailed during the Valentinian dynasty.[28] Ambrose, writing in 392 as bishop of Milan, objected to those senators in Rome who used their influence to request the state financing of cults.[29] Alan Cameron pointed out that the issue at stake was not the scarcity of funds, but rather the desire by traditionalists to provide rites for the general populace: such rites benefited the population as a whole only when they proceeded with public funds.[30] To protect Rome from Alaric in 408, as Zosimus recounts, an Etruscan soothsayer had recommended an act that could only be done properly "if it was performed at public expense, with the senate going up to the Capitol and performing the appropriate ceremonies both there and in the fora of the city."[31] Private financing, by contrast, brought benefits only to the supporters themselves.

It may have been concern over public rites that applied to all residents of a city that motivated the emperor Gratian in 382 to begin questioning the right of temples to maintain endowments and valuable donations.[32] Rita Lizzi Testa has demonstrated that Gratian attempted but did not fully implement a policy that deprived temples of all endowments in 382. The definitive confiscation of temple endowments, she shows, did not occur until 415.[33]

The bishop Ambrose was the most strident voice opposing non-Christian practices. Ambrose wrote a letter to Theodosius I in 388, prior to the decisive anti-pagan legislation of 391, defending Christian mobs who had torn down synagogues in Rome and Callinicum, a city in Syria. The purpose of Ambrose's letter was to persuade the emperor to omit the requirement that bishops rebuild the damaged structures. Ambrose felt that restoring a place Christians deemed worthy of destruction would render it abhorrent, as if "remade from spoils," a lasting emblem of faithlessness.[34] Ambrose's letter celebrating the mobs who attacked synagogues nodded toward the lasting memories that buildings could retain when preserved. Interestingly, the temples of the Forum received substantial repairs during the late fourth century, possibly after 382, in a clear indication that donations continued and that the endowments had not yet been completely taken away.

Some notable Romans continued to seek appointments to *pontifices*, priestly offices of the traditional rites. Vettius Agorius Praetextatus, one of the most illustrious and wealthy residents of Rome to hold numerous traditional priesthoods during the fourth century, was widely respected for the many additional administrative offices that he held, providing his consistent support to the state. Praetextatus' reputation for selfless public service may have derived primarily from his priesthoods; his widow, Fabia Aconia Paulina, composed verses for Praetextatus' funerary monument, set up in 384 near their home, that placed his priestly positions in the context of his disdain for mere status: "Why speak of your honorific offices and the joys others seek in making official requests, which you have always called fleeting and insignificant, well known as you are for wearing the headbands of a priest serving the gods?"[35] Paulina praised Praetextatus' dedication to pursuing lasting rewards, a value that the inscription connected with long-standing religious traditions rather than with

status-driven administrative service. During the fourth century, some powerful senators expressed a desire to see certain ancestral practices continue as a venerable path through which to reconnect with persistent, universal concerns; in short, the traditionalists recast the cults to preserve the nonsacrificial rituals. Despite Praetextatus' apparent abhorrence for the crass pursuit of power, even as he achieved great honor in prestigious positions, his work as a practitioner of certain cultic acts supported a claim to uphold lasting values.

Theodosius I sent a complete ban on sacrifice to the West in 391 and distributed more extensive prohibitions outlawing all forms of cultic offerings to the entire empire in 392.[36] The decisive and strict measures against sacrifice included further provisions against entering temples: "No person shall approach the shrines, shall wander through the temples, or revere the images formed by mortal labor."[37] Clearly, the major restorations of temples ceased thereafter, but Theodosius I never advocated the outright destruction of the buildings.

Before sacrifice was completely banned, temples presented a dilemma to fourth-century civic and imperial officials who maintained all public buildings. Temples in need of repairs presented the greatest challenge of all, since these unstable structures had to serve a useful purpose to warrant conservation. Evidence that civic festivals persisted in Rome, together with the imperial dictates encouraging the repair of public structures after 364, suggest that there was a window of opportunity prior to 391 when elites who practiced ancestral cults were able to maintain the temple structures. One member of this class, Q. Aurelius Symmachus, made a proposal concerning outdoor rites in a letter he sent to his friend Praetextatus in 381:

It has been agreed upon by the public priests that we should entrust attending to the gods to the supervision of the citizens with public ceremony. For the benevolence of the higher power, unless it is cared for with cult, is lost. Thus, with much more splendor than is customary, honor is due to the celestials.[38]

Though Symmachus specifically described the fes-

THE RESTORATION OF THE ROMAN FORUM IN LATE ANTIQUITY

tivities for the people that rendered proper respect to ancestral deities, implicitly the civic rites
he embraced required public architecture. In view
of Symmachus' comments, it could be argued that
late antique temples honoring the gods properly accommodated civic ceremonies for the populace and,
given the problems with entering temples, were remade to encourage outdoor rites.

THE SENATORIAL RESTORATION OF THE PORTICUS DEORUM CONSENTIUM

In 367, Valentinian I appointed Praetextatus to the
urban prefecture of Rome, creating a leadership
role within the senate for one of the most learned
advocates of ancestral customs. Holding an official
post in the imperial administration of Rome offered
Praetextatus the chance to establish a revised format
for temples under a legitimate mandate. During his
year in office, the urban prefect restored the Porticus
Deorum Consentium, which was located at the far
southwest corner of the Roman Forum, nestled into
the slope of the Capitoline Hill (fig. 5.1). The temple
adjoins both the steep cliffs of the Capitol and the
Clivus Capitolinus, along which the triumphal processions had marched prior to the age of Constantine
(see fig. I.8 [14] and [16]). Praetextatus' reconstruction established the last securely dated pagan temple
in Rome for which both archeological and epigraphic testimony survives (fig. 5.2). The current architectural arrangement is hypothetical, since the site
was excavated hastily in the 1830s, rebuilt equally
rapidly in the 1850s, and extensively refurbished in
1942 to make a building whose two colonnades meet
at an obtuse angle, framing a trapezoidal platform.[39]
The format of the Porticus Deorum Consentium
features two adjoined porticoes furnishing access

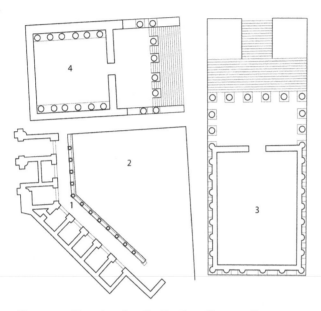

Figure 5.1. Plan showing the Porticus Deorum Consentium, the Temple of Saturn, and the Temple of Vespasian.
Drawing by Brian Doherty.

Figure 5.2. The Porticus Deorum Consentium, as seen from the Palatine Hill. Photo by the author.

Figure 5.3. The Porticus Deorum Consentium, as seen from the Clivus Capitolinus. Photo by the author.

to an outdoor platform framed by colonnades. This arrangement addressed the Clivus Capitolinus in order to frame views experienced by those ascending the Capitol along this path for important civic ceremonies.

What survives from the Porticus offers an approximation of what the author Varro described as a shrine of the "consenting gods." During the first century BCE, Varro made passing reference to "those gods in this city whose gilded images stand in the Forum, six of them male and an equal number female."[40] The building as currently reconstructed features seven chambers arranged on a lower level beneath the trapezoidal podium; these rooms face the late first-century construction of the Temple of Vespasian directly to the north (fig. 5.3). This direct alignment with the adjacent structure provides evidence that the below-grade chambers were part of an intervention in the first century CE. At the upper level, eight chambers arranged behind the two colonnades are separated

from the trapezoidal platform by the porticoes. There is no archeological certainty concerning how many chambers there were originally, since their current number might be the result of the hastily performed nineteenth-century reconstruction.[41] It is curious that gilded statues of the twelve Olympian deities, each of which presumably once resided in an individual cult room, do not correspond with the fifteen extant chambers; but there may have been only twelve chambers in the fourth century. The trapezoidal platform was paved with marble slabs; a few of the original paving stones survive.

The Porticus Deorum Consentium restored by Praetextatus explicitly expressed restitution chiefly by reusing preexisting architectural fragments (see fig. 5.2). This link to the past established the building's historical legitimacy, even though Praetextatus may very well have altered the original sanctuary. Seven of the columns from the fourth-century colonnades were discovered at the site; these are made of fluted *cipollino*

Figure 5.4. Entablature of the Porticus Deorum Consentium showing the inscription of Vettius Agorius Praetextatus (*CIL* 6.102). Photo by the author.

verde, or green marble.[42] The columns are capped by two different series of capitals from the Hadrianic period with trophy motifs; five of the columns currently visible are modern replacements.[43] The purposefully mismatched columns and capitals were assembled as a textured display of *spolia* from a wide array of buildings, since Praetextatus obtained the fragments from many structures and did not reuse columns only from the previous portico.

Assembling mismatched fragments as *spolia* in the fourth-century reconstruction of the portico marked both the alteration of past norms and the partial rejection of novelty, calling attention to the temporal connotations of the building materials. Praetextatus clearly identified this as a restored structure by reusing precious architectural elements. The explicitly excerpted fragments indicate that Praetextatus revised temple architecture, its formats, and its meanings. By gesturing toward the past through the *spolia*, the building employs the antiquity of building materials to map out a trajectory of time rooted in

tradition. As a result, the architecture of the portico adapted *spolia* as fragmented and changing materials that were resilient despite the impending threat of ruin. From a traditionalist point of view, the civic spot had been consecrated by the gods; their statues embodied their immanent presence. The portico therefore advanced the cult, through which the twelve deities once again earned popular support.

Because it was illegal to enter temples, Praetextatus, referencing the statues in an inscription facing the trapezoidal platform, provided outdoor exhibition spots for them. Out of an urgent need to rethink paganism, he thereby changed the format for presenting cultic statuary. Yet his primary concern was to officially restore a properly constituted temple. Praetextatus renewed the pagan sanctuary not as a polemicist, but as a high-ranking administrator of the state making a civic donation. As urban prefect and the holder of numerous pagan priesthoods, Praetextatus fulfilled a traditional role in emphasizing the renewal of cult as a civic responsibility.

The portico's inscription stresses the official patronage that respected the commitment of all twelve deities to the specific topography as well as the cult rituals by which humans acknowledged the localized attachments made by the gods.[44] The inscription (fig. 5.4) reads: "Praetextatus, of the highest senatorial rank and urban prefect, restored the inviolable (*sacrosancta*) statues of the consenting gods and every adornment on behalf of the cult in its ancient form at this place; with Longeius serving as curator."[45] With the documentation of sponsorship by Praetextatus, the inscription clearly indicates that the restoration was an official act, presumably sanctioned by the senate with imperial ratification of the project. Longeius, whose involvement also indicates senatorial participation, probably served as the curator of statues, an office serving under the urban prefect.[46] The duties of this position earlier had entailed maintaining the city's honorific statues displayed in public space; these were now extended to include cultic objects.

The prominent references to the statues and their official dedication by Praetextatus with the help of Longeius suggest that the statues were erected in public space. The epigraphic text establishes this by listing the official positions of the urban prefect and the curator of statues. In addition, the inscribed architrave faced the platform, indicating that the statues could be viewed from there. Thus, by sponsoring the Porticus Deorum Consentium with senatorial permission—and probably receiving imperial agreement as well—Praetextatus provided legitimacy for the maintenance of a temple and its statues.

To reorient the cult, Praetextatus brought the statues out of the interior chambers, liberating them from those tainted locations, which were condemned for having fostered illicit, hidden practices. The statues themselves do not survive. The term characterizing the statues in the inscription, *sacrosancta*, has elicited the observation that the figures were considered "inviolable"; this unprecedented use of *sacrosancta* for statues of divinities suggests that Praetextatus was seeking to establish them as long-lasting.[47] As noted above, fourth-century legal restrictions issued prior to 391 curtailed hidden practices, including nocturnal sacrifices, superstitious divination, and soothsaying, as abhorrent rites. By contrast, the outdoor

installations of cult implements aired them publicly, as if they made the city proud. A digital reconstruction of Praetextatus' portico illustrating a plausible but certainly hypothetical installation of statues suggests that the cult images were located in front of the columns (fig. 5.5). If configured before the colonnades, the images of the twelve Olympian deities would have given an impression of visual unity that emphasized their conceptual cohesion. During the very period in which Christian leaders were trying to prevent people from entering temples, the open-air installation at a temple transformed the traditional deities into publicly accessible and appreciated figures whose statues commemorated the past.

The official reinstatement of the statues by Praetextatus as specified in the inscription advanced the cult. The inscribed architrave further refers to the location where the statues were brought back.[48] Thus, Praetextatus officially activated a place that was designated for the deities. In legislation issued by Ulpian during the third century CE, the method of establishing holy locations was explained: "A sacred place is a place that has been consecrated publicly."[49] Praetextatus abandoned the cultic worship of idols on the interior of shrines and perhaps even neglected sacrificial rites; yet he maintained public festivals and retained the meaning of a consecrated precinct. The specific public cult activities designated for the fourth-century Porticus Deorum Consentium remain unclear. Documentation of the rite called the *lectisternium*, attested during the reign of Marcus Aurelius and presumably continuing thereafter, recounts a dining festivity that commemorated the

Figure 5.5. Digital reconstruction of the Porticus Deorum Consentium showing the late antique installation of statues in front of the colonnades. Experiential Technologies Center, UCLA. © Regents, University of California.

twelve deities by having wicker images of their heads arranged in pairs on couches.[50] There is no record of a fourth-century instance in which Romans staged the ceremonial feast called the *lectisternium*. Nonetheless, Praetextatus may have repaired the Porticus Deorum Consentium for a dining festivity such as this, particularly if it was practiced outdoors.

It should be mentioned that the *Poem against the Pagans* (*Carmen contra paganos*), anonymous verses written in opposition to an unidentified traditionalist, attested to bringing back cult implements to temples. Alan Cameron has proposed that the unspecified pagan in the poem is Praetextatus, and he dates the composition of the verses to shortly after the death of the urban prefect in 384.[51] If this is the case, then these hexameters, which also weigh in against Q. Aurelius Symmachus, who restored the Temple of Flora on the Aventine, imply a link between Praetextatus' rehabilitation of cult objects and the allied revival of temple implements at other sites in Rome.[52]

From a vantage point along the Clivus Capitolinus, facing south while ascending the Capitoline Hill, the Porticus Deorum Consentium seemed to provide a foundation beneath the Temple of Jupiter Optimus Maximus, which loomed above it at the top of the hill. Jupiter's cult precinct had been the center of religious life and the site of culminating sacrifices in triumph processions before the age of Constantine. The most logical arrangement of the statues at the Porticus would have featured Jupiter at the center—namely, where the two colonnades meet, and therefore visible from the Clivus Capitolinus as if directly below the Jupiter temple.[53] There is an indication that Praetextatus even staged a ritual march up the Capitoline Hill, together with a representative group of senators. This procession is mentioned only in a hostile account by Jerome, who reported a public performance by an unspecified "consul-elect." This seems to allude to Praetextatus, who passed away before serving as a consul, a post to which he had already been appointed prior to his death. Jerome did not mention any sacrifices, but nonetheless took offense in his report, stating: "Several days ago all of the city's high-ranking dignitaries processed before him [the consul-elect] as he ascended through the gates of the Capitol like a commander conducting

the triumph."[54] Jerome's account is neither favorable nor completely reliable; yet the senatorial restoration of a temple along the ancient triumphal route for generals does provide the basis for speculating that Praetextatus brought back civic ceremonies that paraded up the Capitoline Hill and passed by the restored Porticus Deorum Consentium. Jerome's complaint may have been prompted by Praetextatus' ability to gain popular support and perform festivities that guaranteed his mass appeal—much like Gelasius' complaints about Andromachus—even if there is no certainty that a triumph ascended the Capitol in the 380s.

For Praetextatus, the concept of restoration was closely connected with his concern for bestowing the cult of the twelve gods upon future generations. Given that Praetextatus' wife disavowed his interest in prestige, the pursuit of status might not have motivated him to recuperate the physical components of the past at the Porticus Deorum Consentium. Instead, Praetextatus plausibly displayed his extensive learning at the portico. The *spolia* in the colonnade and the repositioned statues were presented as if partly tainted, suggesting by means of the fragmented recomposition that ritual practices and antiquarian erudition formed a critical link to the past and contributed to the physical upkeep of the shrine. Praetextatus also worked to maintain a commemoration at the meaningful place along the Clivus Capitolinus where he sustained the topographically rooted cults of the twelve deities and retained the visibility of the statues that retained memories of the deities. Hinting at decomposition as the precedent for restoration in the architecture demonstrated that memory practices, including selective decomposition, regulated the legacy of the twelve gods.

THE TEMPLE OF SATURN AND THE RESTORATION OF THE PAST

The Temple of Saturn, which stands directly across the Clivus Capitolinus from the Porticus Deorum Consentium, provides evident traces of physical renewal (fig. 5.6). This temple, located at the far western end of the Forum, features eight surviving granite columns that still support an entablature inscribed with a record of the restoration: "The Senate and the People of Rome restored [the building] that was consumed by a fire."[55] Six of the eight granite monoliths of the colonnade are grey, flanked on either side by pink granite columns. The heterogeneity of the materials reinforces the expression of recomposition, which is most evident in the clear signs of reuse; the pink column on the eastern edge, for example, is inserted upside down. Although at least three of the granite columns were taken from other colonnades, their arrangement was not haphazard.[56] The weight of the monoliths and the difficulty of setting them up suggest that purposeful decisions preceded the construction of the colonnade. Further, the senatorial body did not economize by reusing granite columns, since the cost of transporting the monoliths and raising them into place would have been astronomical.

The discordant and fragmented colonnade, which features fourth-century Ionic capitals and reused, ill-fitting bases, adds to the impression that the senators installed *spolia* purposefully.[57] Reconstruction of the entire temple occurred during the second half of the fourth century, as Patrizio Pensabene has documented by analyzing the brickwork facing the cement podium and by identifying the Ionic capitals as carved during late antiquity.[58] It remains uncertain which fire caused the damage noted in the inscription, but the occasion to rebuild provided an opportunity in late antiquity that highlighted evident markers of time's passage in the reuse of fragmented *spolia*. Linking material signs of recuperation with the clear discordance among the architectural fragments suggest a tension between decay and restitution. The Temple of Saturn raises concerns, to be addressed below, about recomposing the physical manifestations of the past and how the reconfigured parts can be explained given their fragmented appearance.

The Temple of Saturn's colonnade features columns of inconsistent heights, which support the entablature held by column bases of varying sizes, resulting in a visual expression of restitution. The passage of time, documented by the diversity of materials in the Temple of Saturn, is further accentuated by the inconsistent sizes of the standard architectural elements, in violation of classical rules. Juxtaposed

Figure 5.6. Temple of Saturn. Photo by the author.

to the reused columns are the fourth-century Ionic capitals, perhaps the only components now visible that were newly created during the restoration.[59] Even the inscribed architrave was reused, since the inscribed face is the reverse of the carved side that had been flipped (fig. 5.7). Just as the colonnade combined grey and pink granite monoliths, only two of the bases are of white marble; the remaining six are grey (see fig. 5.6). The evident disregard for the Vitruvian principles of unity and harmony in the temple provided a means of encouraging the veneration of the past in a partly ruined state, achieved by using nonstandard parts and *spolia*. The diverse components of the building appear to be either unfinished or partly diminished so that the assembled elements, while pointing toward the past, anticipate the future. The Temple of Saturn was in part restored to provide lasting civic decoration, allowing for a reconsideration of pagan architecture as implicitly worthy of survival and presenting the fragments as having already endured over the ages. Composed of fragmented elements, the temple presented itself as an "ornament of the city," the term used in imperial laws for repositioned structural components. As cultural property, the spoliate colonnade at the Temple of Saturn linked the legally sanctioned reuse of materials with provisions for situating these materials prominently in public space. Allegedly, no harm was

Figure 5.7. Temple of Saturn, view from the Capitoline Hill. Photo by the author.

done to earlier structures to acquire the reused materials, so the process of recomposition was pursued appropriately.

The Temple of Saturn's height and position gave it imposing prominence in the Forum, particularly given the elevation of the structure above the tall podium (see fig. 5.7). The temple continued to function as the treasury (*aerarium*) into the imperial period, when the storage capabilities of the massive podium were put to use.[60] There is no clear proof that the state treasures continued to be stored in the Temple of Saturn during late antiquity. Nonetheless, the memory of state holdings under senatorial control once having been maintained within the temple gave the late antique structure significance as the emblem of cultural property belonging to the state.

The fourth-century Temple of Saturn honors previous versions of the building that existed at the site. An account written in the fifth century attests that the structure traced its origins back to Tarquin the Proud as early as the sixth century BCE.[61] An important restoration under L. Munatius Plancus is documented in 42 BCE.[62] Neither manifestation gains specific physical expression in the late antique version of the Temple of Saturn; rather, a picture of the struggle to achieve renewal is established. Thus the

spolia at the Temple of Saturn recall the past without specificity and present fragmentation in order to anticipate the future.

One manner of considering historical responses to the late antique Temple of Saturn is to examine the structure's role in Macrobius' *Saturnalia*, a fictional account written at least fifty years after the Forum structure was refurbished. A key issue for Macrobius with respect to the late antique Temple of Saturn concerns the concept of time that is intrinsic to the deity Saturn, also identified as Kronos.[63] Macrobius' text, written in the 430s, discusses rites celebrating Saturn and imagines the long conversations held by historical individuals celebrating the deity during the feast of the Saturnalia. The scene is set in the 380s, when the key characters—prominent pagans— were living, including Nicomachus Flavianus the Elder, Q. Aurelius Symmachus, and Praetextatus.[64]

The Temple of Saturn is discussed as a treasury with its sculptural decorations, but Macrobius omits references to the restoration of the architecture. In the course of analyzing the intricacies of traditional rites, Macrobius recounts discussions about the now-lost pediment at the Temple of Saturn, which featured a statue of Tritons playing trumpets:

That's because from the time of the god's commemoration down to our own day history shines bright and all but speaks, whereas it was previously mute, shrouded in darkness, unknown—as is indicated by the Triton's tails, which are buried beneath the surface and hidden away.[65]

In the learned discussions in which Macrobius describes sculptures, the pediment featuring Tritons is an emblem of the newly reconfigured and recently revealed past. History, then, emphasizes with clarity that which has survived, since those topics that were formerly hidden in the shadows ultimately gain in lucidity. Macrobius characterizes the distant past as having caused things to be obscured and silenced. With this line of argumentation, Macrobius does not simply glorify the past; rather, he is critical of the lapsed ages that had imposed silence. Finally, Macrobius implies, by using the metaphor of shedding light on a topic, that preservation of the old will allow the once-shrouded materials eventually to see the light of day.

The *Saturnalia* also describes the main statue of Saturn on the interior of the temple. The statue's feet were said to have been wrapped in woolen bindings. Macrobius had one of the participants in the learned discussions explain the woolen tethers: "Saturn is bound throughout the year with a woolen bond and is released on the day of his festival, that is, in the month of December."[66] The Saturnalia was celebrated in December, at which point "the seed in the womb, which is held by the delicate bonds of nature until it emerges into the light, quickens and grows."[67] As in the discussion of the pediment, Macrobius deployed the metaphor of light to formulate a contrast with the veil of darkness that the past seems to have imposed. Macrobius' fifth-century text admitted the futility of turning back time, running counter to the concept of a Golden Age under Saturn as a time of perfection that could be fully restored. Macrobius further indicated that shedding light on the past and rejecting darkness would anticipate improvements by increasing the degree of clarity. Also, Macrobius countered the idea that the past can remain intact, since he described the potential for time to generate change when he recounted the legend that Saturn was driven out by his own son: "What does that mean but that as times grow old they are pushed aside by those that come next?"[68] The discussion then returned to the woolen foot bindings, mentioning that the tethers keep each moment connected to the next.

Macrobius' *Saturnalia*, it must be noted, concerns a series of discussions in which the characters display their erudition by remembering antiquarian details about Rome's oldest traditional practices during the feast season of Saturn. Although Macrobius' characters mostly recall lapsed rites, some celebrations must have continued into the fifth century and were apparently important to the preservation of the Temple of Saturn. The Saturnalia itself was celebrated during late antiquity and featured the reversal of social norms, including slaves taking the places of masters. Two late antique calendars mention the December festivities of the Saturnalia, but there is no certainty as to how the Temple of Saturn could have furthered these celebrations.[69] Certainly Macrobius' text documents fifth-century knowledge of the

events practiced during the Saturnalia, including the dining festivities that are described as taking place in senators' homes. By maintaining popular practices in the open and without any taint of illicit activities, a temple could uphold traditional festivities as civic practices in the Forum.

Macrobius offered a set of terms with which to consider the physical structure of the Temple of Saturn. He described how the oldest things had to struggle against the forces that could have diminished them. In doing so, he depicted the surviving parts as optimally equipped to provide clarity, and he used tropes about light to demonstrate that persistence allowed things to shine brightly. Macrobius' line of argumentation, both fictional and dissociated from the physical restoration of the Temple of Saturn, does suggest that recovery, when pursued to acknowledge destructive processes such as ruination, can embolden the fight against loss. Macrobius affirmed the utility of displaying explicitly old antiquities, valorized by having survived the test of time. The relevance of Macrobius to the late antique Temple of Saturn pertains to explaining a reformulated temple that was not brought back to a historic target date, but was presented as a signpost of varied ages to reveal all that appeared to be nobly persistent.

Other instances of rebuilding can be attributed to the fourth century, when damage to the Temple of Castor and Pollux from the fire of Carinus led to the insertion of a staircase on the northern front, projecting before the former tribunal (see fig. I.8 [18]).[70] Somewhat later in the fourth century, the unstable podium at the Temple of Castor and Pollux was repaired to bolster the structure.[71] The entablature of the Temple of Concord at the far western end of the Forum also attested to a senatorial restoration after an unspecified tragedy. The inscription for the Temple of Concord, which recorded that the senate had restored the temple (*restituit*), had been maintained on the façade throughout late antiquity, since the text was recorded in the eighth century by the Einsiedeln pilgrim.[72] Evidence suggests that the Temple of Concord and the Temple of Castor and Pollux might have been repaired for practical reasons; the renovations lack signs that they were undertaken in order to revise the temples' formats, as had been so explicitly done in Praetextatus' reconfiguration of the Porticus Deorum Consentium. Nonetheless, the fourth century witnessed a vast program of rebuilding the Forum's temples.

REHABILITATING THE TEMPLE OF VESTA

It is clear that temples survived intact and were even restored, despite the termination of sacrifice. What concepts, then, allowed Christians to both absorb and rethink the architectural legacy of temples, including the legendary testimony to Rome's foundation? Christian fictional narratives from the fourth and fifth centuries describe the bishop of Rome effectively preserving some of the monuments in the Forum, from a perspective vastly different from the senatorial repairs. The Christian accounts identify potential dangers lurking near the temples without advocating any physical harm whatsoever to the structures. One

legend concerning Pope Silvester placed the bishop's activities during the reign of Constantine close to the Temple of Vesta, where the ancient cult of the perpetual flame and the hidden implements buried underground played important roles (fig. 5.8). There is evidence from the fictional texts that Christians used accounts of architecture to elicit memories embedded in the topography of the Roman Forum; yet the narratives suggest that these memories were used to portray Christianity as having emerged to operate legitimately, as traditional rites were relegated to the dark recesses of the Forum.

The legislation issued by the emperor Theodosius I in 391 extinguished the supposedly eternal flame of Vesta within that deity's temple and thereby obliterated the protection that traditionalists believed the goddess had provided at the hearth. As mentioned earlier, the subterranean chamber of this temple housed objects of the most sacred character, including the statue linked to Rome's foundation, the Palladium. Aeneas was said to have carried the Palladium out of Troy, and it was saved by Lucius Caecilius Metellus from a fire at the Temple of Vesta in 241 BCE.[73] In the last decade of the fourth century, Prudentius wrote a poem with an anti-pagan bent disputing the belief that the Palladium, together with the cult of Vesta, had once protected Rome and its environs from crop failure.

Figure 5.8. Temple of Vesta. Photo by the author.

The land was prone to failures such as these
Ere the Palladium and Vesta saved
The household gods of Troy with hidden fire.[74]

Although the flame had been extinguished at Vesta's temple, Prudentius stated that the protection offered by the Palladium there apparently survived, while other legends revealed how the cult statue had been moved to Constantinople.

In Rome, legends attached to the Temple of Vesta appear in a text that recounts the confrontation between Pope Silvester, Constantine, and a demonic dragon (see fig. 5.8). The text, *Vita seu Actus Silvestri papae et confessoris (Actus Silvestri)*, was widely disseminated: there were nearly 300 Latin variants. The earliest Latin version specifies that the dragon resided at the Temple of Vesta, with subsequent accounts relocating the lair to the cliffs of the Capitoline Hill.[75] In the oldest and longest version of the text, the survival of a temple in the Forum takes on a prominent role. Vestal Virgins are described as providing food to the dragon "at the Temple of Vesta on the first day of every month" in order to prevent its pestilent fury.[76] This topographical marker correlates with an inscription found in the Forum that yields further insights into the dragon. Two fragments originating from one inscribed block were found in two spots: one near the Temple of Vesta, the other close to the Basilica Aemilia.[77] Jaakko Aronen has proposed that the inscription, which includes the term dracen[a], refers to a Dionysian cult.[78] As the inscription plausibly dates to the third century CE, it records a myth concerning the dragon and documents a late antique melding of various cults in the Forum.[79] This site specificity seems to indicate that the anonymous author of the earliest version of the Actus Silvestri had extensive knowledge of Rome's topography.[80] Textual analysis of the Actus Silvestri has positioned the text's composition in the late fourth or early fifth century at the earliest.[81]

In the account, a dragon was threatening Romans and exhaling pestilent fumes from its lair under the Temple of Vesta, the very chasm in which the Palladium had probably been stored. To ward off the dragon's vengeful attacks from below the temple and keep it at bay, the Vestal Virgins made monthly offerings of wheatcakes to it.[82] The emperor Constantine was on the verge of reauthorizing the Vestals' sacrifices to the dragon when, according to the Actus Silvestri, St. Peter appeared to Pope Silvester in a dream and told the bishop to close up the lair and bind the dragon with rope.[83] The pope approached the emperor with this mode of suppressing the dragon and further asserted to an urban prefect named Calpurnius that subduing the dragon would prevent the beast from attacking.[84] The legend reports that the pope descended into the dragon's lair to lock up the creature behind a closed door that could not be opened until Judgment Day.[85]

By furnishing an alternative to pagan sacrifice, Silvester appears to have prevented pestilence after eliminating the cult. Yet the Vestals had also successfully negated the threat of the dragon when they,

according to the Silvester text, made food offerings that kept the beast in its lair, preventing it from killing hundreds each day. Implicitly, the forced enclosure of the dragon caused a cessation in the sacrifices that the Vestal Virgins had offered, as there was no longer any need for them. Silvester, then, established the authoritative role of the bishop in the Roman Forum by quelling the dragon and thus eliminating its threats, such as plagues. In the Silvester text, controlling viewers' responses to antiquities subtly adjusted the temples and allowed them to remain intact. In the darkest recesses of the extant remains of Vesta's temple, the dragon was completely buried—or so says the text. Thus, the legend affirmed that the bishop, acting in coalition with the emperor, both preserved Roman architecture and eliminated any threats it may have contained.

If the Actus Silvestri offers an insightful guide to the topography of the Roman Forum, a perspective that requires a suspension of belief given its colorful details, then the dragon's lair was the former site of the Palladium. According to the Byzantine narratives about the foundation rite of Constantinople, Constantine removed the Palladium from its residence in Rome in order to hide it underneath the porphyry column at the center of a forum in Constantinople. This legend of the Palladium, a hidden talisman concealed first in Rome and then in its new home in Constantinople, is clearly at odds with the evidence of the cult statues at the Porticus Deorum Consentium, which Praetextatus moved outdoors, into the light of day. In the legends of Constantinople's foundation and the Actus Silvestri, the narrative accounts preserve both the talisman and the Temple of Vesta because they facilitate the transference of power either from the emperor to the pope or from Rome to Constantinople. The Temple of Vesta, a dominion of the aristocratic Vestals that the Actus Silvestri also links with the senatorial power of the fictional urban prefect Calpurnius, came to be controlled by the bishop. This temple survived in part due to its former role as the protective hearth for the city of Rome, and its preservation, according to the legend, allowed Silvester and successive generations of bishops to demonstrate their care for the populace at this location. In a parallel manner, the Palladium as a protective statue shifted its beneficial powers to Constantinople.

Silvester locked up the dragon in its cave until the end of time. With this narrative detail, the persistent architecture of the temples was hardly compromised by the bishop who contained the dragon. The narrated dispute between the pope and the Vestals seems to paint the Roman Forum as a site of contention. Yet the preservation of temples indicates the degree to which there was agreement on the architectural integrity of downtown Rome and on the importance of guaranteeing the persistence of Rome's built heritage. In fact, bishops sought the elimination only of altars and sacrifices while maintaining temple structures; at least, the legendary Silvester was careful not to disturb the Temple of Vesta. The subtlety of the *Actus Silvestri* narrative lies in using the dragon's imprisonment as a metaphor for the elimination of cult. Once the sacrificial practices were eliminated and the temples were dissociated from pagan altars, the bishops' concerns receded, and Roman civic religion provided topographical markers for urban life that were sustained throughout late antiquity.

All of the late antique transformations of the temples in the Roman Forum minimized the secrecy of harmful, illicit, or outmoded practices. Exposing the explicitly ancient and heterogeneous columns at the Temple of Saturn and the Porticus Deorum Consentium addressed the outdoor spaces where legal ceremonies were practiced. The very different rites practiced by Pope Silvester in the legend also eliminated the threats from a dark chasm where the dragon resided. The accounts of both fourth-century senators and Christian fictions demonstrate the importance of preserving temples for future generations so that space of the Roman Forum could be used to gain public support.

CHAPTER 6

ROME'S SENATORIAL COMPLEX AND THE LATE ANTIQUE TRANSFORMATION OF THE ELITE

THE SENATE HOUSE (CURIA SENATUS) SYMBOLIZED THE POWER OF ROME'S ARISTOCRACY during late antiquity. The rebuilt Curia, completed around 300 CE, loomed large as the architectural expression of senatorial traditions with ample space to foster cohesion among the members of Rome's elite (fig. 6.1). Prior to the nineteenth-century rediscovery of the Curia by Rodolfo Lanciani, the Senate House's ancient history had been subsumed by its subsequent identity as the church of Sant'Adriano, into which it had been transformed during the seventh century CE.[1] Fascist interventions in the 1930s jettisoned most of the Senate House's medieval transformations to reassert the historical Curia without any evidence that it had been repurposed as a church.[2] Unlike late antique restorers, who appreciated superimposed phases and produced architectural palimpsests, Fascist-era archeologists reversed the historical process to reinstate the late antique building at its moment of completion.

The theme of renewal witnessed at the Curia Senatus after the Tetrarchic rebuilding campaign of about 300 CE continued throughout the fourth and fifth centuries, as senators exerted control over how temporal messages were used and thereby worked to preserve aristocratic dominance at the senatorial complex. Debates sparked by the altar of Victory in the Senate House concerned the fissures dividing traditionalists from Christians among the elite. Despite their differences, both Christian aristocrats and those committed to ancestral practices agreed to uphold the historical significance of the senate as an institution. Later, the aristocrats continued seeking to influence public space, and they expressed this in the physical conservation of the Curia. Yet the efforts of the elite came to be contested in the hagiographic narratives of Sts. Peter and Martina, who separately encroached upon senatorial authority within the Roman Forum. Accounts of saints in the Forum indicate that Christians pondered the lack of visible signs marking the bishop's importance in this part of Rome given the wide array of monuments attesting to aristocratic benefactions and imperial rule.

This chapter presents the restoration projects that had been used to justify the prerogatives of the senatorial elite in the Roman Forum, where aristocrats linked their privileges with the

Figure 6.1. Senate House (Curia Senatus). Photo by the author.

institutional traditions of the senate. Yet the Christian narratives contested that history. Thus, the hagiographic texts hinted to audiences that those bishops who commemorated the saints offered a more favorable path to safeguard the city than the traditional munificence offered by emperors and senators.

RENEWED TIME IN THE CURIA SENATUS

After the fire of 284 CE, a new Curia Senatus was constructed by Diocletian and Maximian upon the foundations of the Curia Julia initiated by Julius Caesar and completed by Augustus. At a different location slightly to the southwest of Diocletian's structure, the older Republican Curia Hostilia once stood.[3] Thus, the Tetrarchs physically connected the Senate House to the previous Curia. As the anonymous author of the *Expositio totius mundi et gentium* states, Rome's

very grand senate possessed rich men, and if you wish to examine its members one by one, you will find that they are all high functionaries or they will be or they could have been; but they do not want it because they would rather protect their own resources in full tranquility.[4]

This picture of dignified leisure and the selfish retention of resources contrasts with the representations of the elite at the Senate House, which emphasized civic munificence and the protection that the aristocrats offered the populace. Reaffirming the senatorial traditions of the past, finally, was vital to the authority of the senate during late antiquity.

Yet the past became a hotly contested terrain after 357 CE, when the emperor Constantius II objected to and removed the altar of Victory from the Senate House. Even though the altar returned to the Curia briefly during the reign of Julian (361–363), the controversy over polytheistic rites flared up again and persisted into the 380s. The terms of the debate usually have been considered as marking a pagan-Christian divide; yet fighting over the traditional altar and its associated statue of Victory was also framed as a negotiation over how to preserve public space.

The removal of the altar of Victory prompted traditionalist senators to consider how best to repossess the past while they attempted in vain to avoid offending Christian senators. Quintus Aurelius Symmachus, the urban prefect in 384, who defended the altar, and Ambrose, bishop of Milan, who rejected it, wrote separately to the emperor Valentinian II (r. 375–392). On the surface, their positions appear to focus on the religious dispute. Yet the members of the senate in Rome, under the leadership of Symmachus, particularly sought ways to retain the historic paths to prestige; for non-Christians this had included serving in pagan priesthoods or adding to temple treasuries. Of course, Symmachus did wish to bring back the altar of Victory, and this was an offensive position to Christian senators. Yet most of the senators shared the goal of restoring the past at the Senate House in the sense of reclaiming the traditional avenues for aristocrats to attain prestige: providing benefactions, maintaining their appointments to prestigious offices, and keeping their privileged connections to emperors. In the wake of senators clamoring for privileges, a structure called the Secretarium Senatus was established adjacent to the Curia during the 390s. There, legal proceedings for aristocrats could be administered separately and advantageously, thus upholding the prerogatives of senators.

THE RENEWAL OF A SPACE FOR SENATORIAL IDENTITY

It is not certain how much the Curia that visitors experience today resembles the fourth-century assembly hall. Working for Mussolini in the 1930s, the archeologist Alfonso Bartoli produced stark expanses of brick in his modern version of plain Tetrarchic construction (fig. 6.2).[5] Even before Bartoli stripped away the medieval and Renaissance features, seventeenth-century pillagers had removed the inlaid marble revetments of the side walls.

The Tetrarchic Curia's vast interior space accommodated the pomp of senatorial meetings: six steep steps flanking a central passageway supported seats for senators (fig. 6.3). Lavish patterns composed of inlaid porphyry and serpentine furnished a richly ornamented pavement between the platforms for the senatorial seats (see fig. 6.2). Opposite the entrance,

Figure 6.2. Interior of the Senate House (Curia Senatus). Photo courtesy of Fototeca Unione (Neg. 10728). © American Academy in Rome.

the hall terminated in an elevated podium, where the urban prefect presided over the senate. The podium retains the brick construction that once supported the altar of Victory as well as the statue of Victory that assuredly was exhibited there; the headless porphyry statue of Hadrianic manufacture that is usually displayed in the hall today was not exhibited inside the Curia during late antiquity (fig. 6.4).

The Tetrarchic emperors fully integrated the new Senate House with the Forum of Caesar. The Curia provided access to the southeast portico of Caesar's Forum through the hall's two rear doors (fig. 6.5). One major consequence of the late antique transfor-

mation was the new ability of the senatorial hall to function coherently with the spaces to its west while maintaining the connection with the Forum of Caesar. An additional feature of the Tetrarchic rebuilding was to furnish a spacious paved plaza to the south of the Curia Senatus that was distinct from the other locus of power at the Forum's central area. The Tetrarchic Curia's façade also featured an elevated portico that required one to ascend steps from the Argiletum onto the porch. At the rear of the Curia, doorways provided passage to the Forum of Caesar's colonnaded portico, with its own access to the Argiletum (see fig. 6.5). Extending to the west of the Curia was

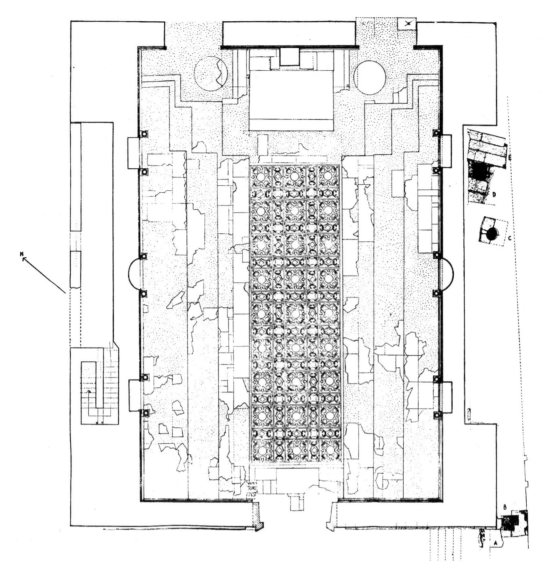

Figure 6.3. Plan of the Senate House (Curia Senatus). Drawing courtesy of Fototeca Unione (Neg. 12.225). © American Academy in Rome.

a series of *tabernae*, or narrow longitudinal halls, that ran parallel to the Curia, and an atrium-like space was situated immediately to the west of the Curia (see fig. I.8 [36]).

By remaking a proper assembly hall at the Curia Senatus, the Tetrarchs formed a clear link to the past. The late antique Curia reused most of the foundations of the Curia Julia, except for the northwestern edge facing the Capitoline Hill.[6] Continuity between the destroyed Curia Julia and the completely reconstructed Curia Senatus helped the Tetrarchy to claim that its political ideas had refounded Rome, as if it had reinstated the principate under Augustus. On the

interior, Diocletian and Maximian installed the same altar of Victory and statue of Victory from Taranto that Augustus had donated to the senate. With its height and decorations, the Tetrarchic Curia provided a suitably grand meeting hall for the senate, focused on the central position of the altar of Victory.

Alfonso Bartoli uncovered six niches for sculptures on the Curia interior that had been masked under the Renaissance and Baroque accretions: each of the Curia's lateral walls contained a central arched niche flanked by a rectangular niche on either side. All of the niches and their projecting consoles are still visible; yet most of the columns supported by

Figure 6.4. Podium originally supporting the altar of Victory and the statue of Victory inside the Senate House (Curia Senatus). The porphyry statue shown here was not displayed inside the Senate House during late antiquity. Photo by the author.

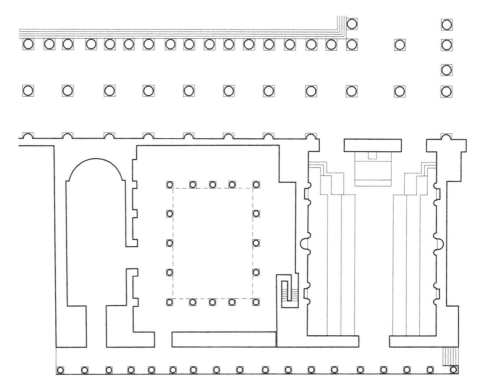

Figure 6.5. Plan of the late antique senatorial complex featuring the Senate House (Curia Senatus), the peristyle courtyard called the Atrium Libertatis, and the Secretarium Senatus occupying a former *taberna* of the Forum of Caesar. Drawing by Brian Doherty.

the consoles are lost (fig. 6.6). One of the consoles from the central niche on the eastern wall features a single figure holding reeds above a cornucopia as a personification of autumn, according to Franz Alto Bauer (fig. 6.7).[7] It seems fairly clear that all four seasons were once depicted on the consoles of the two central niches. The four rectangular corner niches feature different imagery for the consoles (fig. 6.8). Each of the eight corner consoles presents an eagle holding a wreath in its beak (fig. 6.9). These consoles plainly illustrate imperial insignia, and corresponding imagery of an eagle with a wreath was illustrated hovering atop an image of the Tetrarchic emperors from the paintings inside the imperial cult room at Luxor.[8] In the Curia, the four rectangular niches must have held statues installed by the co-ruling Tetrarchs, with the images of eagles permanently installed in the consoles to indicate the everlasting nature of the imperial system. Under the assumption that the imperial statues in the Curia referred to the persistence of the Tetrarchy as Diocletian envisioned it, it is likely that the four outer images were generic presentations of emperors that could have honored any member of the collegial system, rather than the likenesses of individuals; but this cannot be confirmed. It is unclear what statues were placed in the two central niches on each of the Curia's side walls, but it is plausible that images of the deities who watched over the Tetrarchs, Jupiter and Hercules, were installed there. The seasonal motifs in the consoles framing the central statues interjected the Tetrarchic notion of cyclical time. Thus, the interior of the Curia expressed that the regeneration of rulers was synchronized with the seasonal cycles of growth and restoration, offering praise to emperors by reference to regularized sequences.

The theme of seasonal renewal asserted the desire for lasting patterns of succession by co-reigning Tetrarchs on the interior of the Curia. Likewise, outdoor installations displayed in front of the Curia reinforced the concept of regeneration. Public statues honored Diocletian and Maximian with dedications that state: "To the strongest and the most flourishing" (*fortissimo ac florentissimo*).[9] The patterns of seasons charted a path of renewal that led to the empire's

Figure 6.6. Arched niche on the interior of the Senate House (Curia Senatus). Photo by the author.

Figure 6.7. Console with the personification of autumn holding a cornucopia, from the interior of the Senate House (Curia Senatus). Photo by the author.

flourishing, as expressed in the rhetoric of senators inscribed onto statue bases.

The interior of the Curia Senatus as rebuilt under the direction of Diocletian and Maximian was furnished with abundant light streaming in from the three lofty, south-facing windows on the façade.

Sunlight reflected off the rich patterns in the inlaid marble pavement at the center of the floor, as shown in a digital reconstruction (fig. 6.10). The experience of the Curia's interior, therefore, changed with the seasons as the quality of light shifted throughout the year; the light also changed throughout the day according to the orientation of the sun. The play of light conditioned an experience of the statues installed by Diocletian and Maximian on the interior by highlighting the innovative temporal scheme of the decorations.

Late antique sources further praise the Curia's well-lit interior by referring to reflections from gold surfaces, raising the possibility that there was gilded ceiling ornamentation.[10] Two inscriptions dating to the fifth century, if not slightly later, specify that the "hall was shining on account of gold." One instance appears on an inscribed epistyle placed above a doorway that mentions restorations by Flavius Ianuarius, about whom almost nothing is known;

the second inscription is of an equally uncertain date.[11] One of the inscriptions mentioning the shining gold states that there were restorations; it is difficult to determine the exact date of these repairs. The extent of gold may have been limited, since the polished marble walls and floors of the Curia also reflected light.

The lower portion of the interior showcased framed revetments of polychrome marbles that are attested in sixteenth-century descriptions, as shown in the digital model (see fig. 6.10).[12] A different architrave from the one mentioning the gold identifies repairs at the Curia during the urban prefecture of Neratius Palmatus in 412 CE.[13] These repairs clearly reversed the damage after the sack of Rome in 410. The restorations in the wake of this attack are also documented in inscriptions dedicated to the emperors Honorius and Theodosius II (joint reign, 408–423) on blocks that served as architraves over the rear and main entrances.[14]

Figure 6.8. Rectangular niche on the interior of the Senate House (Curia Senatus). Photo by the author.

Figure 6.9. Console with eagle holding a wreath on the interior of the Senate House (Curia Senatus). Photo by the author.

Figure 6.10. Digital reconstruction of the interior of the Senate House (Curia Senatus). Experiential Technologies Center, UCLA. © Regents, University of California.

In the sixth century, under the Ostrogothic rule of Theoderic, the Curia was further consolidated and restored,[15] as indicated by a letter written by Cassiodorus in 527 CE that praises the father of an urban prefect for restoring the Senate House.[16] For the fifth-century restorations prior to Theoderic, it is plausible that the repairs addressed fire damage or thefts of the gilded decorations. The fifth-century repairs brought back the reflective properties of the Curia with newly installed, gleaming materials. The linkages between the Curia and its plaza in front, as well as between the interior and the Forum of Caesar at the rear, were considered vital to the restoration, as the fifth-century inscriptions of renewal above the doorways emphasized (see fig. 6.5).

NOBILITY AND RHETORIC

For senators, the Curia was the space in which to display dignified behavior through elegant speech as well as the proper adherence to protocol in assemblies.[17] The nobility (*nobilitas*) of those belonging to the senatorial order during late antiquity was formed by their association with the authority of the emperor, to whom senators expressed their allegiance.[18] The aristocrats wished to present their eloquence as a formal expression of their ritualized communication with emperors.

Statues, inscriptions, and public oratory also expressed the friendships and allegiances among senators and the rulers. For example, Roman nobles in panegyrics requested that rulers return to the traditional capital in order to repossess the traditional seat of authority over the empire. Inviting emperors back to Rome on such occasions as anniversaries, consulships, or triumphs recalled the lapsed time when the imperial palace had been inhabited. A panegyric composed by the poet Claudian used the literary conceit of the personified Roma speaking directly to the emperor Honorius to anticipate that an official visit of 404 would set the stage for a longer stay in the traditional capital:

Till when, I beg you, will power be exiled from its home, and imperial sway wander far from its own proper dwelling-place? Why do my Palaces, which gave their name to all the others, lie desolate in neglect and decay? And why is it thought that the world cannot be ruled from there?[19]

During the fourth century, the Curia housed the rhetoric expressing the hope that emperors and senators would one day all reside and operate together in Rome. The image of senatorial consensus thus was furthered by the imagined coalitions with emperors and the invitations to the rulers to return to the traditional capital.

The members of the senate also appear to have identified themselves as the global elite. Nazarius, in his panegyric of Constantine written in 317, expresses the emperor's respect for Rome's aristocrats in terms addressing the city:

You felt at last, Rome, that you were the citadel of all nations, and of all lands the queen, when you were promised the best men out of every province for your Curia, so that the dignity of the senate be no more illustrious in name than in face, since it was composed of the flower of the world.[20]

Since they were not based in Rome, fourth-century emperors could only rarely reinforce their links with senators in person. Meanwhile, as imperial appointees, the urban prefects of Rome tried to implement building policies or restorations that brought dignity to the senators. These policies often diverged from those of the rulers, however. Tensions emerged in safeguarding the past at the Senate House, since the aristocratic expressions that furthered elite initiatives clashed with those imposed by distant emperors, disrupting the image of consensus. The past was supposed to sustain the picture of harmony among senators and emperors, but it came to be particularly problematic when late antique aristocrats could no longer operate as a unified group affirming the same past. Specifically, with their objections to sacrifices at altars, Christian senators drew the line over what they would witness within the Senate House. Yet traditionalists, who maintained a deep commitment to customs and a disdain for perceived affronts to their ancestral ways, felt the altar of Victory in the Senate House to be worthy of restoration.

THE ALTAR OF VICTORY

In the fourth-century Senate House, structural restoration was linked to the complex meanings associated with preserving the past. Official texts written by Quintus Aurelius Symmachus when he was the urban prefect of Rome document the significant debate over a statue and altar of the Roman goddess Victory that had once been displayed in the Curia. Symmachus clearly wished to create an alternative to the Christian arguments supporting removal of the statue and altar, but his other goals need to be considered as well. Augustus' original gift of the altar commemorated the relationship between senators and the ruler. Further, the prefect tried to negotiate both the modification of a set of rituals to be practiced at altars and the maintenance of pagan cult objects once the statues were dissociated from offensive practices. The heated discussions about the altar of Victory led to its ultimate removal, illustrating a late antique connection between religious changes and the alterations made to an important public building. But Symmachus' concern with paths to status and the ways that traditional honors were conferred upon pagan priests situate the arguments over religion within a wider debate over elite identity during the fourth century. Nonetheless, the dispute about the altar revealed restrictions on the Senate House during the reign of the emperor Valentinian II (r. 375–392).

Symmachus requested that the altar be restored by implying that, after a subtle modification of rituals, commemorations would renew time harmlessly, providing a vital connection with traditions. Yet the temporal concepts that contributed to Symmachus' worldview clashed with the ideas of the senator's chief adversary, Bishop Ambrose of Milan. To be sure, pagan-Christian conflict today appears to offer an explanatory paradigm for the dispute over the Curia. Yet the larger issues raised by Symmachus often veered away from the altar. Symmachus' letter of 384, which treated both the altar of Victory and the financing of traditional rites, reveals his concern with reviving state subsidies to the cults and priesthoods, framing them as viable institutions that traditionally had advanced senatorial status. As mentioned earlier, proper civic funding guaranteed that rites assisted the entire city. Removing the altar of Victory in response to objections from Christians placed pagan senators in the unexpected position of being religious adversaries. Indeed, Ambrose forced the Roman traditionalists to adopt the position of pagan opponents of Christianity as he set Symmachus and his allies along a path contrary to the tenets of class harmony. As a result, senatorial status, like the definitions of civic space and public architecture, was contested during the 380s, even if the terms of conflict never specifically designated the Senate House as exclusively pagan or Christian. But differing perspectives on time and memory that centered on what deserved to be hidden versus what was worthy of restoration were of greater concern during the late fourth century than the presumed pagan-Christian enmity.

The altar and statue of Victory should be treated as separate objects, since the debate makes a clear distinction between the two. After Augustus brought the statue of Victory from Taranto to the Senate House in 23 BCE,[21] lustrations, oaths, and incense-burning continued in the Curia in honor of the goddess until the mid-fourth century. During the visit of the emperor Constantius II to Rome in 357, the ruler is said to have looked away from the altar with its statue to avoid viewing the polluted objects. He later ordered that only the altar be removed.[22] The altar was temporarily restored—presumably under Julian (361–363)—only to be withdrawn again under Gratian in 382.

Gratian never assumed the title of *pontifex maximus*. Further, he attempted to confiscate—perhaps unsuccessfully—the endowments that had supported both temples and pagan priesthoods, while eliminating some of the benefits accorded to the Vestal Virgins.[23] The emperor, in fact, turned away a delegation of Roman senators requesting a reconsideration of his position on the altar of Victory and the endowments for temples. For unrelated reasons, Gratian was murdered by the usurper Magnus Maximus in 383. The elevation of the teenage Valentinian II to the position of *Augustus* in the West shortly thereafter inspired hope among some senators in Rome that the altar could be reinstated. Q. Aurelius Symmachus' appointment as urban prefect of Rome in 384 led to renewed efforts by some senators to reverse those policies of Gratian that had undermined traditional rites. Symmachus sent a letter to the emperor Valentinian II that pleaded for tolerance of the cult of Victory and restoration of the full cult apparatus, including the altar, to the Senate House.

Symmachus' third *relatio*, one of the letters reporting administrative concerns, was sent to Valentinian II and hints at a modified form of paganism that the prefect hoped would be palatable to Christians; but his letter sparked an angry reply from Ambrose. Based on rumors, without having received a copy of Symmachus' initial correspondence, Ambrose drafted a first letter to Valentinian II; a second letter followed after he had acquired a copy of Symmachus' original dispatch. Symmachus' letter suggests that pagans could perform activities in the Senate House that would remain inoffensive to Christians, as indeed, Constantine had not curtailed the cult of Victory: "Of course, we can list emperors of either faith and either conviction: the earlier emperors venerated our ancestral religious rites, the latter did not abolish them."[24] In contrast to Symmachus' position that retaining some ancestral traditions of the past warranted respect, Ambrose argued that enlightenment requires that the past undergo reassessment. In his letter, the Milanese bishop wrote as if Roma were speaking:

Their failure makes them regretful: the grey hair of old age has brought a blush of shame to the cheek. I do not blush at Rome's conversion after a long life. . . . It is the grey hairs of good character which win praise. There is no reproach in improvement. The only thing I had in common with barbarians was that previously I did not know God.[25]

For Ambrose, the past was filled with shame, and traditionalist senators should atone for the false beliefs held by their ancestors.

The Senate House used the image of winged Victory as an emblem for the institution; the figure crowned the gable of the Curia Julia, and presumably was a feature of the Tetrarchic structure's façade as well. Both Symmachus and Ambrose agreed that the statue of the deity on the interior of the Curia was allowable if considered apart from the altar. Their debate revolved instead around the cult practices localized at a pagan altar, with particular attention to the rites believed by some to safeguard Rome. Prior to 357, oaths were taken at the altar of Victory honoring each new emperor; additional oaths were taken before senatorial meetings.[26] Rome was protected by the traditional rites, according to Symmachus, since "these religious observances (*sacra*) drove Hannibal from [Rome's] walls."[27] Ambrose countered that the rites polluted the space, referring to Christian senators inhaling the ash that the rites produced, which offended them, and he specified that the altar, set up with images, invited the most objectionable acts. Christians would be persecuted, argues Ambrose, if "some pagan were to set up an altar to the images . . . and were to force Christians to assemble there to take part in sacrifices, to have the breath and mouths of the faithful choked with ash from the altar."[28] Perhaps Ambrose also wished to reinforce that the faithful should turn away from the stench of the ash from a pagan altar, and respond only to the sweet smell of liturgical incense.[29] Ambrose focused his attention on the cultic residue such as ash at the altar; a statue, while problematic, presented a lesser problem once its connection with an altar was severed. Indeed, Ambrose seemed to open the door, if only slightly, for the statue to be decontextualized as a work of art after the offensive altar had been removed. Claudian in his panegyric of 404 mentioned the image of Victory, indicating that throughout the debate and for decades thereafter, the statue of Victory remained in the Senate House.[30]

To be sure, Symmachus staked out a conservative position, but his letters demonstrate hints of flexibility. The altar of Victory guaranteed protection, in the arguments of Symmachus, by proving its effectiveness over time: "Who is on such good terms with barbarians as not to need the altar of Victory?" Symmachus asked.[31] Symmachus hinted that he wished to maintain the memory of Victory by continuing to voice honor for the deity nominally at the altar: "We are cautious with regard to the future and avoid omens of change. If she [Victory] cannot be honored as a god, at least let her name be honored."[32] Symmachus claimed that Christians should be able to tolerate those who honored Victory by stating the name alone. But the option Symmachus had floated did not gain traction: addressing Victory by name at the altar was a form of invocation that truly offended Christians.

Symmachus further adduced Roman strategies of regulating memory when considering the altar. The senator hinted that the altar credited Victory with past successes, as these venerable events were recorded with Victory's name, and he proposed that the name could survive in the historical record as people spoke out in honor of Victory. In Symmachus' proposal, therefore, allowing the altar to stand guaranteed that the name of Victory would be remembered; removing the altar, by contrast, constituted a condemnation of memory by means of erasure.[33]

Symmachus' desire to maintain the altar was matched by his advocacy for subsidizing cultic rites and sustaining the endowments for temples. Gratian's attempt to curtail the state financing of polytheism attacked senators sponsoring the old rituals and those who also accrued status through priesthoods. One can hear through the course of Symmachus' arguments a plea for the spiritual protection of Rome that extended to safeguarding the aristocracy. Symmachus suggested that the historical trajectory of Rome's success as well as the status of the pagan elites would be jettisoned by the dismissal of the old rites, since, over time, tradition gained momentum. Symmachus wrote that ancestral practices had entered into the memory over the years:

The divine mind has assigned to different cities different religions to be their guardians. Each man is given at birth a separate soul; in the same way each people is given its own special genius to take care of its destiny. To this line of thought must be added the argument derived from "benefits conferred," for herein rests the most emphatic proof to man of the existence of gods. Man's reason moves entirely in the dark; his knowledge of divine influences can be drawn from no better source than from the recollection and the evidences of good fortune received from them. If long passage of time lends validity to religious observances, we ought to keep faith with so many centuries, we ought to follow our forefathers who followed their forefathers and were blessed in so doing.[34]

Rejecting the ancient traditions, Symmachus feared, struck at the core of ancestral memories that conferred benefits upon pagan aristocrats.

Ambrose proposed an alternate conception of time that cast the pagan past into oblivion while embracing change. Yet Ambrose also registered that Symmachus and others had launched critiques of offensive pagan practices that were illegal by 384:

Those whom the pagans hurled into the sea, the sea restored. The victory of the faith is this, that the pagans themselves feed on the deeds of their ancestors whose activities they condemn. Yet, alas, is it not a strange principle, to request the payments granted to those whose deeds they reject?[35]

A proposed late antique reform of paganism did not soften Ambrose's opposition to the altar's restoration or his rejection of the state paying for cultic rites.

At the end of the debate, neither Ambrose nor Symmachus was a clear winner. The altar was not restored by Valentinian II. On the other hand, the altar did return temporarily in 392, during Eugenius' brief usurpation in the West, and the state subsidies of cults were reinstated at that time.[36] Further, although the altar was permanently removed thereafter, the statue of Victory remained in place.[37]

The survival of the statue of Victory throughout the reign of Valentinian II and into the reign of Honorius suggests that some gesture toward the deity's memory was deemed permissible. Ambrose had specifically objected to the preponderance of pagan statues, writing: "Is it not enough for them [pagans] that their baths, their porticoes and their public squares are crowded with images?"[38] Clearly, Ambrose's complaints about images did not entirely sway Valentinian II. By separating the statue of Victory from the associated cult, and retaining the statue without restoring the altar, Valentinian II allowed the Senate House to become a space for conserving the past, upholding the memories that had proven successful over the ages. The Senate House thus was turned into a monument that retained tradition without welcoming cultic rites. Although Valentinian II's rejection of Symmachus' demand to restore the altar of Victory in the Senate House makes it appear that the prefect lost his struggle, at the same time, Ambrose's request that the statue be removed was not fulfilled either. By regulating senatorial memories, Valentinian II permitted the statue of Victory to be validated as a deconsecrated object. Yet cultic practices were designated as condemned activities belonging to a past that could not be reinstated.

Given the rise of ecclesiastic authorities in the West, the ability of a bishop such as Ambrose to influence civic architecture and urban space seems a foregone conclusion. Despite this, the public's admiration for cult statues as cultural artifacts dissociated from pagan altars was an important point of view advanced by Symmachus. The positions of Ambrose and Symmachus thus introduce the conflict between ecclesiastic and aristocratic authority as a major issue in late antique Rome.

THE ATRIUM LIBERTATIS

Symmachus' thwarted desire to commemorate the name of Victory inside the Curia occurred just prior to efforts that designated zones for preserving the memories of powerful individuals at the Atrium Libertatis, located at the senatorial compound. There are several topographical markers indicating that a large architectural complex surrounding the Senate House was formed during late antiquity. This area may have received particular attention after the sack of Rome in 410. A key feature of the expanded senatorial compound was the Atrium Libertatis, which was relocated

there from another site.[39] One plausible proposal that has been advanced states that prior to its relocation, the Atrium Libertatis held the archives and offices for the censors, and that it was originally accessed from the Tabularium on the Capitoline Hill.[40] While it is certain that the Atrium Libertatis was shifted to some location in the vicinity of the Curia Senatus, there is, unfortunately, no consensus about its precise location during late antiquity.[41] I propose that the Atrium Libertatis retained its archival function and also provided a space for public gatherings during the fifth century, when it occupied a courtyard directly to the west of the Curia; this was a space distinct from the Atrium Minervae, situated in the portico of the Forum of Caesar on the north side of the Senate House.

The best evidence for localizing the late antique Atrium Libertatis comes from an inscription, dating between 491 and 518, that mentions this structure and identifies it as one with seventy columns linked to the Secretarium Senatus.[42] The monument honored both the Ostrogothic king of Italy, Theoderic, and the Byzantine emperor, Anastasius; it was commissioned on the occasion of the restoration of the Atrium's many decaying columns:

To the safety of our lords [Byzantine emperor] Anastasius, ever Augustus, and the most glorious and triumphant man Theoderic. [The statue was set up by] Valerius Florianus, of the highest senatorial rank and illustrious man, once commander of the imperial infantry and once head of a branch of the imperial finance ministry, in the seventy columns of the Atrium Libertatis, which were restored due to their antiquity and which were nearly consumed by the decay [caused by] time, [and] all the things at the site were remade and in the Secretarium Senatus.[43]

The loss of columns over the years makes it difficult to account for them today in the remains of the senatorial complex.

Yet additional epigraphic evidence aids in understanding these many columns and suggests that the Atrium Libertatis was connected to the Secretarium Senatus, the apsidal hall to the west of the Curia that occupied a former *taberna* from the Forum of Caesar (see fig. 6.5).[44] The peristyle courtyard between the Curia and the Secretarium Senatus might account

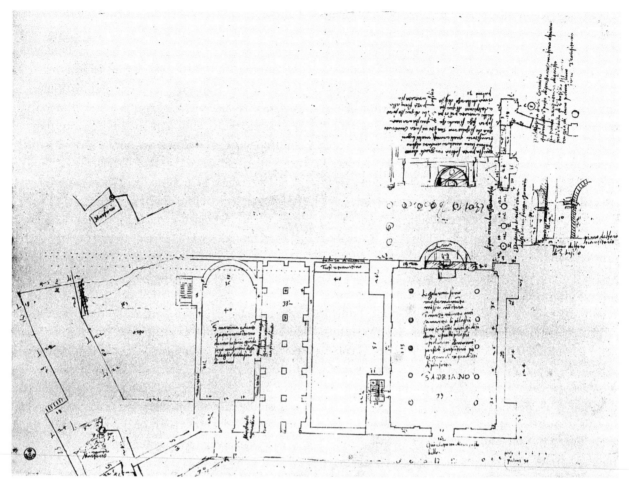

Figure 6.11. Antonio da Sangallo the Younger, sixteenth-century drawing of the Senate House (Curia Senatus) and the Secretarium Senatus. Photo courtesy of Fototeca Unione (Neg. 13774). © American Academy in Rome.

for some of the seventy columns mentioned in the inscription, and there may have been additional ones from the long colonnaded portico joining the Curia's façade with the Secretarium Senatus (see fig. I.8 [34] and [35]). A drawing by Antonio da Sangallo the Younger illustrates the sixteenth-century topography and indicates that the Secretarium Senatus was an apsidal hall, flanking the Senate House but separated from it by other structures that plausibly had been formed out of a late antique peristyle courtyard (fig. 6.11).[45] The columns of this courtyard, together with those from the portico that extended to the west from the Curia's façade, would have been those identified in the inscription dedicated to Anastasius and Theoderic. Thus, I believe that the place named for Liberty can be identified as this peristyle courtyard, which appears to

have been fully integrated into the senatorial complex and to the west of the Curia.

The area dominated by the Curia had long been a site for indicating the affiliations between powerful senators and imperial authorities. In the Atrium Libertatis, honors were on display in statues dedicated to rulers and the top military commanders they appointed, establishing a coherent exhibition strategy together with the plaza in front of the Senate House and the Forum's central area. Both the monument to Anastasius and Theoderic and a statue to the general Aëtius, discussed below, resurrected the traditions of representation that the emperor Honorius and the general Stilicho had implemented close to the Via Sacra at the turn of the fifth century. Further, the public condemnation of those who reported to the officials in the East about the taxable properties owned by Roman senators was expressed in both the ritual acceptance of the Theodosian Code and a statue of Aëtius in the Atrium Libertatis, to be analyzed in fuller detail. Monuments and inscriptions attesting to the negotiated power balance between the imperial bureaucracy and the Roman senate appear at the Atrium Libertatis, the archive that included legal texts, and the Secretarium Senatus, a law court for the senators. The correlations among the monuments from the Atrium Libertatis and the series of monuments from the Forum and the plaza in front of the Senate House suggest a categorical and visual coherence for these sites.

It is important to consider that the administrative roles of senators and their close ties to the rulers were on display in the Atrium Libertatis, presenting senatorial authority in public space. A different function can be ascribed to the Atrium Minervae, which occupied the southeast portico of the Forum of Caesar. Exiting from the Curia through either of the two rear doors, one entered the portico featuring the statue of Minerva; therefore the space was likely known as the Atrium Minervae (see Chapter 3). This lavishly decorated zone for the enjoyment of art accommodated showpieces and therefore should be categorized as distinct from the politicized spaces flanking the south and west sides of the Curia.

The Atrium Libertatis was also close to or within a precinct called "at the Palm" (*ad Palmam*). Meetings of the senate occurred near the location ambiguously identified only as "the Palm"—likely referring to a metallic column in the senatorial plaza that resembled the trunk of a palm tree. This column is mentioned in a biography of Claudius Gothicus as being situated at the Rostra, but it was probably moved from there to the plaza in front of the Senate House after the third century.[46] The likely site of the relocated column was close to the atrium immediately to the west of the Senate House that I have proposed was the Atrium Libertatis (see fig. 6.5). Meanwhile, a text about the martyr Restitutus—possibly written in the fourth century—mentions that the spot at the base of the Capitoline Hill close to the "triumphal arch" (the Arch of Septimius Severus) was called *ad Palmam*. Later, texts reporting Theoderic's address to

the senate in 500 CE localize the event as *ad Palmam* in one account, or close to the *Palma Aurea* in another; the latter term indicates that the palm was gilded bronze.[47] The spot identified with the palm appears to have accommodated public gatherings close to the Curia Senatus.

The home of Anicius Acilius Glabrio Faustus, one of the most prominent Roman elites working at the court of the emperor Valentinian III (r. 425–455), was reportedly near the palm.[48] Faustus was recorded as having attended an imperial wedding of Valentinian III in Constantinople and Theodosius II sent him back to Rome with copies of the Theodosian Code. One copy was presented to the senate at a formal event conducted by Faustus "in his home which is at the Palm (*ad Palmam*)."[49] The publication of the *Codex Theodosianus* in 438 as a legal document ordered by Theodosius II certainly bolstered the authority of emperors as the authors of the law; yet the written record of the pronouncements also provided legal precedents for many issues of concern to Rome's senators. Thus, the presentation of the Theodosian Code in Rome was a highly significant ritual that demonstrated publicly the senatorial acceptance of imperial legal authority.

It is not clear where Faustus' house was situated or why the senate would have met there. The topographical marker *ad Palmam* would at this point have been situated near the plaza in front of the Curia, however. Perhaps Faustus considered himself as performing public roles as if at home while actually he was at the senatorial complex; alternately, Faustus' home plausibly was close to the Curia. Leaving aside the problems of whether or how Faustus could have set up a residence near the public space of the Forum, I propose that the ceremonial presentation of the *Codex Theodosianus* occurred in the atrium to the west of the Senate House, which I have identified as the Atrium Libertatis.

The account of the senate ritually accepting the Theodosian Code in 438 mentions that Faustus informed Romans of their duty to archive copies of the legal text and this important function had been associated with the Atrium Libertatis since the Republic. Senators shouted acclamations in 438 to the emperors and demonstrated their consensus in support of the law, almost as gestures of ratification. All of the senators cried out repeatedly to accept the Code, and exclaimed seventeen chants specifically for Faustus. Yet the ritual acclamations accepting the Theodosian Code featured one caveat: senators wished "to report to the emperors the senate's wishes" that Western laws should avoid "confusion about the rights of landholders."[50] In other words, when the senate assembled at Faustus' "house" near the Curia, they spoke out in unison that the rule by law should help aristocrats maintain their properties. The addendum to the Theodosian Code recording the shouts at the senatorial meeting of 438 indicates that these cries proclaiming consensus were officially documented. Thus, when the Roman senate archived the Theodosian Code, in all likelihood at the archive of the Atrium Libertatis, they entered their own concerns over property into the permanent record.

The assembled senate in 438 also gave fifteen shouts for the military commander of the West, saying, "Hooray, Aëtius."[51] These acclamations that were shouted upon the arrival of the Theodosian Code accorded respect to all of the high-ranking officials, with Theodosius II and Valentinian III receiving the highest honors. Others, such as the consul Faustus and the military general (*magister utriusque militum*) Aëtius received ritual praise at the same time, highlighting the particular esteem in which aristocratic office-holders appear to have been held by the senate at the time.

A base for a statue of Aëtius was discovered close to the Senate House and the inscription identifies its display location as the Atrium Libertatis. It records only part of a lengthy inscription stating that the general was

also a leader of the military (*magister militum*) for Gaul, which region, due to the victories earned during times of war and peace, he has now restored to the Roman empire; who was formerly the commander of both forces [cavalry and infantry = *magister utriusque militiae*] [and] consul twice [and] patrician; always devoted to the state; decorated with every military honor; the Senate and the people of Rome supplied this [statue] on behalf of Italy's security, since he destroyed the subdued people from far away and suppressed the Burgundians and the Goths, conquering

under the command of our lords Theodosius II and Valentinian III (Placidus Valentinianus), most pious rulers. The bronze statue was set up, according to approved custom, to expand upon his genius in the Atrium Libertatis, which it occupies, in honor of his protection of morals, since he was the avenger of shame entrusted with protecting liberty by causing the informers of wealth to flee [and] by defending [us from] the most hostile enemy.[52]

Aëtius was particularly singled out as a protector who made the empire victorious again and restored the liberty of Romans. His position in the Western empire as a military commander working under Valentinian III recalled the position of Stilicho, who had served in the same capacity under Honorius, even though the name of the half-Vandal had been removed from all of the public monuments in Rome, including the statues in the Forum. As Andrew Gillett has pointed out, the memory of Stilicho's quasi-imperial authority prior to 408, the date of the general's condemnation, was recorded in Claudian's verse panegyrics, a poetic genre that the imperial court and the military elite of the West continually used to support the nexus of authority linking the emperors to the topmost military generals.[53] Thus, even though Stilicho was no longer represented physically in the monuments of the Forum after 408, his prominence survived. Claudian's verses celebrating Stilicho inspired poetry for Aëtius by his own panegyrist, Merobaudes. It appears, then, that the public inscriptions for Stilicho prefigured the statue of Aëtius in the Atrium Libertatis—perhaps because, despite erasure, the older monuments displayed signs that Stilicho had once been honored for his military positions. Ironically, Stilicho's erased statues further foreshadowed the assassination and condemnation to oblivion of Aëtius in 455. After Aëtius suffered his own memory sanctions, the legally enforced condemnation led to the destruction of the upper part of Aëtius' monument.

Surprisingly, Valentinian III seems not to have received a publicly displayed statue in the Forum. This might be explained by his shift away from building projects in the Forum and toward the pursuit of both church benefactions at S. Pietro in Vincoli and decorations at S. Paolo fuori le mura and S. Croce in

Gerusalemme.[54] Of course, the loss of an inscription over time could also account for the lack of testimony to Valentinian III. Even the overarching power of the Eastern emperor, Theodosius II, might account for the dearth of monuments at Rome honoring the embattled Valentinian III, as emperor of the West.[55] Certainly, the senate recognized the imperial position of Valentinian III. But the absence of a statue for the emperor, and the presence of statues for both Aëtius and Faustus' father-in-law, Tarrutenius Maximilianus, may also be an indication of the relationship between this emperor and the Roman elite. Aristocrats in Rome deemed Valentinian III incapable of addressing the critical concern of eliminating judicial abuses. The Western emperor was also rumored to have allowed bureaucratic functionaries to work as informers, leaking details about taxable aristocratic properties to the Eastern officials. By contrast, Aëtius held a position in which his military authority and his consular position were celebrated ritually when the senate accepted the Theodosian Code.

Roland Delmaire has argued that, during the ritual acceptance of the Theodosian Code, the senators not only shouted acclamations but also issued cries of condemnation against informers, in an implicit confirmation of Aëtius' role in adjudicating the law and protecting aristocrats.[56] The senatorial shouts, "for those who suppress informers, for those who suppress calumny," were intended as praise for Aëtius, claims Delmaire.[57] As mentioned above, the senate further shouted praise for Aëtius on that day, stating: "Hooray, Aëtius, repeated thirteen times. May you receive a third consulate! Repeated twelve times. Thanks to your efforts, we are safe and secure, repeated twelve times."[58] Since much of the ritual reception of the Theodosian Code indicated how the senators of Rome safeguarded their own interests, Delmaire makes the explicit connection between the acclamations praising those who suppressed informers (*extinctores delatorum*) and the inscription mentioning how Aëtius caused those informing about the taxable wealth of senators to flee (*opum refugo, delatorum*).[59] We can infer from the statues honoring both Tarrutenius and Aëtius that rule by law restored senatorial authority over the favorable ways their properties were taxed while sanctioning elite

lineages. Finally, the acclamations of senators in support of the Theodosian Code and the appreciation of Aëtius' aggression toward the informers were contextualized in the Atrium Libertatis, an archive that also functioned as a place where senatorial consensus was on display.

The Atrium Libertatis was critical to the legal concerns of the senate during late antiquity. In inscriptions, chiefly the one sponsored by Valerius Florianus and the other honoring Aëtius, the Atrium Libertatis functioned as the public space in which the senators advertised their administrative roles and presented aristocratic consensus as the predominant discourse in the city, while also securing elite financial prerogatives. Even if the senatorial acclamations of 438 did not occur in the Atrium Libertatis, the aristocratic concern with condemning informers was linked with the public praise of Aëtius in the minutes of that meeting and was commemorated in the general's statue displayed there. The importance of archiving the Theodosian Code, demonstrating senatorial consensus in acclamations, and obtaining legal exemptions from taxation for senatorial properties all intersected at the Atrium Libertatis. Presumably appearing as a peristyle courtyard flanking the Curia to the west, the Atrium Libertatis offered a public space in which the historical claims of an archive and the public demonstrations of consensus among senators situated the past as sanctioning the aristocratic control over the legal traditions of Rome. These senators were unashamed about honoring Aëtius publicly for defending elite tax privileges, which might have earned Aëtius only a minimal degree of favor before a public who resented those very privileges. Yet after Aëtius' condemnation, the archive at the Atrium Libertatis survived and continued to maintain the documents according financial and legal advantages to senators.

REWRITING URBAN SPACE AT THE SECRETARIUM SENATUS

A row of rectangular halls of the same width extending to the west of the Curia Senatus served as *tabernae* or shops adjoining the Forum of Caesar (see figs. I.8 [35] and [36]). During the 390s, the Secre-

157

tarium Senatus was established inside one of these *tabernae*. The building's remains are now inaccessibly situated beneath Pietro da Cortona's seventeenth-century church, SS. Luca e Martina. The most detailed knowledge of the Secretarium comes from the sixteenth-century plan of Antonio da Sangallo the Younger, which records that it occupied a re-used hall parallel to the Curia, and an atrium must have been situated between the two (see fig. 6.11). The Sangallo drawing shows an apsidal hall without aisles close to and aligned with the Senate House, with two lines projecting away from its entrance that are labeled as an arch.[60] Set slightly apart from the entrance, a late antique reconfiguration of an imperial arch was arranged to mark the trajectory leading into the Secretarium Senatus, according to Alessandro Viscogliosi.[61] The remains of the arch and some of its sculptural reliefs may have been located at the entrance to the Secretarium (fig. 6.12). Recent anal-

ysis of this site has determined that the alignment of the Secretarium Senatus with the Curia brought these two buildings into direct contact with the Roman Forum, even though the rear of each structure was aligned with the portico of the Forum of Caesar.[62]

Building, restoring, and transforming the Secretarium Senatus indicate how texts shaped spatial experiences during late antiquity due to the importance of inscriptions situated on the interior. The foundation of the Secretarium Senatus was provided during the last decade of the fourth century by the urban prefect of Rome, Nicomachus Flavianus.[63] Also known as Flavian the Younger, this prefect possessed a tarnished family legacy, since his father—Nicomachus Flavianus the Elder—had supported the usurper Eugenius in an affront to the emperor Theodosius I. Following the battle where Theodosius defeated Eugenius, the elder Flavian committed suicide. Afterward, Theodosius I condemned the elder Flavian's memory (an action

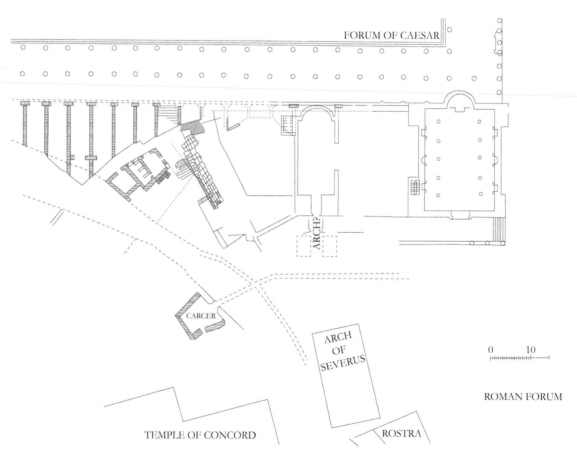

Figure 6.12. Plan of the Secretarium Senatus and the *tabernae* of the Forum of Caesar, after Alessandro Viscogliosi. Drawing by Jacqueline Miles.

that was famously reversed), yet he offered clemency to Flavian the Younger. When it came time to rebuild the Secretarium Senatus after the sack of Rome, the younger Flavian's memory was prominently upheld. A now-lost inscription documents both the creation of the Secretarium Senatus and its early fifth-century conservation by setting up a parallel between the founder and the restorer:

To the safety of our lords Honorius and Theodosius II, the most victorious rulers; Flavian founded the Secretarium of the most expansive senate [which afterward] had been engulfed in deadly flames that the *illustris* Flavius Annius Eucharius Epiphanius repaired and returned to its pristine state.[64]

The original sponsor, Flavian the Younger, founded (*instituerat*) the Secretarium Senatus, and the verb could have alluded to the reuse of a preexisting structure.[65] The urban prefect who served between 412 and 414, Flavius Annius Eucharius Epiphanius, repaired fire damage, presumably from the sack of Rome.[66]

The inscription inside the Secretarium Senatus seems to have linked Epiphanius, who revived a building, with the fame of Flavian the Younger, who belonged to the esteemed Nicomachi family. Memory practices governed concepts that were associated with the architectural restoration. The condemnation of Flavian the Elder had led to the erasure of his name from public inscriptions, and the effort to rehabilitate the family name was relevant to the Secretarium Senatus as a place in which to dispute or uphold senatorial virtue.[67] The Secretarium offered a site in which to conduct the trials of those aristocrats accused of capital crimes. Here, they avoided facing standard judges, and were judged instead by senatorial peers. Potentially the building was a site of exoneration as well as condemnation, so honor was either restored or taken away in this structure. Ernest Nash notes that the Secretarium Senatus was a fourth-century legal innovation providing private—and exclusive—court proceedings for senators accused of crimes.[68] In keeping with the late antique legal policies that were highly advantageous to aristocrats, the institution of senators sitting in judgment over other

senators had been established by legal instructions sent in 376 by the emperors Valens, Gratian, and Valentinian II:

A provincial judge or a judge within Italy shall have the power to institute an examination and to take cognizance of the case . . . against a senator. . . . When the prefect of the city takes cognizance of a case with respect to capital punishment of a senator, a quinqueviral court of especially esteemed men [i.e., senators] shall be associated with him in a trial.[69]

Emperors commanded that senators be given the prerogative to receive their own elite justice, here occurring within the senatorial hall aligned with the Curia, as a result of the forceful leverage senators had over imperial policy.[70]

The Secretarium provided an opportunity for senators to increase their honor and reassert their legal privileges, which they accomplished, ironically, with imperial permission. With the restoration inscription of Epiphanius, the Secretarium Senatus founded by Flavian the Younger paid proper homage to imperial authorities. The oddity of the institution, given the epigraphic commemoration of the emperors there, emerges from imperial authorities allowing senators to bolster the tradition of aristocratic governance of Rome. Epiphanius upheld both the institution expressing the imperial blessings of senatorial power and the revival of senatorial leadership in Rome. In other words, augmenting senatorial authority necessarily occurred in conjunction with expressions of concord with the ruling emperors.

In Rome's late antique culture of honor, an increased amount of respect accrued to one who received a personal rehabilitation when compared to one achieving a first-time success. Due to the role of benefactions in paving the way toward restored virtue, a sponsor could gain the pride of reinstated prestige by supporting architectural conservation. In the case of Epiphanius, his sponsorship of interventions at the Secretarium Senatus implicitly completed the task of the founder, so "restored" status was advantageous in having acquired a historic precedent. Epiphanius renovated the Secretarium Senatus in the fifth century so that it differed from Flavian the Younger's building, allowing the restorer both to earn some credit for what Flavian the Younger had started and to surpass it. Epiphanius also elevated his own status by establishing a link to the Nicomachi family through Nicomachus Flavianus the Younger, who, according to documents, served as urban prefect three times.

The *taberna* that had been converted into the Secretarium Senatus at the end of the fourth century underwent another transformation into the church of S. Martina at an unrecorded moment—in all probability, during the seventh century, when the Curia was converted into the church of Sant'Adriano by Pope Honorius (625–638).[71] Inside S. Martina, an undated and now-lost inscription states: "Here lie the bodies of the holy martyrs: the virgin Martina and her companions Concordius and Epiphanius."[72] St. Epiphanius must have reiterated the name of the old restorer of the Secretarium Senatus, as both the text concerning relics and the earlier inscription were located in the apse.[73] Sts. Concordius and Martina were both venerated on January 1. St. Epiphanius, who was bishop of Salamis in the late fourth century, does not appear to have been particularly venerated in Rome, raising the probability that the name was inscribed as a saintly recapitulation of the fifth-century restorer. Thus, a juxtaposition between the fifth-century inscription and the seventh-century text offered a method of recognizing that the transformation to establish the church of S. Martina continued the tradition set up by Epiphanius' restoration of the Secretarium Senatus.

A hagiographic text recounting the life of St. Martina describes her as a Roman aristocrat persecuted by imperial authorities. St. Martina's biography exists in a Latin version, dated to the seventh century; elements in the text hint at a Greek predecessor.[74] In Martina's story, the saint refused to worship idols at several temples, for which she was condemned to prison, presumably the Mamertine prison or *tullianum* directly opposite the Secretarium Senatus (see fig. I.8 [33]).[75] She thwarted the goals of a fictional emperor named Alexander by crushing the "statues of a temple where there were twelve idols" (*templum ubi erant duodecim idola*), which could be identified as the Porticus Deorum Consentium, at the west-

ern end of the Roman Forum. At the behest of the emperor, a fictional tribune named Limenius is said to have ventured forth from the palace to further punish her. As Limenius proceeded by foot toward Martina's prison cell, he noticed a very pleasant odor. The fragrant scent, emanating from the saint in the text, may have characterized Martina as truthful, honest, and just.[76] The hagiographic account also employs metaphors of light for Martina, arguing for her appeal to the senses:

Proceeding from the palace, Limenius smelled an odor of the utmost sweetness and of spices, and, addressing the assembly of Roman people, he said, "Do you smell the fragrant odor?"—for he was much with the people. But they said: "The citizens have gathered to worship the beloved Martina." . . . When they actually arrived at the prison, the odor had even improved. When Limenius opened the door, at first he saw a great light shining around her. But when he entered inside and approached her cell (for she was in a prison with many cells), around her he saw the great radiance, so that everyone was shaking for fear of him falling to the pavement. He went into the third cell and approached St. Martina, who was seated on an imperial throne. The smell—emanating from the saint—had drawn a crowd to Martina's cell, where she was holding forth while seated on an imperial throne (*in sede imperiali*). Martina read from a tablet, stating, "How magnificent are your works, Lord."[77]

A new perspective on the Roman Forum and the plaza in front of the Senate House emerges in the story, since St. Martina on an imperial throne displaces the connection with the populace that emperors and senators once possessed.

Readers of the St. Martina text must have noted differences between senatorial honor and the status of St. Martina, whose life revealed humble truths. In fact, St. Martina's incarceration might have referenced the *carcer* or prison directly across from the church dedicated to the saint (see fig. I.8 [33]). In the seventh century, the church of S. Martina installed in the Secretarium Senatus exploited material conservation and epigraphic displays to interweave the late antique tradition of munificence and patterns of church sponsorship. Inscriptions at the Secretarium Senatus burnished the status first of Flavian the Younger, then of the urban prefect Epiphanius. Subsequently, in the church of S. Martina, the presence of relics from martyrs, in place of senatorial memories, implicitly shifted honor from an aristocratic to a saintly virtue. The church building effectively restored the Secretarium Senatus with minimal architectural changes. As a result, the church of S. Martina alerted early medieval viewers who read the various inscriptions that the transmission of authority—starting with the senatorial foundation, continuing with the fifth-century restoration, and finally ending with the conversion into a church—made the saints into recipients of honor in inscriptions. Yet the ancient architecture was conserved in order to revise the building's interpretation. Inscriptions for churches and the prominence of Christian benefactors remained excluded from the physical space of the Roman Forum until the sixth century, even though in Rome, aristocratic Christianity developed important points of contact with the old forms of senatorial munificence.[78] The transformation of the Secretarium Senatus into a church rewrote history by juxtaposing the preserved inscription with a new one. Inside the church of S. Martina, the epigraphic connections—especially the pairing of different inscriptions mentioning Epiphanius—demonstrate how a preexisting building could be maintained as a church while carefully manipulating and questioning the late antique culture of individual aristocratic honors.

PUBLIC SPACE FOR SAINTS

Sources that addressed Christian audiences outside of the genre of imperial commemoration depict a critique of the traditional elite honors in the Forum. Biographies of apostles, bishops, and saints filled with colorful episodes and fantastic miracles belonged to an entirely different genre than official historical texts.[79] Like the *Acts of St. Martina*, which features the narrative structure of a legend, the *Acts of St. Peter* belongs to a collection of biographies known as the *Apocryphal Acts of the Apostles*, which narrates the first-century Petrine activities in Rome. A key event in

this narrative occurs in the Roman Forum. Research has indicated that the Latin version of the apocrypha about Peter written down in the codex known as the *Actus Vercellenses* is not a translation of a Greek original, but rather a separate version originating in the late fourth century.[80] A narrative of Peter's competition with Simon Magus in the Forum belongs to this fourth-century version and appears prominently in the Latin editions of the text.[81] The unofficial biographical narrative of Peter challenged the culture of honor that benefited senators through their affiliations with imperial authority, inviting a reconsideration of conscientiously preserved and status-driven public monuments.

The Roman events of the *Acts of St. Peter* alternate between a fictional home, identified as the aristocratic residence of Marcellus, and the Roman Forum, implying that the apostle's goal was to establish both locations as worthy of episcopal intervention. In these scenes, portrait statues or themes relating to the installation of images focus the reader's attention on the civic honors that were paid exclusively to emperors and senators. One implication is that Christian authorities were concerned about the lack of public monuments or physical commemorations establishing the authority of church officials in the fourth-century Forum. At the same time, Christian texts present the "epigraphic habit" of the elite and the striving for status that generated publicly exhibited honors in Rome as reeking of vainglory. Further, the narrative voice in the *Acts of St. Peter* consistently assumes that extensive audiences witnessed the miracles of Peter. The apostle entered the Forum to project his physical presence—according to the text—before a wide public accustomed to gawking at portraits depicting the emperors.

As an apocryphal text, the *Acts of St. Peter* rejected high literary standards as it drew upon folkloric oral narratives, sometimes abruptly interrupted by descriptive passages or scriptural references.[82] Much of the narrative focuses on a series of clashes between Peter and his nemesis, Simon Magus.[83] The story commences in Rome, where a previously pious Christian senator named Marcellus had abandoned the proper church under the corrupting influence of Simon Magus. Though a heretic, Simon held sway over Marcellus and his entire household, leading Peter to arrive with crowds of his followers at Marcellus' residence to persuade all residing therein to reject Simon's errors.[84]

After Peter had used his remarkable skills to displace Simon's influence over Marcellus, a young man in the crowd observing Peter's reconciliation with the senator suddenly became possessed and toppled a great marble statue of "Caesar," which broke into pieces at its display spot in the house's atrium. Marcellus was particularly distraught at the deed, since it implied that the senator had committed an offense against the emperor. In the narrative, Marcellus cried out with fear:

"A great crime has been committed; if Caesar hears of this through some busybody, he will punish us severely." But Peter answered him, "I see you are not the man you were just now; for you said you were ready to spend your whole fortune to save your soul. But if you are truly repentant and believe in Christ with all your heart, take some running water in your hands and pray to the Lord; then sprinkle it in his name over the broken pieces of the statue, and it will be restored as before."[85]

After Marcellus did as Peter had instructed him, the statue was restored.

In Marcellus' atrium, therefore, with the miraculous repair of the statue, faith in Peter's teachings upheld the bonds linking the senator with "Caesar." As a result, Peter, as he appears in the apocryphal text, does not erase the honorific virtues of imperial portraits. Instead, Marcellus receives a rebuke from Peter for prioritizing worldly status over his own soul. Indeed, earlier in the episode, Peter was informed that Simon had asked the senator to dedicate a statue to Simon, "the young God."[86] Again, the narrative appears to criticize the type of munificence that generates status above faith, implying that true belief would instead inspire charity.

The episodes staged in the house of Marcellus concluded with Peter having restored the senator to the proper faith. The apostle then rose and proceeded toward the Forum. Arriving there, senators, prefects, and officers joined together before a crowd to witness a showdown between Peter and Simon.

Under the watch of a fictional urban prefect named Agrippa, in three separate episodes, Simon was unsuccessful in his attempts to revive three boys, all of whom Peter then returned to life. In the first episode, Simon killed a boy by whispering in his ear; Peter then instructed Agrippa to touch the boy after the saint said a prayer that resuscitated the deceased. After this first boy was restored, a widow asked Peter to raise her only son, who had been brought to the Forum on a stretcher and who had provided her sustenance. Peter's prayers also brought the second boy back from the dead. In the third and final contest, Simon bargained with the populace that if he could revive a young man of senatorial status whose mother had transported him to the Forum as if on a funerary procession, then the heretic would earn the right to turn the populace against Peter. At first, the senatorial youth blinked his eyes in response to the apparent cures practiced by Simon. But when the young senator could not stand, and only Peter's prayers caused the deceased to return to life, the veracity of Peter's teachings was upheld. The mother of aristocratic rank informed Peter, by way of thanks, that the funds she had designated for her son's funeral would now be used as the apostle commanded. Peter asked that the money be distributed to widows.

Through these vignettes, the apocryphal text counsels that rather than honoring the elite, munificence should be directed to assist the needy. The repetitive scenes of youths coming back to life through the interventions of Peter would have resonated in the Forum, where there were numerous statues creating redundant series of portraits praising emperors, such as the three images depicting Constantius II. Further, setting up official statues had created proxies for the imperial presence. Statues kept alive memories of esteemed individuals; yet the *Acts of St. Peter* sets forth a clear case for renouncing the trappings of elite self-representation as practiced in the urban public space of late antique Rome.

A final dispute between Peter and Simon Magus took place along the Via Sacra. With slapstick effect, Simon Magus proposed to leap up and fly to prove his valor and the effectiveness of his beliefs. On the given day, "a great crowd gathered at the street called the Sacred Way (*Via Sacra*) in order to see him [Simon] fly."[87] Peter knelt to pray, requesting that Simon be made to fall, but that he not die after crashing to the ground. Peter's wish was granted, and Simon's flight was abruptly terminated. The apostle thereby discredited the heretic publicly.[88]

The competition between Peter and Simon Magus redefined the allegiances of the crowd witnessing the event in the Forum. When Simon crashed, as the apocryphal *Acts* reported, the magician broke some bones, and the audience turned against him, casting stones at his wounded body.[89] Implicitly, the Via Sacra, the avenue for imperial processions, was the route along which emperors performed homecoming rituals during triumphs, anniversaries, and consular celebrations. Thus, the Via Sacra earned Peter a constituency and a public presence in the city through his legendary dispute with Simon. The episode at the Via Sacra marks Rome as the city of St. Peter.

Simon's jump also had topographical specificity. On one level, Simon's leap was a comic reversal of heavenly ascent. On another level, the awkward plunge also reversed the heroic role of Marcus Curtius, who was prominently commemorated in a Forum monument. This legendary Roman hero received his tribute for having plunged into an abyss in the Forum in order to save the populace of Rome; this feat was represented in a relief still preserved in late antiquity and displayed at the Lacus Curtius in the Forum's central area.[90] Simon was a discredited heretic who failed to protect Romans with his leap, in a twisted recapitulation of the Marcus Curtius narrative.

Simon Magus' broken bones and the heretic's failed attempt to protect Romans with a leap suggest an ironic glance at the Forum as well as a reversal of the upright statues that lined the Via Sacra. Specifically, statues on display in the Forum with inscribed bases that noted the affiliations between senatorial officeholders and esteemed rulers expressed how the city benefited from the upkeep and military protection offered by these authorities. Yet popular support was also meaningful for bishops in Rome, particularly given that bitter factional rivalries could emerge.[91] Rather than suggest that the bishop disrupted elite self-presentation in the Forum, the *Acts*

of St. Peter hints that Christian authorities used apocryphal texts to appeal to the public and to find a language with which to acclaim church leaders in the public space of the Roman Forum.

Christian patrons noted the absence of bishops from the representations displayed publicly in the Forum. In a subsequent tradition, Peter, having knelt in prayer, left the imprint of his knees on the Via Sacra. Indentations in stone directly contrasted with the portrait statues. In an account by Gregory of Tours from the sixth century, Peter was accompanied by Paul when they prayed together for the downfall of Simon Magus in the Roman Forum. Both apostles left the permanent traces of their knees in the pavement stones: "Still today at Rome there are two small indentations in the stone upon which the blessed apostles knelt and delivered their oration to the lord against that Simon Magus."[92] In this version of the narrative, the religious conflict emphasized that a monument can symbolize the historic presence of the apostles while capturing their absence. Meanwhile, the *Liber Pontificalis* biography of Paul I (757–767) recounts that "on the Sacred Way (Via Sacra) close to the Temple of Rome . . . even now the kneeprints [of Peter and Paul] can be distinguished on a very hard stone as a testimony to every subsequent generation."[93] The depressions in the pavement both register the saints' knees and reverse the monumentality of imperial installations in the Forum, defining thereby a negative monument. Without disturbing or destroying the aristocratic sponsorship of imperial monuments, the apocryphal account of Peter questioned the materiality of status-driven euergetism. The prints in question may correspond with those on a stone currently installed in the right transept of the church of S. Maria Nova (S. Francesca Romana); the extant indentations could be either footprints or kneeprints (fig. 6.13).

Marking the saints through their absence from the Forum introduced public space as the venue for Christian authorities to question the culture of senatorial honors and to gain support in confronting heretics. In the legendary confrontation between the apostle and the heretic, St. Peter appealed to audiences and persuaded the crowds to reject Simon Magus. The indentations of Peter's feet—or knees—

IN QVESTE
PIETRE POSE
LE GINOCHIA S·PIETRO
QVANDO I DEMONII PORT·
SIMON MAGO
PER ARIA

Figure 6.13. Indentations of the knees (or feet) of St. Peter from the Via Sacra, displayed in the church of S. Francesca Romana, Rome. Photo by the author.

in the pavement suggest that a symbol of modesty gained public acceptance for those leaders who steered people away from heresy. The symbol also deactivated the emblems of status witnessed in the aristocratic and imperial statues.

The *Acts of St. Peter* contests the traditional virtues on display in urban public space by disrupting the learned culture of aristocrats. In Nazarius' panegyric for Constantine performed publicly in 317, discussed earlier, the description of the emperor in public space emphasizes that civic ornament reflects on the ruler much as an aristocratic home reveals the owner's identity: "Truly, as in grand residences where vestibules give access to ornate interiors, so Rome should provide for us the entrance of praise and the doorway of public commendation for we who arrive into the stupendous interior of extensive virtues."[94] Nazarius claims that the praiseworthy qualities of ornamented public spaces in the Forum depicted virtues, masking status under the shared cultural value of rhetorical education and the tight-knit bonds that established formal friendships connecting emperors to other members of the elite.

To praise Theodosius I during his celebration in Rome of a triumph over Maximus in 389, Pacatus delivered a panegyric commending the emperor for his loyalty and the benevolence of spirit that he offered to the upper echelons of society. After listing the appointments that Theodosius had freely and generously made solely on the basis of friendship, namely to the prefecture, the consulship, and the military role of general, Pacatus praised friendship as a noteworthy imperial virtue: "With a novel kind of benevolence, you distributed to your friends honors that were intended to be exclusive to them, so that no benefit might accrue to you from them unless it be the pleasure of giving."[95] In contrast to these honorific models of friendship and ornamental tropes of public space grounded in status, the *Acts of St. Peter* recounts episodes where the bonds among Christians are grounded in belief.

The *Acts of St. Peter* and the biography of St. Martina recount how crowds gathered at sites in the Roman Forum and near the Curia, illustrating how Rome's public space influenced audiences. In the legend of St. Martina, her proximity to the site where aristocrats received favorable legal treatment suggests that her own condemnation before a tribune was unjust. Saints attracted crowds: Martina addressed a group as large as the one that accompanied Peter from the house of Marcellus to the Forum. Both narratives suggest public performances that, in their episodic details and their uses of direct speech, attracted more diverse groups of listeners than the refined phrasing of imperial panegyrics. One could speculate that audiences listened to public storytellers or recitations of these texts, much as the enthroned St. Martina read from a tablet. In the politicized space of Rome, the saints implied that status-driven lay patronage was overbearing. Thus, by contrast to the monuments displaying the excessive power of aristocrats, Peter and Martina gained community support by disavowing the pretentions of senatorial authority. The indentations left by St. Peter in the pavement explicitly negated the figural representations of standing rulers, allowing bishops through reversal to gain authority, while also criticizing the imagery of state officials. Despite the narrative accounts that challenged aristocratic and imperial control of public space, the legends depict the saints seeking alliances with lay patrons and entering the Forum, motivated by the need—at least in narrative texts—to gain popular approval.

The Petrine narratives emphasize that the saint subverted the monumental expressions of aristocratic prestige in Rome. Legends about Peter opened up discussions that implicitly criticized such projects as the Atrium Libertatis and the Secretarium Senatus. These annexes to the Curia instigated the revival of earlier traditions of senatorial governance and secured elite prerogatives during late antiquity. With the increasingly influential role of bishops, church authorities disputed the historical claims of senators as Christian leaders questioned that the past could provide popular appeal. The indentations in the paving stones left by Peter on the Via Sacra and the reversal of the prestige of the senator Epiphanius by a saint of that name at the church of S. Martina point toward modifications in the discourse of senatorial control. Ambrose's letters on the Curia present how the bishop sought to regulate the memories of aristocratic honor by removing a pagan altar. Also, the legend of Peter indicates that the saint disavowed a portrait statue dedicated to an emperor. Finally, the reports on activities of Peter and Martina both reveal that the monuments and buildings of the Forum were preserved to transform historical narratives without destructive measures.

The self-promotion of the elite at the Senate House and in the public space of the Roman Forum reveal the importance of preserving zones in which to display power, even after fissures between paganism and Christianity emerged. The interventions at the Senate House, from the dispute over the altar of Victory to the conflict over St. Martina's opposition to idolatry, should not be understood only as anti-traditionalist polemic. In narrative texts, after all, the saints were presented as helping to preserve many of the monuments in the Forum. Thus, the Senate House in particular reveals how restoration and the maintenance of the past guaranteed the continuation of individual honor over generations; yet the apocrypha and hagiography indicate that the abuse of power by the traditional senatorial aristocracy was relegated to oblivion in the legendary Roman Forum.

PUBLIC SPACE IN
LATE ANTIQUITY

THE SERIES OF PIECEMEAL INTERVENTIONS THAT TRANSFORMED THE ROMAN FORUM during the fourth and fifth centuries CE created a coherent environment, even though they were isolated activities. Significant decorative projects produced the sense that the Forum was restored during this time, as installations updated audiences' perceptions of the past at the civic center. Over these two centuries, the transformations reacted to the empire's bifurcation, the aristocracy's expansion, and the rare occasions when influential emperors resided in Rome. Yet none of these developments was reported negatively in the Forum's inscribed monuments. Neither religious disputes nor the new urban status of bishops received direct attestations in the Forum's inscriptions prior to the sixth century, even though Christian authorities, including emperors, prompted the reconfiguration of temples and the removal of the altar of Victory from the Senate House. Emperors by and large received honor from the images displayed publicly in the late antique Roman Forum because they continued to represent the revived antiquity of the state.

Those who were commemorated by statues individually arranged in the Roman Forum received additional status based on the significance of the images' display spots. Senators who dedicated statues to emperors were seen to have upheld state institutions both at the local level and within the wider empire; the names of aristocrats appeared prominently, inscribed on plinths set up at the most crowded locations. Individual leaders were celebrated in both words and images: emperors appeared to inherit authority from their predecessors at the same time that senators displayed their active participation in governance. Prior to the third century, statues of deities, emperors, and senators had coexisted in civic installations.[1] During the late empire, by contrast, public images of deities were not typically shown in close contact with likenesses of Christian emperors, and there were very few actual portraits on display depicting aristocrats in the Roman Forum. The architectural context in which the installations were located became highly significant in late antiquity as well, since audiences' perceptions of the state were communicated by such structures as the Rostra and the Forum's monumental columns supporting images of rulers. Outside of the Senate House and the Atrium Libertatis were displayed portraits that subtly advanced projects to reinstate the lapsed ages in which aristocrats held power; these goals, oddly, were documented in the inscriptions accompanying images of emperors and the military elite.

Senatorial sponsorship of imperial monuments in busy, reenergized areas of the Forum paved the way for the late antique public to look at their rulers as condoning the elite posts of the local nobles. An installation aligned with the Via Sacra allowed viewers to look at the statue of Honorius undertaken by the local senator Flavius Pisidius Romulus in the foreground against a backdrop of the seven towering columns aligning with the south flank of the Forum's paved central area (see fig. 3.14).[2] Also facing a gathering place were the slightly colossal portraits of Constantius II that the aristocrat Memmius Vitrasius Orfitus had installed; one of the plinths still remains at its original display location facing the plaza in front of the Senate House (see fig. 3.3).[3] The public space for imperial representations where senators also received recognition invited audiences to see the elites as maintaining the Forum. Repaired buildings communicated that patrons earned exalted status through their association with the entire rebuilt zone. Diocletian and Maximian, having undertaken important projects that transformed the central area of the Forum and made provisions for the rebuilt Curia Senatus, created images following a cyclical rhythm of time that was particularly apparent in the two facing installations of five-column monuments. The Tetrarchic sense of imperial stasis was rooted in the comparison between emperors and deities and fell out of favor during the post-Constantinian empire, when displays traced temporal concepts through memories of distinct individuals.

A slightly different picture of restoration emerges at the Basilica Aemilia and the Basilica Julia, which accommodated not only the Roman law courts, but also commerce. In part because the shops furthered the perception that items were available in abundance nearly every day at the *tabernae* of the two basilicas, these buildings served as spaces that were both popular and beneficial to the people.[4] The statues displayed there, at least as far as the recovered

plinths indicate, were shifted from elsewhere in the city or had been "curated" by senators such as Fabius Titianus. The plinths from the Basilica Julia identifying works by the famous Greek artists Polyclitus, Praxiteles, and Timarchus clearly confirm that the opulence of skillfully produced statues was on display.[5] To be sure, there were also signs of imperial honors on view at the Basilica Aemilia—for example, the epistyle set up by Aurelius Anicius Symmachus to commemorate the emperors Honorius and Theodosius II.[6] Nonetheless, it is striking that senators turned these basilicas into sites for statues transferred from elsewhere. The statues moved to the basilicas can be characterized as artworks—a nebulous category, but one defined by indications of beautiful ornamentation or skilled manufacture. Further, the senators' restoration work among these structurally diminished basilicas invited comparisons to the different forms of imperial restoration.

Late antique senators who moved statues and set up artworks, such as Probianus and Fabius Titianus, established spaces for culture at the façades of the basilicas—that is, they set up spaces that were ornamented to give pleasure and to elicit positive reactions from viewers rather than to convey ideology. In so doing, they assumed roles that once had been fulfilled by emperors. Vespasian, for example, had established the lavish, garden-like arrangement of Greek statues in the Temple of Peace, including the impressive masterpieces that Nero had previously collected for his Domus Aurea; he transformed the display contexts of these works as well by moving them from the private into the public sphere. Thus, senators took over the imperial model as the local aristocrats provided for cultural displays and received credit as sponsors of civic ornament at the façades of the basilicas flanking the late antique Roman Forum's central area. Moving statues was not necessarily a result of the closure of temples, then; it was a gesture that provided emblems of sophistication and artworks to be admired as marvels.

Distinguishing political zones, such as the plaza facing the Rostra, from areas for exhibiting artworks, such as the Basilica Aemilia or the Basilica Julia, defines two separate but interrelated projects in the Roman Forum. The busiest public zones of the Forum articulated that senators honored the emperors; the equally crowded but less open zones along the façades of the two basilicas presented culturally meaningful displays as accessible emblems of erudition. All of these expressions of the restored civic realm were articulated in inscriptions; thus public texts were written and revised so as to continually update the space. From the individual works that were installed one by one, late antique viewers gained the sense that senators had revived Rome while working in close collaboration with imperial authorities.

Legitimacy was acquired through the preservation of Rome. During the sixth-century Gothic Wars, in which the East launched military campaigns to reclaim Italy, the Byzantine general Belisarius reportedly issued an impassioned plea for preserving Rome as a city whose built fabric could dictate its own destiny. At the time, Belisarius was about to recapture the city from the Ostrogoths under the king Totila. Aware that political benefits could be gained by protecting the city's built infrastructure, Belisarius aimed to prevent his adversaries from acquiring control over Rome's architectural heritage. In an account of the conflict, Procopius described a persuasive letter written by Belisarius to discourage Totila from setting Rome on fire. Belisarius' words staved off destruction by implying that a leader could achieve fame only by protecting the trajectory of history that was built up in Rome. Burning Rome, by contrast, would taint a ruler's reputation forever. Procopius quoted from the letter:

The destruction of beauty which already exists would be naturally expected only of those who lack understanding, and who are not ashamed to leave to posterity this token of their character. Now among all the cities under the sun Rome is agreed to be the most noteworthy. . . . Little by little have they [previous rulers of Rome] built the city, such as you behold it, thereby leaving to future generations memorials of the ability of them all, so that insult to these monuments would properly be considered a great crime against the people of all time.[7]

Procopius implied that Totila hesitated to destroy Rome because those who harmed monuments were considered despised tyrants.[8] Totila never did burn

Rome, even though the city suffered from numerous sieges during the Gothic Wars. Those who survived the war could inherit the past, Procopius implied, because preserving the "memorials of the ability of them all" appeared in representations that remained intact. These memorials were items that recorded the achievements of esteemed individuals: a wise commander would preserve them, but relegating these "abilities" to oblivion would only sanction villainy. Thus, public space was built up gradually by independent projects that together created an accumulation of memories to be supplemented by just rulers; one could only receive censure by allowing the cultural heritage to perish.

Procopius may have had only the vaguest inkling about the late antique Roman Forum. Nonetheless, public displays in Mediterranean cities illustrated that generations of rulers and powerful aristocrats had inherited the past by restoring buildings. In short, Procopius registered the lasting influence of the senatorial ideas of retrofitting the Forum, where memories of Rome's earliest foundations could be renewed and dramatically reformulated through the zone's transformations. Yet the memories that were by and large preserved in the late antique Roman Forum were those of the specific emperors or the high-ranking senators whose own identities were renewed along with the built fabric.

POSTSCRIPT ON OSTROGOTHIC ROME

The activation of memories that allowed conceptual restoration to further the goals of Italian authorities is strikingly evident during the period of Ostrogothic rule in the late fifth century. Procopius hinted in his account of the decision not to burn Rome that Totila was under the sway of the city's civilizing traditions. Another sixth-century perspective comes from Cassiodorus, a Roman patrician and eloquent voice of an earlier period of Ostrogothic rule: the reign of Theoderic (r. 491–526), who ruled Italy with tacit approval of the Roman emperor, at this point residing in the East. Having written letters to be sent out under Theoderic's signature, Cassiodorus articulated the Ostrogothic king's policies using the eloquent words of an aristocrat.

Reports indicate that Theoderic restored preexisting buildings and reinstated the traditional urban pleasures for which ancient structures were designed. Cassiodorus recorded this strategy in a letter written on behalf of Theoderic, stating: "Let the cities return, then, to their original glory; let no one prefer the delights of the countryside to the public buildings of the ancients. . . . Who does not enjoy conversing with his peers, visiting the Forum, looking on at honest crafts?"[9] Theoderic upheld the physical as well as the cultural health of Rome by providing both water drainage and entertainment places while repairing other civic structures. Taxes on wine (*arca vinaria*) went toward restoration projects, particularly benefiting the palace.[10] Theoderic had also extensively restored the Senate House (Curia Senatus).[11] To supervise these projects, the Gothic king appointed an *architectus* who cared for ancient buildings and repaired venerable monuments.[12] Theoderic even turned his attention to the sewers (*cloacae*) of Rome, thereby earning high rhetorical praise in a letter scripted by Cassiodorus.[13] Texts describing efforts to bolster structures in Rome portrayed the city as a body whose every inner organ deserved maintenance, advancing the notion that the city worked like an organism. Yet Rosella Rea has demonstrated that Theoderic turned to the Colosseum as a quarry of building materials.[14] Such destruction complicated the Ostrogothic claim to have preserved ancient architecture, demonstrating that Theoderic advocated conservationist measures for political effect. In fact, Theoderic's autocratic and oppressive decisions harmed Rome politically, particularly after the king sent the philosopher Boethius and Pope John (523–526) to prison, where both perished. Masking the damage done to the city and its populace, Theoderic insisted upon his reputation as the restorer of other buildings and reaped beneficial publicity from that.

The rule of Theoderic marks a distinct phase in the culture of memory from that of the fourth and fifth centuries. With Cassiodorus, we see record-keeping as a strategy of maintaining memories, perhaps because the built environment in Rome was indeed much more compromised than it had been before. As an archivist himself, Cassiodorus wrote about the public-records office as a repository that functioned optimally by "receiving new additions continually while conserving the old."[15] Cassiodorus sought to ensure the precise wordings of documents that were maintained, which he distinguished from retaining memories that could run the risk of inconsistency.[16] Letters issued under the name of the Ostrogothic king were used more to establish the ruler's identity than were displays in urban public space. In the end, letters written by Cassiodorus offered a discursive method of preserving Theoderic's identity. Inscriptions and statues were in fact put up in honor of Theoderic; but the Ostrogoth used restoration to gain a reputation without negotiating the proper support of local interests and the king did not match his claim to be a preserver with virtuous deeds. Thus, Theoderic did not consistently pursue the affiliations with Romans and the proper respect for aristocratic virtues that connected structural restorations with efforts to reinstate the social cohesion among those who were powerful.

The sixth-century failure to keep up public space seems to have resulted in the loss of memories, compromising the ability of the Forum to accommodate the historical records of esteemed individuals. But these developments remind us of the advantages that the Roman urban center brought during the fourth century. First, outdoor displays of statues representing prominent people were highly visible, not hidden away in the drawers of an archive. Second, during late antiquity the displays presented the illusion that Rome remained a capital, even though the fractured empire had shifted power to the East. Finally, restored buildings reasserted the correct balance between aristocratic individuality, imperial preeminence, and popular support that sustained the most important public memories.

By the period of Theoderic's kingship, the system by which senators believed they mediated the goals of the emperors on behalf of the people had fallen apart. Yet many of the outward forms of late antique practices remained in place. In the year 500, Theoderic commemorated a jubilee year with ritual celebrations that reinstated the tradition of imperial assemblies in the Roman Forum. Arriving from

Ravenna, Theoderic processed into Rome in an official ceremony to mark the longevity of his rule. The ritual high point occurred in front of the Curia, where the king's public address allowed him to acquire proper authority. Theoderic had restored the Curia, as mentioned above. As a result, the link between civic ceremonies and architectural restoration in the Forum as instituted by the Tetrarchs situated Theoderic at the end point of an imperial lineage. This was reinforced by the statues and other monuments that created a historical trajectory.

One account of Theoderic's ceremony in Rome was written by an anonymous chronicler who documented the format of the king's entrance into the city as if it were a recapitulation of the imperial processions celebrated by Constantine, Constantius II, Theodosius I, and Honorius in the Roman Forum. Identifying the event as a thirty-year jubilee, the chronicler established that senators, accompanied by the pope, first greeted Theoderic outside of the city walls. Proceeding toward the Curia, Theoderic met with senators in the Senate House, after which he gave a formal address to the populace. The chronicler states, "Then, arriving inside the city, [Theoderic] entered into the Senate and spoke to the people at the place called the palm (*ad Palmam*), promising that with the help of God he would uphold all of the decrees of earlier Roman rulers."[17] This encounter took place outside of the Senate House, where the metallic palm remained on display at the plaza in front of the Curia. Also on display were statues representing the "earlier Roman rulers" and the tradition of legal authority that had been adjudicated at the Curia. The ritual entrance of Theoderic into the Forum reactivated imperial memories by connecting the physical reconstruction of the Curia with the continuity of the state. In many ways, Theoderic ruled at the time with the tacit approval of the Byzantine emperor Anastasius. But Theoderic's visit to Rome also indicated the dissonance between imperial pomp and cynical audience responses, since he was seen by many as an oppressor.

A mock eyewitness account of Theoderic's visit provides a skeptical voice that gives a Christian perspective. St. Fulgentius of Ruspe was supposedly visiting Rome in 500. According to Ferrandus'

sixth-century biography of Fulgentius, the saint perceived the ancient city as a conceptual rubric for anticipating the heavenly Jerusalem. In Ferrandus' account, Fulgentius felt both admiration and disdain while contemplating the ancient architecture of the Forum. The hagiographic text indicates that Fulgentius witnessed "King Theoderic pronouncing a memorable speech at the place called the *Palma Aurea*," again referring to the gilded column that looked like a palm tree.[18] Ferrandus contended that Fulgentius hesitated to admire Theoderic's boastful pretensions when people shouted out praise of the ruler in front of the Curia. These acclamations reportedly caused Fulgentius to appreciate the humble martyrs more than the vainglorious Theoderic. In the report, however, the saint overcame these qualms, somehow managing to take in the splendor.

[Fulgentius saw] the noble appearance of the Roman senate and the varied ranks of the aristocracy, each with its own distinctive insignia. Hearing with his inexperienced ears the acclamations of a free people, he recognized the nature of the glories of this world. But he was not willing to recognize anything worthwhile in the spectacle, nor did he let himself be tempted by the useless seduction of earthly frivolity. Rather, he was inspired mostly by the aspiration to possess the happiness of the celestial Jerusalem. To his companions, who were standing near him, [Fulgentius] exclaimed the following words. "How beautiful must be the heavenly Jerusalem if the earthly Rome thus shines. And if in this world one can accord so much honor to those who love vanity, then how much this honor and glory will be elevated to the saints who live contemplating the truth."[19]

Fulgentius' response, rooted in Christian apocalyptic thinking, appropriates the late antique concept that civic space points toward a historical trajectory in the individual commemorative monuments that set forth a precedent for the future. Rather than anticipating that a ruler such as an Ostrogothic king gains legitimacy from the past, Fulgentius seems to look toward the end of time. Fulgentius, then, implicitly disputed Theoderic's intention of legitimizing power by reinstating memories through the physical restoration of the Senate House.

ROMAN MEMORY PRACTICES

Architecture provided the tangible context in which either emperors or local senators furnished repairs that launched claims to have repossessed the past. Local aristocrats used late antique statue installations as "restorations" at the Basilica Aemilia and the Basilica Julia to create cultural zones, in a strategy that differed profoundly from the imperial ideology of returning authority to its proper place at the more open zones of the Forum. Thus, physical repairs consistently rebuilt the context in which memories were alternately regulated or valorized. Important architectural developments, such as adaptive reuse and the heterogeneous arrangement of *spolia*, required that viewers conceive of the past in light of individual commemoration. In the account of the life of Fulgentius, as in the legendary tale of Silvester and the dragon, physical architecture was conscientiously maintained, even when it came to be described as somehow threatening.

Modest in scale, yet rich in topographically rooted details about the posturing of late antique elites, the inscriptions that redecorated the Roman Forum were significant in their transformative power. It was, however, precisely the false modesty of restraint that positioned the elite-sponsored interventions as proclamations of virtue when in fact their goal was the accumulation of power. Social relations generated the installations, and a few letters sent by emperors to individual Roman aristocrats were recorded in inscriptions. More frequently, the monuments presented only the illusion that dialogue took place between local Romans and the often distant emperors.

The piecemeal additions of inscribed statues in the Roman Forum recast the built environment into the role of a text whose integrity was constantly subject to reevaluation, allowing the displays to accommodate adaptations over time. As a result, restoration in late antiquity mapped out an atlas of memory that traced the changing circumstances over the years. These were the memories of individuals whose accomplishments were listed in inscriptions. The late antique Roman Forum featured significant restoration projects that were experienced in the context of the memories preserved in portrait statues. Regulating these memories through new installations while preserving that which was already on view explains both the displays of statues and the restored buildings. Even as the structures were altered through the arrangement of *spolia* and as Christians curtailed the activities allowed in temples, the restorations ensured the maintenance of memories. Shifting alliances and statues on the move contributed to these conceptually vast yet physically subtle rearrangements, which supplemented the large-scale initiatives of architectural restoration and allowed the Roman Forum—even if in ruins—to be seen today.

NOTES

INTRODUCTION

1. Giuseppe A. Guattani, *Memorie enciclopediche sulle antichità e belle arti di Roma* (Rome: Stampa Romana, 1819), vol. 2, table 7, shows that excavations during the early nineteenth century at the Column of Phocas revealed the partly concealed inscription of Lucius Naevius Surdinus beneath the column's base.

2. *CIL* 6.31662, 37068: "L(ucius) NAEVIUS L(ucii) F(ilius) SURDINUS PR(aetor)." Some fragments of the Surdinus inscription came to light in the early nineteenth-century excavations of the Column of Phocas, and Boni revealed the additional parts of the inscription in 1905–1906: Cairoli F. Giuliani and Patrizia Verduchi, *L'area centrale del Foro Romano* (Florence: Olschki, 1987), 39–66, 93–94. The original Surdinus repavement was presumably completed after the fire of 14 BCE: Paul Zanker, *Il foro romano: La sistemazione da Augusto alla tarda antichità*, trans. L. Franchi (Rome: De Luca, 1972), 25. Surdinus served as *praetor inter cives et peregrinos*, an office he is presumed to have held around 7 BCE. He also probably served as the *triumvir monetalis* in 15 BCE: *RIC* 1.2, Augustus, 383–386.

3. Alessandra Capodiferro, ed., *Gli scavi di Giacomo Boni al Foro Romano: Documenti dall'archivio della Soprintendenza Archeologica di Roma* (Rome: Flora Palatina, 2003); particularly insightful is the essay there on Boni's collaborators by Miriam Taviani (pp. 35–50). See also Elisabetta Carnabuci, "L'angolo sud-orientale del Foro Romano nel manoscritto inedito di Giacomo Boni," *Atti della Accademia Nazionale dei Lincei: Classe di scienze morali, storiche e filologiche: Memorie*, ser. 9, vol. 1, fasc. 4 (1991): 251–252.

4. Giuliani and Verduchi, *L'area centrale*, 35, 46, 50, 58, 64–66, and 122.

5. Ibid., 65–66.

6. Filippo Coarelli, *Il foro romano*, vol. 2, *Periodo repubblicano e Augusteo* (Rome: Quasar, 1985), 211–222. Coarelli argues on the basis of logic—not archeological data—that a few minor repairs of the Forum plaza might have occurred under the Severans, but not the entire pavement of the plaza. Coarelli rejects the proposal of Giuliani and Verduchi that the pavement was redone in distinct phases: "Ecco così brillantemente risolto il problema della quadratura del cerchio, che consiste nel far convivere la datazione postaugustea del pavimento attuale con la presenza su di esso di un'iscrizione di età augustea: basta introdurre un nuovo e inatteso protagonista, un altro pavimento—questo sì augusteo—che sarebbe poi statto abolito, conservando solo pochi brandelli, a fini che peraltro non sono affatto chiari (perché questa cura per la memoria di un ignoto praetor peregrinus di età augustea?). Ma così si raggiunge perfettamente lo scopo: datare uno o più settori del pavimento non è più sufficente a datare l'insieme" (219). Coarelli did not yet have access to Giuliani and Verduchi's 1987 publication, with full documentation and carefully prepared illustrations that clearly indicate the layers of pavement.

7. Coarelli, *Il foro romano*, 2:220: "È del resto probabile che molte lastre siano state rifatte nel corso della lunghissima vita di questa pavimento."

8. *CIL* 6.1468: "L(ucius) Naevius L(uci) F(ilius) Surdinus / pr(aetor) / inter civis et peregrinos." A replica has been installed in the Roman Forum; the original is displayed in the Capitoline Museums.

9. When writing his volumes on the Roman Forum, Coarelli had access only to the brief, summary publication—Cairoli F. Giuliani and Patrizia Verduchi, *Foro Romano: L'area centrale* (Flor-

ence: Olschki, 1980)—published seven years prior to the more complete analysis with extensive diagrams contained in the book released in 1987. The failure of Giuliani and Verduchi to respond in print to Coarelli's objections may be attributed to the date when their manuscript was submitted; yet the methodology of Giuliani and Verduchi, which relies on physical evidence without acknowledging literary testimony and much of the previous scholarship, has prompted T. P. Wiseman to ask what motive Severus might have had to revive Surdinus' memory in the third century: T. P. Wiseman, "The Central Area of the Roman Forum," *Journal of Roman Archaeology* 3 (1990): 245–247. Wiseman's valid questions do not detract from the physical testimony to the third-century repairs; for the clear evidence of cutting and pasting the inscription during the third century, see Giuliani and Verduchi, *L'area centrale*, 93–94.

10. Diane Favro, "Construction Traffic in Imperial Rome: Building the Arch of Septimius Severus," in *Rome, Ostia, Pompeii: Movement and Space*, ed. Ray Laurence and David J. Newsome (Oxford: Oxford University Press, 2011), 359.

11. For the fire, see Herodian, *Historia* 1.14.4. See also John Curran, *Pagan City and Christian Capital: Rome in the Fourth Century* (Oxford: Oxford University Press, 2000), 5–8.

12. *CIL* 6.1033: ". . . ob rem publicam restitutam imperiumque populi Romani propagatum."

13. Herodian, *Historia* 2.9.5–6.

14. The lack of Severan infill at the central indentation of the Forum plaza that once was associated with the equestrian statue of Domitian was observed by Giuliani and Verduchi (*L'area centrale*, 133–137), who thereby ruled out the possibility that the Severan equestrian monument was inserted into the large gap in the pavement. Giuliani and Verduchi further proposed that the spot directly to the north held the Severan equestrian monument: *L'area centrale*, 117–122. Filippo Coarelli ("Equus: Septimius Severus," in *LTUR* 2:231–232) proposed that the Severan monument occupied what was to become a Constantinian monument adjacent to the western Rostra, but this suggestion has not been widely accepted. Michael Thomas ("[Re]locating Domitian's Horse of Glory: The 'Equus Domitiani' and Flavian Urban Design," *Memoirs of the American Academy in Rome* 49 [2004]: 21–46) proposes that the equestrian statue of Severus stood at the spot that now supports the Column of Phocas. The difficulty of analyzing the material beneath the column prevents confirmation of Thomas's proposal. I agree with Giuliani and Verduchi that the Severan equestrian monument stood on the Forum pavement to the north of the indentation for the Domitian monument.

15. Lukas de Blois, "Emperorship in a Period of Crisis: Changes in Emperor Worship, Imperial Ideology and Perceptions of Imperial Authority in the Roman Empire in the Third Century A.D.," in *The Impact of Rome on Religions, Ritual and Religious Life in the Roman Empire*, ed. Lukas de Blois, Peter Funke, and Johannes Hahn (Leiden: Brill, 2006), 268–278.

16. Ammianus Marcellinus, *Res gestae* 26.6.15. For the im-

portance of the shoes, see Matthew Canepa, *The Two Eyes of the Earth: Art and Ritual of Kingship between Rome and Sasanian Iran* (Berkeley: University of California Press, 2009), 201–204.

17. For Diocletian's system, with the invention of new powerful posts in the empire's administration appointed by the emperors, see Stephen Williams, *Diocletian and the Roman Recovery* (New York: Methuen, 1985), 102–114. For the new ideology of quasi-divine rule, see Frank Kolb, "*Praesens Deus*: Kaiser und Gott unter der Tetrarchie," in *Diokletian und die Tetrarchie: Aspekte einer Zeitenwende*, ed. Alexander Demandt, Andreas Goltz, and Heinrich Schlange-Schöningen (Berlin: Walter de Gruyter, 2004), 27–37; idem, *Herrscherideologie in der Spätantike* (Berlin: Akademie, 2001), 175–186.

18. Lactantius, *De mortibus persecutorum* 17.2: "Quibus sollemnibus celebratis cum libertatem populi Romani ferre non poterat."

19. This observation has been made recently by Paolo Liverani, "Osservazioni sui rostri del Foro Romano in età tardoantica," in *Res bene gestae: Ricerche di storia urbana su Roma antica in onore di Eva Margareta Steinby*, ed. Anna Leone, Domenico Palombi, and Susan Walker, LTUR, suppl. 4 (Rome: Quasar, 2007), 169–194.

20. Ovid, *Fasti* 4.11.819–836; Tacitus, *Annals* 12.24. Dating the wall to the eighth century BCE rests upon the discovery of a cup originating from that era; see Andrea Carandini, *Rome: Day One*, trans. S. Sartarelli (Princeton, N.J.: Princeton University Press, 2011), 59; idem, *La nascita di Roma: Dèi, lari, eroi e uomini all'alba di una civiltà* (Turin: Einaudi, 1997), xxv n. 4.

21. The assertion that Romulus was historical has been rejected by T. P. Wiseman, "Reading Carandini," in *Journal of Roman Studies* 91 (2002): 182–193; idem, review of A. Carandini, *La nascita di Roma*, and M. Bertelli, *Roma: La città prima della città*, *Journal of Roman Studies* 90 (2000): 210–212. Carandini claims that Romulus eventually shifted the city's religious life from the Palatine to the eastern sector of the Roman Forum (*La nascita di Roma*, 46–71). Carandini's claim runs counter to the careful excavations under the auspices of the American Academy in Rome and the Archaeological Superintendent of Rome that associate the early cultic activity near the Regia and the nearby precinct of Vesta, both at the Forum's east end, to the sixth century BCE; see Russell T. Scott, ed., *Excavations in the Area Sacra of Vesta (1987–1996)*, Memoirs of the American Academy in Rome, suppl. 8 (Ann Arbor: University of Michigan Press, 2009), 77–78.

22. Coarelli, *Il foro romano*, vols. 1 and 2.

23. Klaus Freyberger, *Das Forum Romanum: Spiegel der Stadtgeschichte des antiken Rom* (Mainz: Philipp von Zabern, 2009); Franz Alto Bauer, *Stadt, Platz und Denkmal in der Spätantike: Untersuchungen zur Ausstattung des öffentlichen Raums in den spätantiken Städten Rom, Konstantinopel und Ephesos* (Mainz: Philipp von Zabern, 1996), 7–79.

24. Christian Witschel, "Statuen auf spätantiken Platzanlagen in Italien und Africa," in *Statuen in der Spätantike*, ed. Franz

Alto Bauer and Christian Witschel (Weisbaden: Reichert, 2007), 113–169.

25. Cassiodorus, *Variae* 7.13: "populus copiosissimus statuarum, greges etiam abundatissimi equorum."

26. There is a lack of evidence to support the presumption that emperors sponsored buildings and monuments during the high imperial period in the West; see Carlos Noreña, *Imperial Ideals in the Roman West: Representation, Circulation, Power* (Cambridge: Cambridge University Press, 2011), 245–276; Emanuel Mayer, "Propaganda, Staged Applause, or Local Politics? Public Monuments from Augustus to Septimius Severus," in *The Emperor and Rome: Space, Representation, and Ritual*, ed. Björn Ewald and Carlos Noreña (Cambridge: Cambridge University Press, 2010), 111–134; Gregor Kalas, "Writing and Restoration in Rome: Inscriptions, Statues, and the Late Antique Preservation of Buildings," in *Cities, Texts, and Social Networks, 400–1500: Experiences and Perceptions of Medieval Urban Space*, ed. Caroline Goodson, Anne E. Lester, and Carol Symes (Surrey: Ashgate, 2010), 21–43.

27. Noreña, *Imperial Ideals*, 202–218.

28. The reassembled statues are *CIL* 6.1658a and 6.1658b.

29. An important discussion of *spolia* appears in Dale Kinney, "Rape or Restitution of the Past? Interpreting *Spolia*," in *The Art of Interpreting*, ed. Susan Scott (University Park: Pennsylvania State University Press, 1995), 52–65. For the range of definitions of *spolia*, see Kinney, "The Concept of *Spolia*," in *A Companion to Medieval Art*, ed. Conrad Rudolph (London: Blackwell, 2006), 233–252. See also the recent volume edited by Richard Brilliant and Dale Kinney: *Reuse Value: Spolia and Appropriation in Art and Architecture from Constantine to Sherrie Levine* (Surrey: Ashgate, 2011). Current discussions of *spolia* include Caroline Goodson, "Roman Archaeology in Medieval Rome," in *Rome: Continuing Encounters between Past and Present*, ed. Dorigen Caldwell and Lesley Caldwell (Surrey: Ashgate, 2011), 17–34; Marina Prusac, *From Face to Face: Recarving of Roman Portraits and the Late-Antique Portrait Arts* (Leiden: Brill, 2011); Hendrik Dey, "*Spolia*, Milestones, and City Walls: The Politics of Imperial Legitimacy in Gaul," in *Patrons and Viewers in Late Antiquity*, ed. Stine Birk and Birte Poulsen (Aarhus: Aarhus University Press, 2012), 291–310. For a wide-ranging discussion of the development and ideas of architectural *spolia*, see Maria Fabricius Hansen, *The Eloquence of Appropriation: Prolegomena to an Understanding of Spolia in Early Christian Rome* (Rome: "L'Erma" di Bretschneider, 2003), 7–12.

30. Joseph Alchermes, "*Spolia* in Roman Cities of the Late Empire: Legislative Rationales and Architectural Reuse," *Dumbarton Oaks Papers* 48 (1994): 167–178.

31. For current restoration approaches, see Jukka Jokilehto, *A History of Architectural Conservation* (Oxford: Butterworth-Heinemann, 1999), 13–19; Argyro Loukaki, *Living Ruins, Value Conflicts* (Aldershot: Ashgate, 2008), 113–134.

32. An example is *CIL* 6.526, the last line of which mentions that the urban prefect of 474–475 restored a statue of Minerva:

"IN MELIUS / INTEGRO PROVISO PRO / BEATITUDINE TEMPORIS RESTITUIT."

33. See the inscription on the Temple of Saturn, *CIL* 6.937: "SENATUS POPULUSQUE ROMANUS / INCENDIUM CONSUMPTUM RESTITUTO," dated to the fourth century CE. See also Edmund Thomas and Christian Witschel, "Constructing Reconstruction: Claim and Reality of Roman Rebuilding Inscriptions from the Latin West," *Papers of the British School at Rome* 60 (1992): 135–177.

34. The verb *reparare* appears frequently in late antique inscriptions of the Forum, including a series of inscribed statue bases that identifies the movement of statues by Gabinius Vettius Probianus to a basilica in the Forum; see *CIL* 6.1658c: "GABINIUS VETTIUS / PROBIANUS V(ir) C(larissimus) PRAEF(ectus) URBI / STATUAM QUAE BASILI/CAE IULIAE A SE NOVITER / REPARATAE ORNAMENTO / ESSE ADIECIT."

35. M. Aemilius Lepidus the Younger sponsored the images for the restored Basilica Aemilia, according to Pliny (*Historia Naturalis* 35.4). An excellent overview of the culture of euergetism in late antiquity is provided in Ann Marie Yasin, *Saints and Church Spaces in the Late Antique Mediterranean* (Cambridge: Cambridge University Press, 2009), 101–110.

36. Pacatus, *Panegyrici Latini* 2 (12), 45.6–7: "cuncti domibus suis, cuncti coniugibus ac liberis, cuncti denique (quod est dulcius) innocentiae restituti sunt. Vide, imperator, quid hac clementia consecutus sis."

37. Orosius, *Historia adversus paganos* 2.19: "ictu fulminum forum cum imaginibus vanis, quae superstitione miserabili vel deum vel hominem mentiuntur, abiectum est, horumque omnium abominamentorum, quod inmissa per hostem flamma non adiit, missus e caelo ignis evertit." Translation from Orosius, *Seven Books of History against the Pagans*, trans. I. W. Raymont (New York: Columbia University Press, 1936), 106.

38. Bryan Ward-Perkins (*The Fall of Rome and the End of Civilization* [Oxford: Oxford University Press, 2005]) presents a provocative account arguing for the decisive decline of Rome.

39. Alan Cameron, *The Last Pagans of Rome* (Oxford: Oxford University Press, 2011).

40. Harriet I. Flower, *The Art of Forgetting: Disgrace and Oblivion in Roman Political Culture* (Chapel Hill: University of North Carolina Press, 2006).

41. Charles W. Hedrick Jr., *History and Silence: Purge and Rehabilitation of Memory in Late Antiquity* (Austin: University of Texas Press, 2000).

42. Hendrik Dey, *The Aurelian Wall and the Refashioning of Imperial Rome, AD 271–855* (Cambridge: Cambridge University Press, 2011).

43. Paul Zanker, *The Power of Images in the Age of Augustus*, trans. A. Shapiro (Ann Arbor: University of Michigan Press, 1988). See also investigations of Augustan Rome by, e.g., Karl Galinsky, *Augustan Culture* (Princeton, N.J.: Princeton University Press, 1996); Lothar Haselberger, *Urbem adornare: Die Stadt*

Rom und ihre Gestaltumwandlung unter Augustus, Journal of Roman Archaeology, suppl. 64 (Portsmouth, R.I.: Journal of Roman Archaeology, 2007); Elisha Dumser, ed., *Mapping Augustan Rome, Journal of Roman Archaeology*, suppl. 50 (Portsmouth, R.I.: Journal of Roman Archaeology, 2002).

44. Diane Favro, *The Urban Image of Augustan Rome* (New York: Cambridge University Press, 1996), brilliantly captures how Rome was experienced in the first century BCE; see also Ray Laurence and David Newsome, eds., *Rome, Ostia, Pompeii: Movement and Space* (Oxford: Oxford University Press, 2011).

45. Entries featuring the postclassical phases of Roman topographical sites are now available in E. M. Steinby, ed., *Lexicon Topographicum Urbis Romae*, 6 vols. (and supplements) (Rome: Quasar, 1993–2000).

46. See the entries available in the database *Last Statues of Antiquity*, http://laststatues.classics.ox.ac.uk, accessed 8 May 2013.

47. Excellent documentation of find spots is presented in Joyce Reynolds, Charlotte Rouché, and Gabriel Bodard, eds., *Inscriptions of Aphrodisias*, http://insaph.kcl.ac.uk/iaph2007, accessed 8 May 2013. See also Charlotte Rouché, *Aphrodisias in Late Antiquity: The Late Roman and Byzantine Inscriptions*, rev. 2d ed., 2004, http://insaph.kcl.ac.uk/ala2004, accessed 8 May 2013.

48. An important scholarly project has reconstructed the Roman Forum and is featured in the *Digital Roman Forum*; see Diane Favro and Bernard Frischer, *Digital Roman Forum*, http://dlib.etc.ucla.edu/projects/Forum, accessed 24 June 2013. For a spatial consideration using a physical model, see Bernhard Steinmann, Robert Nawracala, and Martin Boss, eds., *Im Zentrum der Macht: Das Forum Romanum im Modell* (Erlangen-Nuremberg: Institut für Klassische Archäologie, 2011). I have not been able to consult Gilbert Gorski and James Packer, *The Roman Forum: A Reconstruction and Architectural Guide* (Cambridge: Cambridge University Press, forthcoming).

49. Reconstructions of Egyptian tombs presenting video formats melding digital models with photographic textures are available in Kent Weeks, Susan Weeks, and Lucy T. Jones, *The Theban Mapping Project*, http://www.thebanmappingproject.org, accessed 24 June 2013.

50. Bernard Frischer, Dean Abernathy, and Kim Dylla, *Rome Reborn*, http://www.romereborn.virginia.edu, accessed 24 June 2013.

51. A widely used scholarly platform for presenting such projects is HyperCities, a joint endeavor of scholars at UCLA and the University of Southern California; see *HyperCities*, http://www.hypercities.com, accessed 24 June 2013. A discussion of the methodological implications of HyperCities is available in Todd Presner, "Digital Humanities 2.0: A Report on Knowledge," in *Emerging Disciplines: Shaping New Fields of Inquiry in and beyond the Humanities*, ed. Melissa Bailar (Houston, Tex.: Rice University Press, 2010), 27–38.

52. Gregor Kalas, Diane Favro, Christopher Johanson, Todd Presner, Marie Saldaña, and Pelin Yoncaci, *Visualizing Statues in the Late Antique Roman Forum*, http://inscriptions.etc.ucla.edu, accessed 5 July 2012. The project was developed at UCLA's Experiential Technologies Center with support provided by the National Endowment for the Humanities. Additional collaborators advanced the project significantly, including Yoh Kawano, Ece Okay, Mike Rocchio, and David Shepard.

53. See both the time-slider in the upper left corner of the window presenting the models, and the time-slider available in the "Mapping Statues" section of *Visualizing Statues*, http://inscriptions.etc.ucla.edu/index.php/mapping-statues, accessed 5 July 2012.

54. Brigitte Ruck, *Die Grossen dieser Welt: Kolossalporträts im antiken Rom* (Heidelberg: Verlag Archäologie und Geschichte, 2007), 41–50.

55. To view the digital models, click on "Launch in Hypercities" from the main page of *Visualizing Statues*, http://inscriptions.etc.ucla.edu, accessed 5 July 2012.

56. See "Inscription Database," in *Visualizing Statues*, http://inscriptions.etc.ucla.edu/index.php/inscription-database, accessed 4 May 2011.

57. To be sure, not all of the statues in the digital reconstruction are securely localized at the original display locations; see Gregor Kalas, "Reconstruction Notes," in *Visualizing Statues*, http://inscriptions.etc.ucla.edu/index.php/statues-and-memory/reconstruction-notes, accessed 5 July 2012.

58. See the "Ritual Experience" section of *Visualizing Statues*, http://inscriptions.etc.ucla.edu/index.php/ritual-experience, accessed 4 May 2011.

59. For a letter sent by Quintus Aurelius Symmachus requesting permission to set up a public statue in honor of a recently deceased senator, Vettius Agorius Praetextatus, see Symmachus, *Relationes* 12.2.

60. For reflections on the late antique fora of Praeneste and Cuicul, see Jinyu Liu, "Late Antique Fora and Public Honor in the Western Cities: Case Studies," in *Shifting Cultural Frontiers in Late Antiquity*, ed. David Brakke, Deborah Deliyannis, and Edward Watts (Surrey: Ashgate, 2012), 225–239.

61. Noreña, *Imperial Ideals*, 82–99.

62. Ibid., 246–247.

63. Robert Chenault, "Statues of Senators in the Forum of Trajan and the Roman Forum in Late Antiquity," *Journal of Roman Studies* 102 (2012): 103–132, esp. 115–117.

64. For a discussion of the context in which the letters of emperors were inscribed on plinths, see John Weisweiler, "Inscribing Imperial Power: Letters from Emperors in Late Antique Rome," in *Rom in der Spätantike: Historische Erinnerung im städtischen Raum*, ed. Ralf Behrwald and Christian Witschel (Stuttgart: Steiner, 2012), 309–329.

65. The entire inscription, *CIL* 6.1698 (and p. 4733), reads: "PHOSPHORII / LUCIO AUR(elio) AVIANIO SYMMACHO V(iro) C(larissimo) / PRAEFECTO URBI CONSULI PRO PRAEFECTIS PRAETORIO IN URBE ROMA FINITI-

MISQUE / PROVINCIIS PRAEFECTO ANNONAE UR/
BIS ROMAE PONTIFICI MAIORI QUINDE/CEMVIRO
S(acris) F(aciundis) MULTIS LEGAT[io]NIBUS / PRO AM-
PLISSIMI ORDINIS DESIDERIIS / APUD DIVIOS PRINCI-
PES FUNCTO QUI / PRIMUS IN SENATU SENTENTIAM
ROGA/RI SOLITUS AUCTORITATE PRUDENTIA ATQ(ue)
/ ELOQUENTIA PRO DIGNITATE TANTI ORDI/NIS MAG-
NITUDINEM LOCI EIUS INPLEVE/RIT AURO INLUS-
TREM STATUAM QUAM / A DOMINIS AUGUSTISQ(ue)
NOSTR(is) SENATUS / AMPLISSIMUS DECRETIS
FREQUENTIB(us) IN/PETRABIT IDEM TRIUMFATORES
PRINCIPES / NOSTRI CONSTITUI ADPOSITA ORATIO-
NE IUS/SERUNT QUAE MERITORUM EIUS ORDINEM
/ AC SERIEM CONTINERET QUORUM PERENNE / IU-
DICIUM TANTO MUNERI HOC QUOQUE AD/DIDIT UT
ALTERAM STATUAM PARI SPLEN/DORE ETIAM APUD
CONSTANTINOPOLIM / CONLOCARET." The attached
oration, the text of which originally had been affixed to the
base, does not survive due to the loss of all but the primary
face. See Heike Niquet, *Monumenta virtutum titulique: Senatori-*
sche Selbstdarstellung im spätantiken Rom im Spiegel der epigraphi-
schen Denkmäler (Stuttgart: Steiner, 2000), 78.

66. This idea draws upon the arguments of Hedrick, *History*
and Silence, 240–246.

67. Carlos Machado, "Building the Past: Monuments and
Memory in the *Forum Romanum*," in *Social and Political Life in Late*
Antiquity, ed. William Bowden, Adam Gutteridge, Luke Lavan,
and Carlos Machado (Leiden: Brill, 2006), 157–192. For recent analyses of the late antique Forum as a space that revived
the past, see Susanne Muth, "Der Dialog von Gegenwart und
Vergangenheit am Forum Romanum in Rom—oder: Wie spätantik ist das spätantike Forum?" in *Rom und Mailand in der Spät-*
antike: Repräsentationen städtischer Räume in Literatur, Architektur
und Kunst, ed. Therese Fuhrer (Berlin: de Gruyter, 2012), 263–
282; Franz Alto Bauer, "Das Forum Romanum als normativer
Raum in der Spätantike," in *Athen, Rom, Jerusalem: Normentransfers*
in der antiken Welt, ed. Gian Franco Chiai, Bardo Gauly, Andreas
Hartmann, Gerhard Zimmer, and Burkardt Zapff (Regensburg:
Friedrich Pustet, 2012), 327–341.

68. This point has been clearly established by Franz Alto
Bauer, "Stadt ohne Kaiser: Rom im Zeitalter der Dyarchie und
Tetrarchie (285–306 n.Chr.)," in *Rom und Mailand in der Spät-*
antike: Repräsentationen städtischer Räume in Literatur, Architektur
und Kunst, ed. Therese Fuhrer (Berlin: de Gruyter, 2012), 65–
70; idem, *Stadt, Platz und Denkmal*, 29–46, 72–79, 401–408.
Chenault ("Statues of Senators," 105) has distinguished between the imperial and military nature of the Roman Forum
and the senatorial representations that predominated in the
Forum of Trajan.

69. John Weisweiler, "From Equality to Asymmetry: Honorific Statues, Imperial Power, and Senatorial Identity in Late-
Antique Rome," *Journal of Roman Archaeology* 25 (2012): 318–
350, esp. 332–336.

70. Jill Harries, *Law and Empire in Late Antiquity* (Cambridge:
Cambridge University Press, 1999), 21–23.

71. *CIL* 6.1119a: "Fortissimo ac / florentissimo /
Imp(eratori) Caes(ari) C(aio) Aur(elio) V(alerio) / Diocletiano
. . .."; *CIL* 6.40722: "FORTISSIMO AC / FLORENTISSIMO /
IMP(eratori) CAES(ari) M(arco) AUR(elio) VAL(erio) / MAXI-
MIANO. . . ." Bauer ("Stadt ohne Kaiser," 16–18) identified the
pendant portraits as commemorating the repairs to the Curia
Senatus during the fifth consulate of Diocletian in 293–295.

72. *CIL* 6.1158.

73. The highly damaged inscription, *CIL* 6.41344a = *CIL*
6.36968 and pp. 5073–5074, has text on two sides. One side
features a reference to the phrase "DECRETUM SENATUS
AM[p]PLISSIMI"; the other side indicates the emperor Valentinian II, "[*Valent*]INIANI," by name and thus quotes the decree.
The monument has been dated to the year 391, during the urban prefecture of Ceionius Rufius Albinus. The damaged text
provides just the letters *FIUS*; though the identification of the
individual is likely, then, it cannot be proved. See the discussion
of this in Niquet, *Monumenta virtutum titulique*, 80; Weisweiler,
"From Equality to Asymmetry," 344.

74. Noreña, *Imperial Ideals*, 273–275.

75. *CIL* 6.40764a = 30562.2: "[felicit]ATIS RESTA[uratori] /
[fundato]RI ET PROPA[gatori] / [pacis auct]ORIQUE [quietis]
/ [d(omino) n(ostro) Fl(avio) Val(erio) Consta]NTIN[o P(io)
F(elici) Aug(usto)] / [– – –]." The inscription is currently in
the Capitoline Museums (inv. no. 20.980). For the term *restitu-*
tor, see Noreña, *Imperial Ideals*, 246–249.

76. Carla M. Amici, *Il foro di Cesare* (Florence: Leo S. Olschki, 1991); Eugenio La Rocca, "La nuova immagine dei fori Imperiali: Appunti in margine agli scavi," *Mitteilungen des Deutschen*
Archäologischen Instituts, Römische Abteilung 108 (2001): 171–
213; Roberto Meneghini, Riccardo Santangeli Valenzani, and
Elisabetta Bianchi, *I Fori Imperiali: Gli scavi del Comune di Roma*
(1991–2007) (Rome: Viviani, 2007); Silvana Rizzo, "Indagini
nei fori imperiali: Oroidrografia, foro di Cesare, foro di Augusto, templus Pacis," *Mitteilungen des Deutschen Archäologischen Ins-*
tituts, Römische Abteilung 108 (2001): 215–244; Johannes Lipps,
"Zur Datierung der spätantike Portikus des Caesarforums:
Literarische Quellen und archäologischer Befund," *Mitteilun-*
gen des Deutschen Archäologischen Instituts, Römische Abteilung 114
(2008): 389–405.

77. The following laws prevented sacrifice at altars: Cod.
Theod. 16.10.3 (346 CE); 16.10.5 (346 CE); 16.10.12 (392
CE).

78. Cicero, *De oratore* 3.133: "M'. vero Manilium nos etiam
vidimus transverso ambulantem foro; quod erat insigne eum,
qui id faceret, facere civibus suis omnibus consili sui copiam."
See Timothy O'Sullivan, *Walking in Roman Culture* (Cambridge:
Cambridge University Press, 2011), 65–71.

79. Rowland Smith, "'Restored Utility, Eternal City': Patronal Imagery at Rome in the Fourth Century AD," in *"Bread*
and Circuses": Euergetism and Municipal Patronage in Roman Italy,

ed. Kathryn Lomas and Tim Cornell (London: Routledge, 2003), 142–166, esp. 158–159.

80. Nicholas Purcell, "Rediscovering the Roman Forum," *Journal of Roman Archaeology* 2 (1989): 156–166.

81. Hedrick, *History and Silence*, 147–170; for the installations of statues representing the harmony among individuals from different eras, see Noreña, *Imperial Ideals*, 132–134.

82. Paul Zanker, "By the Emperor, For the People: 'Popular' Architecture in Rome," in *The Emperor and Rome: Space, Representation, and Ritual*, ed. Björn Ewald and Carlos Noreña (Cambridge: Cambridge University Press, 2010), 45–87.

83. Denis Feeney, *Caesar's Calendar: Ancient Time and the Beginnings of History* (Princeton, N.J.: Princeton University Press, 2007), 131–134.

84. Cassius Dio (56.25.1) mentions the name of Tiberius and his brother, Drusus, inscribed upon the Temple of Concord around 10 CE. For the statues of deities displayed inside and outside of the temple, see Steven Rutledge, *Ancient Rome as a Museum: Power, Identity, and the Culture of Collecting* (Oxford: Oxford University Press, 2012), 266–271; Barbara Kellum, "The City Adorned: Programmatic Display at the *Aedes Concordiae Augustae*," in *Between Republic and Empire: Interpretations of Augustus and His Principate*, ed. Kurt Raaflaub and Mark Toher (Berkeley: University of California Press, 1990), 276–307.

85. Robert Markus, *The End of Ancient Christianity* (Cambridge: Cambridge University Press, 1990), 87–95.

86. Hedrick, *History and Silence*, 183–190.

87. For the letters of Symmachus, see *Epistulae Q. Aurelii Symmachi*, ed. Otto Seeck, *MGH AA* 6.1 (Berlin: Weidmann, 1888); for the Theodosian Code (*Codex Theodosianus*), *Theodosiani libri XVI cum Constitutionibus Sirmondinis*, ed. Theodor Mommsen and Paul Meyer, 2 vols. (Hildesheim: Weidmann, 2000).

88. Pierre Nora, "Between Memory and History: *Les lieux de mémoire*," *Representations* 26 (1989): 7–25.

89. Machado, "Building the Past," 158–160, 186–187.

90. For a distinction between cultural memory, or what can be called "remembrance," and an individual retention of memory, or "remembering," see Aleida Assmann, *Cultural Memory and Western Civilization: Functions, Media, Archives* (Cambridge: Cambridge University Press, 2011), 291–298.

91. The urban prefect, the chief imperial administrator in Rome, was the highest authority supervising public works, including civic buildings, and also presided over the senate. This position was an imperial appointment; see André Chastagnol, *La préfecture urbaine à Rome sous le Bas-Empire* (Paris: Presses universitaires de France, 1960).

92. Cod. Theod. 15.1.19 (1:805, ed. Mommsen): "Nemo praefectorum urbis aliorumve iudicum, quos potestas in excelso locat, opus aliquod novum in urbe Roma inclyta moliatur, sed excolendis veteribus intendat animum. Novum quodque opus qui volet in urbe moliri, sua pecunia, suis operibus absolvat, non contractis veteribus emolumentis, non effossis nobilium operum substructionibus, non redivivis de publico saxis,

non marmorum frustis spoliatarum aedium deformatione convulsis." The text is dated to 376, during the reign of Valentinian I, Valens, and Gratian.

93. Wolfgang Kuhoff, *Diokletian und die Epoche der Tetrarchie: Das römische Reich zwischen Krisenbewaltigung und Neuaufbau (284–313 n. Chr.)* (Frankfurt: Peter Lang, 2001), 147, 594.

94. Adam Gutteridge, "Some Aspects of Social and Cultural Time in Late Antiquity," in *Social and Political Life in Late Antiquity*, ed. William Bowden, Adam Gutteridge, Luke Lavan, and Carlos Machado (Leiden: Brill, 2006), 578.

95. Ibid.

96. *CIL* 6.1158: "RESTITUTORI URBIS ROMAE ADQUE ORB[is]. . . ." The historical importance of acquiring a past so as to establish a trajectory for a path toward the future is argued in Hedrick, *History and Silence*, 147–170.

97. Local aristocrats sponsoring monuments that honored an emperor anticipated rather than reflected centrally issued propaganda, as argued in Noreña, *Imperial Ideals*, 266–283.

98. This can be argued in light of the discovery in 2005 of a colossal-scale portrait of Constantine pointedly set up in the the Forum of Trajan; see Eugenio La Rocca and Paul Zanker, "Il ritratto colossale di Costantino dal Foro di Traiano," in *Res bene gestae: Ricerche di storia urbana su Roma antica in onore di Eva Margaret Steinby*, ed. Anna Leone, Domenico Palombi, and Susan Walker (Rome: Quasar, 2007), 145–168.

99. Elizabeth Marlowe has called attention to Constantine's victory over Maxentius at the Milvian Bridge as a battle in a civil war: "Framing the Sun: The Arch of Constantine and the Roman Cityscape," *Art Bulletin* 88 (2006): 223–225.

100. For legislation concerning breadmakers, see Cod. Theod. 14.3.3, 14.3.4, 14.3.5. For the sale of subsidized wine, see Cod. Theod. 11.2.2, 11.2.3.

101. Legislation kept the senators from pursuing their own building initiatives; see Cod. Theod. 15.1.19, mentioned above, and 15.1.11. See also Andreas Alföldi, *A Conflict of Ideas in the Late Roman Empire: The Clash between the Senate and Valentinian I*, ed. H. Mattingly (Oxford: Clarendon, 1952).

102. Rutilius Namatianus, *De reditu suo* 1.137–140: "Quae restant nullis obnoxia tempora metis, / dum stabunt terrae, dum polis astra feret. / Illud te reparat quod cetera regna resoluvit: / ordo renascendi est crescere posse malis."

103. The restoration by Praetextatus is documented in an inscription, *CIL* 6.102. See also Giuseppe Nieddu, "Il portico degli Dei Consenti," *Bollettino d'Arte* 71 (1986): 37–52.

104. Jelle Wytzes, *Der letzte Kampf des Heidentums in Rom* (Leiden: Brill, 1977).

105. Wilhelm Pohlkamp, "Tradition und Topographie: Papst Silvester I (314–335) und der Drache vom Forum Romanum," *Römische Quartalschrift* 78 (1983): 11–47.

CHAPTER 1: COLLECTIVE IDENTITY AND RENEWED TIME IN THE TETRARCHIC ROMAN FORUM

1. The preponderance of imperial portraits left little room for images of senators, according to Machado, "Building the Past," 179–185. For the earlier competitions between emperors and senators, see Werner Eck, "Senatorial Self-Representation: Developments in the Augustan Period," in *Caesar Augustus: Seven Aspects*, ed. Fergus Millar and Erich Segal (Oxford: Clarendon, 1984), 129–167. The case for interpreting portrait statues as preserving senatorial social structure during the early Roman empire is made by Greg Woolf, "Monumental Writing and the Expansion of Roman Society in the Early Empire," *Journal of Roman Studies* 86 (1996): 22–39.

2. *Chronographus anni 354*, in *Chronica Minora*, ed. T. Mommsen, *MGH AA* 9 (Berlin: Weidmann, 1892), 146: "Operae publicae arserunt senatum, forum Caesaris, basilicam Iuliam, et Graecostadium" (entry for the emperors Carinus and Numerian).

3. Bauer, "Stadt ohne Kaiser," 7–10; Anne Daguet-Gagey, *Les opera publica à Rome (180–305 ap. J.-C.)* (Paris: Institut des Études Augustiniennes, 1997), 70–73.

4. *Chronographus anni 354*, *MGH AA*, 9:148: "Multae operae publicae fabricatae sunt: senatum, forum Caesaris, basilica Iulia, scaena Pompei, porticos II, nymfea III, templa II, Iseum et Serapeum, arcum novum, thermas Diocletianas" (on the works of Diocletian and Maximian).

5. Horst Blanck, *Wiederverwendung alter Statuen als Ehrendenkmäler bei Griechen und Römern* (Rome: "L'Erma" di Bretschneider, 1969), 63.

6. Niquet, *Monumenta virtutum titulique*, 20–22, 55–69; Ruck, *Die Grossen dieser Welt*, 257–258.

7. Ammianus Marcellinus, *Res gestae* 14.6.8: "ex his quidam aeternitati se commendari posse per statuas aestimantes eas ardenter adfectant quasi plus praemii de figmentis aereis sensu carentibus adepturi, quam ex conscientia honeste recteque factorum."

8. Freyberger, *Das Forum Romanum*, 95–99; Bauer, *Stadt, Platz und Denkmal*, 42–43; Martina Jordan-Ruwe, *Das Säulenmonument: Zur Geschichte der erhöhten Aufstellung antiker Porträtstatuen* (Bonn: Habelt, 1995), 110–112; Giuliani and Verduchi, *L'area centrale*, 166–173.

9. Only building restorations are specified in the text, *Chronographus anni 354*, *MGH AA*, 9:148.

10. The clear evidence that local sponsors took the initiative to develop monuments that advanced the goals of the emperors they honored is presented in Mayer, "Propaganda, Staged Applause, or Local Politics?" 111–134. Depicting the emperor as if he possessed a powerful status that made him appear remote was a consequence of new ceremonies of rulership after the late third century, according to R. R. R. Smith, "Roman Portraits: Honours, Empresses, and Late Emperors," *Journal of Roman Studies* 75 (1985): 219–221.

11. Lactantius notes the administrative changes: *De mortibus persecutorum* 7.2, 8.3. The number of provinces is documented in the *Verona List*, a document specifying the provinces in the Roman empire in c. 300 as transcribed in a seventh-century manuscript; see Timothy D. Barnes, *The New Empire of Diocletian and Constantine* (Cambridge, Mass.: Harvard University Press: 1982), 195–208. For the military reforms, see Roger Rees, *Layers of Loyalty in Latin Panegyric, AD 289–307* (Oxford: Oxford University Press, 2002), 26–27. See also Frank Kolb, *Diocletian und die Erste Tetrarchie: Improvisation oder Experiment in der Organisation monarchischer Herrschaft?* (Berlin and New York: Walter de Gruyter, 1987).

12. For an overview of Tetrarchic principles and the adoption by each ruler of a divinized identity associated with either Jupiter or Hercules, see Roger Rees, *Diocletian and the Tetrarchy* (Edinburgh: Edinburgh University Press, 2004), 54–58.

13. Barnes, *New Empire*, 47–87.

14. Ibid., 27.

15. Simon Corcoran, *The Empire of the Tetrarchs: Imperial Pronouncements and Government, AD 284–324* (Oxford: Clarendon, 1996); idem, "The Tetrarchy: Policy and Image as Reflected in Imperial Pronouncements," in *Die Tetrarchie: Eine neues Regierungssystem und seine mediale Präsentation*, ed. Dietrich Boschung and Werner Eck (Wiesbaden: Reichert, 2006), 31–61.

16. Severus and Maximianus Daia joined as *Caesares* in 305. Lactantius (*De mortibus persecutorum* 18.2–5) recounts that Diocletian initially wished to appoint relatives of the currently reigning Tetrarchs, but Galerius dissuaded him.

17. Kolb, *Diocletian und die erste Tetrarchie*, 117–127; Wolfram Weiser, "Die Tetrarchie—Ein neues Regierungssystem und seine mediale Präsentation auf Münzen und Medaillons," in Boschung and Eck, *Die Tetrarchie*, 205–220.

18. Barbara Borg and Christian Witschel, "Veränderungen im Repräsentationsverhalten der römischen Eliten während des 3. Jhs. n. Chr.," in *Inschriftliche Denkmäler als Medien der Selbstdarstellung in der römischen Welt*, ed. Géza Alföldy and Silvio Panciera (Stuttgart: Steiner, 2001), 47–120.

19. For the Roman concept of temporal repetition, see Ellen O'Gorman, "Repetition and Exemplarity in Historical Thought: Ancient Rome and the Ghosts of Modernity," in *The Western Time of Ancient History*, ed. Alexandra Lianeri (Cambridge: Cambridge University Press, 2011), 264–279.

20. Gerhard Zimmer, *Locus datus decreto decurionum: Zur Statuenaufstellung zweier Forumsanlagen im römischen Afrika* (Munich: Bayerische Akademie der Wissenschaften, 1989), 54–63.

21. *Panegyrici Latini* 8 (5), 3.1–2 (C.E.V. Nixon and Barbara S. Rodgers, *In Praise of Later Roman Emperors* [Berkeley: University of California Press, 1994], 544): "O tempus quo merito quondam omnia nata esse credantur, cum eodem nunc confirmata videamus! O kalendae Martiae, sicuti olim annorum volumentium, ita nunc aeternorum auspices imperatorum! Quanta enim, invictissimi principes, et vobis et rei publicae saecula propagatis orbis vestri participando tutelam?"

22. Michele Renee Salzman, *On Roman Time: The Codex-Calendar of 354 and the Rhythms of Urban Life in Late Antiquity* (Berkeley: University of California Press, 1990), 109–110.

23. The sequential patterns of the first Tetrarchy are explored in Kolb, *Diocletian und die Erste Tetrarchie*, 115–127. For the imperial adoption of the temporal ideas tied to the highly conceptual deity Aion, see Andreas Alföldi, "From the *Aion Plutonius* of the Ptolemies to the *Saeculum Frugiferum* of the Roman Emperors," in *Greece and the Eastern Mediterranean in Ancient History and Prehistory: Studies Presented to Fritz Schachermeyr on the Occasion of His Eightieth Birthday*, ed. K. H. Kinzl (Berlin: de Gruyter, 1977), 1–30.

24. *Panegyrici Latini* 8 (5), 4.2 (Nixon and Rodgers, *In Praise of Later Roman Emperors*, 545): "Quippe isto numinis vestri numero summa omnia nituntur et gaudent, elementa quattuor et totidem anni vices et orbis quadrifariam duplici discretus Oceano et emenso quater caelo lustra redeuntia et quadrigae Solis et duobus caeli luminibus adiuncti Vesper et Lucifer."

25. Rees, *Layers of Loyalty*, 108–115.

26. Curran, *Pagan City and Christian Capital*, 49; Barbara Saylor Rodgers, "Divine Insinuation in the 'Panegyrici Latini,'" *Historia* 35 (1986): 69–104.

27. *Panegyrici Latini* 10 (2), 4.2 (Nixon and Rodgers, *In Praise of Later Roman Emperors*, 525): "Praecipitanti Romano nomini iuxta principem subiuisti eadem scilicet auxilii opportunitate qua tuus Hercules Iovem uestrum quondam Terrigenarum bello laborantem magna victoriae parte iuvit probavitque se non magis a dis accepisse caelum quam eisdem reddidisse."

28. *Chronographus anni 354*, *MGH AA*, 9:146 and 148.

29. Machado, "Building the Past," 161–166; La Rocca, "La nuova immagine dei fori Imperiali," 180; Carla Amici, *Il foro di Cesare* (Florence: Leo S. Olschki, 1991), 143–154; Rizzo, "Indagini nei fori imperiali," 228–229. One inscription, *CIL* 6.40726, survives from Maximian's interventions in the Forum of Caesar; see Lipps, "Zur Datierung der spätantiken Portikus des Caesarforums," 389–405.

30. Olivier Hekster, "The City of Rome in Late Imperial Ideology: The Tetrarchs, Maxentius, and Constantine," *Mediterraneo Antico* 2 (1999): 717–748.

31. *CIL* 6.1125, 1126, 1127, and 1128.

32. The key example is the inscription accompanying the equestrian statue of Constantius II, referring to the emperor as "RESTITUTORI URBIS ROMAE ADQUE ORB[is]" (*CIL* 6.1158), discussed below. A monument honoring the emperors Arcadius and Honorius celebrates the end of a usurper's hold over Libya with the words "VINDICATA REBELLIONE / ET AFRICAE RESTITUTIONE LAETUS" (*CIL* 6.1187). An inscription (*CIL* 6.41389) celebrates that which was "restored" by Aëtius on account of successful military campaigns against Goths and Burgundians: "[O]B IURATAS BELLO PACE VICTORIAS ROMANO IMPERIO / REDDIDIT."

33. Giuliani and Verduchi, *L'area centrale*, 159. This interpretation is disputed by Filippo Coarelli, "L'edilizia pubblica a Roma in età tetrarchica," in *The Transformations of* Urbs Roma *in Late Antiquity*, ed. William V. Harris (Portsmouth, R.I.: Journal of Roman Archaeology, 1999), 30.

34. Giuliani and Verduchi, *L'area centrale*, 156; Patrizia Verduchi, "Rostra Diocletiani," in *LTUR*, 4:217–218.

35. Coarelli, "L'edilizia pubblica," 29–30.

36. Bauer, *Stadt, Platz und Denkmal in der Spätantike*, 21–24; Giuliani and Verduchi, *L'area centrale*, 62–65, 156.

37. The date can be inferred from the inscription, *CIL* 6.1141; Giuliani and Verduchi, *L'area centrale*, 51–58, 64, 72–73; Verduchi, "Rostra Diocletiani," in *LTUR*, 4:216–218.

38. Christian Hülsen ("Iscrizione di Giunio Valentino, prefetto della città nel secolo V," *Mitteilungen des Deutschen Archäologischen Instituts, Römische Abteilung* 10 [1895]: 58–63) dates the inscription to 476, but this has been revised. *CIL* 6.32005 = 41405 and 6.8.3:5104–5105: "Salv(is) d[d(ominis)] n[n(ostris)] (duobus) Marciano et Avito p(erpetuis Augustis duobus) Vetti]us Iunius [Va]lentin[u]s [praef(ectus)] urb[i– – –]." Vettius Iunius Valentinus, as urban prefect, has been identified as using this monument to celebrate the victory of Ricimer over the Vandals in the sea battle of 456: Dirk Henning, "CIL VI 32005 und die 'Rostra Vandalica,'" *Zeitschrift für Papyrologie und Epigraphik* 100 (1996): 259–264. But Bauer (*Stadt, Platz und Denkmal*, 24) points out that the date of his prefecture remains uncertain.

39. *PLRE* 2:1140 (Valentinus 5).

40. Bauer, *Stadt, Platz und Denkmal*, 24–25.

41. Giuliani and Verduchi, *L'area centrale*, 151–166; Jordan-Ruwe, *Das Säulenmonument*, 110–112.

42. Heinz Kähler (*Das Fünfsäulendenkmal für die Tetrarchen auf dem Forum Romanum*, Monumenta Artis Romanae 3 [Cologne: M. DuMont Schauberg, 1964], 9–27) proposes that the image of Jupiter stood at the center of the western podium. Liverani ("Osservazioni sui rostri," 177–182) argues that the Jupiter statue elevated upon a column stood at the eastern Rostra; yet Liverani seems to present a misreading of the relief on the Arch of Constantine, according to Bauer ("Stadt ohne Kaiser," 58–59).

43. Emanuel Mayer, *Rom ist dort wo der Kaiser ist: Untersuchungen zu den Staatsdenkmälern des dezentralisierten Reiches von Diocletian bis zu Theodosius II* (Mainz: Römisch-Germanischen Zentralmuseums, 2002), 178–180.

44. The delivery of funeral orations for both emperors and aristocrats from the Rostra in the Forum also featured the presentation of funerary masks of ancestors of the deceased, establishing connections across generations; for the funeral of Septimius Severus, see Herodian 4.2.2–4. See also Diane Favro and Christopher Johanson, "Death in Motion: Funeral Processions in the Roman Forum," *Journal of the Society of Architectural Historians* 69 (2010): 12–37; and Javier Arce, "Roman Imperial Funerals *in effigie*," in *The Emperor and Rome*, ed. Björn Ewald and Carlos Noreña (Cambridge: Cambridge University Press, 2010), 309–323.

45. Zanker, *The Power of Images*, 79–82; Favro, *Urban Image*, 196–200.

46. The lack of individual names in the few recorded inscriptions supports this claim, as argued by Bauer ("Stadt ohne Kaiser," 62–64).

47. Ibid., 64.

48. Giuliani and Verduchi (*L'area centrale*, 155–156) have demonstrated that one set of five columns was supported by the platform of the western Rostra rather than by the hemicycle of steps there.

49. Mary Boatwright argues that Marcus Aurelius was figured in the statue on the left and Hadrian was represented in the one on the right: *Hadrian and the City of Rome* (Princeton, N.J.: Princeton University Press, 1987), 104. L. Richardson Jr. ("The Tribunals of the Praetors of Rome," *Mitteilungen des Deutschen Archäologischen Instituts, Römische Abteilung* 80 [1973]: 232–233) suggests that the left statue depicted M. Salvius Iulianus.

50. Hans Peter L'Orange, "Ein tetrarchisches Ehrendenkmal auf dem Forum Romanum," *Mitteilungen des Deutschen Archäologischen Instituts, Römische Abteilung* 53 (1938): 28.

51. Giuliani and Verduchi, *L'area centrale*, 154–157.

52. Patrizia Verduchi, "Le tribune rostrate," in *Roma: Archeologia nel centro*, Lavori e studi di archeologia 6 (Rome: De Luca, 1985), 1:29–33.

53. A. Pulte, "Rostra: Fünfsäulendenkmal," in *LTUR*, 4:218–219; Giuliani and Verduchi, *L'area centrale*, 154–157.

54. Kähler, *Das Fünfsäulendenkmal*, 9–11.

55. For the fourth-century regionary catalogues, see Roberto Valentini and Giuseppe Zucchetti, eds., *Codice topografico della città di Roma*, Fonti per la storia d'Italia 81 (Rome: Tipografia del Senator, 1940–1953), 1:113 and 173. Augustus' funeral orations were given from two Rostra, the western one and the one at the Temple of the Deified Julius Caesar; see Cassius Dio, *Roman History* 56.34–35.

56. Giuliani and Verduchi, *L'area centrale*, 153–156. Coarelli (*Il foro romano*, 2:318–321) argues that an Augustan Rostra preceded the late antique construction at the eastern end of the Forum square and was situated at a point slightly to the west of the Temple of the Deified Julius Caesar.

57. Giuliani and Verduchi, *L'area centrale*, 156 and fig. 222; for the brick stamp, see *CIL* 15.1650. See also Cairoli Fulvio Giuliani, "Una rilettura dell'area centrale del Foro Romano," in *Présence de l'architecture et d'urbanisme romains*, ed. R. Chavallier, Actes du Colloque, 12–13 Dec. 1981 (Paris: Les Belles Lettres, 1983), 85; Verduchi, "Le tribune rostrate."

58. *CIL* 6.1203. This base was discovered in 1547 in front of the Curia. L'Orange ("Ein tetrarchisches Ehrendenkmal," 1–34) originally connected the surviving Decennalia base with the Tetrarchic monument; see also Kähler, *Das Fünfsäulendenkmal*.

59. *CIL* 6.1204: "AUGUSTORUM VICENNALIA FELICITER"; *CIL* 6.1205: "VICENNALIA IMPERATORUM." See Max Wegner, "Gebälk von den Rostra am Forum Romanum,"

Mitteilungen des Deutschen Archäologischen Instituts, Römische Abteilung 94 (1987): 331–332.

60. Henning Wrede, "Der *genius populi Romani* und das Fünfsäulendenkmal der Tetrarchen auf dem Forum Romanum," *Bonner Jahrbücher des Rheinischen Landesmuseums in Bonn und des Vereins von Altertumsfreunden im Rheinlande* 181 (1981): 111–142, esp. 122–123; Jordan-Ruwe, *Das Säulenmonument*, 105.

61. André Chastagnol, "Aspects concrets et cadre topographique des fêtes décennales des empereurs à Rome," in *L'Urbs: Espace urbain et histoire (Ier siècle av. J.-C.–IIIe siècle ap. J.-C.)*, Collection de l'École française de Rome 98 (Rome: L'École française de Rome, 1987), 493–497.

62. Mayer, *Rom ist dort wo der Kaiser ist*, 176–180.

63. Kolb, *Diocletian und die Erste Tetrarchie*, 125–126.

64. *CIL* 6.1205. Kolb (*Diocletian und die Erste Tetrarchie*) argues that the inscription refers to all four emperors by reflecting on the fulfillment of the vows by the *Augusti* while anticipating the fulfilled vows of the *Caesares*. L'Orange ("Ein tetrarchisches Ehrendenkmal," 23–24) argues that all four emperors were shown on the four sides of the lost plinth, citing a vague description from the Renaissance recounting that there were figures on the reliefs, misinterpreted at the time as priests. The sixteenth-century description of the plinth was written by F. Albertini: "Non longe a tribus columnis hoc anno [1509] multa marmora efossa fuere cum ingenti basi marmorea, in qua erat haec inscriptio forma circulari (vicennalia imperatorum) cum litteris incisa. Ab alia parte visebantur sacerdotes sculpti taurum sacrificantes"; the document was reprinted by Kähler (*Das Fünfsäulendenkmal*, 41 n. 68).

65. Jordan-Ruwe, *Das Säulenmonument*, 106–107.

66. Monuments with columns were discovered at Antinoopolis and other Egyptian cities; see Wolfgang Thiel, "Die 'Pompeius-Säule' in Alexandria und die Vier Säulen Monumente Ägyptens," in Boschung and Eck, *Die Tetrarchie*, 249–322.

67. Hans-Georg Niemeyer, *Studien zur statuarischen Darstellung der römischen Kaiser* (Berlin: Gebr. Mann, 1968), 44, 47, and 88–89; Wrede, "Der *genius populi Romani*," 121–123.

68. *Chronographus anni 354*, 9:148–149: "Genium populi Romani aureum in rostra posuit."

69. *CIL* 6.36975 = 40714 (and p. 4532), with a find spot in the Roman Forum: "[Genio p]OPU[li Romani] / [Dioclet]IANUS E[t Maximianus] / [invi]CTI AU[gusti]."

70. Hans Peter Laubscher, "Beobachtung zu tetrarchischen Kaiserbildnissen aus Porphyr," *Jahrbuch des Deutschen Archäologischen Instituts* 144 (1999): 207–252.

71. Lactantius, *De mortibus persecutorum* 17.1–2 (ed. J. L. Creed [Oxford: Clarendon, 1984], 24): "[Diocletianus] . . . quibus sollemnibus celebratis cum libertatem populi Romani ferre non poterat."

72. The *Chronographus anni 354* mentions this for the joint rule of Diocletian and Maximian, 9:148: "sparserunt in circo aureos et argenteos. partectorum podius ruit et oppressit homines $\overline{\text{XIII}}$."

73. Dirk Schlinkert, *"Ordo senatorius" und "nobilitas": Die Konstitution des Senatsadels in der Spätantike* (Stuttgart: Franz Steiner, 1996), 171–172.

74. The extensive number of officials together with the large household staff and numerous eunuchs in Diocletian's residence is reported by Lactantius, *De mortibus persecutorum* 15.2.

75. Eutropius, *Breviarium* 9.26: "Diocletianus . . . adorari se iussit, cum ante eum cuncti salutarentur. ornamenta gemmarum vestibus calciamentisque indidit. nam prius imperii insigne in chlamyde purpurea tantum erat." The discovery of Maxentius' regalia, including an imperial orb, during excavations on the eastern slope of the Palatine indicates that the use of Tetrarchic insignia continued into the reign of Maximian's son; see Clementina Panella, *I segni del potere: Realtà e immaginario della sovranità nella Roma imperiale* (Bari: Edipuglia, 2011).

76. Harold Mattingly, "The Imperial *Vota*," *Proceedings of the British Academy* 36 (1950): 155–195, and 37 (1951): 219–268; Gutteridge, "Some Aspects of Social and Cultural Time," 569–601.

77. For the Arcus Novus, see Hans Peter Laubscher, "Arcus Novus und Arcus Claudii, zwei Triumphbögen an der Via Lata in Rom," *Nachrichten der Akademie des Wissenschaften in Göttingen* 3 (1976): 65–108; the arch was specified as situated in region 7: see *Libellus de regionibus urbis Romae*, ed. Arvast Nordh (Lund: Gleerup, 1949), 82.

78. The fragment, now in the Villa Medici, Rome, was discovered on the Via del Corso in Rome, near S. Maria in Via Lata, together with other fragments now in the Boboli Gardens, Florence. See Sandro De Maria, *Gli archi onorari di Roma e dell'Italia Romana* (Rome: "L'Erma" di Bretschneider, 1988), 197–200.

79. The phrase "VOTA X ET XX" shortens the phrase *vota soluta X et vota suscepta XX*. This reading of the phrase on the Arcus Nova is argued by Chastagnol, "Aspets concrets," 501–504.

80. Kuhoff, *Diokletian und die Epoche der Tetrarchie*, 147, 594.

81. Testimony attests to more *adventus* rituals staged in the provinces by generals, governors, and other administrators during the late fourth and early fifth century, but the rites must have occurred earlier as well. Hendrik Dey, "Art, Ceremony, and the City Walls: The Aesthetics of Imperial Resurgence in the Late Roman West," *Journal of Late Antiquity* 3 (2010): 21–23; Sabine MacCormack, *Art and Ceremony in Late Antiquity* (Berkeley: University of California Press, 1981), 22–25; Michael McCormick, *Eternal Victory: Triumphal Rulership in Late Antiquity, Byzantium, and the Early Medieval West* (Cambridge: Cambridge University Press, 1986), 252–258; Daniëlle Slootjes, *The Governor and His Subjects in the Later Roman Empire* (Leiden: Brill, 2006), 105–128.

82. *Panegyrici Latini* 10 (2) 1.4–5 (Panegyric of Maximian), in Nixon and Rodgers, *In Praise of Later Roman Emperors*, 523–524: "Iure igitur hoc die quo immortalis ortus dominae gentium civitatis vestra pietate celebratur, tibi potissimum, imperator invicte, laudes canimus et gratias agimus, quem similitudo ipsa stirpis tuae ac vis tacita naturae ad honorandum natalem Romae diem tam liberalem facit, ut urbem illam sic colas conditam, quasi ipse condideris. Re vera enim, sacratissime imperator, merito quiuis te tuumque fratrem Romani imperii dixerit conditores: estis enim, quod est proximum, restitutores et, sic licet hic illi urbi natalis dies, quod pertinet ad originem populi Romani vestri imperii primi dies sunt principes ad salutem."

83. Eutropius, *Breviarum historiae Romanae* 9.27.2 (ed. Franciscus Ruehl [Leipzig: Teubner, 1887], 70): "post triumpham inclitum, quem Romae ex numerosis gentibus egerant."

84. Eutropius (*Breviarium* 9.27.2) mentions that Diocletian and Maximian celebrated the triumph by marching through the streets of Rome with the wife, sister, and children of the conquered Narses on parade. The *Chronographus anni 354* (9:148) also mentions the wife and children of the Persian king on parade, together with elephants and horses.

85. The panegyric read to Maximian in 291 notes that the ceaseless series of battles forestalled celebrations: "sic interim meritorum conscientia triumphatis, dum triomphos ipsos semper vincendo differtis" (*Panegyrici Latini* 11 [3], 4.3 [Nixon and Rodgers, *In Praise of Later Roman Emperors*, 534]).

86. *Chronographus anni 354*, 1:148: "sparserunt in circo aureos et argenteos. . . . regem Persarum cum omnibus gentibus et tunicas eorum ex margaritis numero XXXII circa templa domini posuerunt. elephantes XIII, agitatores VI, equos CCL in urbem adduxerunt."

87. *Panegyrici Latini* 11 (3), 6.3 (Nixon and Rodgers, *In Praise of Later Roman Emperors*, 535): "Qui germani geminive fratres indiviso patrimonio tam aequabiliter utuntur quam vos orbe Romano?"

88. The joint abdication is folded into Eutropius' description of the ceremony in Rome. The single chariot comes up in the description of the family of Narses, the Persian general whom Galerius conquered. Eutropius, *Breviarum* 9.27.2 (ed. Ruehl, 70): "Tamen uterque uno privato habitu imperii insigne mutavit, Nicomediae Diocletianus, Herculius Mediolani, post triumpham inclitum, quem Romae ex numerosis gentibus egerant, pompa ferculorum inlustri, qua Narsei coniuges sororesque et liberi ante currum ducti sunt."

89. *Panegyrici Latini* 6 (7), 15.5–6 (Nixon and Rodgers, *In Praise of Later Roman Emperors*, 580): "puduit imitari, huic illum in Capitolini Iovis templo iurasse paenituit."

90. Lactantius, *De mortibus persecutorum* 17.1 (ed. Creed, 21): "Hoc igitur scelere perpetrato Diocletianus, cum iam felicitas ab eo recessisset, perrexit statim Romam, ut illic vicennalium diem celebraret."

91. Bauer, *Stadt, Platz und Denkmal*, 42–43.

92. Verduchi, "Le tribune rostrate," 31.

93. Fragments of another granite column were discovered nearby: Giuliani and Verduchi, *L'area centrale*, 162 and 167.

94. Herbert Bloch (*I bolli laterizi e la storia edilizia romana* [Rome: Commune di Roma, 1947], 314 n. 238) claimed that these columns should be connected with the Vicennalia cele-

bration of the Tetrarchs. More recently, however, Eva Margareta Steinby has found comparisons for the specific brick stamps: "L'industria laterizia di Roma nel tardo impero," in *Società romana e impero tardoantico*, ed. A. Giardina (Bari: Laterza, 1986), 2:99–165, esp. 117–124. As Steinby notes (p. 119), one stamp type (*CIL* 15.1569.3–4) clearly belongs to the workshop under Domitian, as it reads "OFFSRFDOM" = "OFF(icina) S(ummae) R(ei) F(isci) DOM(itiana)." Another appears to be Constantinian (*CIL* 15.1590.1 compares to one found in the Baths of Constantine; see Steinby, "L'industria laterizia," 123–124).

95. Bauer, *Stadt, Platz und Denkmal*, 43.

96. Jordan-Ruwe, *Das Saülenmonument*, 122.

97. Jordan-Ruwe (ibid., 116) links the propaganda with Maxentius, but the specifics of a political program remain elusive.

98. See Richard Brilliant, *The Arch of Septimius Severus in the Roman Forum* (Rome: American Academy in Rome, 1967). Reliefs on the Arch of Septimius Severus depict victorious campaigns against the Parthians, which are also mentioned in the inscriptions, *CIL* 6.1033 and *CIL* 6.31230. See also Amanda Claridge and Lucos Cozza, "Arco di Settimio Severo," in *Roma, Archeologia nel centro* 1, Lavori e studi di archeologia 6 (Rome: De Luca, 1985), 34–40. For the earlier importance of arches to Augustus' plan for the Roman Forum, see Laura Chioffi, *Gli elogia Augustei del Foro Romano: Aspetti epigrafici e topografici*, Opuscula Epigraphica 7 (Rome: Quasar, 1996), 27–32.

99. The Arch of Tiberius was dedicated on the occasion of a successful recovery mission conducted by Varus, Germanicus, and Tiberius, and it was located close to the Temple of Saturn; see Tacitus, *Annales* 2.41: "Propter aedem Saturni ob recepta cum Varo amissa ductu Germanici auspiciis Tiberii." The foundations were discovered around 1900 by Giacomo Boni, and this evidence is discussed by Fred Kleiner in *The Arch of Nero in Rome: A Study of the Roman Honorary Arch before and under Nero*, Archaeologica 52 (Rome: G. Bretschneider, 1985), 24–28. It is fairly certain that the Parthian Arch of Augustus remained standing throughout late antiquity, and it has been proposed that some of the sculptural reliefs were restored and recarved at that time; see Niels Hannestad, *Tradition in Late Antique Sculpture: Conservation, Modernization, Production* (Aarhus: Aarhus University Press, 1994), 67–71. Gamberini-Mongenet discovered the foundations for a single vault arch, identified as the Arch of Gaius and Lucius, where the Via Sacra reached the Basilica Aemilia, but never published an excavation report. See Bernard Andreae, "Archäologische Funde im Bereich der Soprintendenzen von Rom, 1949–1957," *Archäologischer Anzeiger* 72 (1957): 168–178. The exact location of the Arch of Gaius and Lucius along the Via Sacra remains unclear; see Domenico Palombi, "Contributo alla topografia della Via Sacra: Dagli appunti inediti di Giacomo Boni," in *Topografia Romana: Ricerche e discussioni*, Quaderni di Topografia Antica 10 (Florence: Leo Olschki, 1988), 77–97.

100. Jordan-Ruwe, *Das Saülenmonument*, 119.

101. Zanker, *Il foro romano*, 13–17; Coarelli, *Il foro romano*, 2:320–323.

CHAPTER 2: CONSTANTINE THE RESTORER

1. The phrase "restorer" (*restitutor*) of civic governance or public affairs (*res publica*) appears in an inscription praising Constantine (presumably with Licinius), *CIL* 6.40768: "[fortitudin]E AC VIRTUTE [divina] / [invictis senat]US POPULIQ(ue) R(omani) TAE[terrimis] / [tyrannis extinctis] LIBERATORIBUS [atque rei] / [publicae] RESTITUTORI[bus] / [dd(ominis) nn(ostris) Fl(avio) Val(erio) Const]ANTINO MAX(i)MO [– – –]." In another inscription, Constantine is deemed as the *restitutor* credited with bringing back peace, *CIL* 6.40764a: "[felicit] ATIS RESTA[uratori] / [fundato]RI ET PROPA[gatori] / [pacis auct]ORIQUE [quietis]."

2. Constantine's marriage to Maxentius' sister, Fausta, is a key piece of evidence in establishing the ties between the two prior to the battle of 312. See Maxentius' role in the back story to Constantine's identity as emperor in David Potter, *Constantine the Emperor* (Oxford: Oxford University Press, 2012), 100–135.

3. For the alienation of Christians from public life during the Tetrarchy, see H. A. Drake, *Constantine and the Bishops: The Politics of Intolerance* (Baltimore, Md.: Johns Hopkins University Press, 2000), 157, 192–198.

4. For Maxentius' help in facilitating the election of Marcellus as bishop of Rome in 306, see *Liber Pontificalis*, ed. Louis Duchesne (Paris: Ernest Thorin, 1981), 1:164; the restitution of property to bishops is recorded in Augustine, *Brev. Coll.* 3.34, in *Gesta conlationis Carthaginensis*, ed. Serge Lancel (Turnhout: Brepols, 1974). See also Ramiro Donciu, *L'empereur Maxence* (Bari: Edipuglia, 2012), 143–154.

5. For the Maxentius coinage, see *RIC*, 6:296, no. 130 (minted in Ticinum), reverse legend: "Conserv urb suae." See Mats Culhed, *Conservator urbis suae: Studies in the Politics and Propaganda of the Emperor Maxentius* (Stockholm: Paul Åströms, 1994), 45–59.

6. "RESTITUTORI LIBERTATIS" appears on coins dating to 312–315. *RIC*, 7:165–166 (minted in Trier, nos. 22–26).

7. *RIC*, 6:303–304 (Rome). The following draws upon the arguments of Elizabeth Marlowe, "*Liberator urbis suae*: Constantine and the Ghost of Maxentius," in Ewald and Noreña, *The Emperor and Rome*, 199–219.

8. Marlowe, "*Liberator urbis suae*," 215–219.

9. Steinby, "L'industria laterizia," 117–124; Bauer, *Stadt, Platz und Denkmal*, 42–43.

10. Dale Kinney, "*Spolia*: *Damnatio* and *renovatio memoriae*," *Memoirs of the American Academy in Rome* 42 (1997): 117–148, esp. 124–129; idem, "Roman Architectural *Spolia*," *Proceedings of the American Philosophical Society* 145 (2001): 138–150, esp. 138–145.

11. For the archeological attention to the long afterlife of Roman buildings, see, in particular, Daniele Manacorda, *Crypta Balbi: Archeologia e storia di un paesaggio urbano* (Milan: Electa, 2001); Meneghini, Valenzani, and Bianchi, *I Fori imperiali*. Contextualizing architectural reuse in the discourse of *spolia* has been characterized as "spoliation"; see Dale Kinney, "Spoliation in Medieval Rome," in *Perspektiven der Spolienforschung 1: Spoliierung und Transposition*, ed. Stefan Altenkamp, Carmen Marcks-Jacobs, and Peter Seiler (Berlin: De Gruyter, 2013), 261–286.

12. Lactantius, *De mortibus persecutorum* 48.

13. For the Lateran Basilica, see Herman Geertman, "Forze centrifughe e centripete nella Roma cristiana: Il Laterano, la Basilica Iulia, e la Basilica Liberiana," *Atti della Pontificia Accademia Romana di Archeologia: Rendiconti* 59 (1986–1987): 63–91. The arguments about whether Constantine maintained traditional benefactions in Rome and how he positioned himself vis-à-vis Maxentius are presented in Marlowe, "*Liberator urbis suae*," and idem, "Framing the Sun," 223–242.

14. Hansen, *The Eloquence of Appropriation*, 33–58.

15. Aurelius Victor, *De Caesaribus* 40.25: "adhuc cuncta opera, quae magnifice construxerat urbis fanum atque basilicam, Flavii meritis patres sacravere."

16. Richard Krautheimer, *Three Christian Capitals: Topography and Politics* (Berkeley: University of California Press, 1983), 8–40, 93–121.

17. John Weisweiler, "Inscribing Imperial Power: Letters from Emperors in Late Antique Rome," in *Rom in der Spätantike: Historische Erinnerung im städtischen Raum*, ed. Ralf Behrwald and Christian Witschel (Stuttgart: Steiner, 2012), 309–329.

18. Zosimus, *Historia nova* 2.29.5. Constantine took the traditional ceremonial precaution of purification preceding a triumph in an *evocatio* ritual, which demonstrated that he was fighting to protect Rome and conquering Maxentius to help the city, according to Noel Lenski ("Evoking the Pagan Past: *Instinctu divinitatis* and Constantine's Capture of Rome," *Journal of Late Antiquity* 1 [2008]: 239–247). That Constantine paraded the head of the vanquished Maxentius through the city is also taken as a sign of the ritual's triumphal character, *Panegyrici Latini* 12 (9), 18.3. See Augusto Fraschetti, *La conversione: Da Roma pagana a Roma cristiana* (Rome: Laterza, 1999), 5–127; Johannes Straub, "Konstantins Versicht auf den Gang zum Kapitol," *Historia* 4 (1955): 297–313.

19. The inscription is reported to be stored in the attic of the Arch of Constantine, but it is not fully analyzed in publications. Further, only those working on restoring the arch in the 1980s have seen it; Adriano La Regina only presented this find in an unpublished talk at the ninth *Incontro di Studio sull'Archeologia Laziale*. See Marlowe, "Framing the Sun," 239 n. 40. See also Jonathan Bardill, *Constantine, Divine Emperor of the Christian Golden Age* (Cambridge: Cambridge University Press, 2012), 84–104.

20. Marlowe, "Framing the Sun," and Bardill, *Constantine, Divine Emperor*, 99–100.

21. For a recent discussion that wisely balances Constantine's brand of Christianity and his sustained commitments to the old rites, see Raymond Van Dam, *The Roman Revolution of Constantine* (Cambridge: Cambridge University Press, 2007), 19–34. For Constantine's rejection of Tetrarchic deities, see MacCormack, *Art and Ceremony*, 36.

22. Kinney, "Rape or Restitution," 53–67.

23. Kinney, "*Spolia*."

24. This was originally determined by H. P. L'Orange. See H. P. L'Orange and Armin van Gerkan, *Der spätantike Bildschmuck des Konstantinsbogens* (Berlin: De Gruyter, 1939), 161–191; see also Kinney, "Rape or Restitution," 56–58.

25. These are Ceionius Annius Annulinus, Aradius Rufius, and Rufinus Caeonius Volusianus. The promise of forgiveness for Rome's senators who had allied with Maxentius earned Constantine praise in a panegyric: *Panegyrici Latini* 12 (9), 20.1–2; see also Barnes, *New Empire*, 111–114.

26. Aurelius Victor, *De Caesaribus* 40.29: "Adeo acceptius praestantiusque tyrannorum depulsoribus nihil est, quorum gratia eo demum auctior erit, si modesti ipsi atque abstinentes sint."

27. Lactantius, *De mortibus persecutorum* 44.11. In a brief reaffirmation of the Tetrarchy, after Diocletian's retirement and prior to the senate elevating Constantine's rank, hierarchy had been reintroduced so that the eastern emperor Maximinus Daia (r. 310–313) received the position of senior *Augustus*.

28. Rita Lizzi Testa, "Alle origini della tradizione pagana su Costantino e il senato romano (Amm. Marc. 21.10.8 e Zos. 2.32.1)," in *Transformations of Late Antiquity: Essays for Peter Brown*, ed. Philip Rousseau and Manolis Papoutsakis (Surrey: Ashgate, 2009), 85–128, esp. 111–121; Christopher Kelly, "Bureaucracy and Government," in *The Cambridge Companion to the Age of Constantine*, ed. Noel Lenski (Cambridge: Cambridge University Press, 2006), 183–206; Pierfrancesco Porena, "Trasformazioni istituzionali e assetti sociali: I prefetti del pretorio tra III e IV secolo," in *Le trasformazioni delle élites in età tardoantica*, ed. Rita Lizzi Testa (Rome: "L'Erma" di Bretschneider, 2006), 325–356; André Chastagnol, "Constantin et le sénat," in *Atti dell'Accademia Romanistica Constantiniana: Secondo Convegno Internazionale* (Perugia: Libreria Universitaria, 1976), 51–69.

29. Michele Renee Salzman, *The Making of a Christian Aristocracy: Social and Religious Change in the Western Roman Empire* (Cambridge, Mass.: Harvard University Press, 2002), 31–33.

30. CIL 6.1169: "instinctu divinitatis mentis magnitudine"; Lenski, "Evoking the Pagan Past," 204–257.

31. *Panegyrici Latini* 12 (9), 25.4: "Constantine, et nuper senatus signum dei . . . dedicarunt" (Nixon and Rodgers, *In Praise of Later Roman Emperors*, 331). Timothy D. Barnes (*Constantine and Eusebius* [Cambridge, Mass.: Harvard University Press, 1980], 46) reads manuscript sources using the word *dee* instead of *dei* as abbreviating *deae* to indicate that the senate had dedicated a statue of Victory to Constantine.

32. *Panegyrici Latini* 12 (9), 20.1: "Nam quid ego de tuis in curia sententiis atque actis loquar, quibus senatui auctoritatem pristinam reddidisti, salutem quam per te receperant non

imputasti, memoriam eius in pectore tuo sempiternam fore spopondisti?" (Nixon and Rodgers, *In Praise of Later Roman Emperors*, 325).

33. *Panegyrici Latini* 12 (9), 20.1 (Nixon and Rodgers, *In Praise of Later Roman Emperors*, 325).

34. André Chastagnol, "Remarques sur les sénateurs orientaux au IVème siècle," *Acta Antiqua Accademiae Scientiarum Hungaricae* 24 (1976): 341–356.

35. Chastagnol, *La préfecture urbaine*, 52–53; Donald Strong, "Roman Museums," in *Roman Museums: Selected Papers on Roman Art and Architecture* (London: Pindar, 1994), 19–20. An inscription listing the title of *curator statuarum* for Flavius Magnus Ianuarius, dated to 332–337, documents the introduction of this title during the Constantinian period: *CIL* 6.1708.

36. André Chastagnol, *Les Fastes de la préfecture de Rome au Bas-Empire* (Paris: Nouvelles Éditions Latines, 1962); Noreña, *Imperial Ideals*, 190–244.

37. *Libellus de regionibus urbis Romae*, ed. Nordh, 104: "Equi magni XXII / Dei aurei LXXX / eburnei LXXIIII."

38. *CIL* 6.41320 (pp. 5052–5053): "M(a)ECILIU[s] Hilarianus v(ir) c(larissimum) / [c]ONSU[l ordinarius] / [curavit?]." Silvio Panciera and Silvia Orlandi (*CIL* 6:5052–5053) argued that it can be inferred that Maecilius Hilarianus took the position of curator of statues after his consulship of 332–333 because he set up a statue and inscribed the base with his name in the nominative case. This statue can thus be linked to the Constantinian reforms and the formation of the office of curator of statues: Niquet, *Monumenta virtutum titulique*, 83–84, 219.

39. Niquet, *Monumenta virtutum titulique*, 201–226.

40. Panella, *I segni del potere*.

41. MacCormack, *Art and Ceremony*, 17–50.

42. Götz Lahusen, *Untersuchungen zur Ehrenstatue in Rom: Literarische und epigraphische Zeugnisse* (Rome: Bretschneider, 1983), 14–18; for evolving imperial policies within the memory landscape of Rome, see Tonio Hölscher, "Das Forum Romanum—Die monumentale Geschichte Roms," in *Erinnerungsorte der Antike: Die römische Welt*, ed. Elke Stein-Hölkeskamp and Karl-Joachim Hölkeskamp (Munich: C. H. Beck, 2006), 100–122.

43. *CIL* 1.268, 1.272.

44. Stephan Elbern, "Das Verhältnis der spätantiken Kaiser zur Stadt Rom," *Römische Quartalschrift* 85 (1990): 19–49.

45. McCormick, *Eternal Victory*, 84–91.

46. The tetrarchs had developed the term "VICTORIA AETERNA AUG" in coinage (*RIC* 6:705, 7:754–758). For rituals, the fourth-century *ludi aeterni* were mentioned in *Panegyrici Latini* 12 (9), 19.6. This could be linked with the *evictio tyranni* on 28 October to commemorate Constantine's defeat of Maxentius, which was repeatedly celebrated in the fourth century, according to the Codex-Calendar of 354: Salzman, *On Roman Time*, 121, 141.

47. Lactantius, *De mortibus persecutorum* 44.10: "Confecto tamen acerbissimo bello cum magna Constantinus Maximini perfidiam cognoscit, litteras deprehendit, statuas et imagines invenit."

48. McCormick, *Eternal Victory*, 86. Honorius commenced the consular celebrations in 404, practiced at Rome, with a departure from the Milvian Bridge: Claudian, *Panegyricus de sexto consulatu Honorii Augusti* 534–546.

49. For the decapitated head of Maxentius, see *Panegyrici Latini* 12 (9), 18.3.

50. Salzman, *On Roman Time*, 121.

51. Ibid., 157–162.

52. Ibid., 154–156.

53. Symmachus, *Relationes* 9.4–5: "invenit ordo amplissimus amabilem vicem, qua se gratum probaret. nam familiae vestae et stirpis auctorem, Africanum quondam et Brittannicum ducem, statuis equestribus inter prisca nomina consecravit. . . . sic coluntur, quorum liberi ad bonum publicum nati sunt. at vero populus imperialis munificentiae muneribus expletus in amorem vestrum prompta inclinatione concessit. qui ubi conperit meo praefatu, adfore dona publicorum parentum, portis omnibus in longinqua fusus erupit, feliciorem ceteris iudicans, qui primus bona vestra vidisset. ergo cum expectari munera principiis soleant, nunc accita venerunt. praetereo illum diem, quo elefantos regios per conferta agmina equorum nobilium pompa praecessit." Translation from R. H. Barrow, *Prefect and Emperor: The Relationes of Symmachus, A.D. 384* (Oxford: Clarendon, 1973), 69.

54. One of the most useful general discussions of late antique patronage using epigraphic evidence is provided by Yasin, *Saints and Church Spaces*, 101–109.

55. Each position functioned in an ascending hierarchy of honor, as can be observed in the *Notitia dignitatum*; see J. E. Lendon, *Empire of Honour: The Art of Government in the Roman World* (Oxford: Clarendon, 1997), 107–175.

56. *CIL* 6.40764: "[Consta]NTINO / [Augu]STO / [senatus p]OPULUSQ(ue) / [Roma]NUS." The extant statue base's remains are 104 cm wide and can be reconstructed to 120 cm deep, which could accommodate a double life-size portrait, according to Brigitte Ruck (*Die Grossen dieser Welt*, 252).

57. Schlinkert, "*Ordo senatorius" und "nobilitas*," 171–172.

58. *CIL* 6.36953: "[– – –] / CONSTANTINO MA[ximo] / STATUAM C[ivili habitu] EX AERARIO IN S[– – –]."

59. Rowland Smith, "Measures of Difference: The Fourth-Century Transformation of the Roman Imperial Court," *American Journal of Philology* 132 (2011): 125–151.

60. *CIL* 6.40768: "[fortitudin]E AC VIRTUTE [divina] / [invictis senat]US POPULIQ(ue) R(omani) TAE[terrimis] / [tyrannis extinctis] LIBERATORIBUS [atque rei] / [publicae] RESTITUTORI[bus] / [d(omino) n(ostro) Fl(avio) Val(erio) Const]ANTINO MAX(i)MO [– – –]."

61. *CIL* 6.40764a: "[felicit]ATIS REST[auratori] / [funda]tORI ET PROPA[gatori] / [pacis auct]ORIQUE [quietis] / [d(omino) n(ostro) FL(avio) V(alerio) Consta]NTIN[o P(io) F(elici) Aug(usto)]."

62. This is established by measurements of the surviving statue bases, Ruck, *Die Grossen dieser Welt*, 257–259.

63. *CIL* 6.36951 and p. 4355: "OPTIMO ET VENERABILI / D(omino) N(ostro) CONSTANTINO / MAXIMO VICTORI PIO / SEMPER AUG(usto) / FL(avius) EGNATIUS / LOL-LIANUS V(ir) C(larissimus) CURATOR / AQUAR(um) ET MINIC(iae) D(evotus) N(umini) M(aistati)Q(ue) E(ius)." The *CIL* only records the find spot as being in the Roman Forum, close to the Lacus of Juturna.

64. *CIL* 6.36951 and p. 4355, on the left side: "DEDICATA CUM STATIONE A FL(avio) LOLLIANO C(larissimo) V(iro) CUR(atore) / KAL(endis) MARTIS / IANUARINO ET IUS-TO CONSS(ulibus)."

65. P. Burgers, "Statio Aquarum," in *LTUR*, 4:346–349; Mika Kajava, "Le iscrizioni ritrovate nell'area del Lacus Iuturnae," in *Lacus Iuturnae I*, ed. Eva Margareta Steinby (Rome: De Luca, 1989), 34–35; Gregor Kalas, "Topographical Transitions: The Oratory of the Forty Martyrs and Exhibition Strategies in the Early Medieval Roman Forum," in *Santa Maria Antiqua al Foro Romano: Cento anni dopo lo scavo*, ed. John Osborne, J. Rasmus Brandt, and Giuseppe Morganti (Rome: Campisano, 2004), 201–203.

66. *CIL* 6.37134 (and p. 4822): "[– – –]/[bus i]MMANIBUS OCCUPAT[– – –] / QUI UTRIQUE TRANSITUI FA[ciundo – – –] / ETIAM FORO QUOD RUIN[a – – –] / DESUPER ORNAMENTIS V(ir) C(larissimus) IUDEX SACRARUM C(ognitionum) / RESTITUIT." This inscription is dated by titulature and letter style to Constantine or Constantius II.

67. M. T. W. Arnheim, *The Senatorial Aristocracy in the Later Roman Empire* (Oxford: Clarendon, 1972), 39–48.

68. See Gregor Kalas et al., *Visualizing Statues*, at http://inscriptions.etc.ucla.edu/index.php/ritual-experience-hyper-cities. Digital models such as that seen in the screenshot in fig. 2.4 can be accessed by launching in HyperCities; a discussion of Constantine occurs in the "Ritual Experience" section, chapter 7 ("Late Antique Processional Protocol").

69. *Notitia urbis Romae*, in Valentini and Zucchetti, *Codice topografico*, 1:173: "[Regio VIII, Forum Romanum et Magnum continet]: Rostra III / Genium populi Romani aureum et equum Constantini. / Senatum. / Atrium Minervae. / Forum Caesaris. Augusti. Nervae. Traiani. . . ."

70. The Einsiedeln itinerary mentions the Equus Constantini twice. On the path from the Porta Sancti Petri to the church of S. Lucia in Orfeo, it was mentioned as if between the Arch of Septimius Severus and the Roman Forum: Gerald Walser, *Die Einsiedler Inschriftensammlung und der Pilgerführer durch Rom: Codex Einsiedlensis 326* (Stuttgart: Franz Steiner, 1987), 162–167. On the route from the Porta Aurelia to the Porta Praenestina, the Equus Constantini comes after the Arch of Septimius Severus, the *Umbilicus urbis*, and S. Maria Antiqua, whereas it is listed before SS. Cosma e Damiano and the Roman Forum: ibid., 181–189.

71. The site that once held the obliterated equestrian statue of Domitian should be ruled out. Giuliani and Verduchi defined the cavity framed by surviving blocks of *giallo antico* as the most

logical place for Domitian's statue, but not Constantine's; see Giuliani and Verduchi, *L'area centrale*, 118–122, 133–140, referring to Giacomo Boni's *cartella* 8 from 1903 in the archives of the Soprintendenza del Foro Romano e Palatino at pp. 574–577. See also Johannes Bergemann (*Römische Reiterstatuen: Ehrendenkmäler im öffentlichen Bereich* [Mainz am Rhein: Philipp von Zabern, 1990], 166–167), who believed the equestrian monument for Constantine was displayed close to the Temple of the Deified Julius Caesar.

72. Giuliani and Verduchi, *L'area centrale*, 69–73, 143–147; Patricia Verduchi, "Equus: Constantinus," in *LTUR* 2:226–227. An equestrian statue of Septimius Severus, recorded by Herodian, probably took possession of the foundations for the equestrian statue that had been left empty due to Domitian's official condemnation: Herodian 2.9.6. The larger cavity in the Forum pavement to the west of the smaller, central indentation was ruled out as having held first Domitian's statue and then Septimius Severus' because incised lines of the Severan pavement align instead with the smaller *giallo antico* cavity. Neither the equestrian statue of Domitian nor that of Septimius Severus remained once Constantine's was installed; evidence suggests that the equestrian statue of Constantine was on the far western end of the Forum square.

73. *CIL* 6.1158. This monument is discussed below.

74. The foundations measure approximately 3.4 by 7.4 meters. It is possible to imagine that the equestrian statue of Constantine was even as large as triple life-size, according to Ruck, *Die Grossen dieser Welt*, 85, 252.

75. *CIL* 6.1141: "D(omino) N(ostro) CONSTANTINO MAXIMO / PIO FELICI AC TRIUMPHATORI SEMPER AUGUSTO / OB AMPLIFICATAM TOTO ORBE REM PUBLI-CAM FACTIS CONSULTISQ(ue) / S(enatus) P(opulus)Q(ue) R(omanus) / DEDICANTE ANICIO PAULINO IUNIORE V(iro) C(larissimo) CONS(ule) ORD(inario) PRAEF(ecto) URBI"; for Anicius Paulinus, see *PLRE* 1 (Paulinus 14).

76. The family of Anicius Paulinus was still identified as pagan in the fifth-century poetry of Prudentius, *Contra Symmachum* 552–557; see Cameron, *The Last Pagans of Rome*, 180–181.

77. Georges Depeyrot, "Economy and Society," in *The Cambridge Companion to the Age of Constantine*, ed. Noel Lenski (Cambridge: Cambridge University Press, 2006), 239–245; Jairus Banaji, *Agrarian Change in Late Antiquity: Gold, Labour and Aristocratic Dominance* (Oxford: Oxford University Press, 2007).

78. *CIL* 6.36952 and p. 4355: "DOMINO NOSTRO / CONSTANTINO PIO / FELICI INVICTO / ET BEATISSI-MO / SEMPER AUGUSTO / FILIO DIVI PII / CONSTANTI AUGUSTI / APPIUS PRIMIANUS / V(ir) P(erfectissimus) / RAT(ionalis) / SUMMAE PRIVAT(ae) NUMINI M(aiestati)-Q(ue) / EIUS DICATUS //." The writing on the sides has been identified as erasures from a monument erected during the reign of Gordian III: "[[ded(icata) III Id(us) Sept(embres)]] / [[d(omino) n(ostro) – – – IIII et – – – co(n)s(ulibus)]] / [[cur(antibus)]] / [[– – – IBII – – –E]] / [[pro magg(istris)]]."

See also André Chastagnol, "Le formulaire de l'épigraphie latine officielle dans l'antiquité tardive," in *La terza età dell'epigrafia: Atti del Colloquio AIEGL*, ed. Angela Donati (Faenza: Epigrafia e antichità, 1986), 19.

79. Amici, *Il foro di Cesare*, 39; La Rocca, "La nuova immagine dei fori Imperiali," 179–180; Rizzo, "Indagini nei fori imperiali," 226–228.

80. There is little basis for associating this installation with the western Rostra, as argued by Hennig Wrede ("Der *genius populi Romani*," 130–131). There appears to have been insufficient space for the image of Mars to have been installed next to the northern extension of the Rostra. The rediscovery of the base for the statue of Mars in front of the Senate House also rules out the Rostra as the original display spot; see Bauer, *Stadt, Platz und Denkmal*, 18. After examining the monument upon its rediscovery, Christian Hülsen ("Jahresberich über neue Funde und Forschungen zur Topographie der Stadt Rom," *Mitteilungen des Deutschen Archäologischen Instituts, Römische Abteilung* 17 [1903]: 30–31) determined that the apparently late antique restorations of the basalt plates of the Lapis Niger should be affiliated with the statue base for the Mars statue (*CIL* 6.33856).

81. For analysis of erasure relegating Domitian's name to oblivion, see Flower, *The Art of Forgetting*, 240–262.

82. *CIL* 6.33856: "MARTI INVICTO PATRI / ET AETERNAE URBIS SUAE / CONDITORIBUS / DOMINUS NOSTER / [[Imp(erator) Maxent[iu]s P(ius) F(elix)]] / INVICTUS AUG(ustus)."

83. *CIL* 6.33856, on the right side: "MAGISTR. QUINQ. CO[– – –]L F[– – –]BR[– – –]U[– – –]." The left side of the statue base lists them by name.

84. *CIL* 6.33856, on the right side: "DEDICATA DIE XI KAL(endas) MAIAS / PER FURIUM OCTAVIANUM V(irum) C(larissimum) / CUR(atorem) AED(ium) SACR(arum)." For Furius Octavianus, see *PLRE* 1 (Furius Octavianus 4).

85. *CIL* 6.1220 = 31394a = 33857: "CENSURAE VETERIS / PIETATISQUE SINGULARIS / DOMINO NOSTRO / [max]ENTIO." Assistance in translating the inscription was generously provided by Maura Lafferty.

86. Bauer, *Stadt, Platz und Denkmal*, 18.

87. Coins issued by Maxentius citing the memory of his son, Romulus, with a dedication to eternal memory (*memoriae aeternae*), depict buildings that do not definitively represent the Via Sacra Rotunda; see Emilia Talamo, "Raffigurazioni numismatiche," in *Il "Tempio di Romulo" al Foro Romano*, ed. Gabriella Flaccomio, *Quaderni dell'Istituto di Storia dell'Architettura*, ser. 26, fasc. 157–162 (1980): 23–34; Lizia Luschi, "L'iconografia dell'edificio rotondo nella monetazione massenziana e il 'tempio del divo Romolo,'" *Bullettino della Commissione Archeologica Communale di Roma* 89 (1984): 43–50. The pertinent coin legend reads, "DIVO ROMULO N V BIS CONS." The coin images with this legend are not clearly identified as indicating the Via Sacra Rotunda.

88. Elisha Dumser, "The Architecture of Maxentius: A Study in Architectural Design and Urban Planning in Fourth-Century Rome" (Ph.D. diss., University of Pennsylvania, 2005), 142–150.

89. Richard Krautheimer, "SS. Cosma e Damiano," in idem, *Corpus Basilicarum Christianarum Romae: Le basiliche cristiane antiche di Roma sec. IV-IX* (Vatican City: Istituto di Archeologia Cristiana, 1937–1980), vol. 1, fasc. 3, pp. 140–143.

90. Thomas and Witschel, "Constructing Reconstruction," 135–177.

91. Onofrio Panvinio transcribed the text as "CONSTANTIN[o] MAXIM[o] . . . [– – –]ME[– – –]," Biblioteca Apostolica Vaticana, Codex Vat. Lat. 6780, fol. 45.

92. Pirro Ligorio, in Biblioteca Apostolica Vaticana, Codex Vat. Lat. 3439, fol. 40, records the inscription. One could infer that Ligorio looked at the same inscribed epistyle, interpreting the letters that Panvinio read as *ME*, but proposing a variant reading of *MP*; accordingly, he may have filled in letters to form an epigraphic interpretation of "[triu]MP[h– – –]." The editors of the *Corpus inscriptionum Latinarum*, due to the loss of the original inscribed epistyle, suggest that letters could have been either MP or ME, since the inscription might have read "[cle]ME[ntissimoque principi]," *CIL* 6.1147 (and p. 4329).

93. Marlowe, "*Liberator urbis suae*," 214.

94. F. Paolo Fiore, "L'impianto architettonico antico," in *Il "Tempio di Romulo" al Foro Romano*, ed. Gabriella Flaccomio, *Quaderni dell'Istituto di Storia dell'Architettura*, ser. 26, fasc. 157–162 (1980): 72.

95. Fiore, "L'impianto architettonico antico," 74–81.

96. The curved wall blocked two of the Rotunda's large windows that addressed the Via Sacra. These were filled with bricks once the curved addition was added; see Dumser, "The Architecture of Maxentius," 129–130; Carla Martini, "Opera muraria," in Flaccomio, *Il "Tempio di Romulo" al Foro Romano*, 96–100.

97. Tucci, "Nuove acquisizioni," 277–279.

98. For the importance of the architectural repairs that undergirded the truth claims of Roman rebuilding inscriptions, see Garrett Fagan, "The Reliability of Roman Rebuilding Inscriptions," *Papers of the British School at Rome* 64 (1996): 81–93, an article that responds to the arguments of Thomas and Witschel ("Constructing Reconstruction").

99. Aurelius Victor, *De Caesaribus* 40.25.

100. For the construction of historical claims through erasure and the addition of new inscriptions, see Hedrick Jr., *History and Silence*, 238–239.

101. The hall, originally a library, no longer functioned as such once it received the fourth-century apse, since Maxentius' architects removed the niches for storing scrolls and texts. This *aula* certainly continued to provide passageway from the Via Sacra toward the marble plan of Rome throughout late antiquity. The basilica must have also functioned as a secular audience hall; see Pier Luigi Tucci, "Nuove osservazioni sull'architettura del *Templum Pacis*," in *Divus Vespasianus: Il bimillenario dei Flavi*,

ed. Filippo Coarelli (Milan: Electa, 2009), 158–167.

102. Tucci, "Nuove acquisizioni," 275–293.

103. Tucci (ibid., 276–283) identified the surviving evidence of this door, now at the level of the lower church.

104. Laura Nasrallah, *Christian Responses to Roman Art amid Architecture: The Second-Century Church and the Spaces of Empire* (Cambridge: Cambridge University Press, 2010), 163–164.

105. John Osborne, "The Jerusalem Temple Treasures and the Church of SS. Cosma e Damiano in Rome," *Papers of the British School at Rome* 76 (2008): 173–181, esp. 176–178.

106. Procopius, *Gothic Wars* 8.21.10–16 (ed. and trans. H. B. Dewing, 5:274–275).

107. Margherita Guarducci, *Epigrafia greca*, 4 vols. (Rome: Istituto Poligrafico dello Stato, 1967–1978), 3:419–420.

108. La Rocca, "La nuova immagine dei fori Imperiali," 196–199.

109. Emilio Rodríguez Almeida, *Formae urbis antiquae: Le mappe marmoree di Roma tra la repubblica e Settimo Severo*, Collection de l'École française de Rome 305 (Rome: École française de Rome, 2002), 73–76; Tina Najbjerg and Jennifer Trimble, "Ancient Maps and Mapping in and around Rome," *Journal of Roman Archaeology* 17 (2009): 577–583.

110. Jennifer Trimble, "Visibility and Viewing on the Severan Marble Plan," in *Severan Culture*, ed. Simon Swain, Jaś Elsner, and Stephen Harrison (Cambridge: Cambridge University Press, 2007), 368–384.

111. See the standard scholarly works: Gianfilippo Carettoni et al., eds. *La pianta marmorea di Roma antica* (Rome: Danesi, 1960); Rodríguez Almeida, *Forma urbis marmorea: Aggiornamento generale, 1980* (Rome: Quasar, 1981); Marc Levoy et al., eds., "Stanford Digital Forma Urbis Romae Project," http://forma urbis.stanford.edu, accessed 12 December 2011.

112. The provocative concept of *Bildräume* points out how changing responses by audiences could be shaped through building projects; see Paul Zanker, "Bild-Räume und Betrachter im kaiserzeitlichen Rom," in *Klassische Archäologie: Eine Einführung*, ed. Adolf Borbein et al. (Berlin: Dietrich Reimer, 2000), 205–226.

113. Beat Brenk, "Türen als Spolien und Baureliquien: Nova construere sed amplius vetusta servare," in *Künstlerischer Austausch / Artistic Exchange*, Akten des XXVIII Internationalen Kongresses für Kunstgeschichte, Berlin, 15–20 July 1992, ed. Thomas W. Gehtgens (Berlin: Akademie, 1993), 1:43–54, esp. 45–47.

114. Max Wegner, *Ornamente kaiserzeitlicher Bauten Roms. Soffitten* (Cologne: Böhlau, 1957), 68.

115. Tucci, "Nuove acquisizioni," 278.

116. Rodolfo Lanciani, *Notes from Rome*, ed. Anthony Cubberly (London: British School at Rome, 1988), 80.

117. Nazarius, "Panegyric of Constantine," *Panegyrici Latini* 4 (10), 35.4: "Placidam quippe rerum quietem et profundum Urbi otium gentes perdomitae condiderunt. Vacat remissioribus animis delectamenta pacis adhibere. Celeberrima quaeque Urbis novis operibus enitescunt, nec obsoleta modo per vetustatem redivivo cultu insigniuntur, sed illa ipsa quae antehac magnificentissima putabantur nunc auri luce fulgentia indecoram maiorum parsimoniam prodiderunt." Translation from Nixon and Rodgers, *In Praise of Later Roman Emperors*, 381.

118. Aurelius Victor, *De Caesaribus* 40.27: "urbis fanum atque basilicam, Flavii meritis patres sacravere."

119. The argument that the colossus was recarved from an earlier statue has long been noted. An analysis of the Parian marble reveals that the colossus must predate the reign of Maxentius; see Patrizio Pensabene, Lorenzo Lazzarini, and Bruno Tuni, "New Archaeometric Investigations on the Fragments of the Colossal Statue of Constantine in the Palazzo dei Conservatori," in *Interdisciplinary Studies on Ancient Stone*, ed. J. Hermann Jr., Norman Herz, and Richard Newman, ASMOSIA: Association for the Study of Marble and Other Stone in Antiquity (London: Archetype Publications, 2002), 5:250–255; I wish to thank Brenda Longfellow for this reference. The observation that the original was a bearded figure also rules out Maxentius as the one depicted in the original colossus and has led to the conclusion that Hadrian's likeness had been recarved to form that of Constantine; on this, see Cécile Evers, "Remarques sur l'iconographie de Constantin: À propos des portraits des 'Bons Empereurs,'" *Mélanges de l'École française de Rome: Antiquité* 103 (1991): 785–804, esp. 794–799. The suggestion that the Constantinian statue presented some of the attributes of Jupiter does not rule out the probability that Hadrian's image was reused to form the colossal portrait now in the Capitoline Museums; see Claudio Parisi Presicce, "Costantino come Giove: Proposta di ricostruzione grafica del colosso acrolitico della Basilica Costantiniana," *Bullettino della Commissione archeologica comunale di Roma* 107 (2006): 127–161.

120. Anthony Minoprio, "A Restoration of the Basilica of Constantine, Rome," *Papers of the British School at Rome* 12 (1932): 1–25. A reexamination of the evidence has confirmed that the southern staircase was integral to the original conception of the building; see Carla Amici, "Dal progetto al monumento," in Giavarini, ed., *La Basilica di Massenzio*, 21–74, esp. 38–47.

121. Susanna Buranelli Le Pera and Luca D'Elia, "'Sacra Via': Note topografiche," *Bullettino della Commissione archeologica comunale di Roma* 91 (1986): 241–262, esp. 257–259.

122. Carla Maria Amici, "Le techniche di cantiere e il procedimento costruttivo," in Giavarini, *La Basilica di Massenzio*, 149–159.

123. Marlowe, "*Liberator urbis suae*," 211.

124. The use of the Basilica of Constantine for publicly conducted judicial proceedings accords with the traditional purposes of such halls. Urban prefects serving as appellate judges probably used the basilica after the reign of Constantine; yet the argument that the generic meetings of the urban prefect occurred in the basilica during the reign of Maxentius fails to adequately specify the prefect's judicial responsibilities. The

claim that the Basilica of Constantine held unspecified meetings of the urban prefect was first advanced by Filippo Coarelli, "L'urbs e il suburbio: Ristrutturazione urbanistica e ristrutturazione amministrativa nella Roma di Massenzio," in *Società romana e impero tardoantico*, ed. Andrea Giardina (Rome: Laterza, 1986), 2:1–35.

125. Francesco De Angelis, "The Emperor's Justice and Its Spaces in Rome and Italy," in *Spaces of Justice in the Roman World*, ed. Francesco de Angelis (Leiden: Brill, 2010), 136.

126. Timothy Barnes, "Praetorian Prefects, 337–61," *Zeitschrift für Papyrologie und Epigraphik* 94 (1992): 249–252.

127. Harries, *Law and Empire*, 55.

128. Indications of a large base in the western apse, on which the colossus was displayed, are documented by early modern drawings: Tilmann Buddensieg, "Die Konstantinsbasilika in einer Zeichnung Francescos di Giorgio und der Marmorkoloss Konstantins des Grossen," *Münchner Jahrbuch der Bildenden Kunst* 13 (1962): 37–48.

129. Ruck, *Die Grossen dieser Welt*, 258. The bronze portrait is in the Capitoline Museums.

130. Eusebius, *Historia ecclesiastica* 9.9.10.

131. Bardill, *Constantine, Divine Emperor*, 203–212.

132. Bardill (ibid., 209) argues the case by suggesting that the larger hand, found in 1744, fitted originally onto a now-lost arm for the earlier version of the portrait, which was different in size from the extant arm belonging to the Constantinian transformation.

133. Eusebius, *Historia ecclesiastica* 9.9.11 (translation from Eusebius, *Ecclesiastical History*, trans. J. E. L. Oulton and H. J. Lawler [Cambridge, Mass.: Harvard University Press, 1957], 2:363–365).

134. Henri Grégoire, "La statue de Constantin et la signe de la croix," *L'antiquité classique* 1 (1932): 138–143.

135. Rufinus, *Historia ecclesiastica* 9.9.11 (in Eusebius, *Kirchengeschichte*, ed. Theodor Mommsen, Eduard Schwartz, and Friedhelm Winkelmann [Berlin: Akademie, 1999], 2:833): "quia in hoc singulari signo, quod est verae virtutis insigne, urbem Romam senatumque et populum Romanum iugo tyrannicae dominationis ereptam pristinae libertati nobilitatique restitui."

136. John Noel Dillon, *The Justice of Constantine: Law, Communication, and Control* (Ann Arbor: University of Michigan Press, 2012), 154–155, 252–255.

137. For the argument that writing and editing offered models for constructing the historical record in urban space, see Hedrick, *History and Silence*, 215–222.

138. Aurelius Victor, *De Caesaribus* 40.27.

139. *Chronographus anni 354*, 9:148 (discussing the reign of Maxentius): "templum Romae arsit et fabricatum est."

140. Ernesto Monaco, "Il Tempio di Venere e Roma: Appunti sulla fase del IV secolo," in *Aurea Roma: Dalla città pagana alla città cristiana*, ed. S. Ensoli and E. La Rocca (Rome: "L'Erma" di Bretschneider, 2000), 58–60.

141. Cassiodorus, *Chronica* 2.142.

142. Bauer, *Stadt, Platz und Denkmal*, 60.

143. Prudentius, *Contra Symmachum* 1.215–225: "ut publica festa diesque / et ludor stupuit celsa et Capitolia vidit / laurigerosque deum templis adstare ministros / ac Sacram resonare Viam mugitibus ante / delubrum Romae . . . / vera ratus quaecumque fiant auctore senatu, / contulit ad simulacra fidem dominosque putavit / aetheris, horrifico qui stant ex ordine vultu."

144. Prudentius, *Contra Symmachum* 1.226–231: "illic Alcides, spoliatis Gadibus hospes / Arcadiae, fulvo aere riget, gemini quoque fratres / corrupta de matre, nothi, Ledeia proles / nocturnique equites, celsae duo numina Romae, / inpendent retinente, venu magnique triumphi / nuntia suffuso figunt vestigia plumbo."

1. For the catalogue of the inscribed statue bases considered in this chapter, see Kalas, Favro, Johanson, et al., *Visualizing Statues*, http://inscriptions.etc.ucla.edu. The dates span the reign of Diocletian up to the death of Theoderic. Carlos Machado has identified 102 late antique statues ("Building the Past," 157–192, esp. 165–179), not 101, but I consider the inscription from the Column of Phocas (*CIL* 6.1200), dated 608 CE, to be beyond the scope of this investigation.

2. Kalas, Favro, Johanson, et al., *Visualizing Statues*, http://inscriptions.etc.ucla.edu. One can navigate through the digitally reconstructed space by clicking on the icon, "Launch in HyperCities."

3. In the *Visualizing Statues* website, the catalogue is labeled, "Inscription Database," http://inscriptions.etc.ucla.edu/index.php/inscription-database/.

4. For the letters, see Weisweiler, "Inscribing Imperial Power," 309–329.

5. Franz Alto Bauer, "*In formam antiquam restitutus*: Das Bewahren der Vergangenheit in der Spätantike am Beispiel des Forum Romanum," in *Die "Denkmalpflege" vor der Demkmalpflege*, Akten der Berner Kongresses, 30 June–3 July 1999, ed. V. Hoffmann, Jürg Schweizer, and Wolfgang Wolters (Bern: Peter Lang, 2005), 39–62.

6. Coarelli, "L'edilizia pubblica," 23–33; Franz Alto Bauer, "*Beatitudo temporum*: Die Gegenwart der Vergangenheit im Stadtbild des spätantiken Rome," in *Epochenwandel? Kunst und Kultur zwischen Antike und Mittelalter*, ed. F. A. Bauer (Mainz: Philipp von Zabern, 2001), 75–94.

7. For the renewed attention to Rome starting with the reign of Honorius, see Andrew Gillett, "Rome, Ravenna, and the Last Western Emperors," *Papers of the British School at Rome* 69 (2001): 131–167; Meaghan McEvoy, "Rome and the Transformation of the Imperial Office from the Late Fourth–Mid-Fifth Centuries AD," *Papers of the British School at Rome* 78 (2010): 151–192.

8. The concept of public exhibitions that construct a visual presentation of the historical record accounting for famed individuals is argued in Hedrick, *History and Silence*, 214–225.

9. Flower, *The Art of Forgetting*; Hedrick, *History and Silence*, 147–170.

10. The repeated use of terms such as *felicissimus* and *clementissimus* can be seen in the late antique inscriptions of the Forum.

11. For analysis of the functions of fora in ancient cities, see most recently Ray Laurence, Simon Esmonde Cleary, and Gareth Sears, *The City in the Roman West, c. 250 BC–c. A.D. 250* (Cambridge: Cambridge University Press, 2011), 186–189. For consensus in epigraphic displays, see Flower, *The Art of Forgetting*, 276–283.

12. Bauer, *Stadt, Platz und Denkmal*, 72, 132, 401–405.

13. Machado, "Building the Past," 179–185.

14. Chenault, "Statues of Senators," 103–132.

15. Roberto Meneghini, *I Fori imperiali e i Mercati di Traiano: Storia e descrizione dei monumenti alla luce degli studi e degli scavi recenti* (Rome: Libreria dello Stato, 2009).

16. Weisweiler, "From Equality to Asymmetry," 319–350.

17. Chenault, "Statues of Senators," 110–112; for Claudian, *CIL* 6.1710; for Merobaudes, *CIL* 6.1724; Julian honored Aurelius Victor with a statue, Ammianus Marcellinus, *Res gestae* 21.10.6. A reference to his own statue is made by Sidonius Apollinaris, *Epistulae* 9.16.3, vv. 25–28: "Cum meis poni statuam perennem / Nerva Traianus titulis videret, / inter auctores utriusque fixam / bybliothecae"; for Marius Victorinus, see Jerome, *Chronicon*, anno 354: "Victorinus rhetor et Donatus grammaticus praeceptor meus Romae insignes habentur, e quibus Victorinus etiam statuam in foro Traiani meruit."

18. Chenault, "Statues of Senators," 129.

19. La Rocca, "La nuova immagine dei Fori Imperiali," 195–196, with the mention of newly discovered statue bases identifying the artists Kephisodos, Parthenokles, and Praxiteles at 197–201. See also Alessandra Bravi, *Ornamenta urbis: Opere d'arte greche negli spazi romani* (Bari: Edipuglia, 2012), 167–181.

20. For the works from Jerusalem, see Josephus, *Bellum Iudaicum* 7.162; for the Greek and Pergamene statues, see Pliny, *Naturalis historia* 34.84.

21. Procopius, *Gothic Wars* 8.21.11–14.

22. For a global collection in the Forum of Peace, see Steven Rutledge, *Ancient Rome as a Museum: Power, Identity, and the Culture of Collecting* (Oxford: Oxford University Press, 2012), 272–284; the idea of a cultural zone for happiness is presented in Paul Zanker, "By the Emperor, For the People: 'Popular' Architecture in Rome," in Ewald and Noreña, *The Emperor and Rome*, 45–87; for the metaphors of peace in the display, see Carlos Noreña, "Medium and Message in Vespasian's *Templum Pacis*," *Memoirs of the American Academy in Rome* 48 (2003): 25–43.

23. Bauer, *Stadt, Platz und Denkmal*, 72, 74–75, 401–405.

24. Q. Aurelius Symmachus had written to the emperors Theodosius I, Arcadius, and Valentinian II, informing them that the senate had voted to put up a memorial to Vettius Agorius Praetextatus in the form of a statue: Symmachus, *Relationes* 12.3 (R. H. Barrow, *Prefect and Emperor: The Relationes of Symmachus, A.D. 384* [Oxford: Clarendon, 1973], 78): "Senatus inpatiens dispendii sui solacium petit de honore virtutis vestrumque numen precatur, ut virum nostra aetate mirabilem statuarum diuturnitas tradat oculis posterorum, non quod ille praemia terrena desideret . . . , sed quia ornamentis bonorum incitatur imitatio et virtus aemula alitur exemplo honoris alieni." Symmachus' request was the proper method of granting an honorific statue; the Vestals who wished to set up a statue to the same Praetextatus had not received the appropriate permission. See Symmachus, *Epistulae* 9.108–109.

25. *CIL* 6.1779a: "[Vettio Agorio Praet]EXTATO / [v(iro) c(larissimo) correctori Tusciae et U]MBRIAE / [consulari Lusitaniae proc]ONSULI ACHAIAE / [praef(ecto) urb(i) praef(ecto) praet(orio) Il]YR[i]CI ET ITALIA[e]."

26. Niquet, *Monumenta virtutum titulique*, 178–179. Robert Chenault ("Statues of Senators," 125) ponders whether Praetextatus' death in 385 when he was consul-designate earned him a public funeral and the associated benefit of a public statue.

27. The prohibition had been clearly articulated in the East after 398; see *Codex Iustinianus* 1.24.1.

28. Marietta Horster, "Ehrungen spätantiker Statthalter," *Antiquité Tardive* 6 (1998): 37–59; Slootjes, *The Governor and His Subjects*, 129–152. See the legislation requiring that the one depicted in an installation pay for the statue, *Codex Iustinianus* 1.24.4; the statues probably also diminished after the Vandal attack on Rome led by Gaiseric in 455.

29. Jakob Munk Højte, *Roman Imperial Statue Bases: From Augustus to Commodus* (Aarhus: Aarhus University Press, 2005), 20–24.

30. This is inferred from Symmachus, *Relatio* 12, regarding the statue for Vettius Agorius Praetextatus. See Niquet, *Monumenta virtutum titulique*, 96.

31. Hedrick, *History and Silence*, 126–153.

32. This was recorded for the consulship of Probinus and Olybrius in 395: Claudian, *Panegyricus dictus Probino et Olybrio consulibus* 226–233.

33. Majorian, *Novels* 4.1 ("De aedificiis publicis"), in *Leges novellae ad Theodosianum pertinentes*, ed. Theodor Mommsen and P. Meyer (Berlin: Weidmann, 1905), 161: "Dum necessaria publico operi saxa finguntur antiquarum aedium dissipatur speciosa constructio et ut parvum aliquid reparetur, magna diruuntur."

34. Cassiodorus, *Variae* 25.1: "Nil prodest initia rei solidare, si valebit praesumptio ordinata destruere: illa sunt enim robusta, illa diuturna quae prudentia incipit et cura custodit. atque ideo maior in conservandis rebus quam in inveniendis adhibenda cautela est, quia de initiis praedicatio debetur invento, de custoditis adquiritur laudata perfectio."

35. Symmachus, *Epistulae* 4.4.2 (ed. Seeck, *MGH AA*, 6.1:99: "maius quiddam est honorem restituere quam dedisse."

36. Paul Veyne, *Bread and Circuses: Historical Sociology and Political Pluralism*, trans. Brian Pearce (London: Penguin, 1990); a highly informative review of the culture of benefactions is provided in Yasin, *Saints and Church Spaces*, 102–109.

37. Ammianus Marcellinus, *Res gestae* 27.3.7: "non instaurator, sed conditor."

38. Ammianus Marcellinus, *Res gestae* 27.3.6: "accitos a Vaticano quosdam egentes, opibus ditaverat magnis" (trans. John Rolfe [Cambridge, Mass.: Harvard University Press, 1939], 19).

39. Ammianus Marcellinus, *Res gestae* 27.3.10: "non ex titulis solitis parari iubebat impensas, sed si ferrum quaerebatur, aut plumbum, aut aes aut quicquam simile, apparitores immittebantur, qui velut ementes diversas raperent species, nulla pretia persolvendo" (trans. Rolfe, 19).

40. Ammianus Marcellinus, *Res gestae* 16.10.13: "allocutus nobilitatem in curia, populumque pro tribunali." See Augusto Fraschetti, "'*Veniunt modo reges Romam*,'" in *Transformations of Urbs Roma in Late Antiquity*, ed. William V. Harris, *Journal of Roman Archaeology*, suppl. 33 (Portsmouth, R.I.: Journal of Roman Archaeology, 1999), 235–248, esp. 241–243.

41. The activities of Theodosius I are mentioned in the panegyric by Pacatus, *Panegyrici Latini* 2 (12), 47.3. A description of Honorius' ritual at Rome of 404 appears in Claudian, *De sexto consulatu Honorii Augusti* 587–591.

42. Niquet, *Monumenta virtutum titulique*, 77–78.

43. Noreña, *Imperial Ideals*, 246–255.

44. Ruck, *Die Grossen dieser Welt*, 36–48, 253.

45. Franz Alto Bauer, *Stadt, Platz und Denkmal*, 19.

46. *CIL* 6.31395: "PROPAGATORI IMPERII / ROMANI D(omino) N(ostro) / FL(avio) IUL(io) CONSTANTIO MAXIMO / TOTO ORBE VICTORI AC / TRIUMFATORI SEMPER AUG(usto) / MEMMIUS VITRASIUS ORFITUS V(ir) C(larissimus) / ITERUM PRAEF(ectus) URBI IUD(ex) SAC(rarum) COGN(itionum) / TERTIUM D(evotus) N(umini) M(aiestati)Q(ue) EIUS"; *CIL* 6.1161: "PROPAGATORI IMPERII / ROMANI D(omino) N(ostro) Fl(avio) IULIO / CONSTANTIO MAXIMO / TOTO ORBE VICTORI / AC TRIUMF(atori) SEMP(er) AUG(usto) / MEMMIUS VITRASIUS / ORFITUS V(ir) C(larissimus) ITERUM / PRAEF(ectus) URBI IUDEX / SAC(rarum) COGN(itionum) TERT(ium) D(evotus) N(umini) M(aiestati)Q(ue) E(ius)"; *CIL* 6.1162: "PROPAGATORI IMPERII / ROMANI D(omino) N(ostro) FL(avio) IULIO / CONSTANTIO MAXIMO / TOTO ORBE VICTORI / AC TRIUMF(atori) SEMP(er) AUG(usto) / MEMMIUS VITRASIUS / ORFITUS V(ir) C(larissimus) / PRAEF(ectus) URBI IUDEX / SAC(rarum) COGN(itionum) TERT(ium) D(evotus) N(umini) M(aiestati)Q(ue) E(ius)."

47. Ammianus Marcellinus, *Res gestae* 14.6.1: "seditiones sunt concitatae graves ob inopiam vini."

48. Ammianus Marcellinus, *Res gestae* 16.10.13: "venisset ad rostra, perspectissimum priscae potentiae forum, obstupuit, perque omne latus quo se oculi contulissent, miraculorum densitate."

49. Ammianus Marcellinus, *Res gestae* 16.10.9–10: "Augustus itaque faustis vocibus appellatus, minime vocum lituorumque intonante fragore cohorruit, talem se tamque immobilem, qualis in provinciis suis visebatur, ostendens. Nam et corpus perhumile curvabat portas ingrediens celsas, et velut collo munito, rectam aciem luminum tendens, nec dextra vultum nec laeva flectebat tamquam figmentum hominis: non cum rota concuteret nutans, nec spuens . . . manumve agitans visus est umquam."

50. *CIL* 6.1158: "RESTITUTORI URBIS ROMAE ADQUE ORB[is] / ET EXTINCTORI PESTIFERAE TYRANNIDIS D(omino) N(ostro) FL(avio) IUL(io) CONSTANTIO VICTORI AC TRIUMFATORI / SEMPER AUGUSTO / NERATIUS CERE[a]LIS V(ir) C(larissimus) PRAEFECTUS URBI / VICE SACRA(rum) IUDICANS D(evotus) N(umini) M(aiestati) QUE EIUS."

51. Niquet, *Monumenta virtutum titulique*, 19.

52. Heike Niquet, "Die valentinianische Dynastie und Rom: Das Selbstverständnis der Kaiser und ihre Haltung zur Senatsaristokratie im Licht von Bau- und Ehreninschriften," in *Inschriftliche Denkmäler als Medien der Selbstdarstellung in der römischen Welt*, ed. Géza Alföldy and Silvio Panciera (Stuttgart: Franz Steiner, 2001), 125–147.

53. Cod. Theod. 9.16.7.

54. Alföldi, *A Conflict of Ideas*.

55. *CIL* 6.1174: "MAXIMO PRINCIPI / INDULGENTISSIMO / DOMINO VALENTI TRI/UMFATORI SEMPER AUG(usto) / C(aius) CEIONIUS RUFIUS VOLUSIANUS / V(ir) C(larissimus) PRAEF(ectus) URBI ITERUM IUD(ex) / SACRARUM COGNITIONUM / SERENTITATI EIUS DICATUS."

56. *CIL* 6.36955: "[Maximo p]RINC[ipi] / [indulgent]ISSIMO D(omino) [n(ostro)] / [Valent]INIANO TRI[umfatori] / [semp]ER AUGUSTO / C(aius) CEI[o]NIUS RUFIUS V[olusianus] / V(ir) C(larissimus) P[r]AEF(ectus) URB[i iterum iudex] / SACRARUM C[ognitionum] / SERENIT[ati eius dicatus]." One piece of the inscription was found encased in the portal of the Curia Senatus; the other was recovered at the piazza in front of the Senate House. See the entry by M. Buroni in Silvio Panciera, ed., *Iscrizioni greche e latine del Foro romano e del Palatino* (Rome: Edizioni di storia e letteratura, 1996), 354–355.

57. For C. Caeionius Rufius Volusianus signo Lampadius, see *PLRE* 1 (Volusianus 5).

58. Ammianus Marcellinus, *Res gestae* 27.3.5–10. The court of Valentinian I encouraged Lampadius to offer practical repairs in 364: Cod. Theod. 15.1.11.

59. For the repairs to the Pons Aurelius: *ILS* 769; Ammianus Marcellinus (*Res gestae* 27.3.3) specifies Avianus Symmachus' involvement in the Pons Aurelius. For the bridge in honor of Valens, Valentinian I, and Gratian, see *CIL* 6.1175 and 1176. See also Mark Humphries, "Roman Senators and Absent Emperors in Late Antiquity," *Acta ad archaeologiam et artium historiam pertinentia* 17 (2003): 27–46.

60. Q. Aurelius Symmachus received the exalted post of *comes tertii ordinis*.

61. Franz Alto Bauer, "Das Denkmal der Kaiser Gratian, Valentinian II. und Theodosius am Forum Romanum," *Mitteilungen des Deutschen Archäologischen Instituts, Römische Abteilung* 106 (1999): 213–234. The inscription is *CIL* 6.1184a = 31255: "DOMINIS OMNIUM GRATIANO VALENTINIANO ET THEODOSIO IMPERATORIB(us) ET THEODOSIO / IMPERATORIB(us) AUG(ustis) / L(ucius) Val(erius) SEPT(imus) BASS[us] V(ir) C(larissimus) PRAEF(ectus) URB(i) MAIESTATI EORUM DICAVIT."

62. Bauer ("Das Denkmal der Kaiser," 213–234) has identified an inscribed block found between the Temple of Castor and Pollux and the Temple of Vesta as originally having labeled a doorway at the Rostra; this fragment was separate from the epistyle block and provided additional testimony to Bassus' benefaction; *CIL* 6.37132: "L(ucius) VAL(erius) SEP[timius BASSUS]."

63. Hedrick, *History and Silence*, 3–36.

64. *CIL* 6.3791a = 31413: "EXTINCTORI TYRANNORUM / AC PUBLICAE SECURITATI(s) / AUCTORI / D(omino) N(ostro) VALENTINIANO / PERPETUO AC FELICI SEMPER AUGUSTO / CEIONIUS RUFIUS ALBINUS V(ir) C(larissimus) / PRAEF(ectus) URBI ITERUM / VICE SACRA IUDICAN D(evotus) N(umini) M(aiestati) Q(ue) EIUS"; *CIL* 6.3791b = 31414: "EXTINCTORI TYRANNORUM / AC PUBLICAE SECURITAT[is] / AUCTORI / D(omino) N(ostro) ARCAD[io] / PERPETUO AC FELIC[i] SEMPER AUGUST[o] / CEIONIUS RUFIUS ALBIN[us (vir clarissimus)] / PRAEF(ectus) URBI ITE[rum] / VICE SACRA IUDICAN D(evotus) N(umini) M(aiestati)[q(ue) eius]"; *CIL* 6.36959: "EXTINCTORI TYRANNORUM / AC PUBLICAE SECURITATI(s) / AUCTORI / D(omino) N(ostro) THEODOSIO / PERPETUO AC FELICI SEMPER AUGUSTO / CEIONIUS RUFIUS ALBINUS V(ir) C(larissimus) / PRAEF(ectus) URBI ITERUM / VICE SACRA IUDICAN D(evotus) N(umini) M(aiestati)Q(ue) EIUS." For the inscription of Constantius II, see *CIL* 6.1148: "EXTINCTORI PESTIFERAE TYRANNIDIS." The link between the two installations is argued by Robert Chenault, "Rome without Emperors: The Revival of a Senatorial City in the Fourth Century CE," Ph.D. dissertation, University of Michigan, 2008, 260–262.

65. Chenault, "Rome without Emperors," 261–262.

66. *CIL* 6.36960: "[Thermantia]E / [sanctissimae] AC NOBILISSIMAE / [memoriae femi]NAE CONIUGI DIVI / [Theodosi inlust]RIS COMITIS UTRIUS / [que militiae m]ATRI D(omini) N(ostri) THEODOSI / [perpetui aug(usti)] AVIAE DD(ominorum) NN(ostrorum) / [Arcadi fortis]SIMI PRINCIPIS / [et Honori piis]SIMI IUVENIS. . . ." See also Wolfgang Messerschmidt, "Die statuarische Repräsentation des theodosianischen Kaiserhauses in Rom," *Mitteilungen des Deutschen Archäologischen Instituts, Römische Abteilung* 111 (2004): 558. For a discussion of the statues depicting women from impe-

rial families that were displayed in the Roman Forum from the early principate until the Trajanic period, all of which had presumably been destroyed by the fourth century CE, see Mary T. Boatwright, "Women and Gender in the Forum Romanum," *Transactions of the American Philological Association* 141 (2011): 124–130, 132–133.

67. Bauer, *Stadt, Platz und Denkmal*, 39–41.

68. *CIL* 6.33856; for the text, see Chapter 2, n. 82.

69. Pacatus, *Panegyrici Latini* 2 (12), 44.5: "Vos . . . artifices, vulgata illa veterum fabularum argumenta despicite. . . . Haec potius, haec gesta sollertes manus ducant; his fora . . . decorentur" (trans. Nixon and Rodgers, *In Praise of Later Roman Emperors*, 511).

70. Pacatus, *Panegyrici Latini* 2 (12), 47.3: "Ea vero quae Romae gesta sunt, qualem te Urbi dies primus invexerit; quis in curia fueris, quis in rostris; ut pompam praeeuntium ferculorum curru modo, modo pedibus subsecutus alterno clarus incessu nunc de bellis, nunc de superbia triumpharis; ut te omnibus principem, singulis exhibueris senatorem; ut crebro civilique progressu non publica tantum opera lustraveris sed privatas quoque aedes divinis vestigiis consecrearis" (trans. Nixon and Rodgers, *In Praise of Later Roman Emperors*, 515).

71. Claudian (*De sexto consulatu Honorii augusti* 57–59) mentions that Theodosius I sought to appear as if he were a regular citizen during his ritual visit to Rome in 389.

72. Claudian drew upon the memory of Honorius' childhood visit when the poet commemorated a procession in Rome for Theodosius' son, *De sexto consulatu Honorii augusti* 422–425: "hunc civis dignare chorum conspectaque dudum / ora refer, pompam recolens ut mente priorem, / quem tenero patris comitem susceperat aevo, / nunc duce cum socero iuvenem te Thybris adoret."

73. McEvoy, "Rome and the Transformation of the Imperial Office."

74. Niquet, *Monumenta virtutum titulique*, 68.

75. The now-lost text of Honorius' statue base survives in apparently fragmentary form using terms that are suspiciously similar to those used for Stilicho. But, since the Stilicho inscription (*CIL* 6.1731) survives and is displayed at the Villa Medici in Rome, there is every reason to conclude that there were two silver-plated statues on the Rostra. See *CIL* 6.1195: "DOMINI NOSTRI HONORI AUGUSTI / POPULUS ROMANUS / PRO SINGULARI EIUS / CIRCA SE AMORE / ADQUE PROVIDENTIA / STATUAM EX AERE ARGENTOQUE / IN ROSTRIS AD MEMORIAM / GLORIAE / SEMPITERNAE / CONLOCANDAM DECREVIT."

76. Senators were motivated to pay for statues of rulers in the Forum to secure elevated status after forging links with the emperor, according to Schlinkert, *"Ordo senatorius" und "nobilitas,"* 229. By inference, instructions were provided to Pisidius Romulus how best to commemorate both Honorius and Stilicho, since the latter did not have imperial status.

77. For this claim, see Claudian, *Panegyricus de tertio con-*

sulatu Honorii Augusti 142–162, esp. 151–153; Alan Cameron, *Claudian: Poetry and Propaganda at the Court of Honorius* (Oxford: Clarendon, 1970), 37–45.

78. Honorius' appointment as emperor at Constantinople in 393 allowed the procession of 404 in Rome to serve as a *decennalia* rite, even though the celebration occurred after the anniversary. For Honorius and Stilicho adopting the themes of collegial rulership, see Meaghan McEvoy, *Child Emperor Rule in the Late Roman West, AD 367–455* (Oxford: Oxford University Press, 2013), 167–174.

79. Stilicho's fate and ultimate condemnation in 408 is explored in John Matthews, *Western Aristocracies and the Imperial Court, A.D. 364–425* (Oxford: Clarendon, 1975), 278–283.

80. *CIL* 6.1731: "[Flavio Stilichoni inlustrissimo] / VIRO BIS CONSULI ORDINARIO / MAGISTRO UTRIUSQUE MILITIAE / COMITI DOMESTICORUM / ET STABULI SACRI ADQUE / AB INEUNTE AETATE / PER GRADUS CLARISSIMAE / MILITIAE AD COLUMEN REGIAE / ADFINITATIS EVECTO SOCIO / BELLORUM OMNIUM / ET VICTORIARUM ADFINI / ETIAM DIVI THEODOSI AUGUSTI / ITEMQUE SOCERO / DOMNI NOSTRI HONORI AUGUSTI / POPULUS ROMANUS / PRO SINGULARI EIUS / CIRCA SE AMORE / ADQUE PROVIDENTIA / STATUAM EX AERE ARGENTOQUE / IN ROSTRIS AD MEMORIAM / GLORIAE SEMPITERNAE / CONLOCANDAM DECREVIT / EXEQUENTE FL(avio) PISIDIO ROMULO V(iro) C(larissimo) / PRAEF(ecto) URB(i)."

81. Catherine Ware, *Claudian and the Roman Epic Tradition* (Cambridge: Cambridge University Press, 2012), 99–116.

82. Claudian, *Panegyricus de sexto consulatu Honorii Augusti* 587–589: "hic est ille puer, qui nunc ad rostra Quirites / evocat et solio fultus genitoris eburno / gestarum patribus causas ex ordine rerum" (trans. Dewar, 41).

83. Claudian, *Panegyricus de sexto consulatu Honorii Augusti* 49–50: "volantia signa / nubibus et densum stipantibus aethera" (trans. Dewar, 7). For Claudian's literary strategies and connections between artworks and late antique poetry, see Michael Roberts, *The Jeweled Style: Poetry and Poetics in Late Antiquity* (Ithaca, N.Y.: Cornell University Press, 1989).

84. Claudian, *Panegyricus de sexto consulatu Honorii Augusti* 592–594: "nil cumulat verbisque nil fiducia celat; / fucati sermonis opem mens conscia laudis / abnuit."

85. Claudian, *Panegyricus de sexto consulatu Honorii Augusti* 595–596.

86. Claudian, *Panegyricus de sexto consulatu Honorii Augusti* 597: "adfuit ipsa suis ales Victoria templis."

87. Claudian, *Panegyricus de sexto consulatu Honorii Augusti* 598–602: "Romanae tutela togae: quae divite pinna / patricii reverenda fovet sacraria coetus / castrorumque eadem comes indefessa tuorum / nunc tandem fruitur iunctis atque omne futurum / te Romae seseque tibi promittit in aevum."

88. Claudian, *Panegyricus de sexto consulatu Honorii Augusti* 637–639: "perpetuisque inmoto cardine claustris / Ianus Bella premens laeta sub imagine pugnae / armorum innocuos paci largitur honores."

89. Claudian, *Panegyricus de sexto consulatu Honorii Augusti* 603–604: "hinc te iam patriis laribus Via nomine vero / Sacra refert" (trans. Dewar, 41).

90. Claudian, *Panegyricus de sexto consulatu Honorii Augusti* 551–559: "Romanos vetuit currum praecedere patres / . . . hunc civem, dominos venisse priores."

91. Stilicho's procession through Rome to celebrate the consulship in 399–400 might have set the stage for Honorius' ritual: Claudian, *De consulatu Stilichonis* 2.397–405. See Jacqueline Long, "Claudian and the City: Poetry and Pride of Place," in *Aetas Claudianea: Eine Tagung an der Freien Universität Berlin vom 28. bis 30. Juni 2002*, ed. Wolfgang Ehlers, Fritz Felgentreu, and Stephen Wheeler (Munich: K. G. Saur, 2004), 1–15. For the late antique route for imperial processions in Rome, see Stéphane Benoist, *Rome, le prince et la cité* (Paris: Presses universitaires de France, 2005), 61–101; Pierre Dufraigne, *Adventus Augusti, Adventus Christi: Recherche sur l'exploitation idéologique et littéraire d'un cérémonial dans l'antiquité tardive* (Paris: Institute d'Études Augustiniennes, 1994), 217–221; Fraschetti, "'Veniunt modo reges Romam,'" 240–244; Mark Humphries, "From Emperor to Pope? Ceremonial, Space, and Authority at Rome from Constantine to Gregory the Great," in *Religion, Dynasty, and Patronage in Early Christian Rome, 300–900*, ed. Kate Cooper and Julia Hillner (Cambridge: Cambridge University Press, 2007), 30–37.

92. Claudian, *Panegyricus de sexto consulatu Honorii Augusti* 578–580.

93. Claudian, *Panegyricus de tertio consulatu Honorii Augusti* 144–162; Zosimus 4.59.1–15, 5.4.3. See also Alan Cameron, "Theodosius the Great and the Regency of Stilicho," *Harvard Studies in Classical Philology* 73 (1969), 247–280.

94. Claudian, *Panegyricus de sexto consulatu Honorii Augusti* 422–425: "hunc civis dignare chorum conspectaque dudum / ora refer, pompam recolens ut mente priorem, / quem tenero patris comitem susceperat aevo, / nunc duce cum socero iuvenem te Thybris adoret" (trans. Dewar, 29–31). For Stilicho as the hero of Claudian's panegyric, see Cameron, *Poetry and Propaganda*, 46–48.

95. *CIL* 6.1730 (and p. 4746): "PROGENERO DIVI THEODOSI COMITI DIVI / THEODOSI AUGUSTI IN OMNIBUS BELLIS / ADQUE VICTORIIS ET AB EO IN ADFINITATEM / REGIAM COOPTATO ITEMQUE SOCERO D(omini) N(ostri) / HONORI AUGUSTI AFRICA CONSILIIS EIUS / ET PROVISIONE LIBERATA EX S(enatus) C(onsulto)." The base was discovered in 1539 near the Arch of Septimius Severus in front of the now-lost church of SS. Sergio e Baccho; see Mara Bonfioli, "La diaconia dei SS. Sergio e Bacco nel Foro Romano," *Rivista di Archeologia Cristiana* 50 (1974), 68. For an argument that this statue base also reused an equestrian monument's plinth, see Ruck, *Die Grossen dieser Welt*, 264–265.

96. *CIL* 6.31987: "FIDEI VIRTUTIQ(ue) DEVOTISSIMO-

RUM / MILITUM DOM(i)NORUM NOSTRORUM / AR-CADI HONORI ET THEODOSI / PERENNIUM AUGUS-TORUM / POST CONFECTUM GOTHICUM / BELLUM FELICITATE AETERNI / PRINCIPIS DOM(i)NI NOSTRI HONORI / CONSILIIS ET FORTITUDINE / INLUSTRIS VIRI COMITIS ET / [– – –] / [– – –] / S(enatus) P(opulus) Q(ue) R(omanus) / CURANTE PISIDIO ROMULO V(iro) C(larissimo) / PRAEF(ecto) URBI VICE SACRA / ITERUM IUDICANTE." The two erased lines have been restored as "[magister utriusq(ue) militiae Fl(avi) Stilichonis bis co(n)s(ulis) ord(inarii)]."

97. This facet of the installation was pointed out to me by Chris Johanson. For the "colossal" scale of the two statues, see Ruck, *Die Grossen dieser Welt*, 265.

98. *CIL* 6.41381: "[– – –] / [p]ROV[identissimo duci] / VICTO[rios]ISS[imo dominor(um) nn(ostrorum)] / [c]ON-SULT[o]RI ETIAM [fautori divini] / [ge]NERIS AC NO[minis Romani] / [[Fl(avio) Stilicho]ni [v(iro) c(larissimo) et inl(ustri) – – –?]]."

99. Niquet, *Monumenta virtutum titulique*, 57–58; she reconstructs the width as approximately 125 cm.

100. Chenault, "Statues of Senators," 126–127.

101. The travertine foundations on the Forum pavement were analyzed in their archeological context by Giuliani and Verduchi, *L'area centrale*, 79–82.

102. Bauer, *Stadt, Platz und Denkmal*, 39–42; Paolo Liverani, "Arco di Onorio—Arco di Portogallo," *Bollettino della Commissione Archeologica Comunale di Roma* 105 (2004): 351–370; idem, "Osservazioni sui rostri," 169–193.

103. *CIL* 6.1187; 31256 = 36888: "IMPERATORIBUS IN-VICTISSIMIS FELICISSIMISQUE / DD(ominis) NN(ostris) ARCADIO ET HONORIO FRATRIBUS / SENATUS POPU-LUSQUE ROMANUS / VINDICATA REBELLIONE / ET AF-RICAE RESTITUTIONE LAETUS." This inscription is in two parts; the last section, "[a]RMIPOTENS LIBY[c]UM DEFEN-DIT HONORIU(s)," originates from a much smaller architrave that must have been part of the installation.

104. Claudian, *Panegyricus de sexto consulatu Honorii Augusti* 370–373: "et nominis arcum / iam molita tui, per quem radiante decorus / ingredere toga, pugnae monumenta dicabam / defensam titulo Libyam testata perenni." There was another Arch of Honorius, Arcadius, and Theodosius II in the western Campus Martius; its inscription was recorded in the Einsiedeln itinerary, *CIL* 6.1196: "Imppp. clementissimis felicissimis toto orbe victoribus ddd. nn[n] / Arcadio Honorio Theodosio Auggg. Ad perenne indicium tripho[rum] / quod Getarum nationem in omne aevum doc[u]ere exti[ngui] / arcum simulacris eorum tropaeisq. decora[tum] / SPQR totius operis splendore." See De Maria, *Gli archi onorari di Roma*, 323–324. The Campus Martius arch's inscription does not correlate as closely with Claudian's text as does the one in the Forum.

105. Giuliani and Verduchi (*L'area centrale*, 79) specify that the sector was paved in late antiquity; the continued display of statues from the first century BCE depicting Marsyas and the

fig tree in the fourth century is established by Bernard Frischer (Frischer, Abernathy, and Dylla, "Rome Reborn," www.romereborn.virginia.edu).

106. Claudian, *Panegyricus de quarto consulatu Honorii* 17–25: "Haud indigna coli nec nuper cognita Marti / Ulpia progenies et quae diademata mundo / sparsit Hibera domus . . . hinc processit avus" (trans. Platnauer, 1:287–289).

107. Claudian, *Panegyricus de sexto consulatu Honorii Augusti* 57–59: "te consorte dies, cum se melioribus addens / exemplis civem gereret" (trans. Dewar, 7).

108. Such texts as Ausonius, *Cento Nuptialis*, and Proba's *Cento* feature a bricolage of Virgilian excerpts; see John Curran, "Virgilizing Christianity in Late Antique Rome," in *Two Romes: Rome and Constantinople in Late Antiquity*, ed. Lucy Grig and Gavin Kelly (Oxford: Oxford University Press, 2012), 325–344. For Claudian, see his *Panegyricus dictus Probino et Olybrio consulibus*.

109. Bauer, *Stadt, Platz und Denkmal*, 305.

110. Sarah Bassett, *The Urban Image of Late Antique Constantinople* (Cambridge: Cambridge University Press, 2004), 68–71, 192–204.

111. *CIL* 6.1200: "Optimo clementiss[imo piissim]oque / principi domino n(ostro) F[ocae imperat]ori / perpetuo a d(e)o coronato, [t]riumphatori / semper Augusto, / Smaragdus ex praepos(itus) sacri palatii / ac patricius et exarchus Italiae, / devotus eius clementiae / pro innumerabilibus pietatis eius / beneficiis et pro quiete / procurata Ital(iae) ac conservata libertate, / hanc sta[tuam maiesta]tis eius / auri spend[ore fulge]ntem huic / sublimi colu[m]na[e ad] perennem / ipsius gloriam imposuit ac dedicavit, / die prima mensis Augusti indict(ione) und(ecima) / p(ost) c(onsulatum) pietatis eius anno quinto."

112. F. M. Nichols, "A Revised History of the Column of Phocas in the Roman Forum," *Archeologia* 52 (1890): 187.

113. F. M. Nichols, "The Column of Phocas before Phocas," *Journal of the British and American Archaeological Society of Rome* 3 (1888–1889): 174–178; idem, "A Revised History of the Column of Phocas," 192.

114. G. Boni, *cartella* 8, unpublished document in the Soprintendenza Foro Romano e Palatino; it is discussed in Giuliani and Verduchi, *L'area centrale*, 176.

115. Giacomo Boni, "Foro Romano," in *Atti del congresso internazionale di scienze storiche* 1.9 (Apr. 1903), vol. 5, sec. 4 (Archeologia): 577–579.

116. Giuliani and Verduchi, *L'area centrale*, 176.

117. Ibid., 176–177.

118. Steinby, "L'industria laterizia," 123–124.

119. Bauer, *Stadt, Platz und Denkmal*, 118.

120. Ibid., 45.

121. Ibid., 46.

122. Patrizia Verduchi, in Giuliani and Verduchi, *L'area centrale*, 174.

123. Gillett, "Rome, Ravenna and the Last Western Emperors."

124. *CIL* 6.1767: "... DEORUM PARTICIPI / HOMINUM NUTRICI...."

125. *CIL* 6.1767: "... ANICIUS ANCILIUS GLABRIO FAUSTUS V(ir) C(larissimus) DICAVIT."

126. *CIL* 6.1767: "TARRUTENII / TARRUTENIO MAXI-MILIANO V(iro) C(larissimo) / ELOQUENTISSIMOQUE CONSULARI / PICENI ANNO AETATIS NONO DECIMO / VICARIO URBIS ROMAE LEGATO AMPLIS/SIMI SENATUS SECUNDO SOCERO / EXOPTATISSIMO ANICIUS ACILI-US / GLABRIO FAUSTUS V(ir) C(larissimus) LOCI HUIUS / ORNATOR TOGATAM STATUAM / LIBENS OPTULI."

127. Lorenzo Pignoria, *Le origini di Padova* (Padua, 1625), 153.

128. Amici, *Il foro di Cesare*, 143–157.

129. Rizzo, "Indagini nei fori imperiali," 215–244.

130. *CIL* 6.40726. See Lipps, "Zur Datierung der spätantiken Portikus des Caesarforums," 389–405.

131. *CIL* 6.41384, with an inscription of Virius Nicomachus Flavianus, urban prefect during 392–394, 399–400, and 408. See Chiara Morselli and Edoardo Tortorici, *Curia, Forum Iulium, Forum Transitorium*, 2 vols. (Rome: De Luca, 1989), 253; Bauer, "Stadt ohne Kaiser," 20.

132. Carla Amici, *Lo scavo didattico della zona retrostante la Curia (foro di Cesare): Campagne di scavo 1961–1970* (Rome: Bonsignori, 2007).

133. *CIL* 6.526: "SIMULACRUM MINERBAE / ABOLEN-DO INCENDIO / TUMULTUS CIVILIS IGNI / TECTO CA-DENTE CONFRACTUM / ANICIUS ACILIUS AGINANTIUS / FAUSTUS V(ir) C(larissimus) ET INL(ustris) PRAEF(ectus) URBI / VIC(e) SAC(ra) IUD(icans) IN MELIUS / INTEGRO PROVISO PRO / BEATITUDINE TEMPORIS RESTITUIT."

134. Carlos Machado, "Religion as Antiquarianism: Pagan Dedications in Late Antique Rome," in *Religious Dedications in the Greco-Roman World: Distribution, Typology, Use*, John Bodel and Mika Kajava eds. (Rome: Institutum Romanum Finlandiae, 2009), 331–354; Franz Alto Bauer, "*Beatitudo Temporum*," 87–89.

135. Fausto Zevi, "Atrium Minervae," in *LTUR* 1:135–136; Augusto Fraschetti, "L'Atrium Minervae in epoca tardoantica," *Opuscula Instituti Romani Finlandiae* 1 (1981): 25–40; idem, *La conversione*, 157-159.

136. Cod. Theod. 16.10.8: "... in qua simulacra feruntur posita artis pretio quam divinitate metienda iugiter patere publici consilii auctoritate...."

137. Zanker, "By the Emperor, For the People," 45–87.

138. Peter Stewart, *Statues in Roman Society: Representation and Response* (Oxford: Oxford University Press, 2004), 83–91.

139. Eumenius, *Panegyrici Latini* 5 (9), 6.4 (Nixon and Rodgers, *In Praise of Later Roman Emperors*, 159).

140. *CIL* 6.40768a (see *CIL* 6, pt. 8, fasc. 2, p. 4551): "[co]NSERVATORI ROMANI / [no]MINIS PROPAGATORI / [or]BIS SUI FACTIONUM / [ty]RANNICARUM EXTINCTO-RI / [dom]ITORI GENTIUM BARBARUM / [– – –impera?]-TORI DIVIN[– – –]...."

CHAPTER 4: RESTORED BASILICAS AND STATUES ON THE MOVE

1. Francesco de Angelis, "*Ius* and Space: An Introduction," in *Spaces of Justice in the Roman World*, ed. Francesco de Angelis (Leiden: Brill, 2010), 13.

2. For a summary of the inscriptions, see Witschel, "Statuen auf spätantiken Platzanlagen," 139–140. Understanding the civic space of the ancient city as providing spaces for a cultured, leisurely life is eloquently presented in Zanker, "By the Emperor, For the People," 45–88.

3. The prosopographical record lists two pertinent individuals named Probianus. One served as the urban prefect of Rome in 377 CE (*PLRE* 1 [Probianus 4]) and is mentioned at *Codex Theodosianus* 11.2.3. The other Probianus served as urban prefect of Rome in 416 (*PLRE* 2 [Probianus 1]) and is mentioned at *Codex Theodosianus* 14.10.4.

4. *CIL* 6.1658c: "GABINIUS VETTIUS / PROBIANUS V(ir) C(larissimus) PRAEF(ectus) URBI / STATUAM QUAE BASILI/CAE IULIAE A SE NOVITER / REPARATAE ORNA-MENTO / ESSE ADIECIT." I thank Maura Lafferty for advice on this translation.

5. *CIL* 6.1156a (with p. 4330): "DOMINO NOSTRO / FL(avio) CONSTANTINO / FORTISSIMO HAC / BEATISSI-MO CAESARI / FL(avius) URSACIUS V(ir) P(erfectissimus) / TRIBUNUS COHORTI/UM URBANARUM / X XI ET XII ET FORI / SUAR(i)."

6. *PLRE* 1:985 (Ursacius 4). Ursacius is usually seen as tribune of the urban cohorts in 317 and 337 CE, but clearly he held this position earlier as well.

7. Laura Chioffi, "Forum Suarium," in *LTUR* 2:346–347.

8. *Chronographus anni 354*, 9:148: "Diocletianus et Maximianus ... multae operae publicae fabricatae sunt: senatum, forum Caesaris, basilica Iulia...." The *Chronograph* also specified the fire of 284 that had destroyed the Basilica Julia (p. 146): "His [Carino et Numeriano] imperantibus fames magna fuit et operae publicae arserunt: senatum, forum Caesaris, basilica Iulia et Graecostadium."

9. Cod. Theod. 15.1.1.

10. Cod. Theod., 15.1.37.

11. For a discussion of examples, including the reinstalled portraits of Trajan and Constantine in Thuburiscu Numidarum, see Luke Lavan, "Political Talismans? Residual 'Pagan' Statues in Late Antique Public Space," *The Archaeology of Late Antique "Paganism,"* ed. Luke Lavan and Michael Mulryan (Leiden: Brill, 2011), 467. The public role of transferred statues in the cities of North Africa is discussed further in Anna Leone, *The End of the Pagan City: Religion, Economy, and Urbanism in Late Antique North Africa* (Oxford: Oxford University Press, 2013), 111–114, 125–133.

12. Noreña, *Imperial Ideals*, 271–297.

13. Veyne, *Bread and Circuses*, 70.

14. Yasin, *Saints and Church Spaces*, 102–110.

15. "RESTITUTORI URBIS ROMAE," for example, ap-

pears in the Roman Forum on the equestrian statue base of Constantius II (*CIL* 6.1158).

16. Borg and Witschel, "Veränderungen im Repräsentationsverhalten," 47–120.

17. *CIL* 6.526.

18. For the long-standing phrases of lament over ruins in literary responses, see Catharine Edwards, *Writing Rome: Textual Approaches to the City* (Cambridge: Cambridge University Press, 1996), 10–15.

19. Arguments suggesting that the deconsecration of pagan art led to the public display of statues as art were advanced long ago; see Giovanni Battista De Rossi, "La base d'una statua di Prassitele testè scoperta e la serie di simili basi alla quale essa appartiene," *Bullettino della Commissione Archeologica Municipale* 2 (1874): 174–181.

20. *CIL* 6.41416: "[– – –] / [– – –]ESIN[– – – statuam? ex] / SQUALEN[tibus ruinis – – –? trans]/LATAM LOC[o celeberrimo – – –] / [– – –] / [– – –]."

21. The old view that translated art was *necessarily* removed from a pagan context has been persuasively rejected by John R. Curran, "Moving Statues in Late Antique Rome: Problems of Perspective," *Art History* 17 (1994): 46–58.

22. This argument has been established on the basis of thorough scrutiny of the epigraphic sources by Hugo Brandenburg, "Die Umsetzung von Statuen in der Spätantike," in *Migratio et commutatio: Studien zur alten Geschichte und deren Nachleben (Festschrift Thomas Pekáry)*, ed. Hans-Joachim Drexhage and Julia Sünkes Thompson (St. Katharinen: Scripta Mercaturae, 1989), 235–246.

23. Curran, "Moving Statues," 46–58.

24. Hedrick, *History and Silence*, 230–237. The famous statue rehabilitating the honor of Virius Nicomachus Flavianus (Flavian the Elder) was displayed in the Forum of Trajan, *CIL* 6.1783.

25. This argument is heavily indebted to Paul Zanker ("By the Emperor, For the People," 45–87, esp. 84–87, and *The Mask of Socrates: The Image of the Intellectual in Antiquity*, trans. Alan Shapiro [Berkeley: University of California Press, 1995], 190–194).

26. Cairoli F. Giuliani and Patrizia Verduchi, "Basilica Iulia," in *LTUR* 1:177–179.

27. Bauer, "Stadt ohne Kaiser," 21–25.

28. Ibid., 22–23; Rodríguez Almeida, *Forma urbis marmaorea*, tav. 13, frag. 16e.

29. Steinby, "L'industria laterizia," 140, judging from a brick stamp: *CIL* 15.1569a.

30. Pliny the Younger, *Epistulae* 6.33.4; Leanne Bablitz, "A Relief, Some Letters and the Centumviral Court," in *Spaces of Justice in the Roman World*, ed. Francesco de Angelis (Leiden: Brill, 2010), 225.

31. Bablitz, "A Relief, Some Letters and the Centumviral Court," 223–249.

32. Loud applause from the four concurrent sessions barely overpowered Cicero's voice, which Quintilian mentions to sug-

gest both the noise pollution in the Basilica Julia and the ability of Cicero to speak audibly: *Institutio oratoria* 12.5.6.

33. Bauer, "Stadt ohne Kaiser," 25.

34. See the inscriptions attesting to the *nummularii de basilica Iulia*, *CIL* 6.9709 and *CIL* 6.9711.

35. Francesco Trifilò, "Movement, Gaming and the Use of Space in the Forum," in *Rome, Ostia, Pompeii: Movement and Space*, ed. Ray Laurence and David Newsome (Oxford: Oxford University Press, 2011), 312–331. Trifilò presents legal and epigraphic testimony to skilled game boards in fora, which are distinguished from the boards for games of chance and thus gambling. See also Henri Thédenat, *Le Forum romain et les Forums impériaux* (Paris: Hachette, 1923), 216–221. For gambling, see Freyberger, *Das Forum Romanum*, 75.

36. Trifilò, "Movement, Gaming and the Use of Space," 321.

37. Rouché, *Aphrodisias in Late Antiquity: The Late Roman and Byzantine Inscriptions*, available at http://insaph.kcl.ac.uk/ala2004, inscription nos. 59, 68, 69, 70, 71, and 238; see also Trifilò, "Movement, Gaming and the Use of Space," 326–328.

38. The Basilica Aemilia's repairs are attested by the numerous brick stamps from the time of Diocletian's Tetrarchy: Steinby, "L'industria laterizia," 117–124.

39. Johannes Lipps, *Die Basilica Aemilia am Forum Romanum: Der kaiserzeitliche Bau und seine Ornamentik* (Wiesbaden: Reichert, 2011), 160–166; for an inscription associated with Lucius Caesar and dating to 14 CE at the latest, see *CIL* 6.36908.

40. Steinby, "L'industria laterizia," 140–141; Bauer, *Stadt, Platz und Denkmal*, 32–35.

41. Lipps, *Die Basilica Aemilia*, 171.

42. Richard Reece, "A Collection of Coins from the Centre of Rome," *Papers of the British School at Rome* 50 (1982): 134; idem, "Coins and the Late Antique Economy," in *Theory and Practice in Late Antique Archaeology*, ed. Luke Lavan and William Bowden (Leiden: Brill, 2003), 157–158.

43. Alfonso Bartoli, "Ultime vicende e trasformazioni cristiane della Basilica Emilia," *Rendiconti della reale Accademia dei Lincei* 21 (1912): 759.

44. Lipps, *Die Basilica Aemilia*, 20. There remains evidence of secondary reuse of the façade, with construction dating to the eighth or ninth century creating a residence there: Roberto Meneghini and Riccardo Santangeli Valenzani, *Roma nell'altomedioevo: Topografia e urbanistica della città dal V al X secolo* (Rome: Libreria dello stato, 2004), 166–169.

45. Bauer, *Stadt, Platz und Denkmal*, 32–35; idem, "*Beatitudo temporum*," 84.

46. C. L. Labranche, "*Roma nobilis*: The Public Architecture of Rome, 330–476," Ph.D. dissertation, University of Michigan (1968), 153; Bauer, *Stadt, Platz und Denkmal*, 34; idem, "*Beatitudo temporum*," 84.

47. *CIL* 6.36962: "PRO FELICITATE D(ominorum) NN(ostrorum) HONORI [et Theodosi] / AUR[elius Anicius] SYMMACHUS [v(ir) c(larissimus) praef(ectus) urbi]."

48. Pliny the Elder, *Historia naturalis* 35.4.

49. For the reused granite columns on the façade of the Basilica Aemilia, see Patrizia Pensabene and Claudia Panella, "Reimpiego e progettazione architettonica nei monumenti tardo-antichi di Roma," *Atti della Pontificia Accademia Romana di Archeologia, Rendiconti* 66 (1993–1994): 164–166.

50. "FABIUS TITIANUS V(ir) C(larissimus) CONSUL PRAEF(ectus) URBI CURAVIT": *CIL* 6.1653a, 1653b, 1653c, 31880, 31881, 37107, and 37108.

51. Niquet, *Monumenta virtutum titulique*, 91–93.

52. Humphries, "Roman Senators and Absent Emperors," 18–19; Chenault, "Rome without Emperors," 75–77.

53. The text is transcribed in *Digesta Iustiniani* 43.9.2: "Concedi solet, ut imagines et statuae quae ornamenta rei publicae sunt futurae, in publicum ponantur."

54. Connections between literary education and mythological statues are explored in Lea Stirling, *The Learned Collector: Mythological Statuettes and Classical Taste in Late Antique Gaul* (Ann Arbor: University of Michigan Press, 2005), 153–155.

55. The first Tetrarchic inscription found in the Basilica Julia was sponsored by Turrianius Gratianus, urban prefect from 290 to 291; it might indicate that significant repairs had been completed at the Basilica Julia by that date, *CIL* 6.1128: "CLEMENTISSIM[o ac for]/TISSIMO IMP(eratori) / CAE[s(ari) M(arco) Aur(elio)] / MAXIMIANO PIO [felici] / INVICTO AUG(usto) PONT(ifici) [M(aximo)] / TRIB(unicia) POTEST(ate) CO(n)S(uli) II [p(atri) p(atriae)] / TURRIANI-US GRATIAN[us] / PRAEF(ectus) URBI." The term *tribunicia potestas* refers to the veto power accorded to the emperor. The second inscription can be less precisely dated, but was also found in the Basilica Julia, *CIL* 6.1127: "FORTISSIMO [piissimo] / INVICTISSIM[o principi] / DOMINO NOSTR[o imp(eratori) Caes(ari)] / MARCO AUR(elio) VA[l(erio)] / [M]AXI[mi]AN[o] / [p(io) f(elici) invicto semper Augusto]. . . ."

56. *CIL* 6.804, rediscovered in the sixteenth century behind the Basilica Julia at the Vicus Tuscus. See Jaakko Aronen, "Signum Vortumni," in *LTUR* 4:310–311; Carlos Machado, "Religion as Antiquarianism: Pagan Dedications in Late Antique Rome," in *Religious Dedications in the Greco-Roman World: Distribution, Typology, Use*, ed. John Bodel and Mika Kajava (Rome: Institutum Romanum Finlandiae, 2009), 343.

57. Claude Lepelley, "Le musée des statues divines: La volunté de sauvegarder le patrimoine artistique païen à l'époque théodosienne," *Cahiers Archéologiques* 42 (1994): 5–15.

58. Dio Chrysostom, *Orations* 31.38–39, 31.90.

59. Joseph Alchermes, "Spolia in Roman Cities of the Late Empire: Legislative Rationales and Architectural Reuse," *Dumbarton Oaks Papers* 48 (1994), 167–178.

60. Brandenburg, "Die Umsetzung," 243.

61. Cod. Theod. 15.1.16 (date: 365 CE): "In eo sane larga ac benigna his licentia tribuuntur, ut ornamenta urbium ac decora marmorum, quae in aliquo senium temporis sentiunt, ad speciem pristinam et usum congruae utilitatis instaurent" (trans. Pharr, 424).

62. Cod. Theod. 15.1.19: "Nemo praefectorum urbis aliorumve iudicum, quos potestas in excelso locat, opus aliquod novum in urbe Roma inclyta moliatur, sed excolendis veteribus intendat animum" (trans. Pharr, 425).

63. The late antique statuary of Aphrodisias is particularly well documented; see R. R. R. Smith, "Late Antique Portraits in a Public Context: Honorific Statuary at Aphrodisias in Caria, A.D. 300–600," *Journal of Roman Studies* 89 (1999): 155–189; Roueché, *Aphrodisias in Late Antiquity*, available at http://www.insaph.kcl.ac.uk/ala2004.

64. Portrait statues depicting the highest-ranking officials at the open spaces of the fora have been noted in the North African cities of Cuicul (Djemila) and Thamugadi (Timgad); see Zimmer, *Locus datus decreto decurionum*.

65. Cod. Theod. 15.1.31: "Si qui iudices perfecto operi suum potius nomen quam nostrae perennitatis scribserint, maiestatis teneantur obnoxii" (trans. Pharr, 426).

66. Fagan ("The Reliability of Roman Rebuilding Inscriptions," 81–93) sees the high cost of statues displayed in architectural contexts as furthering a claim of restoration by those who sponsored sculptures; the expense is also documented in Miranda Marvin, "Freestanding Sculptures from the Baths of Caracalla," *American Journal of Archaeology* 87 (1983): 347–384.

67. Bauer (*Stadt, Platz und Denkmal*, 29–30) interprets the need for repairs at the Basilica Julia after the sack of Rome in 410 as an indicator that Probianus completed the repairs in 416, when he claims the second Probianus held the urban prefecture.

68. Santo Mazzarino (*Stilicone: La crisi imperiale dopo Teodosio* [Rome: A. Signorelli, 1942], 383–384) proposes that the fifth-century individual is Rufius Probianus, who held the post of vicar in Rome around 408–416 or earlier, and that these repairs occurred prior to his urban prefecture. This Probianus appeared in a famous ivory diptych held in Tübingen's National Library.

69. Machado, "Building the Past," 170–171.

70. CIL 6.1658a–d, 3864a–b, 31886, 41337, and 41338.

71. *CIL* 6.1658a and 1658b: "GABINIUS VETTIUS / PRO-BIANUS V(ir) C(larissimus) PRAEF(ectus) URB(i) / STATU-AM CONLOCARI PRAE/CEPIT QUAE ORNAMENTO / BASILICAE ESSE POSSET INLUSTRI." Both were discovered near the Senate House. A third close variant is *CIL* 6.41337: "[Ga]VINIUS VETT[ius] / [Pro]BIANUS V(ir) C(larissimus) PRA[ef(ectus) urbi] / [st]ATUAM CONL[ocari] / [pra]ECI-PIT QUAE [or]/[na]MENTO BASIL[icae] / [ess]E POSSIT INLUS[tri]"; it was also found at the Senate House. Plausibly, a fourth statue repeated this wording, but its damaged condition prevents a clear reading; see *CIL* 6.41338: "[Gabinius Vettius] / [Prob]IANUS [v(ir) c(larissimus)] / PRAEF(ectus) URBI / STATUAM CON[locari] / [praecepit – – –?] / [– – –]."

72. *CIL* 6.3864a and 3864b: "GABINIUS VETTIUS / PRO-BIANUS V(ir) C(larissimus) PRAEF(ectus) URB(i) / STATU-AM FATALI / NECESSITATE CON/LABSAM CELEBERRI/MO URBIS LOCO ADHI/BITA DILIGENTIA REPARAVIT."

73. *CIL* 6.38641 and 3864b.

74. Machado, "Building the Past," 184.

75. Ariel Lewin, "Urban Public Building from Constantine to Julian: The Epigraphic Evidence," in *Recent Research in Late Antique Urbanism*, ed. Luke Lavan (Portsmouth, R.I.: Journal of Roman Archaeology, 2001), 27–37.

76. Thomas and Witschel, "Constructing Reconstruction," 135–177.

77. An edict of 364 CE (Cod. Theod. 15.1.11) has been understood as giving blanket permission for senators and urban prefects to undertake restoration as their local responsibility, while emperors pursued new construction; see Niquet, "Die valentinianische Dynastie und Rom, 143–144.

78. *CIL* 6.10040: "OPUS POLYCLIT[i]"; *CIL* 6.10041: "OPUS PRAXITELIS"; *CIL* 6.10042: "OP[u]STIM[a]RCHI."

79. *CIL* 6.41394: "FL(avius) MACROBIUS PL[otinus] / [E] USTATHIUS V(ir) [c(larissimus) et inl(ustris) praef(ectus)] / [urbi – – –] MES(?) OB[– – –] / [ex ab]STRUSIS LOC[is] / [– – –]PAENE(?)." See Bauer, "Beatitudo temporum," 81.

80. Géza Alföldy, "*Difficillima Tempora*: Urban Life, Inscriptions and Mentality in Late Antique Rome," in *Urban Centers and Rural Contexts in Late Antiquity*, ed. T. S. Burns and John Eadie (East Lansing: Michigan State University Press, 2001), 3–24; Cameron, *The Last Pagans of Rome*, 610–613.

81. Eusebius, *Vita Constantini* 8.54.

82. *PLRE* 2:749–751 (Maximus 22).

83. *CIL* 6.36956: "PETRONIUS MAXIMUS / V(ir) C(larissimus) ITERUM PRAEF(ectus) URB(i) / CURAVIT // DOMINO NOSTR[o] / Fl(avio) VALENTI P(io) [F(elici)] / TOTO ORBE VICTOR[i] / AC TRIUMFATORI / SEMPER AUGUSTO / PLACIDUS SEVERUS V(ir) C(larissimus) / A(gens) V(ices) PRAEF(ectus) PRAET(orio) / D(evotus) N(umini) M(aiestati)Q(ue) EIUS." The earlier inscribed face was sponsored in 365 by Placidus Severus.

84. Again, Petronius Maximus described his work with the term *curavit*; see *CIL* 6.37110: "PETRONIUS MAXIMUS / V(ir) C(larissimus) ITERUM PRAEF(ectus) URB(i) / CURAVIT." See Niquet, *Monumenta virtutum titulique*, 93.

85. *CIL* 6.37109: "PETRONIUS MAXIMUS / V(ir) C(larissimus) ITERUM PRAEF(ectus) URB(i) / CURAVIT." See Bauer, *Stadt, Platz und Denkmal*, 78.

86. See the influential article by Ramsay MacMullen, "The Epigraphic Habit during the Roman Empire," *American Journal of Philology* 103 (1982): 233–246. For the placement of statues in "minor" fora in Rome, see Franz Alto Bauer, "Einige weniger bekannte Platzanlagen im spätantiken Rom," in *Pratum Romanum: Gedenkschrift Richard Krautheimer*, ed. R. L. Colella (Wiesbaden: Reichert, 1997), 27–54.

87. Humphries, "Roman Senators and Absent Emperors," 27–46.

88. Woolf, "Monumental Writing," 22–39.

89. Luke Lavan, "*Fora* and *agorai* in Mediterranean Cities during the 4th and 5th centuries A.D.," in *Social and Political Life in Late Antiquity*, ed. W. Bowden et al. (Leiden: Brill, 2006), 195–249.

90. *CIL* 5.3332 = *ILS* 5363: "Hortante beatitudine / temporum ddd(ominorum) nnn(ostrorum) / Gratiani Valentiniani / et Theodosi Auggg(ustorum) / statuam in Capitolio / diu iacentem in / cereberrimo fori / loco constitui / iussit Val(erius) Palladius / v(ir) c(larissimus) cons(ularis) Venet(iae) et Hist(riae)." The inscription dates to 379–383 and originates in the Forum of Verona; see Géza Alföldy, *Römische Statuen in Venetia et Histria: Epigraphische Quellen* (Heidelberg: Carl Winter, 1984), 129, no. 202.

91. Kinney, "Rape or Restitution," 53–67.

92. Cassiodorus, *Variae* 4.51.3 (*MGH AA* 12): "Et ideo theatri fabricam magna se mole solventem consilio vestro credimus esse roborandam, ut quod ab auctoribus vestris in ornatum patriae constat essse concessum, non videatur sub melioribus posteris imminutum."

CHAPTER 5: THE CONTESTED ETERNITY OF TEMPLES

1. John Malalas, *Chronicle* 13.7.

2. The concept of transferring power as conveyed by the legend is argued by Cameron, *The Last Pagans of Rome*, 610–613. Clifford Ando sees the contest over topography in the empire as a religious dispute: *The Matter of the Gods: Religion and the Roman Empire* (Berkeley: University of California Press, 2008), 186–195.

3. Hedrick, *History and Silence*, 85–88.

4. Theodosius I issued the ban on sacrifice and the prohibition of entering temples in a law applicable to Rome and sent to Milan in 391: Cod. Theod. 16.10.10. For the earlier legislation of 356, see Cod. Theod. 16.10.4.

5. Cod. Theod. 16.10.20 (date of 415): "Omnia etiam loca, quae sacris error veterum deputavit, secundum divi Gratiani constituta nostrae rei iubemus sociari ita ut ex eo tempore, quo inhibitus est publicus sumptus superstitioni deterrimae exhiberi, fructus ab incubatoribus exigantur."

6. The letter is one of those assembled in the Avellan Collection (*Collecta Avellana* 100); see Gelasius I, "Letter against Andromachus," in *Gélase Ier: Lettre contre les Lupercales et dix-huit messes du sacramentaire Léonien*, ed. Gilbert Pomarès (Paris: Éditions du Cerf, 1959), 162–185.

7. Markus, *The End of Ancient Christianity*, 133.

8. Gelasius, "Letter against Andromachus" 2 (in *Gélase Ier*, ed. Pomarès, pp. 162–164).

9. For the view that Gelasius probably did not stop the Lupercalia, see Neil McLynn, "Crying Wolf: The Pope and the Lupercalia," *Journal of Roman Studies* 98 (2008): 161–175. In fact, the Lupercalia continued into the tenth century in Constantinople; see T. P. Wiseman, "The God of the Lupercal," *Journal of Roman Studies* 85 (1995): 17.

10. Cod. Theod. 16.10.17: "Ut profanos ritus iam salubri

lege submovimus, ita festos conventus civium et communem omnium laetitiam non patimur submoveri. Unde absque ullo sacrificio atque ulla superstitione damnabili exhiberi populo voluptates secundum veterem consuetudinem, iniri etiam festa convivia, si quando exigunt publica vota, decernimus" (trans. Pharr, 475). This law was sent in 399 to the proconsul of Africa, Apollodorus.

11. Michael Mulryan, "The Temple of Flora or Venus by the Circus Maximus and the New Christian Topography: The 'Pagan Revival' in Action?" in *The Archaeology of Late Antique Paganism*, ed. Luke Lavan and Michael Mulryan (Leiden: Brill, 2011), 216–222.

12. Ovid, *Fasti* 2.422–430, records how the rite aided the fertility of women.

13. Gelasius I, "Letter against Andromachus" 23 (in *Gélase Ier*, ed. Pomarès, p. 180): "Si propter pestilentiam summovendam, ut antiquiora praeteream, ecce, antequam meis temporibus tollerentur, pestilentiam gravem tam in urbe quam in agris hominum pecudumque fuisse non dubium est." For Andromachus, see *PLRE* 2 (Andromachus 2).

14. Gelasius I, "Letter against Andromachus" 25a (in *Gélase Ier*, ed. Pomarès, p. 182): "Numquid Lupercalia deerant quando urbem Alaricus evertit? . . . Cur istis minime profuerunt?"

15. This was speculated by McLynn, "Crying Wolf," 172.

16. Johannes Geffcken, *The Last Days of Greco-Roman Paganism*, trans. Sabine MacCormack (Amsterdam: North Holland, 1978), 225–230.

17. Libanius, *Orations* 30.17. I thank Christine Shepardson for bringing this to my attention. See also her fascinating comments on this oration in her book, *Controlling Contested Places: Fourth-Century Antioch and the Spatial Politics of Religious Controversy* (Berkeley: University of California Press, 2014), 178.

18. Jerome, *Epistle* 107.1: "movetur urbs sedibus suis"; in Jerome, *Epistulae*, ed. I. Hilberg, Corpus Scriptorum Ecclesiasticorum Latinorum 55 (Vienna: Hoeder, Pichler, and Tempsky, 1917). The context of the phrase is the letter to Laeta in which Jerome notes the decline of the Capitol: "Squalet Capitolium, fuligine et ardearum telis omnia Romae templa cooperta sunt, movetur sedibus suis et inundans populus ante delubra semi-ruta currit ad martyrum tumulos."

19. Scott Bradbury, "Constantine and the Problem of Anti-Pagan Legislation in the Fourth Century," *Classical Philology* 89 (1994): 120–139.

20. Cod. Theod. 9.16.2 (*Theodosiani libri XVI*, T. Mommsen ed., vol. 1, part. 2, p. 460): "adite aras publicas adque delubra et consuetudinis vestrae celebrate sollemnia: nec enim prohibemus praeteritae usurpationis officia libera luce tractari." See Timothy D. Barnes, "Constantine's Prohibition of Pagan Sacrifice," *American Journal of Philology* 105 (1984): 69–72.

21. Cod. Theod. 16.9.3.

22. Cod. Theod. 16.10.3: "Quamquam omnis superstitio penitus eruenda sit, tamen volumus, ut aedes templorum, quae extra muros sunt positae, intactae incorruptaeque consistant.

Nam cum ex nonnullis vel ludorum vel circensium vel agonum origo fuerit exorta, non convenit ea convelli, ex quibus populo Romano praebeatur priscarum sollemnitas voluptatum" (trans. Pharr, 472). The law was sent to Catullinus, presumably Catullinus signo Philomathius, praetorian prefect of Italy; see Salzman, *The Making of a Christian Aristocracy*, 118.

23. Cod. Theod. 16.10.2.

24. Cod. Theod. 16.10.4: "Placuit omnibus locis adque urbibus universis claudi protinus templa et accessu vetito omnibus licentiam delinquendi perditis abnegari" (trans. Pharr, 472). Taurus, to whom the law was sent, was the praetorian prefect of Italy and Africa from 355–361: *PLRE* 1:870–880 (Taurus 3).

25. Bradbury, "Constantine and the Problem of Anti-Pagan Legislation," 120–139.

26. Cod. Theod. 15.1.11: "Intra urbem Romam aeternam nullus iudicum novum opus informet, quotiens serenitatis nostrae arbitria cessabunt. Ea tamen instaurandi, quae iam deformibus ruinis intercidisse dicuntur, universis licentiam damus" (trans. Pharr, 424).

27. Christophe Goddard, "The Evolution of Pagan Sanctuaries in Late Antique Italy (Fourth–Sixth Centuries A.D.): A New Administrative and Legal Framework," in *Les cités de l'Italie tardo-antique (IVe–VIe siècle): Institutions, économie, société, culture et religion*, ed. Massimiliano Ghilardi, Christophe Goddard, and Pierfrancesco Porena (Rome: École française de Rome, 2006), 281–308.

28. Roland Delmaire, *Largesses sacrées et res privata: L'aerarium impérial et son administration du IVe au VIe siècle* (Rome: École française de Rome, 1989), 641–645.

29. Ambrose, *De obitu Valentiniani* 52, a funerary oration for Valentinian II.

30. Cameron, *The Last Pagans of Rome*, 43–49.

31. Zosimus 5.3; Cameron, *The Last Pagans of Rome*, 47.

32. Cod. Theod. 16.10.20 (see note 5 above). See also Béatrice Caseau, "Late Antique Paganism: Adaptation under Duress," in *Late Antique Archaeology of "Paganism,"* ed. Luke Lavan et al. (Leiden: Brill, 2011), 111–134; Roland Delmaire, "La législation sur les sacrifices au IV siècle, un essai d'interprétation," *Révue historique de droit français et étranger* 82 (2004): 319–334.

33. Rita Lizzi Testa, "Christian Emperor, Vestal Virgins, and Priestly Colleges: Reconsidering the End of Roman Paganism," *Antiquité Tardive* 15 (2007): 252.

34. Ambrose, *Epistulae* 1a.10 (40.10), in *Epistulae et Acta*, ed. Otto Faller and Michaela Zelzer, CSEL 82, vol. 3 (Vienna: Hoelder-Pichler-Tempsky, 1996). See Shepardson, *Controlling Contested Places*, 224–225.

35. CIL 6.1779, lines 18–21: "QUID NUNC HONORES AUT POTESTATES LOQUAR / HOMINUMQUE VOTIS ADPETITA GAUDIA? / QUAE TU CADUCA AC PARVA SEMPER AUTUMANS / DIVUM SACERDOS INFULIS CELSUS CLUES."

36. Cod. Theod. 16.10.10 (sent to Milan in 391), 16.10.12 (issued in Constantinople in 392).

37. Cod. Theod. 16.10.10: "nemo delubra adeat, templa perlustret et mortali opere formata simulacra suspiciat" (trans. Pharr, 473).

38. Symmachus, *Epistulae* 1.46.2: "Convenit inter publicos sacerdotes, ut in custodiam civium publico obsequio traderemus curam deorum. Benignitas enim superioris, nisi cultu teneatur, amititur. Ergo multo tanto ornatior, quam solebat, caelestis factus est hono." For a discussion of Roman civic religion in late antiquity, see Maijastina Kahlos, *Vettius Agorius Praetextatus: A Senatorial Life in Between* (Rome: Institutum Romanum Finlandiae, 2002), 11–114.

39. For the nineteenth-century excavation, see Antonio Nibby, *Roma nell'anno 1838* (Rome: Tipografia delle Belle Arti, 1838), 1:545–548; for the work in the 1940s, see Giuseppe Nieddu, "Il Portico degli Dei Consenti," in *Roma: Archeologia nel Centro* (Rome: De Luca, 1985), 1:27–28; idem, "Il Portico degli Dei Consenti" (*Bollettino d'Arte*), 39–40.

40. Varro, *On Agriculture* 1.1.4: "sed duodecim deos Consentis; neque tamen eos urbanos, quorum imagines ad forum auratae stant, sex mares et feminae totidem."

41. David Watkin, *The Roman Forum* (Cambridge, Mass.: Harvard University Press, 2009), 79–81.

42. Hansen, *The Eloquence of Appropriation*, 100.

43. For the columns, see Friedrich Deichmann, *Die Spolien in der spätantiken Architektur* (Munich: C. H. Beck, 1975), 10–11; Bauer, *Stadt, Platz und Denkmal*, 27–28. For the Hadrianic capitals, see Nieddu, "Il Portico degli Dei Consenti" (*Roma*), 24–28; idem, "Il Portico degli Dei Consenti" (*Bollettino d'Arte*), 37–52; Patrizia Tucci, "The Portico degli Dei Consenti," *Periodici di Mineralogia* 71 (2002): 247–263.

44. Ando, *The Matter of the Gods*, 164.

45. *CIL* 6.102: "[deorum c]ONSENTIUM SACROSANCTA SIMULACRA CUM OMNI LO[ci totius adornatio]NE CULTU IN [formam antiquam restituto / v]ETTIUS PRAETEXTATUS +V+C+ PRA[efectus u]RBI [reposuit] CURANTE LONGEIO[. . . v c c]ONSUL[ari]."

46. *Notitia Dignitatum Occidentalis* 4.113–114; Chastagnol, *La préfecture urbaine*, 43–63.

47. Bruggisser, "'Sacro-saintes statues,'" 331–356.

48. *CIL* 6.102: "SIMULACRA CUM OMNI LO[ci totius adornatio]NE CULTU IN [formam antiquam restituto]. . . ."

49. Ulpian, *Digest* 1.8.9 pr. 2: "Sacra loca ea sunt, quae publice sunt dedicata."

50. *Scriptores Historiae Augustae* 13.1–2; see also the earlier documentation of the *lectisternium* in Livy 22.10.8.

51. Cameron, *The Last Pagans of Rome*, 273–319.

52. *Carmen contra paganos* 112–115: "sola tamen gaudet meretrix te consule Flora, / ludorum turpis genetrix Venerisque magistra, / composuit templum nuper cui Symmachus heres. / omnia quae in templis positus, tot monstra colebas." See also Cameron, *The Last Pagans of Rome*, 297.

53. This idea was suggested to me by Maya Maskarinec.

54. Jerome, *Epistulae* 23.2 (ad Marcellam de exitu Leae):

"Ille, quem ante paucos dies dignitatum omnium culmina praecedebant, qui quasi de subiectis hostibus triumpharet Capitolinas ascendit arces."

55. *CIL* 6.937: "SENATUS POPULUSQUE ROMANUS / INCENDIO CONSUMPTUM RESTITUIT."

56. John Stamper, *The Architecture of Roman Temples: The Republic to the Middle Empire* (Cambridge: Cambridge University Press, 2005), 111–115.

57. Patrizio Pensabene (*Tempio di Saturno: Architettura e decorazione* [Rome: De Luca, 1984], 103–115) categorizes the capitals as of late antique manufacture; see pp. 91–100 for the argument that the columns are *spolia*. Kristine Iara shared with me insightful comments on the date of the restoration of the Temple of Saturn, which have been of tremendous assistance.

58. Pensabene, *Tempio di Saturno*, 61–62, 151.

59. For the capitals, see Hansen, *The Eloquence of Appropriation*, 103–109.

60. For Pliny's position in the *praefecturam aerarii Saturni*, see Pliny the Younger, *Epistulae* 10.3.1.

61. See the account of this in a text from the 430s, Macrobius, *Saturnalia* 1.8.1; see also Dionysius of Halicarnassus 6.1.4.

62. *CIL* 10.6087; *CIL* 6.1316.

63. Macrobius, *Saturnalia* 1.8.6.

64. Alan Cameron, "The Date and Identity of Macrobius," *Journal of Roman Studies* 56 (1966): 25–38.

65. Macrobius, *Saturnalia* 1.8.4: "quoniam ab eius commemoratione ad nostram aetatem historia clara et quasi vocalis est, ante vero muta et obscura et incognita, quod testantur caudae Tritonum humi mersae et absconditae" (trans. Kaster, 1:87–89).

66. Macrobius, *Saturnalia* 1.8.5: "[Apollodorus is said to speak in the narrative:] Saturnum Apollodorus alligari ait per annum laneo vinculo et solvi ad diem sibi festum id est mense hoc Decembri" (trans. Kaster, 1:89).

67. Macrobius, *Saturnalia* 1.8.5: "semen in utero animatum in vitam grandescere, quod donec erumpat in lucem, mollibus naturae vinculis detinetur" (trans. Kaster, 1:89).

68. Macrobius, *Saturnalia* 1.8.11: "quid aliud est quam tempora senescentia ab his quae post sunt nata depelli?" (trans. Kaster, 1:91).

69. The Calendar of Philocalus from 354 and the Calendar of Polemius Silvius from 448–449 both mention the Saturnalia in December; see Salzman, *On Roman Time*, 74–76, 242–245.

70. Kjell Aage Nilson, Claes Persson, and Jan Zahle, "The Foundation and the Core of the Podium and of the Tribunal," in *The Temple of Castor and Pollux*, vol. 3: *The Augustan Temple*, by Kjell Aage Nilson, Claes Persson, Siri Sande, and Jan Zahle (Rome: "L'Erma" di Bretschneider, 2009), 72–73.

71. Inge Nielsen and Birte Poulsen, eds., *The Temple of Castor and Pollux*, vol. 1: *The Pre-Augustan Temple Phases with Related Decorative Elements* (Rome: "L'Erma" di Bretschneider, 1992), 20, 113–114.

72. *CIL* 6.89: "SPQR / AEDEM CONCORDIAE VETUS-

TATE COLLAPSAM / IN MELIOREM FACIEM OPERE ET CULTU SPLENDIDIORE RESTITUIT." Angela Maria Ferroni, "Concordia, Aedes," in *LTUR* 1:316–320; Carlo Gasparri, *Aedes Concordiae* (Rome: Istituto di Studi Romani, 1979), 1–3. A suggestion that the inscription for the Temple of Concord had been inserted during late antiquity remains possible, if uncertain; see Muth, "Der Dialog von Gegenwart und Vergangenheit," 269.

73. For Aeneas' removal of the Palladium from Troy, see Dionysius of Halicarnassus 1.67–69; for the heroic protection of the Palladium by Metellus, see Ovid, *Fasti* 6.419–436; see also Itala Santinelli, "Alcune questioni attinenti ai riti delle Vergini Vestali," *Rivista di filologia e d'istruzione classica* 30 (1902): 255–268.

74. Prudentius, *Contra Symmachum* 2.965–968 (ed. H. J. Thomson [Cambridge, Mass.: Harvard University Press, 1949–1953]): "Ager vitiis corruptus et ante / subiacuit, quam Palladium, quam Vesta penates / sub lare Pergameo servarent igne reposto" (trans. Eagan, 2:171).

75. Riccardo Santangeli Valenzani, "Il vescovo, il drago e le vergini: Paesaggio urbano e paesaggio del mito nella leggenda di S. Silvestro e il drago," in *Res bene gestae: Ricerche di storia urbana su Roma antica in onore di Eva Margareta Steinby*, ed. Anna Leone, Domenico Palombi, and Susan Walker, *LTUR*, suppl. 4 (Rome: Quasar, 2007), 379–395. The variants of the *Actus Silvestri* identified as version B are characterized by the slight shift of the locale to the Capitoline or its slopes in a separate narrative strand. See Louis Duchesne, "S. Maria Antiqua: Notes sur la topographie de Rome au Moyen Âge," *Mélanges d'archéologie et d'histoire* 17 (1897): 31; Jaakko Aronen, "I Misteri di Ecate sul Campidoglio," *Studi e materiali di storia delle religioni* 51 (1985): 74–75; Daniel Ogden, *Drakon: Dragon Myth and Serpent Cult in the Greek and Roman Worlds* (Oxford: Oxford University Press, 2013), 391–393.

76. *Actus Silvestri* [version A], in *Sanctuarium seu Vitae Sanctorum*, ed. Boninus Mombritius, 3d ed. (publishing a fifteenth-century manuscript) (Hildesheim and New York: Georg Olms, 1978), 2:529: "solebant enim virgines sacrae in templo Vestae omni kalendarum die ad eum [draconem] descendere cibosque ei similagini ministrare."

77. *CIL* 6.30159: "[– – –]veste adv[– – –] / [ne]bride cinctu[– – –] / [– – –]iti dracen[a] / – – –."

78. Jaakko Aronen ("Dragon Cults and ΝΥΜΦΗ ΔΡΑΚΑΙΝΑ in IGUR 974," *Zeitschrift für Papyrologie und Epigraphik* 111 [1996]: 129–136) reads *[– – –ne]bride* as a Latin form of the Greek word *nebris*, referring to a fawn skin used in the cult of Dionysus. *CIL* 6.30159 dates the inscription to the fourth century. Aronen ("Dragon Cults," 129) suggests that a third-century date is plausible.

80. Santangeli Valenzani ("Il vescovo") argues, however, that the text has no bearing on the condition of the Forum's monuments, since the text could have been composed outside of Rome.

81. Wilhelm Pohlkamp ("Tradition und Topographie," 11–15) dates the early version A of the *Actus Silvestri* to the fifth century by establishing a close textual link to the late fourth-century text *Carmen ultimum*, or Carmen 32, by Paulinus of Nola.

82. *Actus Silvestri* (version A) (in *Sanctuarium seu Vitae Sanctorum*, ed. Mombritius, 2:529): "Transactis itaque aliquantis diebus pontifices universi templorum huiusmodi suggestionem augusto Constantino fecisse dicuntur: Sacratissime imperator et semper auguste, populus semper vester Romanus draconis periclitatur afflatu. Solebant enim virgines sacrae in templo Vestae omni kalendarum die ad eum descendere cibosque ei similaginis ministrare. Ex quo autem pietas vestra legem christianam accepit, huic nihil infertur ideoque indignatus cotidie flatu suo populum vexat. Et ideo deprecamur, ut solitas maiestati eius escas iubeas exhiberi, quo possit tuae pietatis civitas Romana de salute suorum omnium civius gratulari."

83. Wilhelm Levison ("Konstantinische Schenkung und Silvester-Legende," in *Miscellanea F. Ehrle: Scritti di storia e paleografia* [Vatican City: Biblioteca Apostolica Vaticana, 1924], 2:159–247 = *Aus rheinischer und fränkischer Frühzeit: Ausgewählte Aufsätze* [Düsseldorf: L. Schwann, 1948], 390–465) identified the two early textual variants; the late fourth- or early fifth-century date for version A is argued in Wilhelm Pohlkamp, "Kaiser Konstantin, der heidnische und der christliche Kult in den Actus Silvestri," *Frühmittelalterliche Studien* 18 (1984): 1–100. A fifth-century date for version A, specifically just after 410, is argued in Vincenzo Aiello, "Costantino, la lebbra e il battesimo di Silvestro," in *Costantino il Grade: Dall'antichità all'umanesimo, Colloquio sul Cristianesimo nel mondo antico*, ed. G. Bonamente and F. Fusco (Macerata, Università degli studi di Macerata: 1990), 38–42. By contrast, version A is attributed to the sixth century by Tessa Canella, *Gli Actus Silvestri: Genesi di una leggenda su Costantino imperatore* (Spoleto: Fondazione Centro Italiano di Studi sull'alto Medioevo, 2006).

84. *Actus Silvestri* (version A) (in *Sanctuarium seu Vitae Sanctorum*, ed. Mombritius, 2:529): "Dixit ei [Calpurnio] sanctus Silvester: Ergo nihil novum fecit draco, qui homines interfecit. Hoc enim ut dicis ipse placabatur, ut minus laederet non ut non laederet. Ego autem illum dico in nomine dei mei Iesu Christi ab omni laesione cessare."

85. *Actus Silvestri* (version A) (in *Sanctuarium seu Vitae Sanctorum*, ed. Mombritius, 2:529): "et adprehendit draconem . . . et ligavit eum per annos mille et misit eum in abussum et clausit et signavit super illum."

CHAPTER 6: ROME'S SENATORIAL COMPLEX AND THE LATE ANTIQUE TRANSFORMATION OF THE ELITE

1. Rodolfo Lanciani, "L'Aula e gli uffici del senato romano (*Curia hostilia iulia: Secretarium senatus*)," *Notizie degli scavi* (1883): 3–32.

2. Morselli and Tortorici (*Curia*) document the extensive material that was removed during the 1930s. For the transformation of the Curia into the Church of Sant'Adriano during the pontificate of Honorius (625–638), see *Liber Pontificalis*, 1:324.

3. Filippo Coarelli, "Curia Hostilia," in *LTUR* 1:331–332; Edoardo Tortorici, "Curia Iulia," in *LTUR* 1:332–334.

4. *Expositio totius mundi et gentium* 453–457 (ed. Giacomo Lumbroso [Rome: Tipografia della R. Accademia dei Lincei, 1903], 73–74): "Habet autem et senatum maximum virorum divitum: quos si per singulos probare volueris invenies omnes iudices aut factos aut futuros esse aut potentes quidem, nolentes autem propter suorum frui cum securitate velle."

5. Alfonso Bartoli, *Curia Senatus: Lo scavo ed il restauro* (Rome: Istituto di Studi Romani, 1963); for the extent of twentieth-century interventions, see David Watkin, *The Roman Forum* (Cambridge, Mass.: Harvard University Press, 2009), 118–119.

6. Morselli and Tortorici, *Curia*, 1:168–169, 229.

7. Bauer, "Stadt ohne Kaiser," 16; Kähler, *Das Fünfsäulendenkmal*, 34.

8. Bauer, "Stadt ohne Kaiser," 16; Johannes Deckers, "Die Wandmalereien im Kaiserkultraum von Luxor," *Jahrbuch des Deutschen Archäologischen Instituts* 94 (1979): 644–645.

9. *CIL* 6.1119a: "FORTISSIMO AC /FLORENTISSIMO / IMP(eratori) CAES(ari) C(aio) AUR(elio) VAL(erio) / DIOCLETIANO / P(io) F(elicii) INVICTO AUG(usto) CONS(uli) V / P(atri) P(atriae) OFF(iciales) A S(criniis?) / CURANTE TIB(erio) Cl(audio) SEVERO V(iro) C(larissimo) / D(evoti) N(umini) M(aiestati)Q(ue) EIUS SEMPER." *CIL* 6.40722: "FORTISSIMO AC / FLORENTISSIMO IMP(eratori) CAES(ari) M(arco) AUR(elio) VALE(rio) / MAXIMIANO / P(io) F(elici) INVICTO AUG(usto) CONS(uli) IV / P(atri) P(atriae) OFF(iciales) A S(criniis?) / CURANTE TIB(erio) CL(audio) SEVERO V(iro) C(larissimo) / D(evoto) N(umini) M(aiestati)Q(ue) EIUS SEMPER." Franz Alto Bauer dates the reconstruction of the Curia to a completion date of 295 on the basis of these inscriptions and compares their ideological content to the Tetrarchic statues found at the western Rostra hemicycle: "Stadt ohne Kaiser," 18.

10. The coffered ceiling visible today was conjecturally reconstructed by Alfonso Bartoli in the 1930s.

11. The fifth-century inscriptions found in the Curia might have referred to features restored or introduced during the Ostrogothic period. See Bartoli, *Curia Senatus*, 64–65; *CIL* 6.41378: ". . . [came]RAM AURO FULGENTEM . . . / . . . [provi]DENTIA PRO GENIO SENATUS AMPLISSI[ma] RESTA[ura]VIT . . . / . . . FL[avius] IANU[arius]. . . ." Flavius Ianuarius is too common a name to indicate a clear date; see Bauer, *Stadt, Platz und Denkmal*, 9. An additional inscription, *CIL* 6.30314, mentions gilded ornament: "[c]AMERIAM AURI FULGORE DOCORATUM SINO[. . .]." See also Lucrezia Spera, "La realtà archeologica: Restauro degli edifici pubblici e riassetto urbano dopo il sacco," in *Roma e il sacco del 410: Realtà, interpretazione, mito (Attie della Giornata di studio, Roma, 6 dicembre 2010)*, ed. Angelo Di Berardino, Gianluca Pilara and Lucrezia Spara (Rome: Institutum Patristicum Augustinianum, 2012), 113–152, esp. 120–142.

12. See the description written on the legend of the plan by Antonio da Sangallo (Bartoli, *Curia Senatus*, tav. 1). The transcription reads: "Le cholonne sono modernamente messe non ci era in mezo niente anticamente; li pilastri sono corintii antichi di fodere e fralli pilastri è foderato di marmi porfidi, serpentini, pezi grandi riquadrati di più sorti." These precious marbles were still in place in 1562, as documented in a letter by Pirro Ligorio, discovered and published by Michele Dattoli, *L'aula del Senato Romano e la chiesa di S. Adriano* (Rome: Maglione & Strini, 1921), 19–20.

13. André Chastagnol (*Les Fastes*, 269–271) analyzed the pertinent inscription from the Curia and identified the urban prefect as Neratius Palmatus while correcting the inscription as published in *CIL* 6.37128: "[Im]PERANT[ibus dd(ominis) nn(ostris) Honorio et Theodosio Augg(ustis) / N]ERATIUS P[almatus, v(ir) c(larissimus) praef(ectus) urb(i) vice sacra iudicans, reparavit, / c]URIAM SEN[atus]." This highly damaged inscription may not have included the term *reparavit*, which Chastagnol proposed in his reconstruction. See also Bauer, *Stadt, Platz und Denkmal*, 9.

14. One inscription, *CIL* 6.41386, was displayed at the rear entrance and reads: "[I]MPERANTIBUS DD(ominis) NN(ostris) HONORIO ET THEO[d]OSIO AUGG[usti]"; see Bartoli, *Curia Senatus*, 43, fig. 36.1. The other inscription, *CIL* 6.41387, belonged to the main entrance and may have indicated a large-scale reconstruction campaign under the emperors Honorius and Theodosius II: "[Imperantibus] DD(ominis) NN(ostris) HONORIO ET THEO[do]SIO AUGG(ustis) / [vice s]ACRA IUDICANS REPAR[avit]"; see Bartoli, *Curia Senatus*, 42–43, fig. 36.2. See also Bauer, *Stadt, Platz und Denkmal*, 8–9.

15. See Ludovico Gatto, "Ancora sull'edilizia e l'urbanistica nella Roma di Teodorico," *Romanobarbarica* 12 (1992–1993): 368–369; Alfonso Bartoli, "Lavori nella sede del Senato romano al tempo di Teodorico," *Bullettino della Commissione Archeologica Comunale di Roma* 73 (1949–1950): 77–90; Giuseppina Della Valle, "Teodorico e Roma," *Rendiconti della Accademia di Archeologia, Lettere e Belle Arti di Napoli*, n.s. 34 (1959): 119–176.

16. Cassiodorus, *Variae* 9.7 (letter to Reparatus, praefectus urbi in *MGH AA*, 12:273): "Comitavae siquidem largitionum praesidens, functus etiam vicibus praefectorum, praetorianam egit integerrimae dignitatem, curiam reparans, pauperibus ablata restituens et quamvis liberalibus studiis fuerit impolitus."

17. Beat Näf, *Senatorisches Standesbewußtsein in spätrömischer Zeit* (Freiburg: Freiburg Universitätsverlag, 1995).

18. Schlinkert, *"Ordo senatorius" und "nobilitas,"* 229.

19. Claudian, *Panegyricus de sexto consolatu Honorii*, 407–411 (ed. Dewar, 28): "quem precor, ad finem laribus seiuncta potestas / exulat imperiumque suis a sedibus errat? / cur mea quae cunctis tribuere Palatia nomen / neclecto squalent senio, nec creditur orbis / illinc posse regi?" (trans. Dewar, 29).

20. Nazarius, "Panegyric of Constantine," in *Panegyrici Latini*

4 (10), 35.2 (Nixon and Rodgers, *In Praise of Later Roman Emperors*, 626): "Sensisti, Roma, tandem arcem te omnium gentium et terrarum esse reginam, cum ex omnibus provinciis optimates viros curiae tuae pignerareris, ut senatus dignitas non nomine quam re esset inlustrior, cum ex totius orbis flore constaret" (trans. Nixon and Rodgers, 380).

21. Cassius Dio, *Roman History* 51.22.2.

22. Ambrose, *Epistula* 18.32. The letters of Symmachus and Ambrose have been assembled by Richard Klein, *Der Streit um den Victoriaaltar* (Darmstadt: Wissenschaftliche Buchgesellschaft, 1972).

23. Gratian's legislation, while not recorded in the legal codices, was mentioned in the letters of both Symmachus and Ambrose: Symmachus, *Relationes* 3.7, 11–14; Ambrose, *Epistulae* 17.3, 18.13–18. For Ambrose objecting to imperial gifts to the priestly colleges, with the properties clearly dissociated from temple endowments, see Neil McLynn, *Ambrose of Milan: Church and Court in a Christian Capital* (Berkeley: University of California Press, 1994), 345–346.

24. Symmachus, *Relationes* 3.3: "Certe dinumerentur principes utriusque sectae utriusque sententiae: pars eorum prior caerimonias patrum coluit, recentior non removit" (trans. Barrow, *Prefect and Emperor*, 36–37).

25. Ambrose, *Epistulae* 18: "Poenitet lapsus: vetusta canities pudendi sanguinis traxit ruborem. Non erubesco cum toto orbe longaeva converti. . . . Erubescat senectus, quae emendare se non potest. Non annorum canities est laudata, sed morum. Nullus pudor est ad meliora transire. Hoc solum habebam commune cum barbaris, quia Deum antea nesciebam." (trans. Croke and Harries, *Religious Conflict*, 42).

26. Symmachus (*Relationes* 3.5). See also Ambrose, *Epistulae* 17.9–10.

27. Symmachus, *Relationes* 3.9: "Haec sacra Hannibalem a moenibus . . . reppulerunt."

28. Ambrose, *Epistulae* 17.9: "si hodie gentilis aliquis, imperator, quod absit, aram statueret simulacris et eo convenire cogeret christianos, ut sacrifantibus interessent, ut oppleret anhelitus et ora fidelium cinis ex ara" (trans. Croke and Harries, *Religious Conflict*, 32).

29. Susan Ashbrook Harvey, *Scenting Salvation: Ancient Christianity and the Olfactory Imagination* (Berkeley: University of California Press, 2006), 22–25.

30. This point has been demonstrated by Santo Mazzarino, "Tolleranza e intolleranza: La polemica sull'ara della Vittoria," in *Il basso impero: Antico, tardoantico ed era costantiniana* (Bari: Dedalo, 1974–1975), 2:339–373; Claudian, *Panegyricus de sexto consulatu Honorii Augusti* 597–604.

31. Symmachus, *Relationes* 3.3: "Quis ita familiaris est barbaris ut aram victoriae non requirat?" (trans. adapted from Barrow, *Prefect and Emperor*, 37).

32. Symmachus, *Relationes*, 3.3.

33. Charles Hedrick Jr., *History and Silence: Purge and Rehabilitation of Memory in Late Antiquity* (Austin: University of Texas Press, 2000), 40–44.

34. Symmachus, *Relationes* 3.8: "varios custodes urbibus cultus mens divina distribuit, ut animae nascentibus ita populis fatalis genii dividuntur. Accedit utilitas, quae maxime homini deos adserit. Nam cum ratio omnis in operto sit, unde rectius quam de memoria atque documentis rerum secundarum cognitio venit numinum? Iam si longa aetas auctoritatem religionibus faciat, servanda est tot saeculis fides" (trans. Barrow, *Prefect and Emperor*, 39–41).

35. Ambrose, *Epistulae* 18.15: "Quos gentiles praecipitarunt, maria reddiderunt. Fidei ista victoria est, quod et ipsi iam facta maiorum carpunt suorum? Sed quae, malum, ratio, ut eorum munera petant, quorum gesta condemnant?" (trans. Croke and Harries, *Religious Conflict*, 45).

36. Paulinus, *Vita Ambrosii* 26.

37. Claudian, *Panegyricus de sexto consulatu Honorii Augusti* 597–604.

38. Ambrose, *Epistulae* 18.31: "Non illis satis sunt lavacra, non porticus, non plateae occupatae simulacris?" (trans. Croke and Harries, *Religious Conflict*, 66).

39. Ferdinando Castagnoli, "Atrium Libertatis," *Rendiconti: Accademia dei Lincei* 8 (1946): 276–291.

40. Nicholas Purcell, "Atrium Libertatis," *Papers of the British School at Rome* 61 (1993): 125–155.

41. Arguments have been advanced that place the Atrium of Liberty at the southeast corner of the Forum of Caesar, but there is insufficient evidence to confirm this. See Fraschetti, *La conversione*, 175–217.

42. Christoph Schäfer, *Der weströmische Senat als Träger antiker Kontinuitäten unter den Ostgotenkönigen (490–540 n. Chr.)* (St. Katharinen: Scripta Mercaturae, 1991), 71–72.

43. *CIL* 6.1794 (fasc. 8, pp. 4570–4571): "[Sal]VIS DOMI-[n]IS NOSTRIS ANASTASIO PERPETUO / AUGUSTO ET GLORIOSISSIMO A[c] TRIUMFALI VIRO / THEODERICO VALERIUS FLORI[an]US V(ir) C(larissimus) ET INL(ustris) / EX COM(es) DOMEST(icorum) EX COM(es) [sacrar(um)] / IN ATRIO LIBERTAT[is – – –] SEPTUAGINARIAS / QUAE VETUS[tate] . . . CARIE FUERANT / [a]T[q]UE CONFEC[tae] . . . OMNIA EIUS LOCI / [re]FECIT . . . [e]T IN SECRETA-RIO / [senatus] . . . VES SIMILI [. . .]TAVIT QUAM EIUS / . . . CAPITOLIUM / FUERAT EX OMNI / IVI LOCO."

44. A large inscribed epistyle was discovered in the Secretarium Senatus after it had been converted into the church of S. Martina; it indicates a link between the Secretarium and the Atrium Libertatis within the senatorial complex, *CIL* 6.470: "SENATUS POPULUSQUE R(omanus) LIBERTATI."

45. Alessandro Viscogliosi, *I fori imperiali nei disegni d'architettura del primo cinquecento: Ricerche sull'architettura e l'urbanistica di Roma* (Rome: Gangemi, 2000), 32–34, arguing on the basis of another drawing by Baldassari Peruzzi in the Uffizi (GDSU, A625r).

46. The column held a statue of Claudius Gothicus on top, which I believe was moved during or before the fire of Carinus in 284. The palm column may have been reinstalled without the portrait statue. *Historia Augusta*, Claudius Gothicus 3.5: "illi

totius orbis iudicio in Rostris posita est columna palmata statua superfixa librarum argenti mille quingentarum."

47. *Acta S. Restituti*, in *Acta Sanctorum*, vol. 7, *Maii collecta*, ed. Jean Bolland, Godefroid Henschler, and Jean-Baptiste Carnadet (Brussels: Culture et civilisation, 1999), 12–13: ". . . decollaverunt extra Capitolium; et extrahentes iactaverunt eum iuxta Arcum Triumphi ad Palmam"; for the visit of Theoderic, the Anonymous Valesianus states that the king arrived at the Senate House and at the Palm, *MGH AA*, 9:324: ". . . venit ad Senatum et ad Palmam populum adlocutus." A report of St. Fulgentius of Ruspe witnessing Theoderic at the Senate House calls the site the "Golden Palm": Ferrandus, *Vita S. Fulgentii*, in *Saint Fulgence de Ruspe: Un évêque catholique africain sous la domination vandale*, ed. Gabriel Lapeyre (Paris: Lethielleux, 1929), 37: "in loco qui Palma Aurea dicitur, memorato Theodorico rege contionem faciente."

48. Tony Honoré, *Law in the Crisis of Empire, 379–455 AD* (Oxford: Clarendon, 1998), 249–251. As discussed in Chapter 3, Faustus installed a statue in honor of his eloquent father-in-law, Tarrutenius Maximilianus, in the Forum in 438 (*CIL* 6.1767). Eloquence was generally emphasized in the inscribed honorific statues of the East; see the important documentation from Aphrodisias: R. R. R. Smith, "The Statue Monument of Oecumenius: A New Portrait of a Late Antique Governor from Aphrodisias," *Journal of Roman Studies* 102 (2002): 134–156.

49. *Gesta Senatus urbis Romae* (in *Codex Theodosianus, Theodosiani libri XVI*, vol. 1, part 2), 2–3: ". . . in domo sua, quae est ad Palmam."

50. *Gesta Senatus urbis Romae* (in *Codex Theodosianus, Theodosiani libri XVI*, vol. 1, part 2), 3: "Desideria senatus ut suggeras, rogamus. . . . His subreptionibus possessorum ius omne confunditur."

51. *Gesta Senatus urbis Romae* (in *Codex Theodosianus, Theodosiani libri XVI*, vol. 1, part 2), 5: "Aeti, aevas."

52. *CIL* 6.41389: "[– – –]R[-]O[– – –] [n]EC NON ET MAGISTRO MILITUM PER GALLIAS QUAS DUDUM /[o]B IURATAS BELLO PACE VICTORIAS ROMANO IMPERIO / REDDIDIT MAGISTRO UTRIUSQ(ue) MILITIAE ET SECUNDO / CONSULI ORDINARIO ATQ(ue) PATRICIO SEMPER REI PUBLICAE / [i]NPENSO OMNIBUSQ(ue) DOMIS MILITARIB(us) ORNATO HUIC / [s]ENATUS POPULUSQ(ue) ROMANUS OB ITALIAE SECURITATEM / QUAM PROCUL DOMITIS GENTIB(us) PEREMPTISQUE / [B]URGUNDIONIB(us) ET GOTIS OPPRESSIS VINCENDO PRAESTIT[it] / IUSSU PRINCIPUM DD(ominorum) NN(ostrorum) THEODOSI ET PLACIDI [Valenti]\[n]IANI PP(iissimorum) AUGG(ustorum) IN ATRIO LIBERTATIS QUAM [ingenio? suo?] / [pa]RENS ERIGIT DILATAT ET TUETUR AEQUE ST[atuam aere(?)]/AM CONLOCAVIT MORUM PROBO OPUM REFUGO DELATO/RUM UT HOSTIUM INIMICISSIMO VINDICI LIBERTATIS / PUDORIS ULTOR(i)."

53. The fifth-century panegyrics are those of Merobaudes, *Panegyrici* 1 and 2, which survive only in fragments; see Andrew Gillett, "Epic, Panegyric, and Political Communication in the Fifth-Century West," in *Two Romes: Rome and Constantinople in Late Antiquity*, ed. Lucy Grig and Gavin Kelly (Oxford: Oxford University Press, 2012), 265–290.

54. Mark Humphries, "Valentinian III and Rome (425–455): Patronage, Politics, Power," in *Two Romes: Rome and Constantinople in Late Antiquity*, ed. Lucy Grig and Gavin Kelly (Oxford: Oxford University Press, 2012), 167.

55. Fergus Millar, *A Greek Roman Empire: Power and Belief under Theodosius II* (Berkeley: University of California Press, 2006), 51–59.

56. Roland Delmaire, "Flavius Aëtius, 'delatorum inimicissimus,' 'vindex libertatis,' 'pudoris ultor' (*CIL* 6.41389)," *Zeitschrift für Papyrologie und Epigraphik* 166 (2008): 291–294.

57. *Gesta Senatus urbis Romae* (in *Codex Theodosianus, Theodosiani libri XVI*, vol. 1, part 2), 2: "extinctores delatorum, extinctores calumniarum."

58. *Gesta Senatus urbis Romae* (in *Codex Theodosianus, Theodosiani libri XVI*, vol. 1, part 2), 3: "Aeti, aevas: dictum XIII. Ter consulem te: dictum XII. Excubiis tuis salvi et securi sumus: dictum XII."

59. Delmaire, "Flavius Aëtius." See also Timo Stickler, *Aëtius: Gestaltungsspielräume eines Heermeisters im ausgehenden Weströmischen Reich* (Munich: C. H. Beck, 2002), 255–273.

60. Sangallo wrote the following vertical notation on his plan: "Questo è un archo grande aperta va fino al tetto."

61. Viscogliosi, *I fori imperiali nei disegni*, 29–39.

62. La Rocca, "La nuova immagine dei fori imperiali," 175.

63. Pietro de Francisci, "Per la storia del Senato Romano e della Curia nei secoli V e VI," *Atti della Pontificia Accademia Romana di Archeologia: Rendiconti* 22 (1946–1947): 301–302; for Flavianus, see *PLRE* 1:345–346 (Flavianus 14).

64. *CIL* 6.1718: "SALVIS DOMINIS NOSTRIS HONORIO ET THEODOSIO VICTORIOSISSIMIS PRINCIPIBUS SECRETARIUM AMPLISSIMI SENATUS QUOD VIR INLUSTRIS FLAVIANUS INSTITUERAT ET FATALIS IGNIS ABSUMPSIT FLAVIANUS ANNIUS EUCHARIUS EPIFANIUS V(ir) C(larissimus) PRAEF(ectus) URB(i) VICE SACRA IUD(icans) REPARAVIT ET AD PRISTINAM FACIEM REDUXIT."

65. Bauer, *Stadt, Platz und Denkmal*, 11–12.

66. For Epiphanius, see *PLRE* 2:399 (Epiphanius 7).

67. Hedrick, *History and Silence*, 28–29.

68. Ernest Nash, "Secretarium Senatus," in *In Memoriam Otto J. Brendel: Essays in Archaeology and the Humanities*, ed. L. Bonfante and H. von Heintze (Mainz: Philipp von Zabern, 1976), 194.

69. Cod. Theod. 9.1.13 (ed. T. Mommsen and P. Meyer [Hildesheim: Weidmann, 2000], vol. 1, part 2, p. 434): "Provincialis iudex vel intra Italiam, cum in eius disceptationem criminalis causae dictio adversum senatorem inciderit, intendendi quidem examinis et cognoscendi causas habeat potestatem, verum nihil de animadversione decernens integro non causae, sed capitis statu referat ad scientiam nostram vel ad inclytas potestates. . . . Sed praefecto urbis cognoscenti de capite senatorum spectatorum maxime virorum iudicium quinquevirale

sociabitur et de praesentibus et de administratorum honore functis licebit adiungere sorte ductos, non sponte delectos."

70. Ernest Nash, "Secretarium Senatus," *Colloqui del Sodalizio* 3 (1970–1972): 69–71.

71. Sixteenth-century descriptions articulate that the now-lost apse mosaic featured Mary with the infant Jesus in the center flanked by two figures, both of whom were possibly popes, and one who was labeled as a pope with the last part of his name surviving at the time. The text, ". . . ORIUS P P," seems to indicate "Honorius, the pious pontifex," the bishop who converted the Curia around 630. B. Platina, *De vitis pontificum Romanorum*, ed. O. Pavinio (1568), 98.

72. Pio Franchi de' Cavalieri, "S. Martina," *Römische Quartalschrift* 17 (1903): 235: "HI(c) REQ(u)IESCU(n)T CO(r)-P(or)A S(an)C(t)OR(um) MAR(tyrum) MA(r)TINE VI(rginis) CO(n)CO(r)DII (et) EPIPHANII CU(m) SOCIO EORU(m)."

73. Pompeo Ugonio, Cod. Vat. Lat. 2160, fol. 165v: "Nella tribuna di questa chiesa si legge si ano(?) fabrica che ancor che piccola mostra di disegno antico. Nelle cornici e scritti cosi al tempo di Honorio et Theodosio."

74. Franchi de' Cavalieri, "S. Martina," 222; Albert Dufourcq, *Étude sur les Gesta Martyrum romains* (Paris: Fontemoing, 1900 [reprint 1988]), 5:361–365.

75. Dufourcq, *Études sur les Gesta Martyrum romains*, 5:361–365.

76. Harvey, *Scenting Salvation*, 11–15.

77. "De S. Martina," in *Acta Sanctorum*, vol. 1, Ian. 1, ed. Jean Bolland, Godefroid Henschler, and Jean-Baptiste Carnadet (Brussels: Culture et civilisation, 1999), 26: "Mane autem iussit Imperator Limenium quemdam Tribunum ambulare in carcerem, et eiicere eam: antea autem adipibus et pinguedinibus eam perungi. Procedens autem Limenius de palatio odoratus est odorem suavitatis, et aromate multo repletus dixit comitibus suis: Odoratis et vos odorem nimium? Erat enim cum populo multo. At illi dixerunt: Quia odorem hunc cives fecerunt pro dilecta Martina. Alii dicebant: Quia Dii propitii apparuerunt ei. Venientes vero ad carcerem multo amplius invenerunt suavitatis odores. Aperiens autem Limenius primam ianuam, vidit lucem magnam circumfulgentem eam: ingresso autem eo in propinquum habitaculum (erat enim carcer multa habens habitacula) circumfulsit eum sicut fulgur, ut prae timores omnes tremerent, ipso prae timore in pavimento cadente. Cum necessitate vero surgens ingressus est in tertium habitaculum et vidit beatam Martinam sedentem in sede imperiali, et multitudo virorum fortium erat circa eam, quorom non erat considerare claritatem: omnes enim erant in albis; ipsa autem tabulam tenebat, et legebat haec: Quam magnificata sunt opera tua Domine, omnia in sapientia fecisti."

78. Bryan Ward-Perkins, *From Classical Antiquity to the Middle Ages: Urban Public Building in Northern and Central Italy, AD 300–850* (Oxford: Oxford University Press, 1984). For a recent summary and insightful analysis of the issues of Christian munificence, see Yasin, *Saints and Church Spaces*, 102–129; see also Salzman, *The Making of a Christian Aristocracy*.

79. Timothy D. Barnes, *Early Christian Hagiography and Roman History* (Tübingen: Mohr Siebeck, 2010), 1–41.

80. Matthew Baldwin, *Whose Acts of Peter? Text and Historical Context of the Actus Vercellenses* (Tübingen: Mohr Siebeck, 2005); see also Gérard Poupon, "Les 'Actes de Pierre' et leur remaniement," in *Aufstieg und Niedergang der römischen Welt*, vol. 2, fasc. 25 (Berlin: De Gruyter, 1988), 4363–4383.

81. Christine M. Thomas, *The Acts of Peter, Gospel Literature, and the Ancient Novel: Rewriting the Past* (Oxford: Oxford University Press, 2003), 17–29.

82. "The Acts of Peter," trans. Wilhelm Schneemelcher, in *New Testament Apocrypha*, vol. 2, ed. and trans. Wilhelm Schneemelcher and R. M. Wilson (Louisville, Ky.: Westminster John Knox Press, 2003), 271–321.

83. Acts 8:9–24.

84. Based on Irenaeus of Lyon (*Adversus Haereses* 1.23.1), who identifies Gnostic heresy as pervasive in Rome, Kristina Sessa argues that the *Acts of St. Peter* could have refuted specific historical religious developments: "The Household and the Bishop: Establishing Episcopal Authority in Late Antique Rome," Ph.D. dissertation, University of California, Berkeley, 2003, 77–95. See also Gerard Luttikhuizen, "Simon Magus as a Narrative Figure in the Acts of Peter," in *The Apocryphal Acts of Peter: Magic, Miracles and Gnosticism*, ed. Jan Bremmer (Leuven: Peeters, 1998), 39–51.

85. *Actus Vercellenses* 59.9–18 (trans. Wilhelm Schneemelcher, "The Acts of Peter," in *New Testament Apocrypha*, ed. Schneemelcher and Wilson, 2:297).

86. *Actus Vercellenses* 57.25: "Simoni iuveni deo."

87. *Acta Petri cum Simone* 32, in *Acta Apostolorum Apocrypha*, ed. Richard A. Lipsius (Leipzig: Hermann Mendelssohn, 1891), 1:83: "Alia autem die turba magna convenit *ad platea quae dicitur sacra via*, ut viderent eum volantem." See also Walter Rebell, *Neutestamentliche Apokryphen und apostolische Väter* (Munich: Kaiser, 1992), 153.

88. *Acta Petri cum Simone* 32 (ed. Lipsius, 83): "Petrus vero clamavit ad dominum Iesum Christum dicens: Si passus fueris hunc quod conatus est facere, omnes qui crediderunt in te scandalizantur, et quaecumque dedisti per me signa erunt fincta. Citius ergo, domine, fac gratiam tuam et ostende omnibus qui me adtendunt virtutem tuam. Sed non peto ut moriatur, sed aliquid in membris suis vexetur."

89. *Acta Petri cum Simone* 32 (ed. Lipsius, 83): "Et continuo caecidit ad terram, fregit crus in tres partes, tunc eum lapidantes omnes fidentes et conlaudantes dominum."

90. The relief is now in the Capitoline Museums; a replica has been inserted in the original display spot. The reverse of the relief bears an inscription, *CIL* 6.1468: "L(ucius) NAEVIUS L(uci) F(ilius) SURDINUS / PR(aetor) / INTER CIVIS ET PEREGRINOS." The inscription is dated to the first century BCE and is attributed to the same Surdinus who sponsored the Forum pavement. The relief on the verso may constitute a reuse of the inscription block that could have been carved as late as the fourth century CE; see Giuliani and Verduchi, *L'area centrale*, 105–116.

91. E.g., the clash between Damasus and Ursinus in 366, a schism between two rival deacons, each of whom claimed the papacy.

92. Gregory of Tours, *In gloria martyrum*, ed. B. Krusch, *MGH, Scriptorum rerum Merovingicarum*, vol. 1, part 2 (Hannover: Hahn, 1967), 53: "Extant hodique apud urbem Romanam duae in lapide fossulae, super quem beati apostoli, deflexu poplite, orationem contra ipsum Simonem magum ad Dominum effuderunt" (trans. Van Dam, 45).

93. *LP* 1:465: " . . . in via Sacra iuxta Templum Romae in honore sanctorum apostolorum Petri et Pauli, ubi ipsi beatissimi principes apostolorum, . . . propria genua flectere visi sunt, in quo loco usque actenus eorum genua pro testimonio omnis."

94. Nazarius, "Panegyric of Constantine," in *Panegyrici Latini* 4 (10), 6.1 (Nixon and Rodgers, *In Praise of Later Roman Emperors*, 611): "Verum ut in magnis domibus interiorem ornatum vestibula ipsa declarant, sic nobis venturis ad ingentium virtutum stupenda penetralia debet laudationis ingressum et praedicationis ianuam Roma praebere."

95. Pacatus, "Panegyric of Theodosius Augustus," in *Panegyrici Latini* 2 (12), 16.4 (Nixon and Rodgers, *In Praise of Later Roman Emperors*, 656): "A te nova benignitate is amicis honos habitus est qui totus esset illorum quibus deferebatur, nihilque ex eo ad te redundaret nisi dandi voluptas."

CONCLUSION

1. Noreña, *Imperial Ideals*, 266–297.

2. The Honorius inscription remains at its original display spot, *CIL* 6.31987.

3. *CIL* 6.31395.

4. This line of reasoning draws heavily from the ideas of Zanker, "By the Emperor, For the People," 45–87.

5. *CIL* 6.10040, 6.10041, and 6.10042.

6. *CIL* 6.36962.

7. Procopius, *Gothic Wars* 7.22.8–11 (ed. and trans. Dewing, 4:345–347).

8. Kinney, "*Spolia*," 128.

9. Cassiodorus, *Variae* 8.31 (ed. Mommsen, *MGH AA*, 12:260): "Redeant igitur civitates in pristinam decus: nullus amoenitatem ruris praeponat moenibus antiquorum. . . . Cui non affectuosum sit cum paribus miscere sermonem, forum petere, honestas artes invisere?" (trans. Barnish, 108).

10. *Excerpta Valesiana* 12.67 (ed. J. Rolfe, in *Ammianus Marcellinus, History, Books 27–31, and Excerpta Valesiana* [Cambridge, Mass.: Harvard University Press, 1972 (first published 1939)], 550–551): "ad restaurationem palatii seu ad recuperationem moeniae civitatis singulis annis libras ducentas de arca vinaria dari praecepit."

11. Ludovico Gatto, "Ancora sull'edilizia e l'urbanistica nella Roma di Teodorico," *Romanobarbarica* 12 (1992–1993): 368–369; Bartoli, "Lavori nella sede del Senato romano," 77–82; idem, *Curia Senatus*, 72; Della Valle, "Teodorico e Roma," 119–176. Evidence from Cassiodorus suggests that the work was accomplished by providing instructions to the urban prefect of Rome; see Cassiodorus, *Variae* 9.7 (letter to Reparatus, Praefectus Urbi) (ed. Mommsen, *MGH AA*, 12:273): "Comitivae siquidem largitionum praesidens, functus etiam vicibus praefectorum, praetorianam egit integerrimae dignitatem, curiam reparans, pauperibus ablata restituens et quamvis liberalibus studiis fuerit impolitus."

12. Cassiodorus, *Variae* 7.15. See also Della Valle, "Teodorico e Roma," 132–133.

13. Cassiodorus, *Variae* 3.30.

14. Rosella Rea, "Il Colosseo e la valle da Teodorico ai Frangipane: Note di studio," in *La storia economica di Roma nell'alto medioevo alla luce dei recenti scavi archeologici*, ed. Paolo Delogu and Lidia Paroli (Florence: All'Insegna del Giglio, 1993), 71–90.

15. Cassiodorus, *Variae* 11.38.6 (ed. Mommsen), with reference to the *scrinium publicum*: ". . . nova iugiter accipiens et vetusta custodiens."

16. M. Shane Bjornlie, *Politics and Tradition between Rome, Ravenna and Constantinople: A Study of Cassiodorus and the Variae, 527–554* (Cambridge: Cambridge University Press, 2013), 228.

17. Anonymous Valesianus, Pars Posterior: Chronica Theodericiana 11 (in *Chronica minora*, ed. Mommsen, *MGH AA* 9.11), 10–11: "Deinde veniens ingressus urbem, venit ad senatum, et ad Palmam populo adlocutus, se omnia, deo iuvante, quod retro principes Romani ordinaverunt inviolabiter sevaturum promittit."

18. Ferrandus, *Vita S. Fulgentii* 9 (*Vie de Saint Fulgence de Ruspe*, ed. Gabriel-Guillaume Lapeyre [Paris: Lethielleux, 1929], 79): "in loco qui Palma Aurea dicitur, memorato Theoderico rege concionem faciente" (trans. R. B. Eno [Washington, D.C.: Catholic University Press, 1997], 25).

19. Ferrandus, *Vita S. Fulgentii* 9 (in *Vie de Saint Fulgence de Ruspe*, ed. Lapeyre, 79): "Romanae curiae nobilitatem, decus ordinemque distinctis decoratam gradibus exspectaret, et favores liberi populi castis auribus audiens, qualis esset huius saeculi gloriosa pompa cognosceret. Neque tamen in hoc spectaculo aliquid libenter intuitur, nec nugis illis saecularibus superflua illectus delectatione consensit: sed inde potuis ad illam supernae civitatis Hierusalem desiderandam felicitatem vehementer exarsit, salubri disputatione praesentes sic admonens: Fratres, quam speciosa potest esse Hierusalem coelestis, si sic fulget Roma terrestris. Et si in hoc saeculo datur tanti honoris dignitas diligentibus vanitatem, qualis honor et gloria et pax praestabitur sanctis contemplantibus veritatem?" (trans. adapted from Eno, 25).

BIBLIOGRAPHY

PRIMARY SOURCES

Acta Petri cum Simone. In *Acta Apostolorum Apocrypha,* edited by Richard A. Lipsius, vol. 1. Leipzig: Hermann Mendelssohn, 1891.

Acta Sanctorum. In *Acta Sanctorum quotquot toto orbe coluntur,* edited by Jean Bolland, Godefroid Henschler, and Jean-Baptiste Carnadet. 13 vols. Brussels: Culture et civilisation, 1965–1999.

Actus Silvestri. In *Sanctuarium seum Vitae Sanctorum,* edited by Boninus Mombritius, 3rd ed., vol. 2. Hildesheim and New York: Georg Olms, 1978. First published in 1910.

Ambrose. *Epistulae et Acta.* Edited by Otto Faller and Michaela Zelzer. *CSEL* 82.1–4. 4 vols. Vienna: Hoelder-Pichler-Tempsky, 1986–1996. Translation in Croke and Harries, *Religious Conflict.*

Ammianus Marcellinus. *Res gestae.* Edited and translated by J. C. Rolfe. In *Ammianus Marcellinus.* 3 vols. Loeb Classical Library. Cambridge, Mass.: Harvard University Press, 1935–1940.

Aurelius Victor. *Liber de Caesaribus.* Edited by Franz Pichlmayr. Leipzig: B. G. Teubner, 1970.

Cassiodorus. *Chronica.* Edited by Theodor Mommsen. In *Chronica minora saec. IV. V. VI. VII, MGH AA 9.2.* Berlin: Weidmann, 1894.

———. *Variae.* Edited by Theodor Mommsen. In *Cassiodori Senatoris Variae, MGH AA 12.* Berlin: Weidmann, 1894. Translation by S. J. B. Barnish: *The Variae of Magnus Aurelius Cassiodorus Senator.* Liverpool: Liverpool University Press, 1992.

Cassius Dio. *Cassii Dionis Cocceiani Historiarum romanarum quae supersunt.* Edited by Ursul Philipp Boissevain. 5 vols. Berlin: Wiedmann, 1895–1931.

Chronica minora, saec. IV. V. VI. VII. Edited by Theodor Mommsen. In *MGH AA* 9, 11, 13. Berlin: Wiedmann, 1892–1898.

Chronicon Paschale. Edited by Theodor Mommsen. In *Chronica minora, MGH AA 9.1.* Berlin: Weidmann, 1892.

Chronographus anni 354. Edited by Theodor Mommsen. In *Chronica minora, MGH AA 9.* Berlin: Weidmann, 1892.

Claudian. *De consulatu Stilichone.* In *Claudian,* translated by M. Platnauer. Loeb Classical Library. Cambridge, Mass.: Harvard University Press, 1922.

———. *Panegyricus de quarto consulatu Honorii Augusti.* In *Claudian,* translated by Maurice Platnauer. Loeb Classical Library. Cambridge, Mass.: Harvard University Press, 1922.

———. *Panegyricus de sexto consulatu Honorii Augusti.* Translated and edited by Michael Dewar. Oxford: Clarendon, 1996.

———. *Panegyricus de tertio consulatu Honorii Augusti.* In *Claudian,* translated by Maurice Platnauer. Loeb Classical Library. Cambridge, Mass.: Harvard University Press, 1922.

Codex Iustinianus. In *Corpus iuris civilis,* vol. 2: *Codex Iustinianus.* Edited by Paul Krueger. Berlin: Weidmann, 1967.

Codex Theodosianus: Theodosiani libri XVI cum constitutionibus Sirmondinis. Edited by Theodor Mommsen and Paul Meyer. 2 vols. Hildesheim: Weidmann, 2000. First published in 1905. Translation by Clyde Pharr: *The Theodosian Code and Novels and the Sirmondian Constitutions.* Princeton, N.J.: Princeton University Press, 1952.

Eusebius. *Historia ecclesiastica.* In *Die Kirchengeschichte,* edited by E. Schwartz. 3 vols. Die Griechischen christlichen Schriftsteller der ersten drei Jahrhunderte 9. Berlin: Akademie, 1991. Translation by J. E. L. Oulton and H. J. Lawlor: *Eusebius: The Ecclesiastical History.* 2 vols. Loeb Classical Library. Cambridge, Mass.: Harvard University Press, 1957.

Eutropius. *Breviarum historiae Romanae*. Edited by Franciscus Ruehl. Leipzig: Teubner, 1887.

Expositio totius mundi et gentium. In *Expositio totius mundi et gentium*, edited by Giacomo Lumbroso. Rome: Tipografia della R. Accademia dei Lincei, 1903.

Ferrandus. *Vita S. Fulgentii*. In *Vie de Saint Fulgence de Ruspe*, edited by Gabriel-Guillaume Lapeyre. Paris: Lethielleux, 1929. Translation by R. B. Eno: Washington, D.C.: Catholic University Press, 1997.

Gelasius I, Pope. "Letter against Andromachus." In *Gélase Ier: Lettre contre les Lupercales et dix-huit messes du sacramentaire Léonien*, edited by Gilbert Pomarès, 162–185. Paris: Éditions du Cerf, 1959.

Gesta Senatus urbis Romae. In *Codex Theodosianus: Theodosiani libri XVI cum constitutionibus Sirmondinis*, vol. 1.

Gregory of Tours. *In gloria martyrum*. Edited by Bruno Krusch. In *MGH, Scriptorum rerum Merovingicarum* 1.2. Hannover: Hahn, 1967. Translation by Raymond Van Dam: *Glory of the Martyrs*. Liverpool: Liverpool University Press, 1988.

Herodian. *Historiae*. In *Herodian*, translated and edited by C. R. Whittaker. 2 vols. Loeb Classical Library. Cambridge, Mass.: Harvard University Press, 1969–1970.

Jerome. *Epistulae*. In *Epistulae*, edited by Isidorus Hilberg. Corpus scriptorum ecclesiasticorum latinorum 54–56. 3 vols. Vienna: Hoeder-Pichler-Tempsky, 1910–1918.

———. *Lettres*. Edited by Jérôme Labourt. 8 vols. Paris: Les Belles Lettres, 1949–1963.

Lactantius. *De mortibus persecutorum*. Edited and translated by J. L. Creed. Oxford: Clarendon, 1984.

Leges novellae ad Theodosianum pertinentes. Edited by Theodor Mommsen and P. Meyer. Berlin: Weidmann, 1905.

Libellus de regionibus urbis Romae. Edited by Arvast Nordh. Lund: Gleerup, 1949.

Liber Pontificalis. Edited by Louis Duchesne. 3 vols. Paris: Ernest Thorin, 1981. First published in 1884.

Macrobius. *Saturnalia*. Translated and edited by Robert A. Kaster. 3 vols. Cambridge, Mass.: Harvard University Press, 2011.

Malalas, John. *The Chronicle of John Malalas*. Edited and translated by Elizabeth Jeffreys and Michael Jeffreys. Melbourne: Central Printing, 1986.

Notitia urbis Romae. In *Codice topografico della città di Roma*, edited by Roberto Valentini and Giuseppe Zucchetti, 1:165–188. Rome: Tipografia del Senato, 1940.

Orosius. *Pauli Orosii Historiarum adversum paganos libri VII*. Edited by Karl Zangemeister. Vienna: C. Geroldi, 1966. First published in 1882. Translation by I. W. Raymont: *Seven Books of History against the Pagans*. New York: Columbia University Press, 1936.

Panegyrici Latini. In *In Praise of Later Roman Emperors*, translated by C. E. V. Nixon and Barbara Saylor Rodgers. Berkeley: University of California Press, 1994.

Procopius. *Gothic Wars*. Translated and edited by H. B. Dewing. 5 vols. Cambridge, Mass.: Harvard University Press, 1914–1928.

Prudentius. *Contra Symmachum*. Edited by H. J. Thomson. 2 vols. Cambridge, Mass.: Harvard University Press, 1949–1953. Translation by Sister M. Clement Eagan: *Poems of Prudentius*. 2 vols. Washington, D.C.: Catholic University of America Press, 1962–1965.

Rufinus. *Historia ecclesiastica*. In *Kirchengeschichte*, edited by Theodor Mommsen, Eduard Schwartz, and Friedhelm Winkelmann, 3 vols. Berlin: Akademie, 1999.

Rutilius Namatianus. *Rutilius Namatianus: Sur son retour*. Edited by Jules Vessereau and François Préchac. Paris: Les Belles Lettres, 1972.

Sidonius Apollinaris. *Carmina*. In *Gai Solii Apollinaris Sodonii epistulae et carmina*, edited by Christian Lütjohann. *MGH AA* 8. Berlin: Weidmann, 1887.

Symmachus. *Epistulae Q. Aurelii Symmachi*. Edited by Otto Seeck. *MGH AA* 6.1. Berlin: Weidmann, 1888.

———. *Relationes*. In *Prefect and Emperor: The* Relationes *of Symmachus, A.D. 384*, translated by R. H. Barrow. Oxford: Clarendon, 1973.

Zosimus. *Zosime: Histoire nouvelle*. Edited by François Paschoud. 3 vols. Paris: Les Belles Lettres, 1970–1993.

SECONDARY SOURCES

Aiello, Vincenzo. "Costantino, la lebbra e il battesimo di Silvestro." In *Costantino il Grande: Dall'antichità all'umanesimo, Colloquio sul Cristianesimo nel mondo antico*, edited by G. Bonamente and F. Fusco, 38–42. Macerata: Università degli studi di Macerata, 1990.

Alchermes, Joseph. "*Spolia* in Roman Cities of the Late Empire: Legislative Rationales and Architectural Reuse." *Dumbarton Oaks Papers* 48 (1994): 167–178.

Alföldi, Andreas. *A Conflict of Ideas in the Late Roman Empire: The Clash between the Senate and Valentinian I*. Edited by H. Mattingly. Oxford: Clarendon, 1952.

———. "From the *Aion Plutonius* of the Ptolemies to the *Saeculum Frugiferum* of the Roman Emperors." In *Greece and the Eastern Mediterranean in Ancient History and Prehistory: Studies Presented to Fritz Schachermeyr on the Occasion of His Eightieth Birthday*, edited by K. H. Kinzl, 1–30. Berlin: de Gruyter, 1977.

Alföldy, Géza. "*Difficillima Tempora*: Urban Life, Inscriptions and Mentality in Late Antique Rome." In *Urban Centers and Rural Contexts in Late Antiquity*, edited by T. S. Burns and John Eadie, 3–24. East Lansing: Michigan State University Press, 2001.

———. "Individualität und Kollektivnorm in der Epigraphik des römischen Senatorenstandes." In *Epigrafia e ordine senatorio*, tituli 4, edited by Silvio Panciera, 37–53. Rome: Edizioni di storia e letteratura, 1982.

———. *Römische Statuen in Venetia et Histria: Epigraphische Quellen*. Heidelberg: Carl Winter, 1984.

Amici, Carla. "Dal progetto al monumento." In Giavarini, ed., *La Basilica di Massenzio*, 125–148.

———. *Il foro di Cesare*. Florence: Leo S. Olschki, 1991.

———. *Lo scavo didattico della zona retrostante la Curia (foro di Cesare): Campagne di scavo 1961–1970*. Rome: Bonsignori, 2007.

———. "Le techniche di cantiere e il procedimento costruttivo." In Giavarini, ed., *La Basilica di Massenzio*, 149–160.

Ando, Clifford. *The Matter of the Gods: Religion and the Roman Empire*. Berkeley: University of California Press, 2008.

Andreae, Bernard. "Archäologische Funde im Bereich der Soprintendenzen von Rom, 1949–1957." *Archäologischer Anzeiger* 72 (1957): 111–358.

Arce, Javier. "Roman Imperial Funerals *in effigie*." In *The Emperor and Rome: Space, Representation, and Ritual*, edited by Björn Ewald and Carlos Noreña, 309–323. Cambridge: Cambridge University Press, 2010.

Arnheim, M. T. W. *The Senatorial Aristocracy in the Later Roman Empire*. Oxford: Clarendon, 1972.

Aronen, Jaakko. "Dragon Cults and ΝΥΜΦΗ ΔΡΑΚΑΙΝΑ in IGUR 974." *Zeitschrift für Papyrologie und Epigraphik* 111 (1996): 129–136.

———. "I Misteri di Ecate sul Campidoglio." *Studi e materiali di storia delle religioni* 51 (1985): 73–80.

Assmann, Aleida. *Cultural Memory and Western Civilization: Functions, Media, Archives*. Cambridge: Cambridge University Press, 2011.

Bablitz, Leanne. "A Relief, Some Letters and the Centumviral Court." In *Spaces of Justice in the Roman World*, edited by Francesco de Angelis, 223–250. Leiden: Brill, 2010.

Baldwin, Matthew. *Whose Acts of Peter? Text and Historical Context of the Actus Vercellenses*. Tübingen: Mohr Siebeck, 2005.

Banaji, Jairus. *Agrarian Change in Late Antiquity: Gold, Labour and Aristocratic Dominance*. Oxford: Oxford University Press, 2007.

Bardill, Jonathan. *Constantine, Divine Emperor of the Christian Golden Age*. Cambridge: Cambridge University Press, 2012.

Barnes, Timothy D. *Constantine and Eusebius*. Cambridge, Mass.: Harvard University Press, 1980.

———. "Constantine's Prohibition of Pagan Sacrifice." *American Journal of Philology* 105 (1984): 69–72.

———. *Early Christian Hagiography and Roman History*. Tübingen: Mohr Siebeck, 2010.

———. *The New Empire of Diocletian and Constantine*. Cambridge, Mass.: Harvard University Press, 1982.

———. "Praetorian Prefects, 337–61." *Zeitschrift für Papyrologie und Epigraphik* 94 (1992): 249–252.

Bartoli, Alfonso. *Curia Senatus: Lo scavo e il restauro*. Rome: Istituto di Studi Romani, 1963.

———. "Lavori nella sede del Senato romano al tempo di Teodorico." *Bullettino della Commissione Archeologica Comunale di Roma* 73 (1949–1950): 77–90.

———. "Il Senato Romano in onore di Ezio." *Atti della Pontificia Accademia Romana di Archeologia: Rendiconti* 22 (1946–1947): 267–273.

———. "Ultime vicende e trasformazioni cristiane della Basilica Emilia." *Rendiconti della reale Accademia dei Lincei: Classe di scienze morali, storiche, e filologiche* 21 (1912): 758–766.

Bassett, Sarah. *The Urban Image of Late Antique Constantinople*. Cambridge: Cambridge University Press, 2004.

Bauer, Franz Alto. "*Beatitudo temporum*: Die Gegenwart der Vergangenheit im Stadtbild des spätantiken Rome." In *Epochenwandel? Kunst und Kultur zwischen Antike und Mittelalter*, edited by F. A. Bauer, 75–94. Mainz: Philipp von Zabern, 2001.

———. "Das Denkmal der Kaiser Gratian, Valentinian II. und Theodosius am Forum Romanum." *Mitteilungen des Deutschen Archäologischen Instituts, Römische Abteilung* 106 (1999): 213–234.

———. "Einige weniger bekannte Platzanlagen im spätantiken Rom." In *Pratum Romanum: Gedenkschrift Richard Krautheimer*, edited by R. L. Colella, 27–54. Wiesbaden: Reichert, 1997.

———. "Das Forum Romanum als normativer Raum in der Spätantike." In *Athen, Rom, Jerusalem: Normentransfers in der antiken Welt*, edited by Gian Franco Chiai, Bardo Gauly, Andreas Hartmann, Gerhard Zimmer, and Burkard Zapff, 327–341. Regensburg: Friedrich Pustet, 2012.

———. "In formam antiquam restitutus: Das Bewahren der Vergangenheit in der Spätantike am Beispiel des Forum Romanum." In *Die "Denkmalpflege" vor der Denkmalpflege*, Akten des Berner Kongresses, 30 June–3 July 1999, edited by Volcker Hoffmann, Jürg Schweizer, and Wolfgang Wolters, 39–62. Berlin: Peter Lang, 2005.

———. "Stadt ohne Kaiser: Rom im Zeitalter der Dyarchie und Tetrarchie (285–306 n. Chr.)." In *Rom und Mailand in der Spätantike: Repräsentationen städtischer Räume in Literatur, Architektur und Kunst*, edited by Therese Fuhrer, 3–85. Berlin: de Gruyter, 2012.

———. *Stadt, Platz und Denkmal in der Spätantike: Untersuchungen zur Ausstattung des öffentlichen Raums in den spätantiken Städten Rom, Konstantinopel und Ephesos*. Mainz: Philipp von Zabern, 1996.

Bauer, Franz Alto, and Christian Witschel, eds. *Statuen in der Spätantike*. Wiesbaden: Reichert, 2007.

Benoist, Stéphane. *Rome, le prince et la cité*. Paris: Presses universitaires de France, 2005.

Bergemann, Johannes. *Römische Reiterstatuen: Ehrendenkmäler im öffentlichen Bereich*. Mainz am Rhein: Philipp von Zabern, 1990.

Bergmann, Marianne. "Der römische Sonnenkoloss, der Konstantinsbogen und die Ktistes-statue von Konstantinopel." *Jahrbuch Braunschweigische Wissenschaftliche Gesellschaft* (1997): 116–125.

Bjornlie, M. Shane. *Politics and Tradition between Rome, Ravenna and Constantinople: A Study of Cassiodorus and the Variae, 527–554*. Cambridge: Cambridge University Press, 2013.

Blanck, Horst. *Wiederverwendung alter Statuen als Ehrendenkmäler bei Griechen und Römern*. Rome: "L'Erma" di Bretschneider, 1969.

Bloch, Herbert. *I bolli laterizi e la storia edilizia romana*. Rome: Commune di Roma, 1947.

Boatwright, Mary. *Hadrian and the City of Rome*. Princeton, N.J.: Princeton University Press, 1987.

———. "Women and Gender in the Forum Romanum." *Transactions of the American Philological Association* 141 (2011): 105–141.

Bonfioli, Mara. "La diaconia dei SS. Sergio e Bacco nel Foro Romano." *Rivista di Archeologia Cristiana* 50 (1974): 55–72.

Boni, Giacomo. "Esplorazione nel Comizio." *Notizie degli scavi di antichità* (1900): 295–340.

———. "Foro Romano." In *Atti del congresso internazionale di scienze storiche* 1.9 (Apr. 1903), vol. 5, sec. 4 (Archeologia): 577–579.

Borg, Barbara, and Christian Witschel. "Veränderungen im Repräsentationsverhalten der romischen Eliten während des 3. Jhs. n. Chr." In *Inschriftliche Denkmäler als Medien der Selbstdarstellung in der römischen Welt*, edited by Géza Alföldy and Silvio Panciera, 47–120. Stuttgart: Steiner, 2001.

Boschung, Dietrich, and Werner Eck, eds. *Die Tetrarchie: Eine neues Regierungssystem und seine mediale Präsentation*. Wiesbaden: Reichert, 2006.

Bradbury, Scott. "Constantine and the Problem of Anti-Pagan Legislation in the Fourth Century." *Classical Philology* 89 (1994): 120–139.

Brandenburg, Hugo. "Die Umsetzung von Statuen in der Spätantike." In *Migratio et commutatio: Studien zur alten Geschichte und deren Nachleben (Festschrift Thomas Pekáry)*, edited by Hans-Joachim Drexhage and Julia Sünskes Thompson, 235–246. St. Katharinen: Scripta Mercaturae, 1989.

Bravi, Alessandra. *Ornamenta urbis: Opere d'arte greche negli spazi romani*. Bari: Edipuglia, 2012.

Brenk, Beat. "Türen als Spolien und Baureliquien: Nova construere sed amplius vetusta servare." In *Künstlerischer Austausch / Artistic Exchange*, Akten des XXVIII Internationalen Kongresses für Kunstgeschichte, Berlin, 15–20 July 1992, edited by Thomas W. Gehtgens, 1:43–54. Berlin: Akademie, 1993.

Brilliant, Richard. *The Arch of Septimius Severus in the Roman Forum*. Rome: American Academy in Rome, 1967.

Brilliant, Richard, and Dale Kinney, eds. *Reuse Value: Spolia and Appropriation in Art and Architecture from Constantine to Sherrie Levine*. Surrey: Ashgate, 2011.

Bruggisser, Philippe. "'Sacro-saintes statues': Prétextat et la restauration du portique des *Dei consentes* à Rome." In *Rom in der Spätantike: Historische Erinnerung im städtischen Raum*, edited by Ralf Behrwald and Christian Witschel, 331–356. Stuttgart: Franz Steiner, 2012.

Buddensieg, Tilmann. "Die Konstantinsbasilika in einer Zeichnung Francescos di Giorgio und der Marmorkoloss Konstantins des Grossen." *Münchner Jahrbuch der Bildenden Kunst* 13 (1962): 37–48.

Buranelli Le Pera, Susanna, and Luca D'Elia. "'Sacra Via': Note topografiche." *Bullettino della Commissione Archeologica Comunale di Roma* 91 (1986): 241–262.

Cameron, Alan. *Claudian: Poetry and Propaganda at the Court of Honorius*. Oxford: Clarendon, 1970.

———. "The Date and Identity of Macrobius." *Journal of Roman Studies* 56 (1966): 25–38.

———. *The Last Pagans of Rome*. Oxford: Oxford University Press, 2011.

———. "Theodosius the Great and the Regency of Stilicho." *Harvard Studies in Classical Philology* 73 (1969): 247–280.

Canella, Tessa. *Gli Actus Silvestri: Genesi di una leggenda su Costantino imperatore*. Spoleto: Fondazione Centro Italiano di Studi sull'alto Medioevo, 2006.

Canepa, Matthew. *The Two Eyes of the Earth: Art and Ritual of Kingship between Rome and Sasanian Iran*. Berkeley: University of California Press, 2009.

Capodiferro, Alessandra, ed. *Gli scavi di Giacomo Boni al Foro Romano: Documenti dall'archivio della Soprintendenza Archeologica di Roma*. Rome: Flora Palatina, 2003.

Carandini, Andrea. *Rome: Day One*. Translated by Stephen Sartarelli. Princeton, N.J.: Princeton University Press, 2011.

———. *La nascita di Roma: Dèi, lari, eroi e uomini all'alba di una civiltà*. Turin: Einaudi, 1997.

Carettoni, Gianfilippo. "Excavations and Discoveries in the Forum Romanum and on the Palatine during the Last Fifty Years." *Journal of Roman Studies* 50 (1960): 192–203.

Carettoni, Gianfilippo, Antonio M. Colini, Lucos Cozza, and Guglielmo Gatti, eds. *La pianta marmorea di Roma antica*. Rome: Danesi, 1960.

Carnabuci, Elisabetta. "L'angolo sud-orientale del Foro Romano nel manoscritto inedito di Giacomo Boni." *Atti della Accademia Nazionale dei Lincei: Classe di scienze morali, storiche e filologiche: Memorie*, ser. 9, vol. 1, fasc. 4 (1991): 247–365.

Caseau, Béatrice. "Late Antique Paganism: Adaptation under Duress." In *Late Antique Archaeology of "Paganism,"* edited by Luke Lavan et al., 111–134. Leiden: Brill, 2011.

Castagnoli, Ferdinando. "Atrium Libertatis." *Rendiconti: Accademia dei Lincei* 8 (1946): 276–291.

Chastagnol, André. "Aspects concrets et cadre topographique des fêtes décennales des empereurs à Rome." In *L'Urbs: Espace urbain et histoire (Ier siècle av. J.-C.–IIIe siècle ap. J.-C.)*, Collection de l'École française de Rome 98, 491–507. Rome: L'École française de Rome 1987.

———. "Constantin et le sénat." In *Atti dell'Accademia Romanistica Constantiniana: Secondo Convegno Internazionale*, 51–69. Perugia: Libreria Universitaria, 1976.

———. *Les Fastes de la préfecture de Rome au Bas-Empire*. Paris: Nouvelles Éditions Latines, 1962.

———. "Le formulaire de l'épigraphie latine officielle dans l'antiquité tardive." In *La terza età dell'epigrafia: Atti del Colloquio AIEGL*, edited by Angela Donati, 11–64. Faenza: Epigrafia e antichità, 1986.

———. *La préfecture urbaine à Rome sous le Bas-Empire*. Paris: Presses universitaires de France, 1960.

———. "Remarques sur les sénateurs orientaux au IVème siècle." *Acta Antiqua Accademiae Scientiarum Hungaricae* 24 (1976): 341–356.

Chenault, Robert. "Rome without Emperors: The Revival of a

Senatorial City in the Fourth Century CE." Ph.D. dissertation, University of Michigan, 2008.

———. "Statues of Senators in the Forum of Trajan and the Roman Forum in Late Antiquity." *Journal of Roman Studies* 102 (2012): 103–132.

Chioffi, Laura. *Gli elogia Augustei del Foro Romano: Aspetti epigrafici e topografici.* Opuscula Epigraphica 7. Rome: Quasar, 1996.

Claridge, Amanda. *Rome: An Oxford Archaeological Guide.* Oxford: Oxford University Press, 1998.

Claridge, Amanda, and Lucos Cozza. "Arco di Settimio Severo." In *Roma, Archeologia nel centro* 1. Lavori e studi di archeologia 6. Rome: De Luca, 1985.

Coarelli, Filippo. "L'edilizia pubblica a Roma in età tetrarchica." In *The Transformations of Urbs Roma in Late Antiquity*, edited by W. V. Harris, *Journal of Roman Archaeology*, suppl. ser. 33, 23–33. Portsmouth, R.I.: Journal of Roman Archaeology, 1999.

———. *Il foro romano.* Vol. 1: *Periodo arcaido.* Vol. 2: *Periodo repubblicano e Augusteo.* Rome: Quasar, 1983–1985.

———. "L'urbs e il suburbio: Ristrutturazione urbanistica e ristrutturazione amministrativa nella Roma di Massenzio." In *Società romana e impero tardoantico*, edited by Andrea Giardina, 2:1–35. Rome: Laterza, 1986.

Corcoran, Simon. *The Empire of the Tetrarchs: Imperial Pronouncements and Government, AD 284–324.* Oxford: Clarendon, 1996.

———. "The Tetrarchy: Policy and Image as Reflected in Imperial Pronouncements." In Boschung and Eck, *Die Tetrarchie*, 31–61.

Cracco Ruggini, Lellia. "Il paganesimo romano tra religione e politica (384–394 d.C.): Per una reinterpretazione del Carmen contra paganos." *Atti della Academia nazionale dei Lincei. Classe di scienze morali, storiche e filologiche* 23 (1979): 124–130.

Croke, Brian, and Jill Harries. *Religious Conflict in Fourth-Century Rome: A Documentary Study.* Sydney: Sydney University Press, 1982.

Culhed, Mats. *Conservator urbis suae: Studies in the Politics and Propaganda of the Emperor Maxentius.* Stockholm: Paul Åströms, 1994.

Curran, John R. "Moving Statues in Late Antique Rome: Problems of Perspective." *Art History* 17 (1994): 46–58.

———. *Pagan City and Christian Capital: Rome in the Fourth Century.* Oxford: Oxford University Press, 2000.

———. "Virgilizing Christianity in Late Antique Rome." In *Two Romes: Rome and Constantinople in Late Antiquity*, edited by Lucy Grig and Gavin Kelly, 325–344. Oxford: Oxford University Press, 2012.

Daguet-Gagey, Anne. *Les opera publica à Rome (180–305 ap. J.-C.).* Paris: Institut des Études Augustiniennes, 1997.

Dattoli, Michele. *L'aula del Senato Romano e la chiesa di S. Adriano.* Rome: Maglione and Strini, 1921.

De Angelis, Francesco. "The Emperor's Justice and Its Spaces in Rome and Italy." In *Spaces of Justice in the Roman World*, edited by Francesco de Angelis, 127–160. Leiden: Brill, 2010.

de Blois, Lukas. "Emperorship in a Period of Crisis: Changes in Emperor Worship, Imperial Ideology and Perceptions of Imperial Authority in the Roman Empire in the Third Century A.D." In *The Impact of Rome on Religions: Ritual and Religious Life in the Roman Empire*, edited by Lukas de Blois, Peter Funke, and Johannes Hahn, 268–278. Leiden: Brill, 2006.

De Francisci, Pietro. "Per la storia del Senato Romano e della Curia nei secoli V e VI." *Atti della Pontificia Accademia Romana di Archeologia: Rendiconti* 22 (1946–1947): 287–309.

De Maria, Sandro. *Gli archi onorari di Roma e dell'Italia Romana.* Rome: "L'Erma" di Bretschneider, 1988.

De Rossi, Giovanni Battista. "La base d'una statua di Prassitele testè scoperta e la serie di simili basi alla quale essa appartiene." *Bullettino della Commissione Archeologica Comunale di Roma* 2 (1874): 174–181.

De Ruggiero, Ettore. *Il Foro Romano.* Rome: Società topografica arpinate, 1913.

Deckers, Johannes. "Die Wandmalereien im Kaiserkultraum von Luxor." *Jahrbuch des Deutschen Archäologischen Instituts* 94 (1979): 600–652.

Degrassi, Attilio. "L'iscrizione in onore di Aezio e l''Atrium Libertatis.'" *Bullettino della Commissione Archeologica Comunale di Roma* 72 (1946): 33–44.

Deichmann, Friedrich. *Die Spolien in der spätantiken Architektur.* Munich: C. H. Beck, 1975.

Delbrück, Richard. *Spätantike Kaiserporträts: Von Constantinus Magnus bis zum Ende des Westreichs.* Berlin: De Gruyter, 1978.

Della Valle, Giuseppina. "Teodorico e Roma." *Rendiconti della Accademia di Archeologia, Lettere e Belle Arti di Napoli*, n.s. 34 (1959): 119–176.

Delmaire, Roland. "Flavius Aëtius, 'delatorum inimicissimus,' 'vindex libertatis,' 'pudoris ultor' (CIL 6.41389)." *Zeitschrift für Papyrologie und Epigraphik* 166 (2008): 291–294.

———. *Largesses sacrées et res privata: L'aerarium impérial et son administration du IVe au VIe siècle.* Rome: École française de Rome, 1989.

———. "La législation sur les sacrifices au IV siècle, un essai d'interprétation." *Révue historique de droit français et étranger* 82 (2004): 319–334.

Depeyrot, Georges. "Economy and Society." In *The Cambridge Companion to the Age of Constantine*, edited by Noel Lenski, 239–245. Cambridge: Cambridge University Press, 2006.

Dewar, Michael, ed. *Claudian: Panegyricus de Sexto Consulatu Honorii Augusti.* Oxford: Clarendon, 1996.

Dey, Hendrik. "Art, Ceremony, and the City Walls: The Aesthetics of Imperial Resurgence in the Late Roman West." *Journal of Late Antiquity* 3 (2010): 3–37.

———. *The Aurelian Wall and the Refashioning of Imperial Rome, AD 271–855.* Cambridge: Cambridge University Press, 2011.

———. "Spolia, Milestones, and City Walls: The Politics of Imperial Legitimacy in Gaul." In *Patrons and Viewers in Late Antiquity*, edited by Stine Birk and Birte Poulsen, 291–310. Aarhus: Aarhus University Press, 2012.

Dillon, John Noel. *The Justice of Constantine: Law, Communication, and Control.* Ann Arbor: University of Michigan Press, 2012.

Donciu, Ramiro. *L'empereur Maxence.* Bari: Edipuglia, 2012.

Dörries, Hermann. Das Selbstzeugnis Kaiser Konstantins. Göttingen: Vandenhoeck und Ruprecht, 1954.

Drake, H. A. *Constantine and the Bishops: The Politics of Intolerance.* Baltimore, Md.: Johns Hopkins University Press, 2000.

Duchesne, Louis. "S. Maria Antiqua: Notes sur la topographie de Rome au Moyen Âge." *Mélanges d'archéologie et d'histoire* 17 (1897): 13–35.

Dufourcq, Albert. *Étude sur les Gesta Martyrum romains.* 5 vols. Paris: Fontemoing, 1900. Reprint, 1988.

Dufraigne, Pierre. *Adventus Augusti, Adventus Christi: Recherche sur l'exploitation idéologique et littéraire d'un cérémonial dans l'antiquité tardive.* Paris: Institute d'Études Augustiniennes, 1994.

Dumser, Elisha. "The Architecture of Maxentius: A Study in Architectural Design and Urban Planning in Fourth-Century Rome." Ph.D. dissertation, University of Pennsylvania, 2005.

———. *Mapping Augustan Rome. Journal of Roman Archaeology,* suppl. 50. Portsmouth, R.I.: Journal of Roman Archaeology, 2002.

Eck, Werner. "Senatorial Self-Representation: Developments in the Augustan Period." In *Caesar Augustus: Seven Aspects,* edited by Fergus Millar and Erich Segal, 129–167. Oxford: Clarendon, 1984.

Edwards, Catharine. *Writing Rome: Textual Approaches to the City.* Cambridge: Cambridge University Press, 1996.

Elbern, Stephan. "Das Verhältnis der spätantiken Kaiser zur Stadt Rom." *Römische Quartalschrift* 85 (1990): 19–49.

Engemann, Josef. "Die religiöse Herrscherfunktion im Fünfsäulenmonument Diocletians in Rom und in der Herrschermosaiken Justinians in Ravenna." *Frühmittelalterliche Studien* 18 (1984): 336–356.

Errington, R. Malcolm. *Roman Imperial Policy from Julian to Theodosius.* Chapel Hill: University of North Carolina Press, 2006.

Evers, Cécile. "Remarques sur l'iconographie de Constantin: À propos des portraits des 'Bons Empereurs.'" *Mélanges de l'École française de Rome: Antiquité* 103 (1991): 785–804.

Ewald, Björn, and Carlos Noreña, eds. *The Emperor and Rome: Space, Representation, and Ritual.* Cambridge: Cambridge University Press, 2010.

Fagan, Garrett. "The Reliability of Roman Rebuilding Inscriptions." *Papers of the British School at Rome* 64 (1996): 81–93.

Favro, Diane. "Ancient Rome through the Veil of Sight." In *Sites Unseen: Landscape and Vision,* edited by Dianne Harris and Dede Ruggles, 111–130. Pittsburgh, Pa.: University of Pittsburgh Press, 2007.

———. "Construction Traffic in Imperial Rome: Building the Arch of Septimius Severus." In Laurence and Newsome, eds., *Rome, Ostia, Pompeii,* 332–360.

———. *The Urban Image of Augustan Rome.* New York: Cambridge University Press, 1996.

Favro, Diane, and Bernard Frischer. *Digital Roman Forum.* http://dlib.etc.ucla.edu/projects/Forum/. Accessed 24 June 2013.

Favro, Diane, and Christopher Johanson. "Death in Motion: Funeral Processions in the Roman Forum." *Journal of the Society of Architectural Historians* 69 (2010): 12–37.

Feeney, Denis. *Caesar's Calendar: Ancient Time and the Beginnings of History.* Princeton, N.J.: Princeton University Press, 2007.

Fiore, F. Paolo. "L'impianto architettonico antico." In Flaccomio, ed., *Il "Tempio di Romolo,"* 63–90.

Flaccomio, Gabriella, ed. *Il "Tempio di Romolo" al Foro Romano. Quaderni dell'Istituto di Storia dell'Architettura,* ser. 26, fasc. 157–162 (1980).

Flower, Harriet I. *The Art of Forgetting: Disgrace and Oblivion in Roman Political Culture.* Chapel Hill: University of North Carolina Press, 2006.

Franchi de' Cavalieri, Pio. "S. Martina." *Römische Quartalschrift* 17 (1903): 222–236.

Fraschetti, Augusto. "L'*Atrium Minervae* in epoca tardoantica." *Opuscula Instituti Romani Finlandiae* 1 (1981): 25–40.

———. *La conversione: Da Roma pagana a Roma cristiana.* Rome: Laterza, 1999.

———. *The Foundation of Rome.* Translated by K. Windle. Edinburgh: University of Edinburgh Press, 2005.

———. "'Veniunt modo reges Romam.'" In *Transformations of Urbs Roma in Late Antiquity,* edited by William V. Harris, *Journal of Roman Archaeology,* suppl. 33, 235–248. Portsmouth, R.I.: Journal of Roman Archaeology, 1999.

Freyberger, Klaus Stefan. *Das Forum Romanum: Spiegel der Stadtgeschichte des antiken Rom.* Mainz: Philipp von Zabern, 2009.

Frischer, Bernard, Dean Abernathy, and Kim Dylla. *Rome Reborn.* http://www.romereborn.virginia.edu. Accessed 12 Nov. 2011.

Gadeyne, Jan. "Function and Dysfunction of the City: Rome in the Fifth Century A.D." Ph.D. dissertation, Katholieke Universiteit Leuven, 2009.

Galinsky, Karl. *Augustan Culture.* Princeton, N.J.: Princeton University Press, 1996.

Gasparri, Carlo. *Aedes Concordiae.* Rome: Istituto di Studi Romani, 1979.

Gatto, Ludovico. "Ancora sull'edilizia e l'urbanistica nella Roma di Teodorico." *Romanobarbarica* 12 (1992–1993): 311–380.

Geertman, Herman. "Forze centrifughe e centripete nella Roma cristiana: Il Laterano, la Basilica Iulia, e la Basilica Liberiana." *Atti della Pontificia Accademia Romana di Archeologia: Rendiconti* 59 (1986–1987): 63–91.

Geffcken, Johannes. *The Last Days of Greco-Roman Paganism.* Translated by Sabine MacCormack. Amsterdam: North Holland, 1978.

Giavarini, Carlo, ed. *La Basilica di Massenzio: Il monumento, i ma-*

teriali, le strutture, la stabilità. Rome: "L'Erma" di Bretschneider, 2005.

Gillett, Andrew. "Epic, Panegyric, and Political Communication in the Fifth-Century West." In *Two Romes: Rome and Constantinople in Late Antiquity*, edited by Lucy Grig and Gavin Kelly, 265–290. Oxford: Oxford University Press, 2012.

———. "Rome, Ravenna, and the Last Western Emperors." *Papers of the British School at Rome* 69 (2001): 131–167.

Giuliani, Cairoli F., and Patrizia Verduchi. *L'area centrale del Foro Romano*. Florence: Olschki, 1987.

———. *Foro Romano: L'area centrale*. Florence: Olschki, 1980.

Goddard, Christophe. "The Evolution of Pagan Sanctuaries in Late Antique Italy (Fourth–Sixth Centuries A.D.): A New Administrative and Legal Framework." In *Les cités de l'Italie tardo-antique (IVe–VIe siècle): Institutions, économie, société, culture et religion*, edited by Massimiliano Ghilardi, Christophe Goddard, and Pierfrancesco Porena, 281–308. Rome: École française de Rome, 2006.

Goodson, Caroline. "Roman Archaeology in Medieval Rome." In *Rome: Continuing Encounters between Past and Present*, edited by Dorigen Caldwell and Lesley Caldwell, 17–34. Surrey: Ashgate: 2011.

Grégoire, Henri. "La statue de Constantin et la signe de la croix." *L'antiquité classique* 1 (1932): 138–143.

Guarducci, Margherita. *Epigrafia greca*. 4 vols. Rome: Istituto Poligrafico dello Stato, 1967–1978.

Guattani, Giuseppe A. *Memorie enciclopediche sulle antichità e belle arti di Roma*. Rome: Stampa Romana, 1819.

Gutteridge, Adam. "Some Aspects of Social and Cultural Time in Late Antiquity." In *Social and Political Life in Late Antiquity*, edited by William Bowden, Adam Gutteridge, Luke Lavan, and Carlos Machado, 569–601. Leiden: Brill, 2006.

Hannestad, Niels. *Tradition in Late Antique Sculpture: Conservation, Modernization, Production*. Aarhus: Aarhus University Press, 1994.

Hansen, Maria Fabricius. *The Eloquence of Appropriation: Prolegomena to an Understanding of* Spolia *in Early Christian Rome*. Rome: "L'Erma" di Bretschneider, 2003.

Harries, Jill. *Law and Empire in Late Antiquity*. Cambridge: Cambridge University Press, 1999.

Harris, William V., ed. *Transformations of Urbs Roma in Late Antiquity. Journal of Roman Archaeology*, suppl. ser. 33. Portsmouth, R.I.: Journal of Roman Archaeology.

Harvey, Susan Ashbrook. *Scenting Salvation: Ancient Christianity and the Olfactory Imagination*. Berkeley: University of California Press, 2006.

Haselberger, Lothar. *Urbem adornare: Die Stadt Rom und ihre Gestaltumwandlung unter Augustus. Journal of Roman Archaeology*, suppl. 64. Portsmouth, R.I.: Journal of Roman Archaeology, 2007.

Hedrick, Charles W., Jr. *History and Silence: Purge and Rehabilitation of Memory in Late Antiquity*. Austin: University of Texas Press, 2000.

Hekster, Olivier. "The City of Rome in Late Imperial Ideology: The Tetrarchs, Maxentius, and Constantine." *Mediterreaneo Antico* 2 (1999): 717–748.

Henning, Dirk. "CIL VI 32005 und die 'Rostra Vandalica.'" *Zeitschrift für Papyrologie und Epigraphik* 100 (1996): 259–264.

Højte, Jakob Munk. *Roman Imperial Statue Bases: From Augustus to Commodus*. Aarhus: Aarhus University Press, 2005.

Hölscher, Tonio. "Das Forum Romanum—Die momentale Geschichte Roms." In *Erinnerungsorte der Antike: Die römische Welt*, edited by Elke Stein-Hölkeskamp and Karl-Joachim Hölkeskamp, 100–122. Munich: C. H. Beck, 2006.

Honoré, Tony. *Law in the Crisis of Empire, 379–455 AD*. Oxford: Clarendon, 1998.

Horster, Marietta. "Ehrungen spätantiker Statthalter." *Antiquité Tardive* 6 (1998): 37–59.

Hülsen, Christian. "Iscrizione di Giunio Valentino, prefetto della città nel secolo V." *Mitteilungen des Deutschen Archäologischen Instituts, Römische Abteilung* 10 (1895): 58–63.

———. "Jahresberich über neue Funde und Forschungen zur Topographie der Stadt Rom." *Mitteilungen des Deutschen Archäologischen Instituts, Römische Abteilung* 17 (1903): 30–31.

———. *The Roman Forum*. Translated by J. B. Carter. Rome: Loescher, 1906.

Humphries, Mark. "From Emperor to Pope? Ceremonial, Space, and Authority at Rome from Constantine to Gregory the Great." In *Religion, Dynasty, and Patronage in Early Christian Rome, 300–900*, edited by Kate Cooper and Julia Hillner, 21–58. Cambridge: Cambridge University Press, 2007.

———. "Roman Senators and Absent Emperors in Late Antiquity." *Acta ad archaeologiam et artium historiam pertinentia* 17 (2003): 27–46.

———. "Valentinian III and Rome (425–455): Patronage, Politics, Power." In *Two Romes: Rome and Constantinople in Late Antiquity*, edited by Lucy Grig and Gavin Kelly, 161–182. Oxford: Oxford University Press, 2012.

Jokilehto, Jukka. *A History of Architectural Conservation*. Oxford: Butterworth-Heinemann, 1999.

Jordan-Ruwe, Martina. *Das Säulenmonument: Zur Geschichte der erhöhten Aufstellung antiker Porträtstatuen*. Asia Minor Studien 19. Bonn: Hambelt, 1995.

Kähler, Heinz. *Das Fünfsaäulendenkmal für die Tetrarchen auf dem Forum Romanum*. Monumenta Artis Romanae 3. Cologne: M. DuMont Schauberg, 1964.

Kahlos, Maijastina. "The Restoration Policy of Vettius Agorius Praetextatus." *Arctos* 29 (1995): 39–47.

———. *Vettius Agorius Praetextatus: A Senatorial Life in Between*. Rome: Institutum Romanum Finlandiae, 2002.

Kajava, Mika. "Le iscrizioni ritrovate nell'area del Lacus Iuturnae." In *Lacus Iuturnae I*, edited by Eva Margareta Steinby, 34–35. Rome: De Luca, 1989.

Kalas, Gregor. "Topographical Transitions: The Oratory of the Forty Martyrs and Exhibition Strategies in the Early Medieval Roman Forum." In *Santa Maria Antiqua al Foro Romano:*

Cento anni dopo lo scavo, edited by John Osborne, J. Rasmus Brandt, and Giuseppe Morganti, 201–203. Rome: Campisano, 2004.

———. "Writing and Restoration in Rome: Inscriptions, Statues and the Late Antique Preservation of Buildings." In *Cities, Texts, and Social Networks, 400–1500: Experiences and Perceptions of Medieval Urban Space*, edited by Caroline Goodson, Anne E. Lester, and Carol Symes, 21–43. Surrey: Ashgate, 2010.

Kalas, Gregor, Diane Favro, Christopher Johanson, Todd Presner, Marie Saldaña, and Pelin Yoncaci. *Visualizing Statues in the Late Antique Roman Forum*. Available at: http://inscriptions.etc.ucla.edu.

Kellum, Barbara. "The City Adorned: Programmatic Display at the *Aedes Concordiae Augustae*." In *Between Republic and Empire: Interpretations of Augustus and His Principate*, edited by Kurt Raaflaub and Mark Toher, 276–307. Berkeley: University of California Press, 1990.

Kelly, Christopher. "Bureaucracy and Government." In *The Cambridge Companion to the Age of Constantine*, edited by Noel Lenski, 183–206. Cambridge: Cambridge University Press, 2006.

Kiilerich, Bente. *Late Fourth-Century Classicism in the Plastic Arts: Studies in the So-Called Theodosian Renaissance*. Odense: Odense University Press, 1993.

Kiilerich, Bente, and Hjalmar Torp. "*Hic est, hic Stilicho*: The Date and Interpretation of a Notable Diptych." *Jahrbuch der deutschen Archäologischen Instituts* 104 (1989): 319–371.

Kinney, Dale. "The Concept of *Spolia*." In *A Companion to Medieval Art*, edited by Conrad Rudolph, 233–252. London: Blackwell, 2006.

———. "Rape or Restitution of the Past? Interpreting *Spolia*." In *The Art of Interpreting*, edited by Susan C. Scott, 52–67. University Park: Pennsylvania State University Press, 1995.

———. "Roman Architectural *Spolia*." *Proceedings of the American Philosophical Society* 145 (2001): 138–150.

———. "*Spolia*: *Damnatio* and *renovatio memoriae*." *Memoirs of the American Academy in Rome* 42 (1997): 117–148.

———. "Spoliation in Medieval Rome." In *Perspektiven der Spolienforschung 1: Spoliierung und Transposition*, edited by Stefan Altenkamp, Carmen Marcks-Jacobs, and Peter Seiler, 261–286. Berlin: De Gruyter, 2013.

Kissel, Theodor. *Das Forum Romanum: Leben im Herzen Roms*. Düsseldorf: Artemis und Winkler, 2004.

Klein, Richard. *Der Streit um den Victoriaaltar*. Darmstadt: Wissenschaftliche Buchgesellschaft, 1972.

Kleiner, Fred. *The Arch of Nero in Rome: A Study of the Roman Honorary Arch before and under Nero*. Archaeologica 52. Rome: G. Bretschneider, 1985.

Kolb, Frank. *Diocletian und die Erste Tetrarchie: Improvisation oder Experiment in der Organisation monarchischer Herrschaft?* Berlin and New York: Walter de Gruyter, 1987.

———. *Herrscherideologie in der Spätantike*. Berlin: Akademie, 2001.

———. "*Praesens Deus*: Kaiser und Gott unter der Tetrarchie." In *Diokletian und die Tetrarchie: Aspekte einer Zeitenwende*, edited by Alexander Demandt, Andreas Goltz, and Heinrich Schlange-Schöningen, 27–37. Berlin: Walter de Gruyter, 2004.

Krautheimer, Richard. *Corpus Basilicarum Christianarum Romae: Le basiliche cristiane antiche di Roma sec. IV-IX*. 5 vols. Vatican City: Istituto di Archeologia Cristiana, 1937–1980.

———. *Three Christian Capitals: Topography and Politics*. Berkeley: University of California Press, 1983.

Kuhoff, Wolfgang. *Diokletian und die Epoche der Tetrarchie: Das römische Reich zwischen Krisenbewältigung und Neuaufbau (284–313 n. Chr.)*. Frankfurt: Peter Lang, 2001.

La Rocca, Eugenio. "La nuova immagine dei Fori Imperiali: Appunti in margine agli scavi." *Mitteilungen des Deutschen Archäologischen Instituts, Römische Abteilung* 108 (2001): 171–213.

La Rocca, Eugenio, and Paul Zanker. "Il ritratto colossale di Costantino dal Foro di Traiano." In *Res bene gestae: Ricerche di storia urbana su Roma antica in onore di Eva Margaret Steinby*, edited by Anna Leone, Domenico Palombi, and Susan Walker, 145–168. *LTUR*, suppl. 4. Rome: Quasar, 2007.

Labranche, C. L. "*Roma nobilis*: The Public Architecture of Rome, 330–476." Ph.D. dissertation, University of Michigan, 1968.

Lahusen, Götz. *Römische Bildnisse: Auftraggeber–Funktionen–Standorte*. Mainz: Philipp von Zabern, 2010.

———. *Untersuchungen zur Ehrenstatue in Rom: Literarische und epigraphische Zeugnisse*. Rome: Bretschneider, 1983.

———. "Zu römischen Statuen und Bildnissen aus Gold und Silber." *Zeitschrift für Papyrologie und Epigraphik* 128 (1999): 251–266.

Lanciani, Rodolfo. "L'Aula e gli uffici del senato romano (*Curia hostilia iulia: Secretarium senatus*)." *Notizie degli scavi* (1883): 3–32.

———. *Notes from Rome*. Edited by Anthony Cubberly. London: British School at Rome, 1988.

Laubscher, Hans Peter. "Arcus Novus und Arcus Claudii, zwei Triumphbögen an der Via Lata in Rom." *Nachrichten der Akademie des Wissenschaften in Göttingen* 3 (1976): 65–108.

———. "Beobachtung zu tetrarchischen Kaiserbildnissen aus Porphyr." *Jahrbuch des Deutschen Archäologischen Instituts* 114 (1999): 207–252.

Laurence, Ray, Simon Esmonde Cleary, and Gareth Sears. *The City in the Roman West, c. 250 BC–c. A.D. 250*. Cambridge: Cambridge University Press, 2011.

Laurence, Ray, and David Newsome, eds. *Rome, Ostia, Pompeii: Movement and Space*. Oxford: Oxford University Press, 2011.

Lavan, Luke. "*Fora* and *agorai* in Mediterranean Cities during the 4th and 5th centuries A.D." In *Social and Political Life in Late Antiquity*, edited by William Bowden, Adam Gutteridge, Luke Lavan, and Carlos Machado, 195–249. Leiden: Brill, 2006.

———. "Political Talismans? Residual 'Pagan' Statues in Late Antique Public Space." In *The Archaeology of Late Antique "Pa-*

ganism," edited by Luke Lavan and Michael Mulryan, 439–477. Leiden: Brill, 2011.

Lejdegård, Hans. "Honorius and the City of Rome: Authority and Legitimacy in Late Antiquity." Ph.D. dissertation, Uppsala University, 2002.

Lendon, J. E. *Empire of Honour: The Art of Government in the Roman World*. Oxford: Clarendon, 1997.

Lenski, Noel. "Evoking the Pagan Past: *Instinctu divinitatis* and Constantine's Capture of Rome." *Journal of Late Antiquity* 1 (2008): 204–257.

———. *Failure of Empire: Valens and the Roman State in the Fourth Century A.D.* Berkeley: University of California Press, 2002.

Leone, Anna. *The End of the Pagan City: Religion, Economy, and Urbanism in Late Antique North Africa*. Oxford: Oxford University Press, 2013.

Lepelley, Claude. "Le musée des statues divines: La volonté de sauvegarder le patrimoine artistique païen à l'époque théodosienne." *Cahiers Archeologiques* 42 (1994): 5–15.

———. "The Survival and the Fall of the Classical City in Late Roman Africa." In *The City in Late Antiquity*, edited by John Rich, 50–76. New York: Routledge, 1996.

Leppin, Hartmut. *Maxentius: Der letzte Kaiser in Rom*. Mainz am Rhein: Philipp von Zabern, 2007.

Levison, Wilhelm. "Konstantinische Schenkung und Silvester-Legende." In *Miscellanea F. Ehrle: Scritti di storia e paleografia*, 2:159–247. Vatican City: Biblioteca Apostolica Vaticana, 1924. Reprinted in idem, *Aus rheinischer und fränkischer Frühzeit: Ausgewählte Aufsätze*, 390–465. Düsseldorf: L. Schwann, 1948.

Levoy, Marc, Natasha Gelfand, Dave Koller, and Jennifer Trimble, eds. "Stanford Digital Forma Urbis Romae Project." http://formaurbis.stanford.edu/. Accessed 2 December 2011.

Lewin, Ariel. "Urban Public Building from Constantine to Julian: The Epigraphic Evidence." In *Recent Research in Late Antique Urbanism*, edited by Luke Lavan, 27–37. Portsmouth, R.I.: Journal of Roman Archaeology, 2001.

Liebenschuetz, J. H. W. G. *The Decline and Fall of the Roman City*. Oxford: Oxford University Press, 2001.

Lipps, Johannes. *Die Basilica Aemilia am Forum Romanum: Der kaiserzeitliche Bau und seine Ornamentik*. Wiesbaden: Reichert, 2011.

———. "Zur Datierung der spätantiken Portikus des Caesarforums: Literarische Quellen und archäologischer Befund." *Mitteilungen des Deutschen Archäologischen Instituts, Römische Abteilung* 114 (2008): 389–405.

Liu, Jinyu. "Late Antique Fora and Public Honor in the Western Cities: Case Studies." In *Shifting Cultural Frontiers in Late Antiquity*, edited by David Brakke, Deborah Deliyannis, and Edward Watts, 225–239. Surrey: Ashgate, 2012.

Liverani, Paolo. "Arco di Onorio—Arco di Portogallo." *Bollettino della Commissione Archeologica Comunale di Roma* 105 (2004): 351–370.

———. "Osservazioni sui rostri del Foro Romano in età tardoantica." In *Res bene gestae: Ricerche di storia urbana su Roma antica in onore di Eva Margareta Steinby*, edited by Anna Leone, Domenico Palombi, and Susan Walker, 169–194. *LTUR*, suppl. 4. Rome: Quasar, 2007.

Lizzi Testa, Rita. "Alle origini della tradizione pagana su Costantino e il senato romano (Amm. Marc. 21.10.8 e Zos. 2.32.1)." In *Transformations of Late Antiquity: Essays for Peter Brown*, edited by Philip Rousseau and Manolis Papoutsakis, 85–128. Surrey: Ashgate, 2009.

———. "Christian Emperor, Vestal Virgins, and Priestly Colleges: Reconsidering the End of Roman Paganism." *Antiquité Tardive* 15 (2007): 251–262.

Long, Jacqueline. "Claudian and the City: Poetry and Pride of Place." In *Aetas Claudianea: Eine Tagung an der Freien Universität Berlin vom 28. bis 30. Juni 2002*, edited by Widu-Wolfgang Ehlers, Fritz Felgentreu, and Stephen Wheeler, 1–15. Munich: K. G. Saur, 2004.

L'Orange, Hans Peter. "Ein tetrarchisches Ehrendenkmal auf dem Forum Romanum." *Mitteilungen des Deutschen Archäologischen Instituts, Römische Abteilung* 53 (1938): 1–34.

———. *Das spätantike Herrscherbild von Diokletian bis zu den Konstantin-Söhnen, 284–361 n. Chr.* Berlin: Mann, 1984.

L'Orange, Hans Peter, and Armin van Gerkan. *Der spätantike Bildschmuck des Konstantinsbogens*. Berlin: De Gruyter, 1939.

Loukaki, Argyro. *Living Ruins, Value Conflicts*. Aldershot: Ashgate, 2008.

Lugli, Giuseppe. *Monumenti minori del Foro romano*. Rome: G. Bardi, 1947.

———. *Roma antica: Il centro monumentale*. Rome: G. Bardi, 1946.

Luschi, Lizia. "L'iconografia dell'edificio rotondo nella monetazione massenziana e il 'tempio del divo Romolo.'" *Bullettino della Commissione Archeologica Communale di Roma* 89 (1984): 43–50.

Luttikhuizen, Gerard. "Simon Magus as a Narrative Figure in the Acts of Peter." In *The Apocryphal Acts of Peter: Magic, Miracles and Gnosticism*, edited by Jan Bremmer, 39–51. Leuven: Peeters, 1998.

MacCormack, Sabine. *Art and Ceremony in Late Antiquity*. Berkeley: University of California Press, 1981.

———. "Roma, Constantinopolis, the Emperor, and His Genius." *Classical Quarterly* 25 (1975): 131–150.

Machado, Carlos. "Building the Past: Monuments and Memory in the *Forum Romanum*." In *Social and Political Life in Late Antiquity*, edited by William Bowden, Adam Gutteridge, Luke Lavan, and Carlos Machado, 157–192. Leiden: Brill, 2006.

———. "Religion as Antiquarianism: Pagan Dedications in Late Antique Rome." In *Religious Dedications in the Greco-Roman World: Distribution, Typology, Use*, edited by John Bodel and Mika Kajava, 331–354. Rome: Institutum Romanum Finlandiae, 2009.

MacMullan, Ramsay. "The Epigraphic Habit during the Roman Empire." *American Journal of Philology* 103 (1982): 233–246.

Manacorda, Daniele. *Crypta Balbi: Archeologia e storia di un paesaggio urbano*. Milan: Electa, 2001.

Markus, Robert. *The End of Ancient Christianity*. Cambridge: Cambridge University Press, 1990.

Marlowe, Elizabeth. "Framing the Sun: The Arch of Constantine and the Roman Cityscape." *Art Bulletin* 88 (2006): 223–242.

———. "*Liberator urbis suae*: Constantine and the Ghost of Maxentius." In Ewald and Noreña, eds., *The Emperor and Rome*, 199–219.

Martini, Carla. "Opera muraria." In Flaccomio, *Il "Tempio di Romolo*," 91–100.

Marvin, Miranda. "Freestanding Sculptures from the Baths of Caracalla." *American Journal of Archaeology* 87 (1983): 347–384.

Matthews, John. "Continuity in a Roman Family: The Rufii Festi of Volsinii." *Historia* 16 (1967): 507.

———. "Symmachus and the Oriental Cults." *Journal of Roman Studies* 63 (1972): 175–195.

———. *Western Aristocracies and the Imperial Court, A.D. 364–425*. Oxford: Clarendon, 1975.

Mattingly, Harold. "The Imperial *Vota*." *Proceedings of the British Academy* 36 (1950): 155–195, and 37 (1951): 219–268.

Mayer, Emanuel. "Propaganda, Staged Applause, or Local Politics? Public Monuments from Augustus to Septimius Severus." In Ewald and Noreña, eds., *The Emperor and Rome*, 111–134.

———. *Rom ist dort wo der Kaiser ist: Untersuchungen zu den Staatsdenkmälern des dezentralisierten Reiches von Diocletian bis zu Theodosius II*. Mainz: Römisch-Germanischen Zentralmuseums, 2002.

Mazzarino, Santo. *Stilicone: La crisi imperiale dopo Teodosio*. Rome: A. Signorelli, 1942.

———. "Tolleranza e intolleranza: La polemica sull'ara della Vittoria." In Il basso impero: *Antico, tardoantico ed era costantiniana*, 2:339–373. Bari: Dedalo, 1974–1975.

McCormick, Michael. *Eternal Victory: Triumphal Rulership in Late Antiquity, Byzantium, and the Early Medieval West*. Cambridge: Cambridge University Press, 1986.

McEvoy, Meaghan. *Child Emperor Rule in the Late Roman West, AD 367–455*. Oxford: Oxford University Press, 2013.

———. "Rome and the Transformation of the Imperial Office from the Late Fourth–Mid-Fifth-Centuries AD." *Papers of the British School at Rome* 78 (2010): 151–192.

McLynn, Neil. *Ambrose of Milan: Church and Court in a Christian Capital*. Berkeley: University of California Press, 1994.

———. "Crying Wolf: The Pope and the Lupercalia." *Journal of Roman Studies* 98 (2008): 161–175.

Meneghini, Roberto. *I Fori imperiali e i Mercati di Traiano: Storia e descrizione dei monumenti alla luce degli studi e degli scavi recenti*. Rome: Libreria dello stato, 2009.

Meneghini, Roberto, and Riccardo Santangeli Valenzani. *Roma nell'altomedioevo: Topografia e urbanistica della città dal V al X secolo*. Rome: Libreria dello stato, 2004.

Meneghini, Roberto, Riccardo Santangeli Valenzani, and Elisabetta Bianchi. *I Fori imperiali: Gli scavi del Comune di Roma (1991–2007)*. Rome: Viviani, 2007.

Messerschmidt, Wolfgang. "Die statuarische Repräsentation des theodosianischen Kaiserhauses in Rom." *Mitteilungen des Deutschen Archäologischen Instituts, Römische Abteilung* 111 (2004): 555–568.

Mieschner, Jutta. "Das Porträt der theodosianischen Epoche I." *Jahrbuch der deutschen Archäologischen Instituts* 105 (1990): 303–324.

———. "Das Porträt der theodosianischen Epoche II." *Jahrbuch des Deutschen Archäologischen Instituts* 106 (1991): 385–407.

Millar, Fergus. *A Greek Roman Empire: Power and Belief under Theodosius II*. Berkeley: University of California Press, 2006.

Minoprio, Anthony. "A Restoration of the Basilica of Constantine, Rome." *Papers of the British School at Rome* 12 (1932): 1–25.

Monaco, Ernesto. "Il Tempio di Venere e Roma: Appunti sulla fase del IV secolo." In *Aurea Roma: Dalla città pagana alla città cristiana*, edited by S. Ensoli and E. La Rocca, 58–60. Rome: "L'Erma" di Bretschneider, 2000.

Morselli, Chiara, and Edoardo Tortorici. *Curia, Forum Iulium, Forum Transitorium*. 2 vols. Rome: De Luca, 1989.

Mulryan, Michael. "The Temple of Flora or Venus by the Circus Maximus and the New Christian Topography: The 'Pagan Revival' in Action?" In *The Archaeology of Late Antique Paganism*, edited by Luke Lavan and Michael Mulryan, 216–222. Leiden: Brill, 2011.

Muth, Susanne. "Der Dialog von Gegenwart und Vergangenheit am Forum Romanum in Rom—oder: Wie spätantik ist das spätantike Forum?" In *Rom und Mailand in der Spätantike: Repräsentationen städtischer Räume in Literatur, Architektur und Kunst*, edited by Therese Fuhrer, 263–282. Berlin: De Gruyter, 2012.

Näf, Beat. *Senatorisches Standesbewußtsein in spätrömischer Zeit*. Freiburg: Freiburg Universitätsverlag, 1995.

Najbjerg, Tina, and Jennifer Trimble. "Ancient Maps and Mapping in and around Rome." *Journal of Roman Archaeology* 17 (2009): 577–583.

Nash, Ernest. "Secretarium Senatus." *Colloqui del Sodalizio* 3 (1970–1972): 68–82.

———. "Secretarium Senatus." In *In Memoriam Otto J. Brendel: Essays in Archaeology and the Humanities*, edited by L. Bonfante and H. von Heintze, 191–206. Mainz: Philipp von Zabern, 1976.

Nasrallah, Laura. *Christian Responses to Roman Art and Architecture: The Second-Century Church amid the Spaces of Empire*. Cambridge: Cambridge University Press, 2010.

Nibby, Antonio. *Roma nell'anno 1838*. 4 vols. Rome: Tipografia delle Belle Arti, 1838.

Nichols, F. M. "The Column of Phocas before Phocas." *Journal of the British and American Archaeological Society of Rome* 3 (1888–1889): 174–178.

———. "A Revised History of the Column of Phocas in the Roman Forum." *Archeologia* 52 (1890): 187.

Nieddu, Giuseppe. "Il Portico degli Dei Consenti." In *Roma: Archeologia nel Centro*, 1:24–28. Rome: De Luca, 1985.

———. "Il Portico degli Dei Consenti." *Bollettino d'Arte* 71 (1986): 37–52.

Nielsen, Inge, and Birte Poulsen, eds. *The Temple of Castor and Pollux*. Vol. 1: *The Pre-Augustan Temple Phases with Related Decorative Elements*. Rome: "L'Erma" di Bretschneider, 1992.

Niemeyer, Hans-Georg. *Studien zur statuarischen Darstellung der römischen Kaiser*. Berlin: Gebr. Mann, 1968.

Nilson, Kjell Aage, Claes B. Petersson, Siri Sande, and Jan Zahle. *The Temple of Castor and Pollux*. Vol. 3: *The Augustan Temple*. Rome: "L'Erma" di Bretschneider, 2009.

Niquet, Heike. *Monumenta virtutum titulique: Senatorische Selbstdarstellung im spätantiken Rom im Spiegel der epigraphischen Denkmäler*. Stuttgart: Steiner, 2000.

———. "Die valentinianische Dynastie und Rom: Das Selbstverstandnis der Kaiser und ihre Haltung zur Senatsaristokratie im Licht von Bau- und Ehreninschriften." In *Inschriftliche Denkmäler als Medien der Selbstdarstellung in der römischen Welt*, edited by Géza Alföldy and Silvio Panciera, 125–147. Stuttgart: Franz Steiner, 2001.

Nixon, C. E. V., and Barbara S. Rodgers, eds. *In Praise of Later Roman Emperors: The Panegyrici Latini*. Berkeley: University of California Press, 1994.

Nora, Pierre. "Between Memory and History: *Les lieux de mémoire*." *Representations* 26 (1989): 7–24.

Noreña, Carlos. *Imperial Ideals in the Roman West: Representation, Circulation, Power*. Cambridge: Cambridge University Press, 2011.

———. "Medium and Message in Vespasian's *Templum Pacis*." *Memoirs of the American Academy in Rome* 48 (2003): 25–43.

O'Flynn, John Micael. *Generalissimos of the Western Roman Empire*. Edmonton: University of Alberta Press, 1983.

Ogden, Daniel. *Drakon: Dragon Myth and Serpent Cult in the Greek and Roman Worlds*. Oxford: Oxford University Press, 2013.

O'Gorman, Ellen. "Repetition and Exemplarity in Historical Thought: Ancient Rome and the Ghosts of Modernity." In *The Western Time of Ancient History*, edited by Alexandra Lianeri, 264–279. Cambridge: Cambridge University Press, 2011.

Osborne, John. "The Jerusalem Temple Treasures and the Church of SS. Cosma e Damiano in Rome." *Papers of the British School at Rome* 76 (2008): 173–181.

O'Sullivan, Timothy. *Walking in Roman Culture*. Cambridge: Cambridge University Press, 2011.

Palmer, Robert. *Studies of the Northern Campus Martius in Ancient Rome*. Philadelphia: American Philosophical Society, 1990.

Palombi, Domenico. "Contributo alla topografia della Via Sacra: Dagli appunti inediti di Giacomo Boni." In *Topografia Romana: Ricerche e discussioni*, Quaderni di Topografia Antica 10, 77–97. Florence: Leo Olschki, 1988.

Panciera, Silvio, ed. *Atti del Colloquio internazionale AIEGL su epigrafia e ordine senatorio*. Rome: Edizioni di storia e letteratura, 1982.

———. *Iscrizioni greche e latine del Foro romano e del Palatino*. Rome: Edizioni di storia e letteratura, 1996.

Panella, Clementina. *I segni del potere: Realtà e immaginario della sovranità nella Roma imperiale*. Bari: Edipuglia, 2011.

Pékary, Thomas. *Das römische Kaiserbildnis in Staat, Kult und Gesellschaft*. Berlin: Gebr. Mann, 1985.

Pensabene, Patrizio. *Tempio di Saturno: Architettura e decorazione*. Rome: De Luca, 1984.

Pensabene, Patrizio, Lorenzo Lazzarini, and Bruno Tuni. "New Archeometric Investigations on the Fragments of the Colossal Statue of Constantine in the Palazzo dei Conservatori." In *Interdisciplinary Studies on Ancient Stone*, edited by John Hermann Jr., Norman Herz, and Richard Newman, ASMOSIA: Association for the Study of Marble and Other Stone in Antiquity, 5:250–255. London: Archetype Publications, 2002.

Pensabene, Patrizio, and Claudia Panella. "Reimpiego e progettazione architettonica nei monumenti tardo-antichi di Roma." *Atti della Pontificia Accademia Romana di Archeologia, Rendiconti* 66 (1993–1994): 111–283.

Pflaum, H.-G. "Titulaire et rang social sous le Haut-Empire." In *Recherches sur les structures sociales de l'antiquité classique*, edited by Claude Nicolet, 159–185. Paris: Éditions du centre nationale de la recherche scientifique, 1970.

Pohlkamp, Wilhelm. "Kaiser Konstantin, der heidnische und der christliche Kult in der Actus Silvestri," *Frühmittelalterliche Studien* 18 (1984): 357–400.

———. "Tradition und Topographie: Papst Silvester I (314–335) und der Drache vom Forum Romanum." *Römische Quartalschrift* 78 (1983): 1–100.

Porena, Pierfrancesco. "Trasformazioni istituzionali e assetti sociali: I prefetti del pretorio tra III e IV secolo." In *Le trasformazioni delle élites in età tardoantica*, edited by Rita Lizzi Testa, 325–356. Rome: "L'Erma" di Bretschneider, 2006.

Potter, David. *Constantine the Emperor*. Oxford: Oxford University Press, 2012.

Poupon, Gérard. "Les 'Actes de Pierre' et leur remaniement." In *Aufstieg und Niedergang der römischen Welt*, vol. 2, fasc. 25, 4363–4383. Berlin: De Gruyter, 1988.

Presicce, Claudio Parisi. "Costantino come Giove: Proposta di ricostruzione grafica del colosso acrolitico della Basilica Costantiniana." *Bullettino della Commissione archeologica comunale di Roma* 107 (2006): 127–161.

Presner, Todd. "Digital Humanities 2.0: A Report on Knowledge." In *Emerging Disciplines: Shaping New Fields of Inquiry in and beyond the Humanities*, edited by Melissa Bailar, 27–38. Houston, Tex.: Rice University Press, 2010.

Prusac, Marina. *From Face to Face: Recarving of Roman Portraits and the Late-Antique Portrait Arts*. Leiden: Brill, 2011.

Purcell, Nicholas. "Rediscovering the Roman Forum." *Journal of Roman Archaeology* 2 (1989): 156–166.

Rebell, Walter. *Neutestamentliche Apokryphen und apostolische Väter*. Munich: Kaiser, 1992.

Reece, Richard. "Coins and the Late Roman Economy." In *The-*

ory and Practice in Late Antique Archaeology, edited by Luke Lavan and William Bowden, 139–170. Leiden: Brill, 2003.

———. "A Collection of Coins from the Centre of Rome." Papers of the British School at Rome 50 (1982): 116–145.

Rees, Roger. Diocletian and the Tetrarchy. Edinburgh: Edinburgh University Press, 2004.

———. Layers of Loyalty in Latin Panegyric, AD 289–307. Oxford: Oxford University Press, 2002.

Reynolds, Joyce, Charlotte Roueché, and Gabriel Bodard, eds. Inscriptions of Aphrodisias. http://insaph.kcl.ac.uk/iaph2007. Accessed 8 May 2013.

Richardson, L., Jr. "The Tribunals of the Praetors of Rome." Mitteilungen des Deutschen Archäologischen Instituts, Römische Abteilung 80 (1973): 232–233.

Rizzo, Silvana. "Indagini nei fori imperiali: Oroidrografia, foro di Cesare, foro di Augusto, templum Pacis." Mitteilungen des Deutschen Archäologischen Instituts, Römische Abteilung 108 (2001):215–244.

Roberts, Michael. The Jeweled Style: Poetry and Poetics in Late Antiquity. Ithaca, N.Y.: Cornell University Press, 1989.

Rodgers, Barbara Saylor. "Divine Insinuation in the 'Panegyrici Latini.'" Historia 35 (1986): 69–104.

Rodríguez Almeida, Emilio. Formae urbis antiquae: Le mappe marmoree di Roma tra la repubblica e Settimo Severo. Collection de l'École française de Rome 305. Rome: École française de Rome, 2002.

———. Forma urbis marmorea: Aggiornamento generale, 1980. Rome: Quasar, 1981.

Roueché, Charlotte, ed. Aphrodisias in Late Antiquity: The Late Roman and Byzantine Inscriptions. Rev. 2d ed. 2004. http://insaph.kcl.ac.uk/ala2004.

Ruck, Brigitte. Die Grossen dieser Welt: Kolossalporträts im antiken Rom. Heidelberg: Verlag Archäologie und Geschichte, 2007.

Rutledge, Steven. Ancient Rome as a Museum: Power, Identity, and the Culture of Collecting. Oxford: Oxford University Press, 2012.

Salzman, Michele Renee. The Making of a Christian Aristocracy: Social and Religious Change in the Western Roman Empire. Cambridge, Mass.: Harvard University Press, 2002.

———. On Roman Time: The Codex-Calendar of 354 and the Rhythms of Urban Life in Late Antiquity. Berkeley: University of California Press, 1990.

Sande, Siri, and Jan Zahle, eds. The Temple of Castor and Pollux. Vol. 3, The Augustan Temple. Rome: "L'Erma" di Bretschneider, 2009.

Santangeli Valenzani, Riccardo. "Il vescovo, il drago e le vergini: Paesaggio urbano e paesaggio del mito nella leggenda di S. Silvestro e il drago." In Res bene gestae: Ricerche di storia urbana su Roma antica in onore di Eva Margaret Steinby, edited by Anna Leone, Domenico Palombi, and Susan Walker, 379–395. LTUR, suppl. 4. Rome: Quasar, 2007.

Santinelli, Itala. "Alcune questioni attinenti ai riti delle Vergini Vestali." Rivista di filologia e d'istruzione classica 30 (1902): 255–268.

Schäfer, Christoph. Der weströmische Senat als Träger antiker Kontinuitäten unter den Ostgotenkönigen (490–540 n. Chr.). St. Katharinen: Scripta Mercaturae, 1991.

Schlinkert, Dirk. "Ordo senatorius" und "nobilitas": Die Konstitution des Senatsadels in der Spätantike. Stuttgart: Franz Steiner, 1996.

Schneemelcher, Wilhelm, and R. M. Wilson, eds. and trans. New Testament Apocrypha. 2 vols. Louisville, Ky.: Westminster John Knox Press, 2003.

Scott, Russell T., ed. Excavations in the Area Sacra of Vesta (1987–1996). Memoirs of the American Academy in Rome, suppl. 8. Ann Arbor: University of Michigan Press, 2009.

Sessa, Kristina. The Formation of Papal Authority: Roman Bishops and the Domestic Sphere. Cambridge: Cambridge University Press, 2012.

———. "The Household and the Bishop: Establishing Episcopal Authority in Late Antique Rome." Ph.D. dissertation, University of California, Berkeley, 2003.

Shepardson, Christine. Controlling Contested Places: Fourth-Century Antioch and the Spatial Politics of Religious Controversy. Berkeley: University of California Press, 2014.

Slootjes, Daniëlle. The Governor and His Subjects in the Later Roman Empire. Leiden: Brill, 2006.

Smith, R. R. R. "Late Antique Portraits in a Public Context: Honorific Statuary at Aphrodisias in Caria, A.D. 300–600." Journal of Roman Studies 89 (1999): 155–189.

———. "Roman Portraits: Honours, Empresses, and Late Emperors." Journal of Roman Studies 75 (1985): 209–221.

———. "The Statue Monument of Oecumenius: A New Portrait of a Late Antique Governor from Aphrodisias." Journal of Roman Studies 92 (2002): 134–156.

Smith, R. R. R., and Bryan Ward-Perkins, eds. Last Statues of Antiquity. Available at: http://laststatues.classics.ox.ac.uk.

Smith, Rowland. "Measures of Difference: The Fourth-Century Transformation of the Roman Imperial Court." American Journal of Philology 132 (2011): 125–151.

———. "'Restored Utility, Eternal City': Patronal Imagery at Rome in the Fourth Century AD." In "Bread and Circuses": Euergetism and Municipal Patronage in Roman Italy, edited by Kathryn Lomas and Tim Cornell, 142–166. London: Routledge, 2003.

Sodini, Jean-Pierre. "Images sculptées et propaganda imperiale du IVe au VIe siècle: Recherches récentes sur les colonnes honorifiques et les reliefs politiques à Byzance." In Byzance et les images, edited by A. Guillau and J. Durand, 41–94. Paris: Louvre, 1994.

Spera, Lucrezia. "La realtà archeologica: Restauro degli edifici pubblici e riassetto urbano dopo il sacco." In Roma e il sacco del 410: Realtà, interpretazione, mito (Attie della Giornata di studio, Roma, 6 dicembre 2010), edited by Angelo Di Berardino, Gianluca Pilara, and Lucrezia Spera, 113–152. Rome: Institutum Patristicum Augustinianum, 2012.

Stamper, John. The Architecture of Roman Temples: The Republic to the Middle Empire. Cambridge: Cambridge University Press, 2005.

Steinby, Eva Margareta. "L'industria laterizia di Roma nel tardo impero." In *Società romana e impero tardoantico*, edited by A. Giardina, 2:99–165. Bari: Laterza, 1986.

——, ed. *Lexicon topographicum urbis Romae*. 6 vols. Rome: Quasar, 1993–2000.

Steinmann, Bernhard, Robert Nawracala, and Martin Boss, eds. *Im Zentrum der Macht: Das Forum Romanum im Modell*. Erlangen-Nuremberg: Institut für Klassische Archäologie, 2011.

Stewart, Peter. *Statues in Roman Society: Representation and Response*. Oxford: Oxford University Press, 2004.

Stichel, Rudolf. *Die römische Kaiserstatue am Ausgang der Antike: Untersuchungen zum plastischen Kaiserporträt seit Valentinian I. (364–375 v. Chr.)*. Rome: Bretschneider, 1982.

Stickler, Timo. *Aëtius: Gestaltungsspielräume eines Heermeisters im ausgehenden Weströmischen Reich*. Munich: C. H. Beck, 2002.

Stirling, Lea. *The Learned Collector: Mythological Statuettes and Classical Taste in Late Antique Gaul*. Ann Arbor: University of Michigan Press, 2005.

Straub, Johannes. "Konstantins Versicht auf den Gang zum Kapitol." *Historia* 4 (1955): 297–313.

Strong, Donald. "Roman Museums." In *Roman Museums: Selected Papers on Roman Art and Architecture*, 19–20. London: Pindar, 1994.

Talamo, Emilia. "Raffigurazioni numismatiche." In Flaccomio, ed., *Il "Tempio di Romulo,"* 23–34.

Thédenat, Henri. *Le Forum romain et les Forums impériaux*. Paris: Hachette, 1923.

Thiel, Wolfgang. "Die 'Pompeius-Säule' in Alexandria und die Vier Säulen Monumente Ägyptens." In Boschung and Eck, *Die Tetrarchie*, 249–322.

Thomas, Christine M. *The Acts of Peter, Gospel Literature, and the Ancient Novel: Rewriting the Past*. Oxford: Oxford University Press, 2003.

Thomas, Edmund, and Christian Witschel. "Constructing Reconstruction: Claim and Reality of Roman Rebuilding Inscriptions from the Latin West." *Papers of the British School at Rome* 60 (1992): 135–177.

Thomas, Michael. "(Re)locating Domitian's Horse of Glory: The 'Equus Domitiani' and Flavian Urban Design." *Memoirs of the American Academy in Rome* 49 (2004): 21–46.

Trifilò, Francesco. "Movement, Gaming and the Use of Space in the Forum." In Laurence and Newsome, *Rome, Ostia, Pompeii*, 312–331.

Trimble, Jennifer. "Visibility and Viewing on the Severan Marble Plan." In *Severan Culture*, edited by Simon Swain, Jaś Elsner, and Stephen Harrison, 368–384. Cambridge: Cambridge University Press, 2007.

Tucci, Patrizia. "The Portico degli Dei Consenti." *Periodici di Mineralogia* 71 (2002): 247–263.

Tucci, Pier Luigi. "Nuove acquisizioni sulla basilica dei Santi Cosma e Damiano." *Studi Romani* 49 (2001).

——. "Nuove osservazioni sull'architettura del *Templum Pacis*." In *Divus Vespasianus: Il bimillenario dei Flavi*, edited by Filippo Coarelli, 158–167. Milan: Electa, 2009.

Valentini, Roberto, and Giuseppe Zucchetti, eds. *Codice topografico della città di Roma*. Fonti per la storia d'Italia 81. 4 vols. Rome: Tipografia del Senato, 1940–1953.

Van Dam, Raymond. *The Roman Revolution of Constantine*. Cambridge: Cambridge University Press, 2007.

Varner, Eric. *Mutilation and Transformation: Damnatio memoriae and Roman Imperial Portraiture*. Leiden: Brill, 2005.

——. "Tyranny and the Transformation of the Roman Visual Landscape." In *From Caligula to Constantine: Tyranny and Transformation in Roman Portraiture*, 13–14. Atlanta, Ga.: Michael Carlos Museum, 2001.

Verduchi, Patrizia. "Le tribune rostrate." In *Roma: Archeologia nel centro*, Lavori e studi di archeologia 6, 1:29–33. Rome: De Luca, 1985.

Veyne, Paul. *Bread and Circuses: Historical Sociology and Political Pluralism*. Translated by Brian Pearce. London: Penguin, 1990.

Viscogliosi, Alessandro. *I fori imperiali nei disegni d'architettura del primo cinquecento: Ricerche sull'architettura e l'urbanistica di Roma*. Rome: Gangemi, 2000.

Walser, Gerald. *Die Einsiedler Inschriftensammlung und der Pilgerführer durch Rom: Codex Einsiedlensis 326*. Stuttgart: Franz Steiner, 1987.

Ward-Perkins, Bryan. *The Fall of Rome and the End of Civilization*. Oxford: Oxford University Press, 2005.

——. *From Classical Antiquity to the Middle Ages: Urban Public Buildings in Northern and Central Italy, AD 300–850*. Oxford: Oxford University Press, 1984.

——. "Re-using the Architectural Legacy of the Past: *Entre idéologie et pragmatism*." In *The Idea and the Ideal of the Town between Late Antiquity and the Early Middle Ages*, edited by G. P. Brogiolo, 225–244. Leiden and Boston: Brill, 1999.

Ware, Catherine. *Claudian and the Roman Epic Tradition*. Cambridge: Cambridge University Press, 2012.

Watkin, David. *The Roman Forum*. Cambridge, Mass.: Harvard University Press, 2009.

Wegner, Max. "Gebälk von den Rostra am Forum Romanum." *Mitteilungen des Deutschen Archäologischen Instituts, Römische Abteilung* 94 (1987): 331–332.

——. *Ornamente kaiserzeitlicher Bauten Roms. Soffitten*. Cologne: Böhlau, 1957.

Weiser, Wolfram. "Die Tetrarchie—Ein neues Regierungssystem und seine mediale Präsentation auf Münzen und Medaillons." In Boschung and Eck, *Die Tetrarchie*, 205–220.

Weisweiler, John. "From Equality to Asymmetry: Honorific Statues, Imperial Power, and Senatorial Identity in Late-Antique Rome." *Journal of Roman Archaeology* 25 (2012): 318–350.

——. "Inscribing Imperial Power: Letters from Emperors in Late Antique Rome." In *Rom in der Spätantike: Historische Erinnerung im städtischen Raum*, edited by Ralf Behrwald and Christian Witschel, 309–329. Stuttgart: Steiner, 2012.

Welinn, Erik. *Studien zur Topographie des Forum Romanum*. Lund: Gleerup, 1953.

Williams, Stephen. *Diocletian and the Roman Recovery*. New York: Methuen, 1985.

Wiseman, T. P. "The Central Area of the Roman Forum." *Journal of Roman Archaeology* 3 (1990): 245–247.

———. "The God of the Lupercal." *Journal of Roman Studies* 85 (1995): 1–22.

———. "Monuments and the Roman Analysts." In *Past Perspectives: Studies in Greek and Roman Historical Writing*, edited by I. S. Moxon, J. D. Smart and Anthony J. Woodman, 87–100. Cambridge: Cambridge University Press, 1986.

Witschel, Christian. "Statuen auf spätantiken Platzanlagen in Italien und Afrika." In *Statuen in der Spätantike*, edited by Franz Alto Bauer and Christian Witschel, 113–169. Weisbaden: Reichert, 2007.

Woolf, Greg. "Monumental Writing and the Expansion of Roman Society in the Early Empire." *Journal of Roman Studies* 86 (1996): 22–39.

Wrede, Hennig. "Der *genius populi Romani* und das Fünfsäulendenkmal der Tetrarchen auf dem Forum Romanum." *Bonner Jahrbücher des Rheinischen Landesmuseums in Bonn und des Vereins von Altertumsfreunden im Rheinlande* 181 (1981): 111–142.

Wytzes, Jelle. *Der letzte Kampf des Heidentums in Rom*. Leiden: Brill, 1977.

Yasin, Ann Marie. *Saints and Church Spaces in the Late Antique Mediterranean: Architecture, Cult, and Community*. Cambridge: Cambridge University Press, 2009.

Zanker, Paul. "Bild-Räume und Betrachter im kaiserzeitlichen Rom." In *Klassische Archäologie: Eine Einführung*, edited by Adolf Borbein, Tonio Hölscher, and Paul Zanker, 205–226. Berlin: Dietrich Reimer, 2000.

———. "By the Emperor, For the People: 'Popular' Architecture in Rome." In Ewald and Noreña, eds., *The Emperor and Rome*, 45–87.

———. *Il foro romano: La sistemazione da Augusto alla tarda antichità*. Translated by L. Franchi. Rome: De Luca, 1972.

———. *The Mask of Socrates: The Image of the Intellectual in Antiquity*. Translated by Alan Shapiro. Berkeley: University of California Press, 1995.

———. *The Power of Images in the Age of Augustus*. Translated by Alan Shapiro. Ann Arbor: University of Michigan Press, 1988.

Zimmer, Gerhard. *Locus datus decreto decurionum: Zur Statuenaufstellung zweier Forumsanlagen im römischen Afrika*. Munich: Bayerischen Akademie der Wissenschaften, 1989.

INDEX

of the church of S. Martina, 160; of the Column of Phocas, 97–98; as conveying administrative ideals, 60; dedication terminology in, 79; in honor of saints, 161; mentioning a distant location, 121; with names of Greek artists, 121; with references to busy locations, 119; with references to cults near the Temple of Vesta, 139; with references to damage or decay, 101, 119, 153; with references to moving statues, 106, 119, 122; with references to ornament, 119; with references to restoration, 13, 15–16, 106, 108, 119, 133, 153, 159; of the Secretarium Senatus, 158–161; of the Senate House, 148–149; terms and nomenclature for patronage for, 79; of the Tetrarchs, 36–37, 147; vague terms in, 102

Jerome (saint), 127, 134
Jewish antiquities, 65, 78
Jewish War, 78
Johanson, Christopher, 12
John I (pope), 170
Jordan-Ruwe, Martina, 37, 43, 44
Jovian (emperor), 77
jubilees (imperial). *See* imperial rituals: imperial jubilees; imperial rituals: jubilee celebrations at five-column monuments
Julian (emperor), 128, 143, 151
Julius Caesar, 33, 34, 143
Jupiter, 26, 27, 30, 33, 34, 38, 39, 41, 42, 43, 45, 48, 51, 57, 134, 147

Krautheimer, Richard, 51
Kronos, 136

Lactantius, 39, 41
Lacus Curtius, 4, 163
Lacus of Juturna, 57; statue of Constantine displayed nearby, 57
Lampadius. *See* Volusianus, Caeionius Rufius Volusianus (*signo* Lampadius)
Lanciani, Rodolfo, 141
Lapis Niger, 60–62, 87, 89
Lateran, 50
laws: offering exclusive courts for aristocrats, 159; offering tax advantages to aristocrats, 102, 155, 157
lectisternium, 133–134
Lenski, Noel, 53
Libanius, 127
liberalitas, 13
Liber Pontificalis, 163
Libya, 95
Ligorio, Pirro, 64
Limenius (fictional senator), 160
Lizzi Testa, Rita, 129
Lollianus, Flavius Mesius Egnatius, 57

Longeius, 133
L'Orange, Hans Peter, 34
Lucifer, 29–30
Lupercalia. See rituals: *Lupercalia*
Lysippus, 65

Machado, Carlos, 15, 18, 78
Macrobius, 136–137
Macrobius (Flavius Macrobius Plotinus Eustathius), 121
Magnentius (usurper), 81, 83, 116
Majorian (emperor), 80
Malalas, John, 125
Mamertine prison, 160
Mamertinus, 118
Manilius, Manius, 16
marble plan of Rome. See *Forma Urbis Romae*
Marcellus (fictional senator), 161–162, 165
Marcian (emperor), 31, 33
Marcus Aurelius (emperor), 50, 52, 133, 181n49
Marcus Curtius, 163
Maria (daughter of Stilicho), 91
Mars, 36, 60–62, 73, 89, 187n80
Marsyas, 96
Martina (saint), 21, 141, 160–161, 165
Maxentius (emperor), 19, 20, 27, 45, 47, 49, 51, 53, 54, 55, 60, 62, 63, 64, 67, 68, 70, 71, 72, 73, 83, 89, 99, 101, 188n119, 188n124; ceremonial lances and standards belonging to, 54, 182n75; as conserver, 48, 50
Maximian (emperor), 5, 15, 18, 20, 21, 23–45, 48, 49, 50, 51, 55, 60, 77, 101, 102, 107, 109, 111, 112, 117, 143, 145, 147, 148, 168
Maximus, Magnus (usurper), 10, 85, 87, 89, 151, 164
Mayer, Emanuel, 36
memory, 14–15, 17–18, 79, 150; of paganism, 100, 125, 138; as preserved over time, 152; as preserving identities of aristocrats and emperors, 89, 169; retained in cult objects, 152; retained in restored buildings, 129, 134, 137, 157. *See also* memory sanctions
memory sanctions, 122, 158–159; of Aëtius, 156; applied to paganism, 151–152; of Maxentius, 60–62; of Stilicho, 90, 93; of Theodosius the elder, 87
Merobaudes, 78, 156
Mese (street in Constantinople), 97
Minerva, 101–102, 108, 155
moving statues, 74, 106–108, 116–123, 131
Munatius Plancus, L., 136
Myron, 65, 67, 78

Narses (Persian general), 41
Nash, Ernest, 159
Natalis Martis, 29
Nazarius, 68, 149, 164
Nero, 51, 65, 66, 67, 78, 105, 168

Ingram Content Group UK Ltd.
Milton Keynes UK
UKHW050229270323
418963UK00020B/354

9 781477 309933